General Agriculture

Questions Bank for Ready Reference to the Students, Teachers and Researchers for JRF, SRF, ARS, Civil Service Examinations (State and Central), NET, SET, Ph.D. and Allied Examinations

About the Authors

Dr. Bagde Abhaykumar S. completed Ph.D Agril. Entomology from Dr. B.S.K.K.V Dapoli in 2010 M.Sc. (Agriculture) with specialization in Agricultural Entomology from Mahatma Phule Krishi Vidyapeeth, Rahuri in 2001. He has also qualified ICAR-NET examination in 2003 & 2007. He has teaching experience of 15 years. He has published 3 books, 22 research articles in recognized journals & 16 popular articles. Presently working as Assistant Professor in M.P.K.V Rahuri.

Dr. Namdeo Gopal Patil - retired Professor of Entomology, He had 33 years of experience in Research, Teaching and Extension and had been awarded - ICAR Fellowship and University Merit Scholarship for his earlier education. Subsequently, he has been awarded Commonwealth Fellowship by the Government of Trinidad and Tobago for his Doctoral studies at CAB, International Institute of Biological Control, Trinidad during the year 1988 to 1992. He published 30 research papers in well-reputed Indian and foreign journals and wrote one Book chapter on white grub and worked as **Principal Investigator** for Ad-hoc Research Project on *"Survey and study of Sugarcane woolly aphid - Ceratovacuna lanigera, Zehnt. in Western Maharashtra."* sanctioned by the Government of India, Ministry of Science and Technology, Department of Science and Technology, Technology- Bhavan, New Delhi and recorded natural enemies first time during 2004 -06.

Khadtare Rajendra Maruti. completed M.Sc. (Agriculture) with specialization in Plant Pathology from Mahatma Phule Krishi Vidyapeeth, He has teaching experience of 15 years. He has published 5 books chapter, Thirty four research articles in recognized journals & 17 popular articles. Presently working as Assistant Professor in M.P.K.V Rahuri

Dr. Sangram Sahebrao Dhumal completed Ph.D. (Hort.) in Fruit Science. in distinction from Post Graduate Institute, MPKV, Rahuri in 2012. Dr. Dhumal concluded his post-doctoral fellowship in the Department of Horticulture & School of Packaging, Michigan State University (USA) with specialization in Post Harvest Physiology and Technology. He has also completed a Postgraduate Diploma in Geoinformatics from Shivaji University, Kolhapur. He has published a large number of publications, which includes 43 research articles, 18 technical articles and 42 popular articles including two book viz. "Pomegranate Processing Technology" and Production technology of Spices, Aromatics, Medicinal and Plantation Crops: A Practical Manual. He is presently working as an Associate Professor of Horticulture at the College of Agriculture, Karad.

Prof. Ranjit R. Patil obtained M. Sc. (Agriculture Entomology) from Vasantrao Naik Marathwada Krishi Vidyapeeth He has teaching experience of 5 years. with he has also qualified ICAR-NET examination in 2018 and published four research articles in recognized journals. Presently working as Assistant Professor, D.Y. Patil College of Agriculture, Talsande Dist. Kolhapur.

Prof.Rushikesh P. Shinde obtained B.Sc. (Agri.) from Mahatma Phule Krishi Vidyapeeth, ABM CSIBER, Kolhapur. He has teaching experience of 2 years. Presently working as Superintendent in DY Patil college of Agriculture, Talsande Dist. Kolhapur

Sarde Shital Ashok. B.Sc. (Agri) First class with distinction. She obtained M. Sc. (Agriculture Entomology) First class with distinction from Mahatma Phule Krishi Vidyapeeth.

Kadgaonkar Tejusvini S. She obtained M. Sc. (Agriculture Entomology) from Mahatma Phule Krishi Vidyapeeth with She has also qualified ICAR-NET examination in 2018 and published four research articles in recognized journals. Recently working as Assistant Professor.

General Agriculture

A Ready Reference to the Students, Teachers and Researchers for JRF, SRF, ARS, Civil Service Examinations (State and Central), NET, SET, Ph.D. and Allied Examinations

A.S. Bagde
N.G. Patil
R.M. Khadtare
S.S. Dhumal
R.R. Patil
R.P. Shinde
S.A. Sarde
T.S. Kadgaonkar

NEW INDIA PUBLISHING AGENCY

New Delhi – 110 034

NEW INDIA PUBLISHING AGENCY
101, Vikas Surya Plaza, CU Block, LSC Market
Pitam Pura, New Delhi 110 034, India
Phone: + 91 (11)27 34 17 17 Fax: + 91(11) 27 34 16 16
Email: info@nipabooks.com
Web: www.nipabooks.com

Feedback at feedbacks@nipabooks.com

ISBN No. 978-93-87973-89-3

Composed, Designed & Printed in India

Preface

Agriculture, one of the important subject which having an increasing importance day by day. The general understanding of this subject must be in simple way in new era. For various competitive as well as civil examinations in this subject need to be simplified for better understanding of the student. In this book we have tried to simplify the questions in multiple choice with bold answers which is simple to remember & easy to study.

This book covers different topics of Agriculture such as Agronomy, Plant Breeding and Genetics, Horticulture, Soil Science, Agriculture Enggineering, Dairy, Plant Protection, Extension, Economics etc. and this book will be great use to specially students appearing for JRF, SRF, NET/ARS as well as Ms.CET, State entrance exam.

We acknowledge our teachers, students, friends. Special thanks to Dr. A.G. Chandele, Prof. P.K. Dharne, Dr. S.B. Kharbade, Dr. P.B. Mohite, Prof. S.A. Patil, Agril. Asst. R.K. Patil, Amit Chavan, Mrs. C.A. Mane, Atul Pandav Arvind Kayende, Mahesh Supekar, Akshay Patil, Answers by Wahidhusen Peerzade, Sanjib B. Samant, who inspired to write this book. We also grateful to our family members for supporting us. It is my great pleasure to express my sincere thanks to Prof. A.B. Deshmukh, Librarian, College of Agriculture, Pune.

Criticism & suggestions for the improvement of the book will be appreciated.

Authors

Contents

1

Agronomy

1. The Fraction of incident radiation which is reflected back is called as.................
   a) Short wave radiation
   b) Long wave radiation
   c) Albedo
   d) U.V radiation
2. Hulling percent in Rice crop.........
   a) 60-70%
   b) 40-50%
   c) 80-90%
   d) 20-25%
3. SPAC concept was given by.........
   a) Philips
   b) Waksman
   c) James Lovelock
   d) Joseph Lister
4. Safflower contains ....% Linoleic acid which is good for heart patient.
   a) 50-60%
   b) 76-78%
   c) 80-85%
   d) 71-72%
5. Sugar-beet have........% sugar content and.......% sugar recovery.
   a) 15-16%,10-12%
   b) 14-18%,12-14%
   c) 10-12%,8-9%
   d) 20-25%,18-20%
6. *Linum ustiattissium* is a botanical name of ....
   a) Safflower
   b) Sunflower
   c) Linseed
   d) Mustard
7. ....crop is called as king of the legume fodder.
   a) Maize
   b) Luceren
   c) Berseem
   d) Cow Pea
8. The adiabatic lapse rate (DALR) is.........
   a) Dry adiabatic lapse rate
   b) Dry adiabatic lower rate
   c) Both a and b
   d) None of the above

9. Jowar stubble reduces..........available to the succeeding crop.

a) Nitrogen b) Phosphorus

c) Iron d) Sulphur

10. Scheduling irrigation at IW/CP ratio of ....is suitable for most of the systems.

a) 0.40 to 0.50 **b) 0.5 to 1.0**

c) 0.60 to 0.80 d) 0.30 to 0.20

11. Which of the following is complete root parasite of tobacco

a) Witch weed **b) Orobanche**

c) Cuscuta d) Loranthus

12. Which of the following nitrobacteria convert ammonia in to nitrite

a) Nitrosomanas b) Nitobacter

c) Bacillus d) Pesudmonas

13. Conversion of nitrogen from organic to inorganic forms called as......

a) Immbolization b) Ammonification

c) Mineralization d) Nitrification

14. In heavy rainfall area soil........is a limiting factor crop growth

a) Acidity b) Alkalinity

c) Salininity d) Saline alkaline

15. Exchangeable sodium percentage ESP of an alkali soil should be brought down to............forcrop production purpose.

a) 5 b) 10

c) <15 d) 20

16. In rise or paddy field nitrogenous fertilizer are placed are in..........zone for avoiding learning losses.

a) Oxidation **b) Reducing**

c) Root zone d) Sub soil

17. Upland rice cultivation is practiced in area receiving .... mm rainfall.

a) 250-750 mm b) 800- 1000 mm

c) 500-750 mm **d) 1250-3000 mm**

18. The associated with study of precipitation are........

a) Cirrus **b) Nimbo-stratus**

c) Cumulus d) Cumulo-nimbus

19. Example of straight water soluble phosphate fertilizer is
    a) Mono-calcium phosphate
    b) Di-calcium phosphate
    c) Tri- calcium phosphate
    d) Di-ammonium phosphate

20. The solid precipitation on the ground in the form of small particle of clear ice is called as
    a) Snow b) Glaze
    c) Sleet d) Hail

21. The direction from which the wind blows is
    a) Leeward **b) Windward**
    c) Seaward d) None

22. Balloon is a modified papery calyx that encloses the fruit loosely with entrapped airis seen in.........weed.
    a) *Phyllanthus niruri* b) Calotropis
    c) *Physalis minima* **d) Ground cherry**

23. All the three types, namely enforced, innate and induced dormancies are present in the weed plant.
    a) *Phalaris minor* **b) Wild oat**
    c) Both d) None

24. The urea is mixed with Stamp F-34 (Propanil) then it increases...........in the plant.
    a) Absorption **b) Penetration**
    c) Movement d) None

25. Weed competition in rice is more severe in.........
    a) Direct seeded crop b) Transplanted crop
    c) Late sown crop d) Flooded crop

26. The world's most problematic weed is
    a) Ambrosia **b) Parthenium**
    c) *Utrica* spp. d) *Cyprus rotundus*

27. ....is an objectionable weed in lucern
    a) Amaranthus **b) Dodder**
    c) Echinocloa d) *Agropyron repens*

28. The movement of water after rain or irrigation after 48-72 hrs, the soil is said to be at

a) Ultimate wilting point
b) Field capacity
c) Permanent wilting point
d) None

29. The moisture which is present in the form of continuous film outside of the hygroscopic water around soil particles and microspore space is called as

a) Available water
b) Inter-space water
c) Capillary water
d) None

30. One cusec of water is equivalent to......... Lit/min of water

a) 16.66
b) 28.31
c) 1698.96
d) 101.94

31. When plants cannot absorb any water and get died this condition is termed as

a) Ultimate wilting point
b) Field capacity
c) Hygroscopic water
d) PWP

32. The tillage practice in which primary tillage is completely avoided and secondary tillage is restricted to seedbed preparation in the row zone only is known as

a) Minimum tillage
b) Row zone tillage
c) Zero tillage
d) Plough plant tillage

33. Which of the following nitrogenous fertilizer is neutral fertilizer?

a) Ammonium sulphate
b) Anhydrous ammonia
c) Urea
d) CAN (Calcium ammonium nitrate)

34. Which of the following fertilizer is the richest source of sulphur?

a) Ammonium sulphate
b) Single super phosphate
c) Gypsum
d) Potassium magnesium sulphate

35. Potassium chloride or MOP is not suitable for sugar crops as it affects on..........

a) Sugar recovery b) Sugar synthesis

c) Sugar accumulation d) Sugar translocation

36. When one row is skipped and the population is adjusted by decreasing intra-row spacing is known as

a) Square planting b) Rectangular planting

c) Paired-row planting **d) Replacement series**

37. Botanical name of white gram is

a) *Cicer arientinum* **b) *Cicer kabulium***

c) Both d) None

38. Crop which is grown for food, fodder, manuring and soil conservation is

a) Mung b) Maize

c) Cowpea d) None

39. Which one of the following varieties of pigeon pea is an extra early maturing?

a) Pusaageti b) Type-I

c) Mukta **d) Prabhat, UPAS-120**

40. A soil auger having height of 20 cm and inside diameter of 10 cm will have..........cm^3 volume of soil core

a) 1070 **b) 1570**

c) 200 d) 2.00

41. Flow of water in channel using V notch is computed by formula

a) $Q=0.0138^{5/2}$ b) $Q=0.0138^{5}$

c) $Q=0.0138^{2}$ d) None

42. The amount of water that would cover an acre of land to a depth of one foot assuming no seepage evaporation and run-off loses is called

a) Acre foot of water b) Acre inch

c) Acre yard d) None

43. ....involves expenditure of energy in contrast to imbibition and osmosis

a) Active absorption b) Mass flow

c) Passive absorption d) None

44. CCC (Cycocyel) is a .... type of anti-transparents

a) Film forming
b) Stomatal closing
c) Growth retardant
d) All

45. Horti/silvi-pastoral system is suitable for ....lands

a) Arable
b) Non arable
c) Hills
d) All

46. Who discovered the essentiality of boron to plants?

a) Sprengel
b) L. Sommer and P. Lipman
c) K. Warringgton
d) I Arnonand P. R. Stout

47. Which of the following ratios between nursery area and transplantation is correct when rice seeding are raised by "Dapog method"

a) 1:50
b) 1:25
c) 1:10
d) 1:250

48. Propanil (Stam F-34) herbicide should be applied in rice after transplanting

a) 2-4 DAT
b) 6-8 DAT
c) 10-14 DAT
d) 2 weeks

49. The inflorescence in cotton is

a) Axillary
b) Panicle
c) Spikelet
d) Era

50. "Boll shading" in cotton is due to

a) Plant is over loaded with bolls
b) Inhibitory effect of ABA (Abscisic acid)
c) Heavy dressing of urea
d) Frequent irrigation

51. The autumn planting of sugarcane is most successful when planted in month of

a) September
b) October
c) November
d) February

52. Sesamum seed normally contains protein and oil per cent

a) 25 and 40
b) 20 and 48
c) 45 and 26
d) 43 and 22

53. Fruit of Green gram is known as ....

a) Pod
b) Caryopsis
c) Siliquae
d) Dutum

54. Triticale is a cross between
    a) Wheat X Rye b) Oat X Barley
    c) Wheat X Barley d) None

55. In *Cynadon ductylon* the vegetative propagation is through.........
    a) Seeds b) Suckers
    c) Rhizomes d) Underground stems

56. Moisture stress in soils and plants during crop growth due to imbalance between soil moisture and evapo-transpiration of a crop is......
    a) Agricultural drought b) Hydrological drought
    c) Meteorological drought **d) Physiological drought**

57. Which of the following antitranspirant belongs to stomatal closing group
    a) Cycocel **b) PMA**
    c) Silicon d) Paraquat

58. The condition favorable for precipitation is
    a) Low moisture content c) High moisture content
    c) Cooling of air d) Descending air

59. The term trickle irrigation is used synonymously with
    a) Sprinkler irrigation **b) Drip irrigation**
    c) Both d) None

60. Which one of the following is a *Kharif* crop
    a) Pearl millet b) Lentil
    c) Mustard d) Wheat

61. Which of the following is commonly referred to as muriate of potash
    a) Potassium nitrate **b) Potassium chloride**
    c) Potassium sulphate d) Potassium silicon

62. For applying 100 Kg of nitrogen, how much urea would one use
    a) 45 Kg b) 111 Kg
    c) 217.39 Kg d) 333 Kg

63. The species of rice (*Oryza*), other than *O. sativa*that is cultivated is
    a) *O. rufipugons* b) *O. longisteminata*
    c) O. glaberrima d) *O. nivara*

64. All weather phenomena like rain, fog and mist occurs in ....
    a) Troposphere b) Mesosphere
    c) Ionosphere d) Ozonosphere

65. A strain resulting from exposure to a particular environment is termed as

a) Ecotype b) Ideotype

c) Ecophone d) Ecotone

66. The practice of cross ploughing the young crop of rice to reduce weeds and vegetative growth of crop is called

a) Puddling b) Beushening

c) Khelua d) Taungya

67. Which of the following sub-species of *Zea mays*is used as a popular snack food

a) Indurate **b) Avarta**

c) Ceretina d) Amylacea

68. Water potential of pure water is

a) 0 bar b) 1 bar

c) 100 bar d) 10^6 bar

69. In Cotton, Zn deficiency is known as

a) White bud **b) Little leaf**

c) Mottle leaf d) Fern leaf

70. *Phalaris minor* has developed resistance against which herbicide

a) 2,4-D **b) Isoproturon**

c) Sulphosulphan d) Oxadiazon

71. Hydrocyanic acid in sorghum is synthesized in ....

a) Leaves b) Stem

c) Roots d) Flower premordia

72. Which of the following weed is used as vegetable (Sag)

a) *Chinopodiummurale* b) *Convolvulus arvensis*

c) *Avena sativa* **d) *Chinopodium album***

73. Optimum seed rate of sugar beet (*Beeta vulgaris* L.) is

a) 3.6 Kg/ha b) 18-20 Kg/ha

c) 28-30 Kg/ha d) 38-40 Kg/ha

74. Which of the following crop is called as Hill millet

a) Kodo millet b) Horse millet

c) Finger millet d) Proso millet

75. Pusa Dofasali and Pusa Barsati are the improved varieties of ....

a) Green gram b) Pigeon pea

c) Cowpea d) Black gram

76. Topping operation is done in cotton at ......DAS for controlling the vegetative growth

a) 50-60 DAS **b) 70-75 DAS**

c) 80-90 DAS d) 30-45 DAS

77. The boll bearing branches or reproductive branches in cotton is called as...........

a) Sympodial b) Asympodial

c) Lower old branches d) New upper branches

78. Sugarcane + Mustard+ Potato is example of ......type of cropping system

a) Inter cropping b) Companion cropping

c) Multistoried cropping d) Parallel cropping

79. Those crops grown from February to May are called as.........

a) Decoy crop **b) Zaid crop**

c) Summer crop d) Off season crop

80. Tensiometer is suitable for ....type of soil

a) Clay loam **b) Sandy loam**

c) Clayey soil d) Loamy soil

81. Dried pods of Phaseolus vulgaris are called as...............

a) French bean **b) Rajma**

c) Wal d) None

82. Wherever one irrigation is available, the wheat crop should irrigated at ......

a) CRI stage b) Tillering stage

c) Flowering stage d) Milking stage

83. Safflower oil contains ....% linoleic acid

a) 55-80 b) 25-35

d) 35-45 d) 45-55

84. Rachna and Harbhajan are varieties of

a) *Pisum sativum var. hortens* b) ***Pisum sativum* var. *arvense***

c) *Pisum sativum var .gardens* d) None

85. The flowering time of tur is

a) **September- November** b) December- February

c) February- April d) May- June

86. A potato tuber represents

a) **Enlarged underground stem**

b) Enlarged underground root

c) Enlarged underground nodule

d) None

87. The inflorescence of sugarcane is

a) Silique **b) Open panicle**

c) Spikelet d) Ear

88. Common snail is a bio-agent to control.........aquatic weeds.

a) Typha **b) Water hychianth**

c) Hydrilla d) All

89. A short duration crop in between two main Crops is termed as.........

a) Cash crop **b) Catch crop**

c) Companion crop d) Ephemerals

90. A fodder for pasture legume is

a) Glyricidia b) Stylosanthus

c) Cowpea **d) Sesbania**

91. The rate of increase in reaction for every 10^0 C temperature is called

a) Q_{10} b) K_{10}

c) C_{10} d) T_{10}

92. Low salt tolerance crops is/are

a) Pulses **b) Pea**

c) Sesamum d) All

93. Splash and sheet erosion are also known as

a) Inter-rill erosion b) Gully erosion

c) Both a and b d) None

94. Chlorosis is observed in upland rice due to deficiency of

a) S **b) Fe**

c) Zn d) Mn

95. Irrigation interval is a function of

a) Crop
b) Soil
c) Both
d) None

96. ....is a leaf reflectant type of anti-transpirant

a) PMA
b) Kaolin
c) Mobileaf
d) All

97. Couch grass is

a) Sorghum
b) Sugarcane
c) Striga
d) *Agropyronrepens*

98. Mat type nursery is releted to

a) Tobacco crop
b) Paddy crop
c) Onion crop
d) Brinjal crop

99. Brace roots in maize originated from

a) Radicle
b) Plumule
c) Endosperm
d) Nodes

100. Which of the following is TPS variety of potato

a) JH 222
b) HPS 1/113
c) PJ 376
d) Jr 5857

101. 2-4 D Herbicide should not be used in ....

a) Sorghum
b) Jute
c) Cotton
d) Maize

102. Kundan is Variety of.........

a) Bajara
b) Maize
c) Onion
d) Wheat

103. Gypsum used for Agriculture purpose should be ......% pure.

a) 1
b) 65
c) 100
d) 10

104. .... is primary stage of water erosion.

a) Gully erosion
b) Splash erosion
c) Rill erosion
d) Sheet erosion

105. .... is used for cold cloud formation.

a) Silver iodide
b) Sodium chloride
c) HCL
d) Both a & b

106. Stomp is the trade name of .... herbicide.
a) Simazine **b) Pendamethaline**
c) Fluchloraline d) Propanil

107. Specific heat is higher in ....
a) Sand b) Silt
c) Clay **d) Humus**

108. Major pest of Groundnut is............. .
a) White grub b) Aphid
c) Tikka **d) All**

109. Diseased plant produced due to repeated cultivation known as.......... .
a) Chemoalexin b) Alexin
c) Phytoalexin **d) None**

110. Colour of ozone gas is.........
a) Green b) Yellow
c) Light blue d) Colourless

111. Which seed is commanly used by farmers for commercial crop production?
a) Certified seed b) Breeder seed
c) Nucleus seed d) All above

112. The secondary tillage operation are restricted in ....
a) Zero tillage b) Minimum tillage
c) Both a& b d) Only b

113. Cultivation of crop is restricted after ....in land capability classification.
a) Class-1 b) Class-7
c) Class-3 **d) Class-5**

114. Linear strip plantation is the example of ....
a) Agro-forestry b) Farm forestry
c) Social extension forestry d) Forestry

115. .... Is the poor man's substitute for ghee.
a) Groundnut **b) Sesamum**
c) Soybean d) Lentil

116. Term Green revolution coined by ....
a) MS. Swaminathan b) Norman Borlaug
c) Vasantrao Naik **d) William gaud**

117. World Meteorology Day is celebrated on ....
a) 21 March
b) 23 March
c) 16 Sept
d) 4 December

118. Which crop show all three kinds of Dormancy?
a) Wild oat
b) Chickpea
c) Castor
d) Rye

119. In which five year plan Agro-climatic zone were classified by planning commission?
a) 6th
b) 7th
c) 8th
d) None of these

120. Approximate net irrigated area of India is (Mha).....
a) 30
b) 63
c) 80
d) 58

121. The fruit of rapeseed and mustard is known as........ .
a) Pod
b) Grain
c) Siliqua
d) Caryopsis

122. The origin of man made cereal triticale is......... .
a) India
b) USA
c) Switzerland
d) Sweden

123. One ha.cm is equivalent to ...... m^3 of water.
a) 100
b) 1000
c) 28.3
d) 10000

124. Hydrated calcium sulphate is called as ....
a) MOP
b) Gypsum
c) SSP
d) Urea

125. 2017 is designated as International year of ....
a) Family farming
b) Dal year
c) Sustainable tourism for development
d) Soil

126. One bale of Cotton is ......
a) 170 kg
b) 180 kg
c) 160 kg
d) 165 kg

127. Entry of water in the soil is referred as ………

a) Percolation **b) Infiltration**

c) Seepage d) Osmosis

128. CRIDA is Located at…….

a) Banglore b) New Delhi

c) Nagpur **d) Hyderabad**

129. Asymbiotic nitrogen Biofertilizer is………

a) BGA **b) Azatobacter**

c) Beijerinkia d) Rhizobium

130. Jute belongs to family ………

a) Pedaliaceae b) Poaceae

c) Tiliaceae d) Leguminaceae

131. Kaoline is ……… type of Antitranspirant.

a) Stomatal closing b) Film forming

c) Growth retardant **d) Reflecting**

132. During 2 years period 8 crops are grown on same piece of land in rotation. What is rotational intensity?

a) 400 b) 200

c) 600 d) 100

133. Triticale is a cross between ……

a) Wheat x Barley **b) Wheat x Rye**

c) Rice x Wheat d) Rye x Wheat

134. Cation exchange capacity of soil depends on content of ……… .

a) Sand b) Silt

c) Clay d) All the these

135. Present agriculture growth rate of India estimated in 12th five year plan …..

a) 4 % **b) 1.6 %**

c) 4.8 % d) 12 %

136. Delinting of cotton seed may be done with ……..

a) H_2SO_4 b) NAOH

c) NH_4CL d) HNO_3

137. The term mansoon is derived from ……..word.

a) Latin **b) Arabic**

c) Greek d) Roman

138. Which crop is most drought toleran.......

a) Toria
b) Taramira
c) Rai
d) Yellow sarson

139. Fluchloralin can be used for weed control in soybean as........

a) Pre-emergence
b) Pre-plant incorporation
c) Through irrigation
d) None

140. In maize plant ....

a) Silk appears first
b) Tassel appears first
c) Both at same time
d) None

141. Retting temperature for jute is ....

a) 14°C
b) 28°C
c) 26°C
d) 34°C

142. Set line cultivation is followed in .... in Gujrat.

a) Cotton
b) Groundnut
c) Sugarcane
d) Both a & b

143. Moisture % in grain should be reduced to ....% before storage.

a) 20
b) 16
c) 11
d) 18

144. ....is submerged aquatic weed.

a) Typha
b) Hydrilla
c) Water hyacinth
d) Water lily

145. .... crop is known as unpredictable legume.

a) Groundnut
b) Green gram
c) Pigeon Pea
d) Soybean

146. .... used as pollution indicator.

a) Wild castor
b) Wild mustard
c) Wild niger
d) *Opuntia* spp

147. First organic state in India is......

a) Assam
b) Sikkim
c) Kerala
d) Both b & c

148. Gram is a .....

a) Pulse crop
b) Rabi crop
c) Leguminous crop
d) All of these

149. Trickle irrigation is also known as ....irrigation.

a) Surface b) Subsurface

c) Drip d) Sprinkler

150. Objectionable weed present in lucern is.........

a) Chinchorin **b) Cuscuta**

c) Argimone d) Melilotus

151. MSP Price declared by CACP for comman Rice crop is.......Rs in 2016-17 was.

a) 1470 b) 1520

c) 1400 d) 2050

152. Productivity of Sugarcane is highest in ....

a) Maharashtra b) Uttar Pradesh

c) Tamilnadu d) Karnataka

153. "Krushi pandit" title is awarded by ....

a) ICAR b) IARI

c) President of India d) FAO

154. Most destructive disease of Sugarcane is..........

a) Mosaic b) Grassy shoot

c) Red rot d) None of these

155. .... is camel crop.

a) Bajara **b) Sorghum**

c) Barley d) Maize

156. Smell at soil after fresh shower as due to .....

a) Ray fungi b) Algae

c) Actinomycetes **d) Both a & c**

157. Broad bed furrow (BBF) evolved by ICRISAT used in which soil.

a) Black soil b) Clay loam soil

c) Sandy soil d) Loam soil

158. Farm building are necessary evil is stated by American author ......

a) Johnsan b) Jethro Tull

c) Wilson **d) Efferson**

159. It has been observed that soil pH Increase in.......

a) Summer **b) Winter**

c) Zaid d) Mansoon season

160 Thinning is carried out ……. Weeks after sowing of crops.

a) 1 **b) 2-3**

c) 3-4 d) 4-5

161. Mentha is propagated by ………

a) Bulb b) Sucker

c) Tuber **d) Seed**

162. Process of flue curing is related to ……..

a) Chewing **b) Cigarrate**

c) Bidi d) Snuff

163. The temp of mean sea level is……..

a) 20 **b) 15**

c) 14 d) 8

164. Crop infected with weed show deficiency of………

a) K b) P

c) S **d) N**

165 Which of the following is/are variety of mustard developed through Somatic hybridization in India?

a) Pusa kisan b) Pusa Jay

c) Pusa Jay kisan d) Both a & c

166. First Hybrid variety of Cotton (H4) is developed in…….year.

a) 1870 **b) 1970**

c) 1986 d) 1973

167. Rice grain is deficient in ……..

a) Lysine b) Leucine

c) Methionine d) Gluten

168. Chromosome number of *Cicer arietinum* is…….

a) 14 **b) 16**

c) 24 d) Both a & b

169. Inflorescence of Sugarcane is called as……..

a) Arrow b) Open panicle

c) Both a & b d) Spike

170. Paira and Utera Cropping system is closely related to ....

a) Sugarcane **b) Rice**

c) Jowar d) Gram

171. Agriculture is Latin word developed from .....

a) Ager b) Agar

c) Agur d) Agir

172. CIMMYT related to ....crop /crops.

a) Maize b) Wheat

c) Wheat + maize d) Rice

173. Indian meteorological department is established at Pune in.......

a) 1875 b) 1885

c) 1884 d) 1874

174. Black revolution is related to ......

a) Food processing b) Fertilizer production

c) Jathropa production d) Onion

175. In India highest irrigation potential is of the state.....

a) Maharashtra b) Kerala

c) Haryana **d) Punjab**

176. Prakash, Parvati is the variety of ....crop.

a) Babycorn **b) Sweetcorn**

c) Bajara d) Gram

177 The average annual rainfall of India is about ....

a) 1194 mm b) 1180 mm

c) 1094 mm d) 1199 mm

178. Botanical name of Indian Mustard is..........

a) *Brassica nigra* **b) *Brassica juncea***

c) *Brassica comprestris* d) *Eruna sativa*

179. Full form of SAR........

a) Sodium Absorption ratio **b) Sodium Adsorption ratio**

c) Silica Absorption ratio d) None of these

180. Ephemerals plants complete their life cycle within ......

a) 2-4 weeks b) 2-4 months

c) 2-4 days d) 2-4 years

181 Raising of crop with least tillage operations is called........
a) Minimum tillage b) Zero tillage
c) No tillage **d) All of these**

182. Tokyo is the variety of ....
a) Wheat **b) Buck wheat**
c) Durum wheat d) Tritacle

183. In series both crops are called as component crops.
a) Replacement b) Additive
c) Inter d) Intra

184. Origin of Potato is.......
a) South America b) North America
c) Brazil d) Africa

185 Which crop is used for making paint, vernish ....
a) Safflower b) Sunflower
c) Both a & b d) Linseed

186. Best source of Nitrogen in Normal soil is.......
a) Urea b) Ammonium sulphate
c) CAN d) All of these

187. Which of the following is C4 plant?
a) Pea b) Gram
c) Potato **d) Maize**

188. Which plant is used for sodium deficiency indicator ......
a) Sugarbeet b) Carrot
c) Potato d) Mustard

189. The most critical stage of irrigation in wheat crop is.........
a) Tillering **b) Crown root initiaton**
c) Flowering d) Flag leaf

190. *Triticum aestivum*is ......
a) Hexaploid b) Diploid
c) Tetraploid d) Euploid

191. Which crop is Firstly marketed by AGMARK.....
a) Soybean b) Sunhemp
c) Sunflower **d) Maize**

192. The crop having highest pesticide use .....
 a) Maize **b) Cotton**
 c) Rice d) Wheat
193. Soil air content CO_2 %......
 a) 0.03 b) 0.30
 c) 0.25 d) 0.025
194. Crop logging is done ......
 a) Sugarcane b) Maize
 c) Tobacco d) Cotton
195. The practice of growing arable crops between two subsequent rows of leguminous shrubs is called as......
 a) Lay farming b) Alley farming
 c) Alley cropping d) Alternate land use
196. Annedation refers to ....interaction which occurs both in space & time.
 a) Supplementary b) Independent
 c) Complementary d) Antagonastic
197 Cropping scheme is the........
 a) List of crops **b) Crops plan**
 c) Plan of enterprises d) Plan of operations
198. Sugarcane variety is famous as Wondercane......
 a) CO-671 b) CO-527
 c) CO-0238 d) CO-449
199. Pusa composite 701 is newly release variety of ...... crop.
 a) Wheat **b) Pearl millet**
 c) Jowar d) Seasamum
200. Succeeding crop in relay cropping is called as ......
 a) Relay crop **b) Catch crop**
 c) Cash crop d) Ratoon crop
201. Study of Grasses is called as........
 a) Agro-forestry b) Agro-ecology
 c) Agrostology d) Weeds
202. Slope of Zing terracing & Bench terracing is.........% & ....% .
 a) 3-10 & 16-33 b) 2-5 & 3-10
 c) 10-15 & 16-33 d) 16-33 & 3-10

203. Celite is the example of........ type of Antitranspirant.
   a) Film forming b) Stomata closing
   c) Reflecting d) Growth retardant
204. Trade name of Dicamba is........
   a) Basalin **b) Banvel**
   c) Mechate d) Lasso
205. The value of solar constant is........
   a) 1.94 cal/cm/min b) 0.94 cal/cm/min
   c) 1.94 cal/cm/sec d) 1.94 cal/m/min
206. The vertical movement of wind is called as ....
   a) Wind **b) Air current**
   c) Both a & b d) None of these
207. Rise in temperature with rise in altitude called as........
   a) Inversion **b) Lapse rate**
   c) Adiabatic lapse rate d) All of these
208. National Research Centre for Agroforestry is situated at.......
   a) Ghaziabad **b) Jhansi**
   c) Hyderabad d) Banglore
209. Which one of the following is an organic fertilizer ....?
   a) Anhydrous ammonia b) SSP
   c) Urea d) Diammonium phosphate
210. Indicate the formula for leaf area index ......
   a) Leaf weight / leaf area b) Land area / leaf area
   c) Leaf area / land area d) Leaf area / leaf duration
211. Toxin produced by soyabean plant .....
   a) Gossypol **b) Goitrogen**
   c) HCN d) Neurotoxin
212. Olivine is the source of ....nutrient.
   a) Iron b) Nitrogen
   c) Boron **d) Molybdenum**
213. Parboiling operation is followed in.......crop.
   a) Rice b) Groundnut
   c) Cotton d) Sugarcane

214. Pulse crop that does not fix N ....

a) Rajma
b) French bean
c) Groundnut
d) Cowpea

215. Family of Buckwheat is.....

a) Linaceae
b) Pedaliaceae
c) Gramineae
d) Polygonaceae

216. General recommendation of fertilizer dosese for pulse crop......

a) 4:2:1
b) 3:2:1
c) 1:2:1
d) 2:2:1

217. Fruit type of Groundnut is ....

a) Legume
b) Pod
c) Lomentum
d) All of these

218. Test weight of Basmati rice is.....gm.

a) 21
b) 28
c) 25
d) 55

219. Acid rain is caused due to pollutants like......

a) Sulfur dioxide
b) Nitrogen oxide
c) Both a& b
d) Only a

220. .... zone is called as Zone of Illuviation.

a) O
b) A
c) B
d) E

221. The word Meteorology is derived from .... word.

a) Greek
b) Latin
c) Anglosexon
d) French

222. In munsell colour chart the variable 'Hue' denotes ....

a) Relative lightness
b) Purity of colour
c) Dominant wavelength
d) None

223. Water has maximum density at......°C.

a) 3.5
b) 4
c) 4.5
d) 5.2

224. Sand drawn disease in tobacco is caused due to ......element.

a) Magnesium
b) Potassium
c) Phospharus
d) Sulfur

225. Botanical name of Flint corn is……

a) *Zea mays indentata* **b) *Zea mays indurata***

c) *Zea mays amylacea* d) *Zea mays everta*

226. A noxious weed, whose seeds are difficult to separate, once mixed with crop.

a) Satellite weed **b) Objectionable weed**

c) Obligate weed d) Both a & b

227. First manufactured fertilizer in India is …….

a) SSP b) MOP

c) Urea d) All of these

228. Tz (Tetrazolium) test is done for …….

a) Viability of seeds b) Seed germination

c) Disease identification d) N Fix

229. NABARD was set up on the recommendation of…….

a) Shivraman committee b) Mehta committee

c) Nariman committee d) None

230. Indian Journal of Agriculture Sciences is published by …….

a) IARI **b) ICAR**

c) FAO d) Agricultural Universities

231. Pusa giant is the variety of …..

a) Berseem b) Napier

c) Both a & b d) Only a

232 Crop which has highest k+ uptake ……

a) Tea **b) Potato**

c) Wheat d) Cowpea

233. Father of golden revolution is……..

a) Dr. K. L. Chadha b) M. L. Troug

c) Nirpakh Tutej d) J. V. Liebig

234. PAR is measured by …….

a) Quantom sensor b) Lysimeter

c) Altimeter d) Both a & b

235. Lines joining points of equal depth of rainfall called ……..

a) Isohyets **b) Isopluvial**

c) Isotere d) Isotherm

236. The instrument which is used to measure Root pressure ....

a) Manometer b) Altimeter

c) Barometer d) Auxanometer

237. Which of the following is semi root parasite?

a) Loranthus b) Cuscuta

c) Orabanche **d) Striga**

238. Base temperature of Wheat is about......

a) 5°C b) 10°C

c) 4°C d) 12°C

239. First agricultural university in India was established in 1960 at

a) New Delhi b) Udaipur

c) Pantnagar d) Hissar

240. In which of the following crop earthing up is not recommended,

a) Cotton b) Potato

c) Sugarcane d) Sugarbeet

241. In wheat "Ear cockle" disease is caused by ....

a) Fungi b) Nutrient deficiency

c) Nematode d) Actinomycetes

242. High salt tolerant crop is ....

a) Moong bean **b) Sugarbeet**

c) Pea d) Muskmelon

243. Foundation seed is produced from.......

a) Nucleus seed **b) Breeder seed**

c) Truthful seed d) Certified seed

244. Cross pollination in Bajara occurs due to.......

a) Protoandry **b) Protogyny**

c) Cleistogamy d) None of these

245. HS 542 (Pusa Kiran) is new release variety of .... Crop.

a) Wheat b) Pearl millet

c) Castor d) Rice

246. Minimum support price for soybean in 2016 declared by CACP is........

a) 4220 b) 3950

c) 1330 **d) 2775**

247. GST is passed first by which state ……

a) Assam b) Maharashtra

c) Bihar d) Odissa

248. When C:N ratio exceed 30:1 , ……….. occurs.

a) Mineralization **b) Immobilization**

c) Both a & b d) Nitrification

249 Which cake has highest % of N …….

a) Safflower cake b) Cotton cake

c) Groundnut cake d) Neem cake

250. Highest use of potassic fertilizer in the state is……..

a) Gujrat b) Bihar

c) Punjab **d) Maharashtra**

251. Which *Rhizobium Spp.* is used for groundnut …….

a) *R. trifoli* **b) *R. japonicum***

c) *R. meliloti* d) *R. phaseoli*

252. Which of the following is the example of benificial nutrients ?

a) Vanadium b) Silicon

c) Cobalt **d) All of these**

253. Agriculture year in India is from …… to……

a) 1st April to 31st March **b) 1st June to 31st May**

c) 1st August to 31^{St} July d) None of these

254. ICRISAT is established in year ……..

a) 1970 **b) 1972**

c) 1975 d) 1980

255. Long form of IRDP …….

a) Integrated Rural Development Programme

b) Intensive Rural Development Project

c) Integrated Rural Development Project

d) Imperical Rural Development programme

256 The gas responsible for Bhopal gas tragedy in 1984…….

a) MIC b) Nitrogen oxide

c) CFC d) Methane

257. The name of Vitamin- E is……

a) Calciferol b) Phylloquinone

c) Ascorbic acid **d) Tocopherol**

258. World Food Day celebrated on.......

a) 5th June
b) 16th July
c) 16th October
d) 21st March

259. Vertical mulch is used in soils ....

a) Black cotton soil
b) Red soil
c) Laterite soil
d) All of these

260. Rancidity in sunflower oil is due to ......

a) Reduction
b) Oxidation
c) Both a & b
d) None of these

261. Origin of Moong is ....

a) Africa
b) China
c) S. W. Asia
d) India

262. ICARDA is located at ....and established in year........

a) Syria, 1945
b) Hyderabad, 1972
c) Geneva, 1977
d) Syria, 1977

263. The botanical name of Little millet is ....

a) *Setaria italica*
b) *Panicum sumatrense*
c) *Hordeum vulgare*
d) All of these

264. The colour of Registered seed is ....

a) White
b) Golden yellow
c) Purple
d) No colour

265. Seed plot technique is followed in .... Crop .

a) Potato
b) Wheat
c) Groundnut
d) Lentil

266. Paraquat and Diquat are the example of .... herbicide.

a) Pre-emergence
b) Post-emergence
c) Contact herbicide
d) Both a & c

267. The word Social forestry is first time used by Westoby in .... Year.

a) 1977
b) 1968
c) 1984
d) 1970

268. .... is also called as Extension forestry.

a) Farm forestry
b) Rural forestry
c) Urban forestry
d) All

269. Statement “Remove poverty” is related with which five year plan?

a) 4th **b) 5th**
c) 6th d) 7th

270. Which of the following ephemeral is used for curation of Jaundise.

a) Vasantvel b) Amaranthus
c) Niruri d) Cock’s comb

271 What the LER (land equivalent ratio) indicator, when it is more than one.

a) No gain, No loss **b) Yield advantage**
c) Yield loss d) None of these

272. C:N ratio of Normal soil is .....

a) 10:1 b) 20:1
c) 400:1 d) 80:1

273. Tensiometer works upto limit of ....atm.

a) 8.0 b) 0.08
c) 0.8 d) 0.008

274. ....is called as heart of Sprayer.

a) Pump b) Spray lance
c) Nozzle d) Agitator

275. In “Jenny’s equation” – t indicator........

a) Topography **b) Time**
c) Parent material d) Texture

276. First KVK is started at ....

a) Solan **b) Poducherry**
c) Bikaner d) Rahuri

277 Novjot is the variety of ..... crop.

a) Potato b) Wheat
c) Maize d) Bajara

278 Most abundant soil group in india is ....

a) Black b) Red
c) Alluvial d) All of these

279. Acid soil can be managed by ....

a) Add lime material b) Use basic fertilizer
c) Grow acid tolerant crop **d) All**

280. Which is the oil seed cum fiber crops?
   a) Linseed b) Sesame
   c) Groundnut d) Mustard
281. Chemical used for breaking seed dormancy of potato is....
   a) Thiourea b) Sodium thiocynate
   c) G.A. d) All of these
282. Pseudo cereal crop is .....
   a) Buck wheat b) Wheat
   c) Bajara d) Rice
283. Green leaf hopper is the vector of ...... disease.
   a) Hopper burn b) Blast
   c) Rice tungro d) Bacterial blight
284. Silicon is accumulated mostly in which crop....
   a) Rice b) Groundnut
   c) Wheat d) Barley
285. Long form of IMF.......
   a) International money fund b) International marginal fund
   c) Indian money fund **d) International monetary fund**
286. Central tuber crop research institute is located at ....
   a) Kasargord b) Jhansi
   c) New Delhi **d) Thiruvananthapuram**
287. .... soil having highest pore spaces.
   a) Clay b) Silt
   c) Sand d) Loamy
288. The smallest unit of soil classification is the .....
   a) Order b) Family
   c) Subgroup **d) Series**
289. Recently formed soil order is .....
   a) Gelisol b) Vertisol
   c) Entisols d) Endisols
290. The Bemlen factor is ....
   a) 1.68 b) 1.78
   c) 1.88 **d) 1.72**

291. The soil (Sandy soil) is transported by wind is called ....

a) Loess **b) Aeolian**

c) Glacial d) Alluvial

292. Biuret toxic to plants hence, Concentration in urea should not exceed ....%

a) 0.5 b) 1.00

c) 1.5 d) 2.5

293 Which of the following is the example of Immobile Nutrient?

a) Calcium b) Boron

c) Both a & b d) Only a

294. Soil having usually less than 20% organic matter is called as ....

a) Organic soil **b) Mineral soil**

c) Regosol d) None of these

295. A+B+C horizons called as ......

a) Solum b) Organic layer

c) Regolith d) All of these

296. White bud of maize is due to deficiency of ....

a) Zinc b) Molybdenum

c) Magnese d) Chlorine

297. The year 2015 is declared as ....

a) Dal year **b) Soil year**

c) Tourism year d) None of these

298. The present (till late 2018) Governor of RBI was ....

a) Dr. Raghuram Rajan **b) Dr. Urjit Patel**

c) Dr. Adam Smith d) Dr. D. Subha Rao

299 .....is used for preparation of alcohol.

a) Molasses b) Bagasses

c) Press mud d) All of these

300. Mutant variety of Gram is ....

a) RS-11 b) ICCC-2

c) C-235 **d) BGM-547**

301. Which of the following is the partial stem parasite of mango
   a) Cuscutta
   b) Loranthus
   c) Orobanche sp.
   d) Striga
302. Which of the following is a scientific name of 'B-7' vit.
   a) Biotin
   b) Folic acid
   c) Cyanocobalamin
   d) Pantothenic acid
303. Groundnut pegs when developed in the soil forms
   a) Fruits
   b) Roots
   c) Tubers
   d) Stems
304 Which of the following is not correct.
   a) Inter cropping : wheat after rice
   b) Multi-tier cropping : coconut pepper – cacao – pineapple
   c) Sole cropping : potato
   d) Relay cropping : sowing pulse in rice crop prior to harvest
305. Which of the following parts of the tobacco plant synthesizes nicotine.
   a) Branch
   b) Stem
   c) Root
   d) Leaf
306 The most popular 'extra early maturing variety in pigeon pea is
   a) UPAS – 120
   b) Type – 7
   c) Gulbarga
   d) Type – 17
307 Cropping intensity & Gestation period of the crops grown are
   a) Not inter related
   b) Directly related
   c) Exponentially related
   d) Inversely related
308. The intercultural operation in standing broadcast rice crop is
   a) Pudding
   b) Spudding
   c) Pudding
   d) N.O.T.
309. In cotton the maturity of fibre is judged by
   a) Altimeter
   b) Arealometer
   c) Auxenometer
   d) Aerometer

Fill in the Blanks

1. Parthenium is classified as **Annual** weed on the basis of life cycle.
2. **Basalin** is the trade name of **Fluchloralin** herbicide.
3. Botanical name of wild rice ***Echinochlo cruslis***.

4. ***Tridex procumbence*** belongs to Composite family.
5. Complete destruction of weed is known as **Eradication**.
6. Parthenium weed is controlled biologically by using Mexican beetle (***Zygogramma bicularata).***
7. Weed moves from its origin to new environment is called as **Alien weeds.**
8. Glyphosate is suitable herbicide for control of ***Cynadon dactylon*** weed.
9. Fast growing and fast shading crop is called smoother crop.
10. Degrading and chaining method mainly used to remove the weeds from **aquatic area**.
11. Short lived annual weeds are called **Ephemeral**.
12. *Lantana camera* weed can be control by using seed fly ***Crocidoscma lantana*** bioagents.
13. **Aghada** is classified as Indigenous weed on the basis of origin of weeds.
14. The trade name of Alachlor is **Lasso**.
15. Translocate/Non selective is suitable herbicide for ***Cynadon dactylon***.
16. **Atrazin** is selective herbicide used in maize as pre emergence application.
17. The critical period of crop weed competition is **20-30** days.
18. Germination of striga can be initiated by Sorgum.
19. Smoother effect of weed can be achieved by cultivating **sweet potato, mataki, Hulga.**
20. Typha spp. is aquatic weed.
21. ***Calotropis gigantae*** is the botanical name of Rui/Rander plant.
22. Enforced dormancy is due to **deep placement seed**.
23. Water hyacinth is an **aquatic weed.**
24. The herbicide applied before of crop swoing are called as **PPI herbicide.**
25. Weed compete with crop plant mainly for **Nutrition.**
26. Harmful effect of one plant on another plant through the production of toxic chemical compound is refered as **Allopathy**.
27. A chemical used for killing the trees/weeds is known as **brush** killer.
28. Wild rice is the example of mimicry weed in **rice crop.**
29. Glyphosate is suitable herbicide for control of weed in non **cropped area.**
30. Lotus and water hyacinth are examples of **aquatic** weeds.

31. Striga and orobanch are example of root **Parasitic weed**.
32. In non-cropped aera **Glyphosate**, Paraqut wewe used for controlling the weed.
33. Math, Tandulja and Kalemath were example of weeds belongs to the family **amranthaceae**.
34. Two example of **periannial** weed-Hariyali, Nutgrass.

2

Soil Science & Agricultural Chemistry

1. The example of trisaccharide is————————.

   a) Raffinose b) Maltose

   c) Glucose d) Sucrose

2. Betaoxidation of fatty acid was proposed by ——————.

   a) Rose **b) Knoop**

   c) J.B Sumner d) Bloor

3. The first essential amino acid is discovered by ——————in 1935.

   a) Carl Neuberg b) J.B. Sumner

   c) Rose d) Knoop

4. The process of formation of soap is called ——————.

   a) Haloganation b) Rancidity

   c) Saponification d) Acid value

5. The iodine value is the measure of——————————in fatty acid.

   a) Degree of unsaturaton b) Saponification

   c) Rancidity d) Acid value

6. Power house of energy of living cell is ——————.

   a) Vacuoles **b) Mitochondria**

   c) Nucleus d) Ribosome

7. Pentose phosphate pathway is the sourse of ——————.

   a) Glucose b) Maltose

   c) Pentose sugar d) Sucrose

8. The transformation of sugar to glycogen is known as——————.

   a) Photosynthesis b) Respiration

   c) Photophosphorelation **d) Glycogenesis**

9. ——————————— is the only non-reducing sugar.
   a) Lactose **b) Sucrose**
   c) Maltose d) Galactose

10. The term Biochemistry was first introduced by German scientist——— ——————— in 1903.
   a) Knoop b) Antoine Lavoieier
   c) J.B. Sumner **d) Carl Neuberg**

11. Deficiency of vitamin C leads to ———————.
   a) Ricket b) Pellegra
   c) Scurvy d) Bery-bery

12. The gradual change in specific rotation is known as ———————.
   a) Reducing power **b) Mutarotation**
   c) Dehydration d) Methylation

13. Hydrolytic product of simple and compound lipids are known as ——— ———
   a) Fatty acid b) Glycerol
   c) Amino acid **d) a+b**

14. ——————— is the blood sugar controlling hormone.
   a) Insulin b) Heamoglobulin
   c) Myoglobulin d) Saliva

15. ——————— is the protein present In hair.
   a) Collagen b) Elastin
   c) Keratin d) Fibroin

16. ——————— pigment impart yellow colour in plant leaves.
   a) Carotene b) Chlorophyll
   c) Anthocyanin d) Xanthophyll

17. ———————is the father of modern enzymology.
   a) Rose b) knoop
   c) J.B Sumner c) Bloor

18. All enzymes are ——————— in nature.
   a) Carbohydrate **b) Protein**
   c) Lipid d) Vitamins

19. All monosaccharides are ——————— sugar.
   a) Reducing b) Non Reducing
   c) Disaccharide d) Trisaccharide

20. The end product of glycolysis is ——————
    a) Ascorbic acid **b) Pyruvic acid**
    c) Citric acid d) Acetic acid
21. —————— cell oragnel is responsible for photosynthesis.
    a) Vacuoles b) MitochondrIa
    c) Nucleus **d) Chlorophyll**
22. The substance upon which an enzyme acts is known as ——————
    a) Substrate
    b) Active site
    c) Enzyme-substrate complex
    d) None of these
23. Vitamin D is also called as ——————.
    a) Niacin b) Retinol
    c) Calciferol d) Tocopherol
24. Lock and key model of enzyme mechanism is given by ——————
    a) F.W. Kuhne b) J. B. Sumner
    c) Watson and Crick **d) Emil Fischer**
25. ——————method is used for estimation of available nitrogen in soil.
    a) Olsen's method **b) Alkaline permanganate method**
    c) Rapid titration method d) Turbidity method
26. —————— refers to a situation in which a crop need more of a given element, yet has shown no deficiency symptoms.
    a) Hidden hunger b) Toxicity
    c) Deficiency d) None of these
27. Deficiency of Zinc in rice is called ——————disease.
    a) Akiochi b) Whip tail
    c) Khaira d) Chlorosis
28. The alkali soil where the nitrates are in excess and given a brown colour to the soil ,such soil is known as——————
    a) White alkali b) Black alkali
    c) Degraded alkali d) Saline soil
29. ——————nitrogen fixing bacteria is associated with root nodules of leguminous plants.
    a) Symbiotic b) Non symbiotic
    c) Free living d) None of these

30. % K = % K_2O * ————.

a) 0.43 **b) 0.83**

c) 1.33 d) 2.24

31. Water soluble form of phosphorus is ————.

a) H_3PO_4 b) H_2PO^{-4-}

c) HO^{-4} d) $PO^{------4}$

32. The boron deficiency leads to ———— in cauliflower.

a) Akiochi b) Whip tail

c) Khaira **d) Hallow stem**

33. ———— is common used soil amendment for acidic soil.

a) Lime b) Gypsum

c) Iron pyrite d) Sulphur

34. Apetite is a source of ———— plant nutrient.

a) Nitrogen b) Potassium

c) Phosphorus d) Sulphur

35. Yellowing start on young leave is due to deficiency of————.

a) Phosphorus b) Copper

c) Manganese d) Sulphur

36. Capacity of soil to supply nutrient to plant in adequate form is called————.

a) Soil Fertility b) Soil productivity

c) Soil profile d) Soil microbes

37. PH of alkali soil is ————.

a) PH 7 b) PH 6.5-7.5

c) Less than 7 **d) More than 8.5**

38. Paddy absorbs nitrogen in ———— form.

a) Nitrate b) Amide

c) Ammonium d) Ammonium Nitrate

39. Fine texture soils have ———— CEC.

a) Higher b) Lower

c) Medium d) None of these

40. Unit of electrical conductivity is ————

a) Percentage b) gm/cc

c) dS/m d) me/lit

41. Carbon is ——————— plant nutrient.
 a) Macronutrient b) Beneficial
 c) Micronutrient d) Secondary nutrient

42. Molybdenum is essential component of——————— enezym.
 a) Urease b) Zymase
 c) Lipase **d) Nitrate reductate**

43. Orthoclase is source of ——————— plant nutrient.
 a) Nitrogen **b) Potassium**
 c) Phosphorus d) Sulphur

44. Essentiality of Mo was discovered by ———————.
 a) R.M. Welch b) E.E. Cary
 c) P.H. Brown **d) Arnon & Stout**

45. Cracking of fruits are developed due to deficiency of ———————
 a) Molybdenum b) Iron
 c) Boron d) Zinc

46. ——————— is macronutrient which is taken up both in cationic & anionic form.
 a) Nitrogen b) Potassium
 c) Phosphorus d) Sulphur

47. After a long period of submergence the pH of soil will be———————.
 a) Alkaline b) Neutral
 c) Acidic d) None of these

48. Marble is the product of——————— metamorphism of limestone.
 a) Hydro **b) Dynamo**
 c) Thermo d) None of these

49. The first scientific classification of soil was proposed in 1886 by Russian ———————.
 a) Hens Jenny b) E.W. Hilgard
 c) K.D. Glinka **d) V.V. Dokuchaive**

50. In most mineral soils the mean density of particle is about ———————gm/cc.
 a) 2.65 b) 1.77
 c) 1.35 d) 1.65

51. Basalt is ———————— type of rock.

a) Intrusive **b) Extrusive**

c) Plutonic d) Coarse crystalline

52. The mineral theory of plant nutrition is put forth by————.

a) Hens Jenny b) E.W. Hilgard

c) K.D. Glinka **d) Justus Von Liebig**

53. The Dynamo metamorphosis is due to ———— which brought about by folding of rocks due to crust movement of earth.

a) Heat b) Water

c) Pressure d) None of these

54. Soil air contain much greater proportion of ________than atmospheric air.

a) Oxygen **b) Carban dioxide**

c) Nitrogen d) Hydrogen

55. ———————— is science dealing with the genesis, survey and classification of soils in nature.

a) Pedology b) Petrology

c) Soil conservation d) Soil physics

56. The gaseous envelop that covers the earth surface is the————.

a) Lithosphere b) Biosphere

c) Hydrosphere **d) Atmosphere**

57. ———————— formulated the equation of soil forming factorsas S = f(Cl,o,r,p,t….).

a) Hens Jenny b) E.W. Hilgard

c) K.D. Glinka d) Justus Von Liebig

58. The intrusive rocks consolidated in vertical cracks and formed wall like masses are called ————.

a) Vein **b) Dykes**

c) Sills d) None of these

59. The material transported and deposited by the wind is known as————

a) Marine b) Colluvium

c) Loess d) Glacial

60. At wilting co-efficient water is held at ————.

a) -15 bar b) 15 bar

c) 31 bar d) 1 atm

61. ―――――――― is the example of transparent mineral.

a) Copper pyrite | b) Iron pyrite
c) Milk quartz | d) Mica

62. Pedogenic process in which remove of silica and accumulation of Al & Fe oxide takes place known as ――――――――.

a) Laterization | b) Podzolization
c) Calcification | d) Eluviation

63. Horizon A and B collectively known as ――――――――.

a) Organic horizon | **b) Solum**
c) Eluviation | d) Soil profile

64. The irregular and narrow cracks are deposited by molten material and which consolidated is known ――――――――.+

a) Vein | b) Dykes
c) Sills | d) None of these

65. ―――――――― is active factor of soil formation.

a) Parent material | b) Topography
c) Climate | d) Time

66. The pH unit was first proposed by――――――――.

a) Sorenson | b) E.W. Hilgard
c) K.D. Glinka | d) Justus Von Liebig

67. In earth crust the predominant mineral is ――――――――.

a) Mica | **b) Feldspar**
c) Quartz | d) Dolomite

68. C:N ratio of normal soil――――――――.

a) 400:1 | **b) 10:1**
c) 80:1 | d) 200:1

69. ―――――――― is example of 2:1 type of expanding silicate clay mineral

a) Chlorite | b) Kaolinite
c) Montmorillonite | d) Mica

70. ―――――――― is the fundamental soil forming process.

a) Podzolization | **b) Humification**
c) Laterization | d) Calcification

71. Soil Particle have size less than 0.001 mm is called as――――――――.

a) Soil colloid | b) Clay
c) Sand | d) Silt

72. —————————— is the colour of the powder of a mineral.

a) Lustre b) Monometric

c) Hardness **d) Streak**

73. Mohr's scale is used to measure the —————————— of mineral.

a) Lustre b) Monometric

c) Hardness **d) Streak**

74. Physical weathering is essentially a process of ——————————.

a) Decomposition **b) Disintegration**

c) Hydration d) Soluton

75. Decomposition of organic matter produces CO_2 because of increased— ——————.

a) Microbial activity b) Root respiration

c) Diffusion of CO_2 d) Supply of CO_2 from air

76. Calcium cynamide and urea are —————————— type of fertilizers.

a) Ammonical b) Nitrate

c) Ammonical& nitrate **d) Amide**

77. Mycorrhizais the —————————— association of fungi with root vascular plant.

a) Free living b) Associative

c) Symbiotic d) Non Symbiotic

78. Diammonium phosphate contain —————————— % of phosphorus.

a) 21% **b) 46%**

c) 16% d) 60%

79. —————————— is used to reduce or completely suppress the reproduction ability of insect.

a) Chemosterilant b) Defoliant

c) Repellant d) Insecticide

80. —————————— type of phytohormone induce uniform ripening.

a) Gibbrellin b) Auxin

c) Cytokinin **d) Ethylene**

81. The botanical name of the sunhemp is——————————

a) Pongamia pinnata **b) Crotaloria juncea**

c) Sesbania aculeata d) Cyamopsistetra gonoliba

82. C:N ratio of the Wheat straw is ——————————.

a) 400:1 b) 100:1

c) 80:1 d) 20:1

83. ——————————- is referred as anti ageing agent.

a) Vit. A **b) Vit. C**

c) Vit. B d) Vit. D

84. Substances that drain moisture out of plants causing them to dry are called ——.

a) Chemosterilant b) Defoliant

c) Repellant **d) Desiccant**

85. Derris elliptica pyrethrin is derived from the dried flowers of————————————.

a) Chrysanthemum b) Rose

c) Tobacco d) Neem

86. The process which involves conversion of soil nitrate in to gaseous nitrogen or nitrous is called——————————.

a) Nitrification **b) Denitrification**

c) Ammonification d) Ammification

87. K_2O content of biogas slurry is—————————— %.

a) 5.0-8.0 b) 2 .0-2.5

c) 0.8-1.2 d) 1.1-2.0

88. Recommended dose of vermicompost is ——————————.

a) 5 t/ha b) 10 t/ha

c) 2 t/ha d) 8 t/ha

89. The chemical which is used to killed the ticks and mites are called————————

a) Bactericide **b) Acaricide**

c) Herbicide d) Chemosterilant

90. —————————— is example of undecomposed bulky organic manure.

a) Vermicompost b) Compost

c) FYM **d) Green manure**

91. Raw bone meal contains——————————%of phosphorus.

a) 2.5% **b) 20-25%**

c) 2-4% d) 10-12%

92. Calcium ammonium nitrate is———————— in reaction.

a) Basic b) Acidic

c) Neutral d) None of these

93. According to elemental composition of undecomposed organic matter contain ———————— % of ash

a) 40% b) 10%

c) 8% d) 25%

94. Undecomposed organic matter contain ———————— % of Protein

a) 10% **b) 5%**

c) 25% d) 60%

95. C:N ratio of the microorganism is————————.

a) 100:1 b) 400:1

c) 10:1 **d) 4:1-9:1**

96. ———————— are the any substance or mixture of substances used to prevent, destroy, repell or migrate any insect, rodent, nematode, fungi, weeds or any other form of terrestrial or aquatic plant or animal life or microorganism.

a) Pesticide b) Fertilizer

c) Growth hormone d) Fungicide

97. The Fertilizer control order came in to force in————————.

a) 1955 b) 1970

c) 1965 d) 1957

98. ———————— is example of zoocide (Rodenticide)

a) Rotenoue b) Vartarin

c) 2-4-D d) Penecillin

99. ———————— are compounds which added in soil to increase the availability of micronutrient and make them slowly available over a long period.

a) Chelate b) Fertilizer grade

c) Filler d) Conditioner

100. Chloride form potassic fertilizer should not be used in ———————— crop.

a) Wheat b) Chilli

c) Tobacco d) Jute

101. Father of soil science

a) J. V. Liebig b) Boussingaut

c) V. V. Dokuchaiev d) Walne

102. Study of soil in relation to growth, nutrition and yield of crops is called as:
   a) Pedology **b) Edaphology**
   c) Soil chemistry d) Petrology
103. Which of the following mineral is abundant on earth soil.
   a) Feldspar **b) Hornblende**
   c) Quartz d) Clay
104. Which of the following mineral is secondary mineral.
   a) Clay b) Mica
   c) Quartz d) Apatite
105. Which is the formula of Gypsum.
   a) SiO_2 b) Fe_2O_2
   c) $CaSO_4$ $2H_2O$ d) $CaCO_3$
106. Which is the most hard mineral.
   a) Quartz b) Gypsum
   c) Talc **d) Diamond**
107. The Intrusive rocks which consolidated at or in vertical crakes are called as:
   a) Dykes b) Sills
   c) Vein d) Plutonic
108. Granite is a
   a) Extrusive rock **b) Intrusive**
   c) Basic d) Ultra Basic
109. Limestone is a… type of rock.
   a) Igneous **b) Sedimentary**
   c) Metamorphic d) None of these
110. Marble is a …….. type of rock.
   a) Sedimentary b) Hydro metamorphic
   c) Thermo metamorphic **d) Dynamo metamorphic**
111. Process of moving out of Fe &Al is known as….
   a) Decalcification **b) Laterization**
   c) Solodization d) Podzolization
112. Process of Mixing of soil is known as…..
   a) Pedoturbation b) Gleization
   c) Salinization d) Solonization

113. 'O' horizon is present in
   a) Forest soil b) Arable soils
   c) Grass land d) None of these
114. Top most mineral horizon is
   a) 'O' horizon b) E horizon
   c) A horizon d) R horizon
115. Zone of Illuviation is present in
   a) O Horizon b) A Horizon
   c) E Horizon **d) B Horizon**
116. Canker nodule are found mostly in
   a) Black soil **b) Red soil**
   c) Laterite d) Calcareous
117. Laterite Soils dominant in
   a) Maharashtra b) Tamil Nadu
   c) Karnataka d) Kerla
118. Recently formed soils are called
   a) Entisols b) Aridisols
   c) Inceptisols d) Mollisols
119. Hydrated Iron oxides gives ..... colour to the soil
   a) Red b) Black
   c) Gray **d) Yellow**
120. At maximum water holding capacity, the tension is
   a) 15 bar b) 31 bar
   c) 0 bar d) 1/3 bar/0.33 bar
121. In high rainfall area, soil is
   a) Acidic b) Alkaline
   c) Laterite d) Saline
122. Vermiculite is a.... type of mineral
   a) 1:1 **b) 2:1 expanding**
   c) 2:1 Slightly expanding d) 2:1:1 non expanding
123. The unit of cation exchange capacity is
   a) dsm^{-1} b) $Cmol_{100}Kg^{-1}$
   c) $m.eq.100g^{-1}$ **d) Both b & c**
124. Kaolinite mineral have.... AEC than Montsmorillnite
   a) High b) Low
   c) Equal d) Very low

125. Golden green algae are the....

a) Cynophyta b) Bacilliophyta

c) Chrysophyta d) Xanthophyta

126. Thiobacillus Ferrooxidans are the

a) Sulphur Oxidizer b) Iron Oxidizer

c) Autotrophic Bacteria **d) Both b & c**

127. Azolla is a which type of nitrogen fixing Bacteria

a) Symbiotic heterotroph b) Non symbiotic heterotroph

c) Symbiotic Autotroph d) Non symbiotic autotroph

128. Aetinomycetes are more common in

a) Acidic soil b) Basic soil

c) Neutral soil **d) Both b & c**

129. Clay micelle have charge

a) +ve **b) -ve**

c) Neutral d) Only a

130. Fructose is a which type of sugar

a) Monosaccharides

b) Reducing disaccharides

c) Non reducing disaccharides

d) Polysaccharide

131. On hydrolysis of cellobiase it yields

a) Glucose + Glucose b) Galactose + glucose

c) Glucose + fructose d) Glucose + Fructose + Galactose

132. Pectins is a

a) Heteropolysaccharides

b) Homopolysaccharides

c) Structural Polysaccharides

d) Both A&C

133. The 'Lipid' term was first used by

a) Bloor b) Funk

c) Berzelius d) Kuhne

134. The source of Arachidonic fatty acid is...

a) Bacterial Fat **b) Animal fat**

c) Plant fat d) Cotton seed oil

135. Sulphur containing amino acid are
   a) Tryptophan b) Methionine
   c) Cysteine **d) Both b & c**
136. Which of the following is a non essential amino acid
   a) Cystine b) Tyrosine
   c) Proline **d) All**
137. Legumes are deficient in which protein
   a) Lysine b) Methionine
   c) Tryptopran **d) Bot b & c**
138. Elastin protein found in
   a) Hair **b) Insect wing**
   c) Muscle d) Horns
139. Hordein protein obtained from
   a) Wheat b) Corn
   c) Oat d) Rice
140. Vitellin protein present in
   a) Egg white b) Milk
   c) Egg yolk d) Milk whey
141. Serum albumin present in
   a) Muscle b) Blood plasma
   c) Egg white d) Sperm
142. Thrombin is a example of which protein
   a) Regulatory b) Structural
   c) Carrier **d) Defence**
143. The wheat protein is called as
   a) Zein **b) Gliadin**
   c) Hordein d) None of these
144. Nucleotide is a
   a) Acid + Pentose sugar **b) Acid + sugar + Nitrogenous bases**
   c) Nucleoside + Sugar d) Both b and c
145. Conversion of DNA into mRNA is called
   a) Transcription b) Translation
   c) Protein synthesis d) DNA replication

146. Which one is true regarding nitrogenous base pairs

a) A = T | b) A °T
c) A = G | d) G = C

147. DNA contain pyramidine bases

a) Uracil | b) Guanine
c) Thymine | d) Both b & c

148. Enzymes are denatured at

a) 0°C | b) 45°C
c) 60°C | d) 95°C

149. Hormone related to drought tolerance is

a) ABA | b) IBA
c) NAA | d) GA3

150. Ethylene hormone discovered by

a) G. H. Smith | **b) Burg & Thimann**
c) Yabuta and Hayashi | d) Beyliss and Starling

151. When energy is consumed for biosynthesis of cell components, that process is called

a) Metabolism | b) Catabolism
c) Anabolism | d) None of these

152. Estimation of crude fat done by the method

a) Benedict's method | **b) Soxhlet method**
c) Lowry's method | d) Fehling test

153. Plant usable form of Nitrogen is

a) NO_3- | b) NH_4^+
c) NO_2^- | **d) Only a & b**

154. Secondary nutrients are

a) N, P, K | b) C, H, O
c) Ca, Mg, S | d) Fe, Zn, Cu

155. The immobile elements in plant is

a) N | **b) Ca**
c) Mg | d) P

156. Diffusion distance of Phosphorus element is

a) 1 cm | b) 0.2 cm
c) 0.002 cm | d) 0.02 cm

157. Calcium taken by plant by the process

a) Mass flow b) Diffusion

c) Ion exchange **d) Root interception**

158. Opening and closing of stomata is regulated by

a) Nitrogen b) Phosphorus

c) Potassium d) Magnesium

159. Which element increases oil quality

a) Phosphorus b) Potassium

c) Sulphur d) Magnesium

160. Pollen viability is affected by

a) Mg **b) B**

c) Mo d) Cu

161. Male flower sterility is due to deficiency of

a) Cu b) Co

c) Mo d) B

162. Organic nitrogenous fertilizer are

a) CAN **b) Urea**

c) $CaCN_2$ d) Both b & c

163. In high pH soil the nitrogen loss due to

a) Leaching **b) Volatization**

c) Denitrification d) Both a & c

164. For reclamation of Alkaline soil use

a) Gypsum b) Dolomite

c) Lime **d) Both a & c**

165. Leaching is practiced in

a) Acidic soil **b) Saline soil**

c) Sodic soil d) Saline alkali

166. Which are the chloride loving plants

a) Grape **b) Oil palm and coconut**

d) Tobacco and Tomato d) Onion

167. Availability of K is high in pH

a) 3 to 4 b) 6.5 to 7.5

c) 6 to 10 d) >10

168. Fe & Mn deficiency most common in
    a) Calcareous soil   b) Acidic soil
    c) Alkaline soil   d) Black soil
169. Formula of calculating % K is
    a) % K_2O × 0.83   b) % K_2O × 0.43
    c) % K_2O × 1.20   d) % K_2O × 2.29
170. Boron sensitive crop is
    a) Sugarbeet   **b) Cabbage**
    c) Onion   d) Grape
171. In Acidic soil, the toxicity of
    a) Ca   b) Mg
    c) P   **d) Al**
172. The calcareous soils observed in
    a) Temperate region   **b) Arid region**
    c) High rainfall area   d) Medium rainfall area
173. Zn deficiency in Rice causes
    a) Akochi   b) Whiptail
    c) **Khaira**   d) None of these
174. Estimation of available phosphorus in calcareous soil by
    a) Alkaline permagnate method
    b) Olsens method
    c) Bray's method
    d) Flame photometer
175. The indicator plant of copper is
    a) Citrus   b) Sugarbeet
    c) Mustard   d) Potato
176. The C:N ratio of humus is
    a) 4:1 to 9:1   b) 20:1 to 30:1
    c) 10:1 to 12:1   **d) 10:1**
177. Slowly decomposing organic compound is
    a) Lignins   b) Crude protein
    c) Cellulose   d) Waxes

178. Which fertilizer used for explosive purpose

a) CAN b) $CaCN_2$

c) Ammonium Nitrate d) Ammonium Chloride

179. DAP contains N:P:K

a) 18:46:00 b) 20:20:0

c) 82:0:0 d) 11:52:00

180. Fulvic acid is a

a) Acid soluble b) Base soluble

c) Both acid & base soluble d) Insoluble

181. Potassium chloride not used as a potassic fertilizer in

a) Potato b) Tomato

c) Tobacco **d) All**

182. Copper sulphate is a

a) Algicides b) Bactericide

c) Molluscides d) Avicides

183. Molluscides is used to control

a) Birds b) Vegetative part

c) Snail & slug d) Fish

184. Pyrethrum damages the

a) Digestive system b) Respiratory system

c) Circulatory system **d) Nervous system**

185. Blood meal and meat meal are effective for

a) Oil crops b) Fruit Crops

c) Vegetable crops d) Ornamental crops

186. The precursor of ABA is

a) Terpenoids **b) Caratenoids**

c) Adenine d) Trytophane

187. Essential commodity Act passes in

a) 1914 **b) 1955**

c) 1995 d) 1994

188. Detection of adulteration in fertilizers by

a) Rapid test b) Ignition method

c) Gravimetric method d) EDTA method

189. Determination of water soluble phosphorus in super phosphate by
a) Ignition method **b) Pumberton method**
c) Flame photometer d) Devardas alloy method

190. Central soil and water conservation research and training institute is at
a) Karnal b) Bhopal
c) Dehradun d) Kanpur

191. The process of transportation of weathered material is called as
a) Deposition b) Podzolization
c) Denudation d) Soil genesis

192. Granular type of soil structure is
a) Porus **b) Non porus**
c) Both Porus and non porus d) None of these

193. Average particle density of soil is (g/cm^3)
a) 1.33 **b) 2.65**
c) 2.55 d) 1.50

194. Dominant spectral colour is called
a) Value **b) Hue**
c) Chroma d) None of these

195. Soil: water ratio of normal soil is
a) 1:1 **b) 2.5:1**
c) 1:2.5 d) 3:1

196. Which following element encourage deflocculation
a) H b) Ca
c) Mg **d) Na**

197. 1 atm is equal to
a) 1.013 bar b) 101.3 kpa
c) 101.3 bar d) Both a & b

198. The pF scale of capillary water is
a) 2.54 to 4.2 **b) <2.54**
c) 4.5 to 7 d) 1 to 0

199. The thermal conductivity high in
a) Sand b) Clay
c) Peat d) Loam

200. The slope of channel bunding is

a) 6% b) 3-10%

c) 2-10% d) 16-33%

201. Soils with high pH are generally deficient in

a) zn & Mn **b) B & Fe**

c) cu & Mo d) ca & Mg

202. Deficiency symptoms of calcium on plants are first noticed at

a) Growing point b) New leaf

c) Middle leaf d) Older leaf

203. Control soil salinity research institute is located at

a) Jodhpur **b) Karnal**

c) Dehradoon d) Hyderabad

204. The rate of water absorption by plants is decreased due to deficiency of

a) Boron b) Iron

c) Potassium d) Magnecium

205. The core metal in chlorophyll is

a) Fe **b) Mg**

c) Mn d) Zn

206. SAR of alkali soil is

a) < 15 b) < 13

c) > 13 d) > 15

207. The ratio of organic carbon to organic matter in soils is

a) 1.0 : 1. 7 b) 1.0 : 2.0

c) 1.7 : 1.0 d) 20.0 : 1.0

208. Which one of the following is a static property of soil

a) Soil structure b) Soil porosity

c) Soil colour **d) Soil texture**

209. Name the first phase of water erosion

a) Sheet erosion b) Rill erosion

c) Gully erosion **d) Splash erosion**

210. The process of deposition of soil material in the lower layer is called

a) Eluviation **b) Illuviation**

c) Podzalization d) Pedoturbation

211. Moderately mobile nutrient is

a) Cu
b) B
c) Zn
d) Ca

212. The bulk density of sandy soil is always

a) Equal to clay soil
b) Higher than clay soil
c) Less than clay soil
d) None of these

3

Agricultural Engineering

1. Length of Gunter's chain is……..ft

   a) 15 b) 25

   c) 66 d) 30

2. Chain is made up of thick galvanized iron wire of…..... mm in diameter

   a) 2 **b) 4**

   c) 3.5 d) 5

3. The longest of main survey line is also known as….............

   a) Check line b) Tie line

   c) Main survey line **d) Baseline**

4. In …… surveying the curvature of earth is taken into account

   a) Land b) Traverse

   c) Geodetic d) Plain

5. …… Station are the ends of lines which command the boundaries of the survey

   a) Tie b) Subsidiary

   c) Main survey **d) Main**

6. The working edge of alidade is called as...……

   a) Offset b) Right

   c) Plain **d) Fiducial**

7. The Revenue chain is divided into……. link

   a) 40 **b) 16**

   c) 15 d) 100

8. 8 furlong =……....

   a) 1 mile b) 1 degree

   c) 1 sq. kilometer **d) 1.6 km**

9. The method of surveying in which the field work and plotting are done simultaneously is called .... surveying

a) Triangulation b) Traverse

c) Plane tabling d) Intersection

10. 1 nautical mile =.......

a) 100 km^2 **b) 1852 m**

c) 1.6 km d) 4047 m^2

11. The fundamental principle of surveying upon which various survey methods are based is to work from......

a) Triangles b) Rectangles

c) Part to the whole **d) Whole to the part**

12. 100 ha = ...

a) 4047 sq. m **b) 1 sq. km**

c) 2.47 acres d) 1 sq. mile

13. The length of each link in engineer's chain is......ft

a) 15 b) 25

c) 66 **d) 01**

14. .... is used centering in plane table surveying

a) Cross staff b) Offset

c) Plumb bob d) Arrow

15. .... is a fixed reference point of known elevation

a) Contour b) Ranging rod

c) Reduced level **d) Bench mark**

16. The last reading in leveling is always..........

a) Fore sight b) Back sight

c) Intermediate sight d) None of the above

17. The safe limit of soil erosion.......t/ha/yr

a) 7 to 8 **b) 2 to 5**

c) 1to 2 d) 3 to 4

18. ...... erosion is the trasition stage between sheet erosion and gullying

a) Splash b) Stream bank

c) Rill d) Soil

19. The unit of peak runoff rate is expressed as.........

a) m^3 **b) m^3/sec**

c) cm^3 d) cm^3/sec

20. .... is defined as the rate of fall of rainfall, expressed as depth per unit time

a) Runoff b) Infiltration

c) Intensity d) Precipitation

21. The graded bunding is recommended in the region where the annual rainfall is.......

a) <600 mm b) > 700 mm

c) <700 mm **d) >600 mm**

22. The agronomical measures are adopted when the land slope is less than.......

a) 5 % b) 3 %

c) 2 % d) 1 %

23. ...... Weirs are used to measure comparatively large discharge accurately

a) Triangular **b) Rectangular**

c) Circular d) Cippoletti

24. The scientific unit of power is.....

a) Joule b) kg

c) Newton **d) Watts**

25. .... is the ratio of the power output to the power input of the pump

a) Capacity **b) Efficiency**

c) Shaft horse power d) Water horse power

26. Spiral separator separates the grains on the basis of ....

a) Weight b) Density

c) Roundness d) Relative length

27. LSU dryer is ....

a) Batch type dryer

b) Continuous flow type dryer

c) Continuous flow mixing type dryer

d) Continuous flow non mixing type

28. Pulses are major source of ....

a) Carbohydrates **b) Proteins**

c) Fats d) Vitamins

29. The removal of few large particles in an initial process is ....
    a) Scalping b) Cleaning
    c) Sorting d) Grading
30. Raisin obtained from ....
    a) Banana b) Mango
    c) Grape d) Jackfruit
31. Losses in case of fruits and vegetables vary from ....
    a) 0-20 % b) 10-30 %
    c) 20-40 % d) 30-50 %
32. The covering material in a greenhouse should be ....
    a) Transparent b) Translucent
    c) Opaque **d) Either (1) or (2)**
33. In rigid panel greenhouses, the covering materials used ....
    a) PVC b) Fibre glass
    c) Acrylic **d) All of above**
34. Which not a temperature measuring apparatus ....
    a) Thermistor **b) Pyranometer**
    c) Thermocouple d) Thermometer
35. Drying is basically which type of action ....
    a) Thermal-physical b) Physical-chemical
    c) Heat transfer d) All of above
36. For safe storage of paddy, harvested paddy should be dried to moisture content ————
    a) 18 % **b) 14 %**
    c) 20 % d) 22 %
37. Which is not a mechanical drying process ....
    a) LSU dryer b) Batch type dryer
    c) Tunnel dryer **d) Osmotic drying**
38. Full form of LSU is..........
    a) Ludhiana State University **b) Louisiana State University**
    c) Longwal State University d) None of above
39. Capacity of morai storage structure is ....
    a) 3.5 to 18 tones b) 05 to 18 tones
    c) 15 to 18 tones d) 1 to 18 tones

40. In India ......% of fruits and vegetables are processed for value addition

a) 2 % b) 12 %

c) 10 % d) 22 %

41. Hammer mill works on the principle of ....

a) Shearing b) Crushing

c) Impact d) Grading

42. The ball mills are run at ....of their critical speed.

a) 55 to 70 % b) 60 to 90 %

c) 65 to 80 % d) 100 %

43. Milling means..........

a) Size reduction b) Size production

c) Size expansion d) None

44. Full form of FPO...........

a) Fruit Product Order b) Fruit Produce Order

c) Fruit Production Order d) Fruit Product Organization

45. HACCP is ....

a) Hazards Analysis Critical Control Point

b) Hazard Analysis Critical Controls Point

c) Hazard Analysis Critical Control Points

d) Hazard Analysis Critical Control Point

46. Full form of QMS ....

a) **Quality Management system**

b) Quality Manages system

c) Quality Management society

d) None of above

47. ISO 9000 deals with ....

a) Taste of product **b) Quality of product**

c) Shelf life of product d) None

48. ISO 18000 deals with ....

a) Water quality b) Product quality

c) Workers safety d) Environment

49. WHO is ....

a) World Happy Organization

b) World Health Organization

c) World Hazard Organization

d) World Help Organization

50. Pressure required for operation of drip irrigation is ....kg/cm^2.

a) 0.01 b) 0.1

c) >1 d) 10

51. Mechanization possibility is strongly influenced by

a) Farm size

b) Cost of farm power

c) Availability of suitable machines

d) All of the above

52. The application of engineering and technology in agricultural operations to do a better way to improve productivity

a) Custom hiring **b) Farm mechanization**

c) Farm machinery d) All of the above

53. When ploughing one hectare of land once by bullocks having 15 cm. furrow width, has to walk about (km)

a) 55 b) 65

c) 66 d) 67

54. The field capacity (ha/day) of traditional implements is about

a) 0.3-0.4 b) 0.4-0.5

c) 0.5-0.6 d) 0.6-0.7

55. Farmers depends upon the animal drawn implements (%) about

a) 70 **b) 80**

c) 90 d) 60

56. Energy efficient equipments are

a) Rotovator b) Disc harrow

c) Cultivator **d) All of the above**

57. Tractor drawn rotovator is energy efficient equipments it saves time (%)

a) 32-35 b) 35-40

c) 40-45 d) 45-50

58. Selection and use of farm machinery mainly depends upon
   a) Power source b) Land holding
   c) Soil type **d) All of the above**

59. Most of the farmers use threshers, which are operated by
   a) 0-5 hp **b) 5-12 hp**
   c) 12-15hp d) More than 15 hp

60. Tractor rotovators save time and energy (%) to the extent in heavy soil about
   a) 30-35 b) 35-40
   c) 40-45 d) 45-50

61. The width of implement can be calculated from the following formula
   a) Wi= Di/ndpR in cm b) Wi= Di/dpR in cm
   c) Wi= Di+ndpR in cm d) Wi= Di-ndpR in cm

62. Which of the following types of forces acting on MB plough are
   a) Draft b) Side draft
   c) Vertical component **d) All of the above**

63. The best throat angle of share of MB plough is
   a) 45+x **b) 45-x**
   c) 45xx d) 45/x

64. The force encountered by the landside is about
   a) 10-20 % of longitudinal force acting on the plough bottom
   b) 15-20 % of longitudinal force acting on the plough bottom
   c) 25-50 % of longitudinal force acting on the plough bottom
   d) 50-60 % of longitudinal force acting on the plough bottom

65. The width of landside is taken as
   a) One third of throat width of share of plough bottom
   b) One forth of throat width of share of plough bottom
   c) One fifth of throat width of share of plough bottom
   d) One half of throat width of share of plough bottom

66. The thickness of landside is given by following expression
   a) Ft=W.Le2/3t2 b) Ft=W.2Le2/3t2
   c) Ft=W.3Le2/3t2 d) Ft=W.4Le2/3t2

67. The frog of MB plough is made up of

a) Pressed steel sheet b) Cast steel

c) Welded steel **d) All of the above**

68. For heavy duty cast iron should be

a) 160-260 HB b) 260-300 HB

c) 300-350 HB d) 400-450 HB

69. The dia of disc is given by the following expression is

a) Dd= k.dp/cosâ in cm b) D= k.dp/cosâ in cm

c) Dp= k.d/cosâ in cm d) Dd= k./cosâ in cm

70. The width of cut of disc plough is given by

a) W= Dd/3 b) W= D/3

c) W= Dp/3 d) W= Dd/2

71. The radius of curvature of disc is given by

a) R= Dd/2 sinx in cm b) R= Dd/3sinx in cm

c) R= Dd/4 sinx in cm d) R= Dp/2 sinx in cm

72. The thickness of disc for heavy soil is given by

a) Td= 0.006Dd+1 b) Td= 0.009Dd+1

c) Td= 0.007Dd+1 **d) Td= 0.008Dd+1**

73. The tractor drawn rotavator is an excellent

a) Rotary Secondary tillage implements

b) Rotary primary tillage implements

c) Rotary tillage implements

d) Mulching tillage implements

74. The tractor drawn rotavator specially designed for

a) Primary tillage implement

b) Secondary tillage implements

c) Mulching purpose

d) **Wetland cultivation in paddy crops**

75. The main functions of rotavator are

a) Churns the soil

b) Mix the soil

c) Disperses the finer particles in muddy conditions

d) **All of the above**

76. Rotavator work on principle of

a) **Rotary motion** b) Vibrating motion

c) Reciprocating motion d) None of the above

77. The rpm of rotavator tynes are

a) 150-200 b) 200-250

c) **250-350** d) None of the above

78. Which of the following types of tynes are used in rotavator

a) **L shaped** b) U shaped

c) V shaped d) None of the above

79. The no. of cutting blade on each flange of rotavator is

a) 5 b) **6**

c) 7 d) 8

80. The angle between two cutting blade of rotavator is

a) 50 b) **60**

c) 70 d) 80

81. The material used for cutting blade of rotavator is

a) Carbon steel b) **High carbon steel**

c) Low carbon steel d) Medium carbon steel

82. Which of the following types of direction of blade rotation used in rotavator is

a) Reverse b) **Forward**

c) Backward d) None of the above

83. Which of the following types of safety devices are used in PTO drive

a) The over load clutch b) The elastic clutch

c) The over-running clutch d) **All of the above**

84. The selection of overload or over-running clutch for the PTO drive is determined by

a) The type of implement to be

b) The anticipated operating conditions over protected

c) The torque characteristics

d) **All of the above**

85. Which of the following types of bearing used in standard disc plough is

a) Roller bearing **b) Taper roller bearing**

c) Ball bearing d) All of the above

86. The functions of well designed seed drill are

a) Meter seed of different sizes and shapes place the seed in the acceptable pattern of distribution

b) Place the seed accurately and uniformly at the desired depth in the soil

c) Cover the seed and compact the soil around it to be enhance germination and emergence

d) All of the above

87. The heart of sowing machine is

a) Seed box

b) Seed tube

c) Seed metering mechanism

d) All of the above

88. The functions of seed metering mechanism are

a) To meter the seed

b) To distribute the seed

c) To distribute seeds uniformly at the desired application rates

d) None of the above

89. Which of the following physiological properties of seed affect the flow rate of seed in seed drill

a) Size of seed

b) Shape of orifice

c) Shape and dimensions of seed box

d) All of the above

90. Harvesting and threshing consumes, the total energy (%) for farming about

a) 5-10 **b) 10-35**

c) 35-40 d) 40-45

91. The object of surveying is to prepare a

a) Drawing b) Cross section

c) Map d) None of the above

92. The main principle of surveying is to work from
    a) The center of the boundary
    b) The whole to the part
    c) Both
    d) None of these

93. The walking step of a man is considerd equal to
    a) 80 cm b) 70 cm
    c) 60 cm d) 50 cm

94. Compensating error is proportional to
    a) L1/2 b) L1/3
    c) L1/4 d) L1/5

95. The survey stations are located on the ground by
    a) Reference sketch b) Imaginary sketch
    c) Horizontal sketch d) None of the above

96. The working principle of the optical square is based on
    a) Double reflection b) Single reflection
    c) Multiple reflection d) All of the above

97. In chain survey the area is divided into
    a) Triangles b) Square
    c) Rectangle d) Hexagonal

98. Chain survey is recommended when the area is
    a) Fairly level b) Rough level
    c) Not good d) All of the above

99. In a prismatic compass the zero is marked on the
    a) South end b) North end
    c) West end d) None of the above

100. The compass is made of
    a) Brass **b) Aluminum**
    c) Iron d) Bronze

101. The compass box is made of
    a) Brass b) Aluminum
    c) Iron d) Bronze

102. At the magnetic pole, the dip is

a) 900 b) 100

c) 120 d) 140

103. The surface of the still water is considerd to be

a) Level b) Unlevel

c) Level d) None of the above

104. The fixed ration that every distance on the plane bears with corresponding distance on the ground

a) Scales b) Map

c) Error d) All of the above

105. The degree of perfection obtained by

a) Accuracy b) Precision

c) Error d) Map

106. It is the degree of perfection used in the instruments, the methods and the observations

a) Accuracy **b) Precision**

c) Error d) Map

107. Soil erosion is a Three phase phenomena

a) Detachments b) Transportation

c) Deposition **d) All**

108. Gully erosion is the

a) Last stage of rill formation

b) Advanced stage of rill formation

c) Pre stage

d) None of these

109. The sequence of water erosion is

a) Splash, sheet, rill, gully

b) Sheet, gully, rill

c) Rill, Splash, sheet

d) Gully erosion, Splash, sheet, rill

110. Gully development is accomplished under

a) Four b) Three

c) Two d) One

111. Gabion structure are

a) Flexible b) Permeable

c) Both d) None of these

112. The drop spill way are Constructed at the depth height of

a) More than 3 feet b) More than 8 feet

c) More than 10 feet d) More than 12 feet

113. Wind erosion will be higher from

a) A barren sandy soil b) Clay soil

c) Sandy soil d) Loam soil

114. Wind velocity is less at

a) Ground surface b) Above the ground

c) Below the groun d) All of the above

115. Wind velocity higher at

a) 50 m height from the ground

b) 80 m height from the ground

c) 100 m height from the ground

d) 150 m height from the ground

116. Wind turbulence is increases with increase in

a) Friction velocity b) Velocity

c) Pressure d) Temprature

117. Wind turbulence is greater on

a) Rough surface b) Smooth surface

c) Undulating surface d) None of the above

118. The magnitude of wind turbulence is greater at

a) Ground surface b) Rough surface

c) Smooth surface d) None of the above

119. Soil erosion is the function of

a) Erosivity b) Erodibility

c) Both d) None of these

120. Erosivity is the function of

a) Rainfall intensity b) Rainfall

c) Runoff d) Temperature

121. Land capability unit refers to the

a) Classifying the land b) Grade the land

c) Both d) None of these

122. Class-III lands of LUCC are

a) Moderately good for cultivation

b) Good for cultivation

c) Not good for cultivation

d) None of the above

123. Mulch tillage increases

a) Moisture content in the soil

b) Presence of air

c) Flow of water

d) All of the above

124. Bunds are constructed for the purpose of

a) Retaining water b) Controlling soil loss

c) Both d) None of these

125. Rill erosion is also called as

a) Micro channel irrigation

b) Major channel irrigation

c) None of the above

d) All of Above

126. The process by which liquid water is converted into vapor

a) Evaporation b) Transpiration

c) Vapor d) All of the above

127. The process by which water vapor leaves the living plant body and enters the atmosphere

a) Evaporation **b) Transpiration**

c) Vapor d) All of the above

128. Potential evapotranspiration was suggested by

a) Thomthwait (1948) **b) Darcy (1987)**

c) Harrige (1958) d) Gorge (1978)

129. Which of the following instrument is used for measuring evaporation?

a) Pan evaporometer b) Penetrometer

c) Tentiometer d) All of the above

130. The number of days between irrigation during periods without rainfall

a) Irrigation frequency **b) Irrigation interval**

c) Irrigation periods d) None of the above

131. The number of days that can be allowed for applying one irrigation to a given design area during the peak consumption use period of the crop being irrigated

a) Irrigation interval b) Irrigation frequency

c) Irrigation periods d) None of the above

132. The production per unit of water applied

a) Water use efficiency b) Base periods

c) Irrigation sequence d) None of the above

133. Total geographical area of the India about

a) 329 mha b) 350 mha

c) 346 mha d) 378 mha

134. Average rainfall of India is about

a) 1190 mm b) 1140 mm

c) 1150 mm d) 1180 mm

135. Gross irrigation potential of India is

a) 155 mha b) 140 mha

c) 150 mha d) 160 mha

136. CADA stands for:

a) Command area development agencies

b) Common area development agencies

c) Command area divert agencies

d) Commodity area development agencies

137. CADA execute the works on land leveling and construction of field channels

a) Construction of drains b) Reconstruction of drains

c) Construction of mole d) Construction of channel

138. CCA stand for:
   a) Culturable command area
   b) Cultibable common area
   c) Common catchment area
   d) Catchment area agency
139. Delta represents
   a) Total depth of water required by a crop
   b) Total depth of water required by a yield
   c) Total depth of water required by a year
   d) Total depth of water required by a season
140. Of the total crop lands of world the area under irrigation is about
   a) 15% b) 18%
   c) 17% d) 20%
141. In India, the present utilization of ground water is about
   a) 13 mha-m b) 15 mha-m
   c) 20 mha-m d) 40 mha-m
142. The actual area irrigated in a year from an outlet is called as
   a) Duty of water b) Delta of water
   c) Both d) None of these
143. Unit of base is
   a) Days b) Hr
   c) Months d) Year
144. The period for which water is supplied to a crop is called as
   a) Base b) Delta
   c) Duty d) None of the abov
145. The process of distribution of irrigation water is
   a) Regulation **b) Restoring**
   c) Both d) None of these
146. An average man can develop maximum power of about
   a) 75 watts b) 1 Hp
   c) Both d) None of the above

147. The power developed by an average pair of bullocks is about
a) 750 KW
b) 1 hp
c) Both
d) None of the above

148. A draft animal can exert about, for doing farm work
a) 1/10 of its body weight
b) 1/20 of its body weight
c) 1/30 of its body weight
d) 1/40 of its body weight

149. The thermal efficiency (%) of diesel engine varies from
a) 28-32
b) 32-38
c) 38-42
d) 42-52

150. The thermal efficiency (%) of petrol engine varies from
a) 15-25
b) 25-32
c) 32-38
d) 38-40

151. The most popular tractor is found in (hp) country
a) 20-30
b) 31-40
c) 40-50
d) 50-60

152. Tractor manufacturing was started in India in the year
a) 1951
b) 1961
c) 1971
d) 1981

153. Farm holdings belong to small and marginal farmers about (%)
a) 68
b) 78
c) 58
d) 48

154. Farm holdings belong to semi-medium, medium and large farmers about (%)
a) 12
b) 22
c) 32
d) 42

155. The m/c which convert chemical energy into mechanical energy
a) Heat engine
b) Generator
c) Motor
d) Battery

156. The combustion of fuel takes place outside the cylinder is called
a) External combustion engine
b) Internal combustion engine
c) Two stroke engine
d) Four stroke engine

157. The combustion of fuel takes place inside the cylinder is called
   a) External combustion engine
   b) Internal combustion engine
   c) Two stroke engine
   d) Four stroke engine

158. A series of events that repeat themselves in a regular sequence
   a) Thermodynamic cycle b) Otto cycle
   c) Diesel engine d) All of the above

159. The heat is taken at one constant volume and rejected at another constant volume of cylinder
   a) Thermodynamic cycle **b) Otto cycle**
   c) Diesel engine d) All of the above

160. The heat is taken at one constant pressure and rejected at another constant volume of cylinder
   a) Thermodynamic cycle b) Otto cycle
   c) Diesel cycle d) All of the above

161. When the cycle is completed in two revolution of the crankshaft
   a) Four stroke engine b) Two stroke engine
   c) Petrol engine d) Diesel engine

162. When the cycle is completed in one revolution of the crankshaft
   a) Two stroke engine b) Four stroke engine
   c) Diesel engine d) Petrol engine

163. The engine in which liquid fuel is atomized, vaporized and mixed with air in correct proportion before entering into the engine cylinder
   a) Two stroke engine b) Four stroke engine
   c) Diesel engine **d) Petrol engine**

164. The fuel is injected into the cylinder through injector at a very high pressure ranging from
   a) 120 to 200 kg/cm^2 b) 100-110 kg/cm^2
   c) 80-100 kg/cm^2 d) 60-100 kg/cm^2

165. In compression stroke, the engine attains high pressure ranging from
   a) 30 to 45 kg/cm^2 **b) 45-50 kg/cm^2**
   c) 50-55 kg/cm^2 d) 55-60 kg/cm^2

166. The removal of moisture from grains and other product to a predetermined level

a) **Drying** b) Dehydration

c) Both d) None of these

167. The removal of moisture to very low level

a) Drying **b) Dehydration**

c) Both d) None of these

168. Removal of moisture from wet materials by vaporization depends on the rate of

a) **Heat and mass transfer** b) Heat transfer

c) Mass transfer d) All of the above

169. The specific heat of a product is not dependent on its

a) **Mass density** b) Density

c) Mass diffusivity d) Bulk density

170. The heat transfer rate in solid agricultural product of any shape is

a) Mass density b) Density

c) Mass diffusivity d) Bulk density

171. The LSU dryer was develoved at

a) **The Lousiana State University**

b) London State University

c) Ludhiana State University

d) None of these

172. The world food production is damaged by insect during storage

a) **5-10%** b) 10-15 %

c) 15-20 % d) 20-25%

173. The capacity of kothar type storage structure is

a) **9 to 35 tonnes** b) 10-35 tonnes

c) 20-40 tonnes d) 40-50 tonnes

174. The improved kothar type structure generally made of

a) **5 cm thick** b) 10 cm thick

c) 15 cm thick d) 20 cm thick

175. The capacity of mud kothi storage structure varies from

a) 1 to 40 tonnes **b) 1 to 50 tonnes**

c) 1 to 20 tonnes d) 1 to 30 tonnes

176. The capacity of kanaj varies between

a) 1 to 10 tonnes **b) 1 to 20 tonnes**

c) 1 to 30 tonnes d) 1 to 40 tonnes

177. Which storage structures are used in rural areas of up and Bihar

a) Kuthla b) Bins

c) Both d) None of these

178. A squate silo has a wall height to diameter ratio is

a) 0.10 or even less **b) 0.50 or even less**

c) 0.60 or even less d) 0.5 or cven less

179. The process of moving air through stored grain at low flow rates to maintain its quality

a) Aeration b) Air flow

c) Terminal velocity d) Drag force

180. The main object of aeration

a) Is cool the grain and slow down the insect activity

b) By cooling the grain, aeration prolong the effectiveness of pesticides

c) It can provide an appreciably drying function

d) A and B

4

Agricultural Botany

1. The initiator of a food web is
   a) Carnivores
   b) Herbivores
   c) Plants
   d) Decomposers
2. Fauna is term for
   a) Plant kingdom
   b) Both (plant and animals)
   c) Animals
   d) None of the above
3. The gas responsible for global warming is
   a) NO_2
   b) CO_2
   c) SO_2
   d) H_2
4. Which is a great source of energy without any pollution
   a) Wood
   b) Radioactive element
   c) Coal
   d) Sun
5. Energy flow in food web is
   a) Unidirectional
   b) Bilateral
   c) All directional
   d) None of the above
6. Rainy day is counted when rainfall exceeds
   a) 2.4 mm
   b) 5.0 mm
   c) 1.5mm
   d) 10.0 mm
7. A layer in atmosphere which protect us from UV radiation is
   a) Gaseous layer
   b) Hydrogen layer
   c) Ozone layer
   d) CO_2 layer
8. Drought escaping plants are known as
   a) Ephemerals
   b) Dry
   c) Xeric
   d) Halophytes

9. The radioactive pollution is measured in
   a) B.O.D. **b) ppm**
   c) Curie d) Decibel (db)
10. The example of amphibious hydrophytes is
    a) Pankanis b) Pistia
    c) Water hycinth d) Hydrilla.
11. The ability of Plant Cell to perform all the functions of development is known as
    a) **Totipotency** b) Regeneration
    c) Sprouting d) Fertilization
12. The technology used for long term storage of cells/tissues in liquid nitrogen is known as
    a) Biotechnology **b) Cryobiology**
    c) Histobiology d) Nanotechnology
13. Shoot regeneration is promoted by
    a) Gibberalins b) Auxines
    c) **Cytokinene** d) None of the above
14. Embryo derived from somatic cells is known as
    a) Parthenogenetic embryo b) Zygotic embryo
    c) **Somatic Embryo** d) None of the above
15. Tissues and cell culture on an agar gelled medium form an unorganised mass of cells called as
    a) Embryo clumps b) Embryoids
    c) Meristemoids d) **Callus**
16. Testing plants for presence or absence of viruses is called
    a) **Virus indexing** b) Virus elimination
    c) Virus infection d) None of the above
17. Variability obtained through anther cultures is called as
    a) Variation b) Somaclonal variation
    c) **Gamatoclonal variation** d) None of the above

18. Isolation of protoplast is readily achieved by treating cells/tissues with
    a) Ethyl alcohol
    b) Hydrocloric acid
    c) **Cell wall degrading enzymes**
    d) Sodium peroxide

19. The formation of protein using mRNA as template is known as
    a) Transformation b) Transduction
    c) **Translation** d) Transcription

20. Micro-organisms employed to enhance availability of nutrients to the crops are called
    a) Biopesticides b) Bioinsecticide
    c) Bioherbicide d) **Biofertilizers**

21. Virus free planting material is produced by
    a) Embryo culture b) Cell culture
    c) Meristem culture d) None of these

22. First time haploid plants are produced by
    a) Willams b) Edward Cocking
    c) Robert Hook d) **Maheshwari and Guha**

23. The phenomenon of the reversion of mature cells to the meristematic state leading to the formation of callus is known as
    a) Redifferentiation b) **Dedifferentiation**
    c) Organogenesis d) Embryogenesis

24. Haploid plants are produced through
    a) Anther culture b) Embryo culture
    c) Colchicine d) None of these

25. Father of tissue culture
    a) Haberlandt b) Smith
    c) Carry mullis d) Hippocrates

26. The technique used to overcome the post fertilization barrier to obtain interspecific cross is
    a) Embryo rescue technique b) In vitro pollination
    c) Anther culture d) None of these

27. Plants carrying genes from other unrelated organism is called as
    a) Distant hybrid b) Hybrid
    c) Cybrid **d) Transgenics**
28. Genes governing extrachromosomal characters resides in
    a) Chloroplast **b) Ribosome**
    c) Golgi body d) None of these
29. Urasil is the component of
    a) DNA **b) RNA**
    c) Amino acid d) None of these
30. Double helical structure of DNA was discovered by
    a) Robert hook **b) Watson and Crick**
    c) Leaderburg d) Flaming
31. Father of genetic engineering
    a) Haberlandt b) Smith
    c) Carry mullis d) **Paul Berg**
32. PCR reaction invented by
    a) Haberlandt b) Smith
    c) Carry mullis d) Hippocrates
33. The term restriction enzyme coined by
    a) Haberlandt **b) Smith**
    c) Carry mullis d) Hippocrates

5

Agricultural Biotechnology

1. Important objective of biotechnology in agriculture sector is
   a) To increase the nitrogen content
   b) To decrease the seed number
   c) To produce pest resistant varieties of plants
   d) To increase the plant weight
2. The main technology involved in agriculture biotechnology is called
   a) Tissue culture b) Plant breeding
   c) Transformation d) DNA replication
3. Which of the following organelles is related with genetic engineering?
   a) Golgi apparatus **b) Plasmids**
   c) Lysosomes d) Mitochondria
4. A plant part that is excised from its original location and used for initiating a culture is termed?
   a) Callus **b) Explants**
   c) Suspension culture d) Protoplant
5. Growth regulator commonly used in plant tissue culture is /are
   a) BAP b) 2, 4-D
   c) Auxins and cytokinins **d) All of the above**
6. Shoot regeneration is promoted by
   a) NAA **b) BAP**
   c) 2,4-D d) IBA
7. Which of the following is used to obtain single cell protein used as food or feed?
   a) Algae and fungi b) Yeast
   c) Bacteria **d) All of the above**

8. A west African plant produces a protein called *Pentadiplandra brazzeana* which is about 2000 times as sweet as sugar

   a) Brazzein b) Saccharin

   c) Monelin d) None of the above

9. A transgene expression can achieve which of the following?

   a) Prevent expression of native gene

   b) Modify an existing biosynthetic pathway

   c) Produce protein that itself produces the phenotype of interest or is the product of interest

   d) All of the above

10. The first relatively pure enzyme was prepared by

    a) Selman Waksman **b) Christian Hansen**

    c) Alexander Fleming d) Edward Jenner

11. Agar-agar is obtained from

    a) Moulds b) Sea weed

    c) Algae d) Eggprotein

12. The vinegar means

    a) Bitter wine b) Sweet wine

    c) Sour wine d) None of the above

13. Heating milk or any other liquid at 65 °C and then sudden cooling is known as

    a) Fermentation b) Sterilization

    c) Pasterurization d) Preservation

14. Most of the microorganism which produce antibiotics live in the soil because

    a) Darkness favours synthesis of antibiotics

    b) By the phenomenon antibiotics their growth, nutrition and survival value and enhanced in competitive world of microflora of the soil

    c) They cannot get nutrition outside the soil

    d) No one easily misuses their antibiotics

15. Who of the following scientists showed that *Saccharomyces cerevisiae* caused fermentation products such as beer and buttermilk?

    a) Louis Pasteur b) Sach

    c) Alexander Fleming d) Selman Waksman

16. Which enzymes are used for converting corn starch into high fructose syrup?
    a) Glucoisomerase
    b) Amylases
    c) Glucoamylases
    d) All of these
17. Germinating barley seeds are employed in the preparation of
    a) Cheese
    b) Beer
    c) Wine
    d) Lactic acid
18. The enzyme diastase was identified by
    a) Payon and Persoz
    b) Alexander Fleming
    c) Christian Hansen
    d) S.A. Waksman
19. Which enzymes are used for manufacturing of detergents?
    a) Lactases
    b) Amylases
    c) Glucoamylases
    d) Proteases
20. Hybridomas are employed for
    a) Killing cancer cells
    b) Production of somatic hybrids
    c) Synthesis of monoclonal antibodies
    d) Synthesis of antibiotics
21. The method of growing microorganisms as a thin layer on nutrient medium is known as
    a) Thin layer growth system
    b) Suspended growth system
    c) Support growth system
    d) None of these
22. Vitamin B_2 is commercially obtained from
    a) Escherichia coli
    b) Leuconostoc mesenteroids
    c) Closteridium butyricum
    d) Streptomyces alivacaeus
23. Tissue plasminogen activator is
    a) A vitamin
    b) A chemical that stimulates tissue differentiation
    c) An enzyme
    d) An electric device
24. Dextran is used in
    a) Bleeding
    b) Blood Transfusion
    c) Blood Clotting
    d) Blood Pressure

25. Utility of fungi for steroid conversion was demonstrated by
    a) Kohler and Milstein **b) Murray and Peterson**
    c) Pasteur and Jaubert d) Waksman and Woodruff
26. Biotechnology utilizes new organisms developed from present organisms utilizing
    a) Mutation b) Recombinant DNA Technology
    c) Both (a) and (b) d) None of these
27. Which of the following is not concerned with biotechnology?
    a) Biogas production b) Biofertilizers
    c) Sewage treatment **d) Wood seasoning**
28. The technique by which virus detection can be made both in plants and animals is known as
    a) Enzyme Linked Immunoabsorbent Assay (ELISA)
    b) Electrophoresis
    c) Electron microscopy
    d) Immunofluorescence
29. Azotobacter and Bacillus polymyxa are
    a) Decomposers **b) Non-symbiotic nitrogen fixers**
    c) Symbiotic nitrogen fixers d) Pathogenic bacteria
30. Bioreactors are used for
    a) Production of ethanol
    b) Production of enzymes on large scale
    c) Production of cell culture on large scale
    d) All of the above
31. Methanogenic bacteria are
    a) Anaerobic in nature b) Aerobic in nature
    c) Micro aerophillic in nature d) Saprophitic in nature
32. Which yeast strain is naturally used for ethanol production?
    a) Saccharomyces cereviciae b) S. diastaticus
    c) Both of these d) None of these
33. What are the components of PCR reaction?
    a) Buffer, Taq polymerase dNTPs, primer and template
    b) Buffer, dNTPs, primer and template
    c) Buffer, Taq polymerase, primer and template
    d) Buffer, Taq polymerase, dNTPs, and template

34. Which of the following is a dominant marker?
    a) RAPD b) RFLP
    c) SSR d) AFLP
35. High density molecular map can be developed by
    a) RFLP b) RAPD
    c) AFLP **d) SNPs**
36. Double stranded DNA can be isolated from ssDNA or RNA by using
    a) Ion exchange column b) Sephadex column
    c) Hydroxyapatite column d) Affinity chromatography
37. Which of the histone protein is known as linker protein
    a) H1 b) H2A
    c) H2B d) H3
38. Translation of histone proteins occur during
    a) S phase of cell division only
    b) Gl phase only
    c) Gl and G2 phase
    d) M phase only
39. Histone octomer comprise of
    a) H1, H2A, H2B and H3 b) HI, H2A, H2B, H3 and H4
    c) HI, H2B, H3 and H4 **d) H2A, H2B, H3 and H4**
40. Histone proteins are .....in nature
    a) Acidic b) Basic
    c) Neutral d) Both (a) and (b)
41. Chaperone present in *E. coli* is
    a) Hsp60 b) Hsp43
    c) Hsp80 **d) Bip protein**
42. Chaperones play an important role in
    a) Protein folding b) Protein denaturation
    c) Protein trafficking d) Protein synthesis
43. Which gene is used for development of salt tolerant crops?
    a) LEA genes
    b) Genes involved in proline biosynthesis
    c) Heat shock proteins
    d) All to the above

44. One of the following would be called VNTR

a) TTTTCCCC **b) GTGTGTGT**

c) GGTTGGTT d) GGGGTTTT

45. Disease causing organisms are identified by using

a) MAb's b) Gene transfer

c) DNA probes d) Microprojectiles

46. The process of using living organisms to remove contaminants, pollutants or unwanted substances from soil or water is known as

a) Biotechnology b) Biomagnification

c) Biodegradation **d) Bioremediation**

47. A method used to insert DNA molecules into cells by using short electrical impulses is known as

a) Biolistics b) Microinjection

c) Liposomes **d) Electroporation**

48. Genomic library can be prepared by

a) Colony hybridization **b) Shotgun experiment**

c) PCR technique d) All of these

49. Genetically engineered bacteria is used for the production of

a) Ephedrine b) Cortisoles

c) Thyroxine **d) Human insulin**

50. Manipulation of the genetic material towards a desired end in a directed and predetermined way is called

a) Genetic engineering b) Gene cloning

c) Recombinant DNA technology d) All of the above

51. The molecular scissors used to cut DNA into specific genes of interest are called

a) Polymerases **b) Restriction endonucleases**

c) Ligases d) None of these

52. A set of disease resistance mechanisms that are not specific to a particular pathogen comes under

a) Active immunity **b) Innate immunity**

c) Passive immunity d) None of these

53. Which of these is/are the characteristic/s of the specific immunity
    a) Antigenic specificity
    b) Diversity and self/non-self recognition
    c) Immunologic memory
    d) All of the above
54. Microbes have a relatively … that allows the chemical conversions possible.
    a) High metabolic rate b) Large surface area
    c) High multiplication rate **d) All of the above**
55. The medium is added continuously to the fermentor tank to replace that, which has been fermented. This is true in case of
    a) Batch technique **b) Continuous flow technique**
    c) Both (a) and (b) d) None of these
56. Removal of the topological strain by inducing to the negative supercoiling is carried out by
    a) Topoisomerases **b) DNA gyrases**
    c) Ligases d) DNA polymerases
57. Chromosomal aberration in which two breaks occur in a chromosome and the intercalary segment reunites in a reverse order is categorized as
    a) Translocation b) Deletion
    c) Inversion d) None of these
58. ABO blood groups is a good example for both and multiple allelism.
    a) Co-dominance b) Dominance
    c) Recessiveness d) Over dominance
59. Why is the gene that was used by Sheller et al. to produce spider silk in transgenic plants called a "synthetic" gene?
    a) It produces silk fibre, which is a synthetic product in plants
    b) It is assembled from synthesized DNA oligomers
    c) It is a synthesis of proteins from different types of spiders
    d) It is encodes synthetic components such as an epitope tag
60. Which of the following statements about astaxanthin is false?
    a) It has antioxidant properties
    b) It is normally produced by salmon
    c) It is a red-orange pigment
    d) It is produced from terpenoids

61. For cloning eukaryotic gene in prokaryotes, genes should be isolated from

a) cDNA library b) Genomic library

c) Eukaryotic host d) Prokaryotic host

62. Essential constituents of a cloning vector are

a) Replicon, promoter and selectable marker

b) Replicon, unique restriction site and selectable marker

c) Promoter, operatop and restriction site

d) Replicon, unique restriction site and promoter

63. Essential constituents of an expression vector are

a) Replicon, promotor and selectable marker

b) Replicon, unique restriction site, selectable marker and promoter

c) Promoter, operator and restriction site

d) Replicon, unique restriction site and promoter

64. Restriction site for cloning should be

a) Tetranucleotide **b) Palindromic in nature**

c) Repeated sequence d) Hexdanucleotide

65. GAATTC is restriction sequence of

a) CTTAAG b) Nco I

c) Sau 3 d) None of these

66. Antibiotic resistance is used as a selectable marker for

a) Selection of vector b) Selection of recombinant vectors

c) Selection of transformed cells d) Selection of resistant bacteria

67. Commonly used host in gene cloning is

a) *E. coli* b) Pseudomonas

c) Nitromonas d) Bacillus

68. Bacteria possessing restriction enzymes get not affected because

a) Their genome is demethylated

b) Their genome is methylated

c) These enzymes are present in less concentration

d) Their genome lack unique restriction sites. for enzymes

69. Which of the following vector can be used for cloning bigger DNA fragments?

    a) YACs b) Cosmids

    c) Plasmids d) *E.coli*

70. Marker free selection can be done by

    a) Co-transformation b) Deletion

    c) Insertion d) None of these

71. Which vector was used for development of hepatitis vaccine?

    a) Phagemids b) PUC 18

    c) Cosmid d) Yeast expression vector

72. In tissue culture disease resistance can be obtained by

    a) Somaclonal variation b) Embryo culture

    c) Somatic hybridization d) Anther culture

73. You want to know whether the enzyme you have introduced as a transgene in poplar is being expressed in the intended cells at the intended developmental stage. Which technique would be most informative?

    a) QRT-PCR b) Immunolocalization

    c) RNA in situ hybridization d) Promoter fusion

74. When producing human serum albumin (HSA) in transgenic plants, what would be an advantage of incorporating the transgene into the chloroplast genome?

    a) HSA diverts too many amino acids if expressed in cytoplasm

    b) HSA becomes allergenic if expressed in cytoplasm

    c) HSA is toxic to plants if expressed in cytoplasm

    d) HSA is degraded by plant enzymes if expressed in cytoplasm

75. Which of the following transgenic methods were used (in separate experiments) in an attempt to increase the prevalence of certain amino acids in seeds?

    a) Altered tRNA gene; overexpression of sunflower seed albumin (SSA)

    b) Altered tRNA gene; overexpression of human serum albumin (HSA)

    c) Altered rRNA gene; overexpression of sunflower seed albumin (SSA)

    d) Altered tRNA gene; repression of sunflower seed albumin (SSA) expression

76. How was luciferase (LUC) with an artificial stop codon used as a control in the experiments involving altered tRNA?

a) Diminished LUC expression demonstrated that the altered tRNA could properly recognize stop codons.

b) LUC expression demonstrated that the gene was being induced by Lys.

c) LUC expression demonstrated that Lys was being substituted for the stop codon by the altered tRNA.

d) The artificial LUC is an example of a synthetic gene.

77. Which of the following are NOT possible uses for fructans as presented in class?

a) Natural insecticides b) Fat substitute

c) Amino acids **d) Sweeteners**

78. Which of the following statements is true regarding the production of transgenic cassava

a) A non-toxic cyanide derivative was production by metabolic engineering

b) The release of cyanide was inhibited by antisense gene regulation i

c) The release of cyanide was inhibited by immunolocalization

d) The production of cyanide was enhanced by overexpression of an enzyme

79. Biosensers are used as

a) Purified enzymes b) Antibodies

c) Whole microbial cells **d) Any of the above**

80. DNA chip is a wafer of

a) Silicon b) Al

c) Carbon d) Iron

81. DNA chip carries a large number of

a) Oligonucleotides b) cDNAs

c) DNA probes **d) Any of the above**

82. The combination of biology and IT is

a) Cell biology b) Biotechnology

c) Bio-informatics d) Nanotechnology

83. Technique for sequencing DNA and protein is
   a) NMR spectroscopy b) X-ray crystallography
   c) Electron microscopy d) All of the above
84. Structural DNA nanotechnology is for
   a) Nanoelectronics b) Nanorobotics
   c) Smart material **d) All of the above**
85. Microsatellites are also known as
   a) VNTRs b) RFLPs
   c) STRs d) RAPDs
86. Minisatellites are also known as
   a) VNTRs b) RFLPs
   c) STRs **d) RAPDs**
87. Example of tandem gene cluster is id) rRNA genes
   a) Histone gene b) Histone gene cluster
   c) Both (a) and (b) d) None of these
88. RNA molecules involved in splicing are
   a) Sn rRNA b) 5s rRNA
   c) 16s RNA d) mRNA
89. During splicing of mRNA which part is removed
   a) Exons **b) Introns**
   c) Exteins d) Inteins
90. Which amino acid plays role in splicing of proteins?
   a) Serine b) Glycine
   c) Cysteine d) Tryptophan
91. Which amino acid provide twists in tertiary structure of proteins?
   a) Arginine b) Glycine
   c) Proline d) Tryptophan
92. Which among the following is released in photorespiration?
   a) Serine b) Cysteine
   c) Glycine d) Trypophan
93. During the process of reverse transcription
   a) mRNA is synthesized from DNA
   b) DNA is synthesized from DNA

c) Proteins are formed from mRNA

d) DNA is synthesized from mRNA

94. Which enzyme plays important role in reverse transcription?

a) DNA polymerase b) RNA polymerase

c) Reverse transcriptase d) Isomerase

95. Which of the following statements regarding manipulation of the flavonol bio-synthetic pathway in tomato is true?

a) Decreased flavanol production increased carotenoid production

b) Increased flavonol production led to increased carotenoid production

c) Increased flavonol production did not affect carotenoid production

d) Decreased flavanol production did not increase carotenoid production

96. Which method enhances vitamin C production?

a) Polymerization of a series of simple sugars

b) Partitioning of ascorbate into seed storage proteins

c) Derivatization of tocopherols from the shikimate pathway

d) Enzymatic reduction of a component of pectin

97. Which of the following statements concerning the RNA/DNA hybrid oligonucleotides is incorrect?

a) They hybrid molecule must be introduced into the cell using a binary vector

b) They may be synthesized to contain a mutation that will be incorporated into the host genome

c) They provide a mechanism for targeted alteration of the plant genome

d) They are incorporated using a mechanism that involves host DNA repair machinery

98. What is a disadvantage of the current use of transgenic anitbody fragments to induce resistance to the herbicide picloram?

a) Each antibody molecule can neutralize only one herbicide molecule

b) Picloram is an auxinic herbicide, thus the antibodies will neutralize endogenous auxin

c) The antibodies induce morphological defects (e.g. epinasty)

d) The antibodies are quickly degraded by host enzymes, so they have little effect on picloram

99. Which of the following attempts to increase the utility of fungal herbicides succeeded?

    a) Expression of a phytotoxic protein at abnormally high levels in Fusarium

    b) Expression of a phytotoxic protein from Fusarium in another fungal species

    c) Expression of a phytotoxic protein from Fusarium in a crop plant

    d) Expression of a phytotoxic protein from Fusarium in a weed

100. Which of the following was an unexpected result connected to the transgenic production of the terpenoid linalool

    a) Increased production of linaloon resulted in lower levels of GA hormones

    b) Increased transgene expression was not strongly correlated with increased levels of linalool

    c) Increased transgene expression resulted in higher levels of herbivory

    d) Linalool accumulation was localized to the nectar.

6

Plant Breeding and Genetics

1. Mendel presented his results in the form of
   a) Two paper in French langua
   b) Two paper in German language
   c) One paper in German language
   d) None of the above

2. The alternative forms of a gene are called
   a) Allelomorph
   b) Gene
   c) Alleles
   d) None of these

3. G.J. Mendel was born in the year and place
   a) 1822, Holland
   b) 1821, Germany
   c) 1823, Brunn
   d) 1822, Brunn

4. Mendel presented his paper in the year
   a) 1866
   b) 1865
   c) 1867
   d) 1870

5. Which of the following legume crop does not fix atmospheric nitrogen through symbiotic N. fixation?
   a) Frenchbean
   b) Clusterbea
   c) Lathyrus
   d) Mungbean

6. Land races are
   a) Advanced strains
   b) Local varieties
   c) All of these
   d) None of these

7. Lysine is limiting amino acid in
   a) Cereals
   b) Pulses
   c) Green vegetables
   d) None of these

8. In pulses, limiting amino acids are
   a) Methionine
   b) Tryptophan
   c) Alanine
   d) Both (a) and (b)

9. The low neurotoxin variety of Lathyrus is
   a) Pusa 6 b) Pusa 8
   c) Pusa 12 **d) Pusa 24**
10. Pusa Sugandha-5 is new variety of
   a) Rice b) Rose
   c) Marigold d) Gladiolus
11. Shaktiman is the new variety of
   a) Wheat **b) Maize**
   c) Lentil d) Chickpea
12. Pusa Gold is a new variety of
   a) Rice **b) Wheat**
   c) Mustard d) Cotton
13. Pusa 1088, Pusa 1103 and Pusa 1105 are new varieties of
   a) Chickpea b) Maize
   c) Mango d) Lentil
14. Pusa Karishma and Mahak are new varieties of
   a) Palak b) Radish
   c) Mustard d) Amarantha
15. Pusa Arunima and Pusa Surya are new varieties of
   a) Mango b) Guava
   c) Citrus d) Litchi
16. Poorva, Urja and Pusa Vishesh are new varieties of
   a) Bajra **b) Wheat**
   c) Rice d) Chickpea
17. Pusa Ratna is a new variety of
   a) Wheat b) Soybean
   c) Rice **d) Mungbean**
18. Source of dwarfing gene in wheat is
   a) Dee-Gee-Woo-Gen **b) Norin – 10**
   c) Opaque d) Hipsoli
19. An organism which has acquired a heritable variation as a result of sudden change in the hereditary material is called as a
   a) Albino b) Biotype
   c) Mutant d) None of these

20. A polyploid having chromosome sets from different sources such as different species is known as
    a) Autopolyploid b) Aneuploid
    c) Tetraploid **d) None of these**

21. Sex form in most cucurbits including melons
    a) Hermaphrodite **b) Monoecious**
    c) Dioecious d) None of these

22. The increased performance of F_1 hybrid over its parents is called
    a) Dominance **b) Heterosis**
    c) Crossing over d) None of these

23. Ratio of the genetic variance to the total variance which determines the relationship between phenotype and genotype is known as
    a) Genetic advance b) Penetrance
    c) Heritability d) Dominance

24. Mass pedigree selection method of breeding is particularly, useful for improvement of
    a) Self pollinated crops
    b) Self compatible cross pollinated crops
    c) Self incompatible crops
    d) Dioecious crops

25. Emasculation of flower is necessary for hybridization in
    a) Male sterile plants **b) Self pollinated plants**
    c) Self incompatible plants d) Dioecious plants

26. Leafy vegetables like palak, amaranthus, spinach, are
    a) Highly cross pollinated b) Cross pollinated
    c) Often pollinated d) Self pollinated

27. The modern hybrid tea roses were evolved a result of which of the following crossing
    a) Hybrid perpetuals x Tea roses
    b) Hybrid perpetuals x Floribunda
    c) Floribunda x Tea roses
    d) Tea roses x Polyanthus

28. Mendel did not face the problem of linkage however, seven characters studied by him we located on how many chromosomes

    a) Four b) Six

    c) Three d) Five

29. Test cross ratio in case of duplicate gene action will be

    a) 2:1 b) 1:1:1:1

    c) 4:1 **d) 3:1**

30. A condition in which F* plants of an inter specific cross are vigorous and fertile but their F2 progeny is weak and sterile is called

    a) Hybrid sterility b) Hybrid inviability

    c) Hybrid breakdown d) None of these

31. Inability of a hybrid to produce viable offspring is known as

    a) Hybrid sterility b) Hybrid inviability

    c) Hybrid breakdown d) None of these

32. Term heterosis was introduced by

    a) Davenport (1908) **b) Shull (1914)**

    c) Hull (1945) d) Muller (1936)

33. Highest uniformity is present in

    a) Three way cross b) Multiple cross

    c) Single cross d) None of these

34. Double top cross refers to

    a) (AxB) x OPV b) A x B x C x D

    c) A x B x C d) All of these

35. The dominance hypothesis of heterosis was first proposed by

    a) Davenport (1908) b) Knight (1908)

    c) Hull (1945) d) Shull (1914)

36. The method(s) used for fixation of heterosis

    a) Apomixis b) Polyploid

    c) Asexual reproduction **d) All of these**

37. In cross pollinated species, a true breeding line obtained by continuous inbreeding is called

    a) Inbreed b) Clone

    c) Composite variety d) None of these

38. Progeny of a single plant obtained by asexual reproduction is
    a) Pure line
    b) Clone
    c) Strain
    d) None of these
39. The progeny of a single homozygous self pollinated plant is known as
    a) Pure line
    b) Clone
    c) Strain
    d) Inbreed
40. The 'pure line' theory was proposed by
    a) Bateson
    b) Johannsen
    c) Watson
    d) Mendel
41. The term genetics is coined by
    a) Johannsen
    b) Bateson
    c) Muller
    d) Morgan
42. The phenomenon of linkage was first observed by
    a) Bateson and Punnet
    b) Nilson
    c) Hugo de Vries
    d) Mendel
43. A : T ratio in one strand of DNA duplex is 2, what will be the ratio in the complementary strand
    a) 2.0
    b) 0.5
    c) 3.5
    d) 3.0
44. The term gene was coined by
    a) Mendel
    b) Robinson
    c) Morgan
    d) Johannsen
45. Number of chromosomes in wheat endosperm is
    a) 23
    b) 68
    c) 63
    d) 14
46. Cytoplasmic male sterility is best suited for hybrid seed production in
    a) SP crops
    b) CP crops
    c) Vegetatively propagated crops
    d) All of the above
47. An example of a heterozygous but homogeneous population is
    a) Pure line
    b) Open pollinated variety
    c) Hybrid variety
    d) None of these

48. The cross of an inbreed line with an pollinated variety is known as
    a) Double cross **b) Top cross**
    c) Three way cross d) Test cross
49. The first artificial hybrid was made by
    a) Mendel **b) Thomas Fairchild**
    c) Koelreuter d) Morgan
50. Systematic hybridization on a scientific basis began with the work
    a) Shull-Maize **b) Patel-Cotton**
    c) Koelreuter -Nicotiana d) Knight-Fruits
51. Double cross plan was suggested by
    a) Beal b) Shull
    c) Jones d) Knight
52. Who gave the concept of circular chromo some in *E.coli*
    a) Cairns b) Meselson
    c) Watson d) Mendel
53. Sex in plants was discovered by
    a) Grew **b) Camerarious**
    c) T. Fairchild d) Linnaeus
54. Who produced puppies through artificial insemination in dogs
    a) de Graaf b) O. Hertwig
    c) Spallanzani d) Tyndall
55. The 'one gene one enzyme' hypothesis was proposed by
    a) Beadle and Tatum b) Hugo de Vries
    c) Watson and Crick d) Mendel
56. The 'operon concept' of gene regulation was proposed by
    a) Beadle and Tatum b) Jacob and Monod
    c) Watson and Crick d) Muller and Stadler
57. Dr. Har Govind Khurana was awarded the Nobel Prize in 1968 for his work on
    a) Mutation
    b) Amino acids synthesis
    c) Genetic code and in vitro synthesis of DNA
    d) RNA synthesis

58. Which one of the following sets is the correct sequence of events in the cell

a) Transcription, translation, protein synthesis

b) Transcription, protein synthesis, translation

c) Transcription, protein synthesis, transcription

d) None of these

59. The performance of a double cross hybrid (A x C) x (B x D) can be predicted from the average performance of the combination of

a) A x B, A x C, C x B and C x D

b) A x B, A x D, B x C and C x D

c) A x B, A x C, A x D and B x C

d) A x B, C x D, A x C and B x D

60. The number of single crosses will be equal to

a) n(n-1)/2

b) n(n-1) (n-2)/8

c) n(n-1) (n-2) (n-3)/8

d) n(n+1) (n+2)/4

61. The number of double crosses will be equal to

a) n(n - l)/2

b) n(n - 1) (n - 2)(n - 3)/8

c) n(n- l)(n-2)/4

d) n(n + 1) (n - 2)/6

62. The number of three way crosses are

a) n(n- 1) (n - 2)/2

b) n(n + 1) (n + 2)/2

c) n(n - 1) (n - 2)(n - 3)/8

d) n(n - 1) (n + 2)(n - 3)/6

63. The variety of wheat developed from spring x winter wheat crosses is termed as

a) Veery

b) Sonalika

c) WL711

d) None of these

64. The immediate effect of pollen on the character of endosperm is called

a) Metaxenia

b) Xenia

c) Epistasis

d) Hyperxenia

65. An individual with gametic chromosome number is

a) Euploid

b) Haploid

c) Dihaploid

d) Polyploid

66. The individuals with 2n ± 1 chromosomes are commonly known as
a) Euploid **b) Aneuploid**
c) Heteroploids d) Polyploid

67. Concept of epigenesis was proposed by
a) Watson b) Bonnet
c) Wolf d) Darwin

68. 'Origin of species' was published in
a) 1770 b) 1859
c) 1960 d) 1895

69. Germplasm theory was proposed by
a) Darwin **b) Weisman**
c) Aristotle d) Phillips

70. Cell linkage theory was proposed by
a) Virchow b) Nagali
c) Schlieden and Schwan d) Hooke

71. The chromosomes are most condensed at
a) Prophase b) Metaphase
c) Anaphase d) Telophase

72. DNA synthesis is takes place in which stage
a) G_1 phase b) G_2 stage
c) S phase d) None of these

73. In the DNA double helix G/A is equal to
a) C/G b) C/A
c) T/A **d) C/T**

74. Harshey and Chase in their experiments labelled DNA with
a) 3H b) 35S
c) 32P d) All of the above

75. The number of bases in the single turn of the DNA helix is
a) 15 b) 8
c) 10 d) 12

76. The common form of DNA present in the living organisms is the
a) A form b) Z form
c) C form **d) B form**

77. DNA polymerase I was discovered by
 a) Harshey and Chase b) Yanofsky
 c) Kornberg d) Crick
78. The DNA replicating enzyme in bacteria
 a) DNA Pol I b) DNA Pol II
 c) DNA Pol III d) None of these
79. Protein involved in keeping the DNA single stranded during replication is
 a) Ligase b) Helicase II
 c) Topoisomerase **d) SSB protein**
80. Pollination and fertilization in an unopened flower bud is the situation called
 a) Cleistogamy b) Chasmogamy
 c) Homogamy d) Heterogamy
81. The situation in which one gene hides the effect of a second gene when both are present in a chromosome is called
 a) Dominance **b) Epistasis**
 c) Both (a) and (b) d) None of these
82. An individual with 2n-l-l chromosome constitution is called
 a) Monosomic **b) Double monosomic**
 c) Tetrasomic d) Double trisomic
83. Which one of the following statements regarding selfing is correct
 a) It improves heterozygosity
 b) It does not have any effect on heterozygosity
 c) It reduces heterozygosity
 d) None of these
84. Triticale is
 a) Interspecific cross b) Intraspecific cross
 c) Intergeneric cross d) Intrageneric cross
85. Cabbage is cross pollinated owing to
 a) Floral morphology b) Protandry
 c) Self incompatibility d) None of these

86. In maize, cross pollination occurs due to

a) Protandry **b) Protogyny**

c) Self incompatibility d) Floral Morphology

87. Bulk population breeding is suitable for

a) Fruit crops b) Vegetable crops

c) Small grain crops d) Flower crops

88. In sugarcane breeding the initial selection after hybridization is done in the generation

a) F_2 b) F_0

c) F_4 d) F_1

89. In a synthetic variety of maize produced by combining 10 lines, the loss of excess vigour in F_2 generation will be

a) 1/10 b) 1/5

c) 1/4 **d) 1/2**

90. The equilibrium in random mating population is disturbed by selection, mutation, inbreeding, migration and genetic drift in which situation the population may regain its original composition

a) Inbreeding and selection b) Selection

c) Migration d) Genetic drift

91. Consider the following genotypes

a) Breeding lines **c) Land races**

b) Variety under cultivation

92. What is the correct sequence of these in terms of their importance to farmers

a) 1, 2 and 3 **b) 2, 3 and 1**

c) 3, 1 and 2 d) 1, 3 and 2

93. Okazaki fragments are formed due to synthesis of DNA in direction

a) 5'-3' b) 3'-5'

c) Both (a) and (b) d) None of these

94. Deamination of adenine lead to the formaoenn of

a) Xanthine b) Thymine

c) Hypoxanthine **d) Cytosine**

95. Maximum absorbance of DNA molecule is at ....O_A wave length.

a) 260
b) 380
c) 400
d) 530

96. In Drosophila 16A region of X chromosome cause normal eye. If the region is repleated the eye produced is

a) Yellow
b) White
c) Barr
d) Normal

97. The resulting two daughter cells produced by bridge-breakage fusion cycle will have

a) Duplication
b) Deficiency
c) Both (a) and (b)
d) None of these

98. A tautomeric shift in adenine (amino to imino) allows it to pair with .... only.

a) Cytosine
b) Uracil
c) Guanine
d) Thymine

99. In humans, an XO individual has how many barr body in her cells

a) Four
b) One
c) Three
d) None of these

100. Nucleolus plays important role in production of

a) RNA
b) tRNA
c) mRNA
d) All of these

7

Crop Physiology

1. The rice plant belongs to

   a) Short day plant b) Long day plant.

   c) Day neutral plant d) Etiolated

2. Cycoceal is a growth

   a) Growth inhibitor b) Growth hormone

   c) Growth regulator d) Growth stimulant

3. When respiratory substrate is fat, then the value of R.Q. is

   a) 1.00 b) 0.50

   c) 0.70 d) 2.00

4. The theories which assumes that the living cells are essential for ascent of sap are called as

   a) Physical **b) Vital**

   c) Chemical d) Biological

5. The outer wall of guard cell is

   a) Thinner b) Thicker

   c) Broad d) Narrow

6. The elements required in small quantity is known as

   a) Macro elements **b) Microelements**

   c) Trace elements d) None of above.

7. During photosynthesis first stable product in C3 plant is

   a) 3 GAP b) PGAL

   c) 3 PGA d) PEP

8. During the process of respiration gas absorbed is

   a) Oxygen b) Carbon dioxide

   c) Nitrous oxide d) Helium

9. The plants which grows under high salts content are called as
   a) Mesophyte b) Xerophyte
   c) Halophyte d) Hydrophyte
10. The 'S' shape of curve is not observed in
   a) Banana **b) Jowar**
   c) Fruit crops d) Sugarcane
11. Short day plants require light period
   a) More than 12 hrs day length **b) Less than 12 hrs day length**
   c) 24 hrs per day d) Light is not required
12. In plant cell, the power house of cell is known as
   a) Mitochondria b) Golgi bodies
   c) Cell wall d) Cytoplasm
13. In C4 plants photoxidation is
   a) Absent b) Present
   c) Very limited d) None of these
14. In non-cyclic phosphorylation photosynthetic pigment involved are
   a) PS – I b) PS – II
   c) Both PS – I & II d) None of these
15. In plants transpiration occurs through
   a) Stomata b) Guttation
   c) Root d) None of these
16. Maize plant is
   a) Long day plant **b) Short day plant**
   c) day neutral plant d) None of these
17. The term guttation was coined by
   a) Stephan Hales b) Dixon & Jolly
   c) Burgestin d) Boehm
18. Translocation of organic solutes in plant takes place in phloem by process of
   a) Downward movement
   b) Upward movement
   c) None of these
   d) Both Upward and downward movement

19. Exudation of liquid from uninjured part of the plant is called
    a) Transpiration   **b) Guttation**
    c) Respiration   d) Photosynthesis
20. Die-back of citrus causes due to deficiency of the element
    a) Nitrogen   b) Phosphorous
    c) Copper   d) Potash
21. The osmotic pressure of the pure water is
    a) Zero   b) One
    c) Less than one   d) None of these

8

Plant Physiology

1. A man supplied excess fertilizer and water the grass well. After sometime the leaves turn brown because

   a) Due to water logging

   b) It decreases photosynthesis

   c) Fertilizer is drained in lower layer of soil

   d) Osmosis occurs in root and root dies

2. If roots of plant are removed and plant is placed in water, then what will be happen?

   a) Passive absorption will continue

   b) Imbibition will continue

   c) Active absorption will continue

   d) None of these

3. The relay pump theory was given by

   a) Burg b) Unger

   c) Strasburger **d) Godlewski**

4. Maximum transpiration occurs from

   a) Dermal tissue b) Procambium

   c) Ground tissue of scale leaves **d) Periderm and lenticels**

5. Dry seeds when placed in water swell up due to

   a) Absorption b) Diffusion

   c) Imbibition d) Adsorption

6. The following percentage of water absorbed by herbaceous plants is lost in transpiration

   a) 60 b) 40

   c) 80 **d) 99**

7. Uniformly sweet taste of Tea or Coffee is due to
   a) Spreading
   b) Diffusion
   c) Osmosis
   d) None of these
8. Root pressure is maximum when
   a) Transpiration is low, absorption high
   b) Transpiration is high, absorption low
   c) Both transpiration and absorption high
   d) Both transpiration and absorption is low
9. Endosmosis of water occurs when water potential of the cell sap is
   a) Higher
   b) Lower
   c) Equal
   d) None of these
10. Rate of water absorption is slow near freezing point because
    a) Cell membranes become more viscous
    b) Transpiration is reduced
    c) Water absorption is a metabolic process
    d) Cell growth stops
11. Cells absorb water through
    a) Osmosis only
    b) Imbibition only
    c) Both (a) and (b)
    d) None to these
12. Maximum transpiration occurs in
    a) Algal cells
    b) Xerophytic plants
    c) Mesophytic plants
    d) Hydrophytic plants
13. Plants exchange water with environment through structures by two cells
    a) Hydathodes
    b) Lenticells
    c) Stomata
    d) All of these
14. Amount by which water potential is reduced due to presence of solute is called
    a) Solute potential
    b) Matric potential
    c) Pressure potential
    d) None of these
15. For ascent of sap capillary force theory was first proposed by
    a) Dixon and Jolly
    b) Sachs
    c) Strasburger
    d) Christian Wolf

16. Rate of transpiration is related to
    a) Light, temperature and wind
    b) Light and temperature
    c) Soil and temperature
    d) Light, temperature, atmospheric humidity and wind
17. Chlorophyllous cells fewer in number, unique in shape with inner walls thicker are
    a) Guard cells b) Passage cells
    c) Subsidiary cells d) Bulliform cells
18. Risk of spoilage is less in salted pickles as it cause
    a) Diffusion **b) Plasmolysis**
    c) Guttation d) Imbibition
19. Which is not associated with ascent of sap in tall
    a) Continuity of water column
    b) Transpiration pull
    c) Pressure of tracheary elements
    d) Cohesion and adhesion of water molecules
20. An antitranspirant is
    a) Potassium **b) Phenyl mercuric acetate**
    c) Mercury d) Cobalt chloride
21. Rate of transpiration is high in
    a) C3 plants b) C4 plants
    c) CAM plants d) Both (a) and (b)
22. Which can preserve food stuff?
    a) Sugar and vinegar b) Salt and sugar
    c) Vinegar **d) All of these**
23. Cell 'A' with O.P. = 10 atm and T.P. = 5 atm. is contact with cell 'B' having O.P. = 15 atm. and T.P. = 12 atm. The flow of water will be
    a) From A to B b) Equal flow
    c) From B and A d) No flow
24. Water drops present on leaf margins of Tropaeolum, Balsam and grasses in early morning are due to
    a) Guttation b) Osmosis
    c) Dew d) Transpiration

25. Enzymes connected with opening and closing of stomata is
    a) Pyruvic kinase **b) PEP carboxylase**
    c) RuBP carboxylase d) a-amylase
26. Rate of transpiration is measured by
    a) Auxanometer b) Respirometer
    c) Porometer **d) Ganong's potometer**
27. Wooden doors swell up and get stuck during rainy season due to
    a) Capillarity **b) Imbibition**
    c) Endosmosis d) Exosmosis
28. In plants water moves from
    a) Less nagative to more nagative gradient
    b) More negative to less negative gradient
    c) Similar gradient
    d) Zero gradient
29. If turgor pressure becomes equal to osmotic pressure
    a) Water leaves the cells
    b) Water enter the cell
    c) No exchange of water takes place
    d) Solute pass out of the cell
30. When half the leaves are removed randomly, transpiration will show
    a) Lower magnitude but higher flux
    b) Higher magnitude but lower flux
    c) Both magnitude and flux increase
    d) Both magnitude and flux decrease
31. Arrange root hair cell inner, cortical cell and mesophyll cell in ascending order of DPD
    a) Mesophyll cell, Root hair cell and Cortical cell
    b) Cortical cell, Mesophyll cell and Root hair cell
    c) Root hair cell, Cortical cell and Mesophyll cell
    d) Root hair cell, Mesophyll cell and Cortical cell
32. Temporary wilting is due to
    a) Photosynthesis b) Transpiration
    c) Respiration d) None of these

33. Stomata open when the guard cells possess
   a) Less K+ **b) More K+**
   c) More ABA d) All of the above
34. Plasmolysis is due to
   a) Exosmosis b) Endosmosis
   c) Adsorption d) Osmosis
35. High CO_2 concentration in leaf interior will cause
   a) Stomatal opening **b) Stomatal closure**
   c) No effect on stomata d) Stomata are destroyed
36. Which one explains ascent of sap
   a) Cohesion-tension theory of Dixon and Jolly
   b) Photosynthesis
   c) Starch-sugar interconversion
   d) None of these
37. Water supply in plant is due to
   a) Guttation b) Osmosis
   c) Imbibition **d) Cohesion force**
38. A cell placed in solution get deplasmolysed. The solution is
   a) Hypotonic b) Hypertonic
   c) Isotonic d) Ditonic
39. DPD is abbreviated form of
   a) Daily photosynthetic deficit b) Daily phosphorus deficit
   c) Diffusion pressure deficit d) Daily pressure deficit
40. Which can function as carrier in active absorption?
   a) Cytochrome b) Lecithin
   c) Ferredoxin d) Plastoquinone
41. Element responsible for maintainig turgor is
   a) Na b) Ca
   c) K d) Hg
42. Active transport occurs
   a) Against concentration gradient and requires ATP
   b) Against concentration gradient but does not require ATP
   c) Along concentration gradient but requires ATP
   d) Along concentration gradient but does not require ATP

43. Phenyl mercuric acetate

a) **Reduces transpiration** b) Reduces photosynthesis

c) Decreases water absorption d) Kills the plant

44. Amino acids are mostly synthesised from

a) Mineral salts b) Volatile acids

c) a-ketoglutaric acid d) Fatty acids

45. Active and passive transports across cell membrane differ in

a) Passive transport is along the concentration

b) Passive transport is along the concentration gradient while active transport is due to metabolic energy

c) Active transport is more rapid

d) Passive transport is confined to anions while active transport in confined to cations

46. Which is not an essential elements for plants?

a) Iron b) Potassium

c) Zinc **d) Sodium**

47. Plants use zinc as

a) Zn^{2+} b) Zn

c) $ZnSO_4$ d) $Zn(SO_3)_2$

48. Plants growing in urea sprayed but Mg deficient soil will show

a) Deep green foliage b) Loss of pigmentation in petals

c) Early flowering **d) Yellowing of leaves**

49. Nitrogen fixing enzyme found in root nodules is

a) Nitrogen esterase **b) Nitrogenase**

c) Nitrase d) None of these

50. Major role of minor elements inside living organisms is to act as

a) Binder of cell structure

b) Constituent of hormones

c) Building blocks of important amino acids

d) Cofactor of enzyme

51. Plant deficient in zinc, show reduced biosynthesis of growth hormone

a) Cytokinin **b) Auxin**

c) Abscisic acid d) Ethylene

52. Nitrogen is not a constituent of

a) Invertase
b) Pepsin
c) Bacteriochlorophyll
d) Idioblast

53. Boron assists in

a) Sugar transport
b) Photosynthesis
c) Activation of enzymes
d) Acting as enzymes cofactor

54. Grey spots of oat are caused by deficiency of

a) Cu
b) Zn
c) Mn
d) Fe

55. Which of the following is present in the core of chlorophyll molecule?

a) Fe
b) K
c) Mn
d) Mg

56. A crop plant which can grow in nitrogen deficient soils without external supply of it is

a) Cajanus cajan
b) Allium sativum
c) Helianthus annus
d) Gossypium herbaceum

57. Potassium is involved in

a) Photosynthesis
b) Promoting many enzymatic activities that regulate plant processes
c) Providing reddish pigmentation to fruits
d) Formation of vascular cambium

58. Phosphorus brings about

a) Fruit ripening
b) Retarded plant growth
c) Retardation of protein synthesis
d) Healthy root growth

59. Zinc is essential for

a) Biosynthesis of IAA
b) Oxidation of carbohydrates
c) Stomatal closing
d) Stomatal opening

60. Essential macronutrients are

a) Produced by growth hormones
b) Absorbed from soil
c) Produced by enzymes
d) Manufactured during photosynthesis

61. Major role of phosphorus in plant metabolism is
   a) CO_2 evolution during respiration
   b) Create anaerobic conditions
   c) O_2 evolution during photosynthesis
   d) Generate metabolic energy
62. Organic compound invariably contain
   a) Carbon b) Sulphur
   c) Phosphorus d) Magnesium
63. Element essential for photolyisis of water is
   a) Nitrogen **b) Manganese**
   c) Carbon d) Sulphur
64. Which is absent in plant ash?
   a) Mineral elements **b) Nitrogen**
   c) Trace elements d) Essential elements
65. Sink is related to
   a) Phytochrome b) Enzymes
   c) Stomata **d) Transport of minerals**
66. Inorganic nutriens are present in the soil as
   a) Atoms b) Molecules
   c) Electrically charged ions d) Colloids
67. Ions are absorbed by plants through
   a) Carriers and pumps b) Difference in water potential
   c) Difference in DPD d) Molecular diffusion
68. Passage of minerals from topsoil to subsoil through seepage of water is known as
   a) Leaching b) Percolation
   c) Conduction d) Transpiration
69. Phytotron is meant for
   a) Controlled humidity
   b) Induced mutations
   c) Growing plants under controlled environment
   d) Controlled irradiation

70. Micronutrient absorbed by foliage is

a) Zinc
b) Iron
c) Aluminium
d) Phosphorus

71. Hydroponics is

a) Growing of plants inside water
b) Growing of floating aquatic plants
c) Growing of aquatic plants
d) Soil-less cultivation of plants

72. Permeability of protoplasm is accelerated by

a) Ca
b) P
c) K
d) Na

73. Nitrogen is an important constituents of

a) Polyphosphates
b) Proteins
c) Carbohydrates
d) Lipids

74. Nitrogen absorbed by plants is

a) Reduced to ammonia
b) Changed to nitrite
c) Combined with oxygen
d) Converted to nitrate

75. Which is a wrong combination?

a) N_2-Amino acid
b) Fe-Cytochrome
c) Mg-Chlorophyll
d) Na-Protein

76. Which is the role of molybdenum?

a) Flower induction
b) Carbon assimilation
c) Chromosome contraction
d) Nitrogen fixation

77. Which one is an essential mineral, not constituent of any enzyme but stimulates the activity of many enzymes?

a) Zn
b) K
c) Mn
d) Mg

78. Role of inorganic nutrients plant growth and metabolism was first discovered by

a) Knoop
b) Steward
c) Woodward
d) None of these

79. Plant require Fe and Mg for
    a) Synthesis of chlorophyll
    b) Translocation of carbohydrate
    c) Opening and closing of stomata
    d) Energy transfer during photosynthesis and respiration

80. Molybdenum is involved in plant metabolism in
    a) Typtophan synthesis
    b) Ascorbic acid synthesis
    c) Nitrate reduction
    d) Translocation of solutes

81. First experiments in hydroponics were performed by
    a) Knop
    b) DeSassure
    c) Hoagland
    d) Sachs

82. In plants, nitrate is reduced to ammonia state in two steps. In second step, electrons are donated by
    a) Nitrate reductase
    b) Nitrite reductase
    c) Ferredoxin
    d) Cytochrome b_5

83. Number of organelles required for photorespiration is
    a) One
    b) Two
    c) Three
    d) Four

84. Photorespiration occurs in
    a) Green parts
    b) All living cells
    c) Mitochondria
    d) Root

85. Protoplasmic streaming theory of translocation of organic solutes was first proposed by
    a) Van den Honert
    b) Cany and Thanie
    c) de Vries
    d) Curtis

86. In Maize, mesophyll cells perform photosynthetic cycle
    a) C_4
    b) C_3
    c) C_2
    d) C_1

87. Three carbons of phosphoglyceric acid formed during carbon fixation are derived from
    a) PEP + CO_2
    b) RuBP
    c) CO_2
    d) RuBP + CO_2

88. Kranz anatomy is typical of

a) C_4 plants b) C_3 plants

c) C_2 plants d) CAM plants

89. Sugarcane shows high efficiency of CO_2 fixation because it performs

a) Calvin cycle b) EMP pathway

c) Hatch and Slack pathway d) TCA cycle

90. What is true for photosynthesis?

a) Both carbon dioxide and water are oxidised

b) Both carbon dioxide and water are reduced

c) Carbon dioxide is oxidised and water reduced

d) Carbon dioxide is reduced and water oxidised

91. A photosynthetic organism which does not release oxygen is

a) Blue-green alga **b) Green sulphur bacterium**

c) Green alga d) Algal component of lichen

92. Flashing light experiments on photosynthesis were performed by

a) Hill b) Calvin

c) Blackmann **d) Emerson and Arnold**

93. At high oxygen concentration, the rate of photosynthesis decreases due to

a) Warburg effect b) Pasteur effect

c) Emerson effect d) Richmond Lang effect

94. Which is sensitive to longer wavelengths of light?

a) PS II **b) PS I**

c) Phosphor ylation d) Photolysis

95. Photosynthetic enhancement with flashing light was first observed by

a) Benson and Calvin b) Hill and Calvin

c) Hatch and Slack **d) Emerson and Arnold**

96. CAM occurs in

a) Thin green leaves with reticulate venation

b) Thin green leaves with parallel venation

c) Thin coloured leaves

d) Fleshy green leaves

97. Light energy is converted into chemical energy in the presence of

a) Chloroplasts b) Pyrenoids

c) Ribosomes d) Mesosomes

98. Photorespiration is characteristic of

a) C_3 plants b) C_4 plants

c) CAM plants d) All of these

99. Calvin cycle occurs in

a) Cytoplasm b) Mitochondria

c) Glyoxysomes **d) Chloroplasts**

100. Element essential for photolysis of water is

a) Nitrogen b) Oxygen

c) Chlorine d) Carbon

9

Plant Pathology

1. .... is the father of plant pathology.

   a) T J Burril **c) Anton De Barry**
   b) Needham d) E J Butler

2. .... first time reported that plant diseases are caused by bacterium.

   a) Robert Koch c) Kuhn
   b) E F Smith d) T J Burril

3. Founder of Virology is ....

   a) Beijerinck c) W M Stanley
   b) A E Mayer d) T O Diener

4. A bacterial cell having large number of flagella all over it's body then it is knoun as...........

   a) Atrichous c) Lophotrichous
   b) Amphitrichous **d) Peritrichous**

5. In bacteria, variability is caused by...........

   a) Conjugation c) Transduction
   b) Transformation **d) All of these**

6. Blackleg in potato is caused by ....pathogen.

   a) *Erwiniaamylovora* c) *Agrobacterium tumefaciens*
   b) *Erwinia caratovora* d) *Pseudomonas solanacearum*

7. J. C. Luthra and his associates developed the solar heat treatment of wheat seeds for the control of ....

   a) Black rust c) Seed gall
   b) Loose smut d) Brown rust

8. .... done most of his work on rust diseases in India

   a) R Prasad c) B BMundakur
   b) K C Mehta d) E J Butler

9. Bacterial leaf blight of rice is commonly controlled by .... Chemical.

   a) Streptocycline c) Aretan

   b) Agrimycin d) RH-893

10. Sandal spike disease in sandal is caused by...........

    a) Bacteria **c) MLO**

    b) Fungi d) Virus

11. .... are the sexual spores in fungi

    a) Chlamydospores c) Zoospores

    b) Sporangiospores **d) Zygospores**

12. Ascospores are .... in number.

    a) 4 **c) 8**

    b) 6 d) 10

13. The perfect (sexual) stage not seen in.........

    a) Zygomycotina c) Basidiomycotina

    b) Ascomycotina **d) Deuteromycotina**

14. Basidiospores are .... in number.

    a) 4 c) 8

    b) 6 d) 10

15. Tundu disease of wheat is caused by..........

    a) Bacteria c) Virus

    b) Nematode d) Phytoplasma

16. Sandal spike disease of wheat is caused by............

    a) Fungi b) Bacteria

    c) Virus **d) MLO**

17. .... are the sexual spores of fungi.

    a) Chlamydospores b) Sporangiospores

    c) Zoospores **d) Zygospore**

18. Ascospores are................ in number.

    a) 2 b) 4

    c) 6 **d) 8**

19. The perfect (sexual) stage not seen in...............

    a) Zygomycotina b) Ascomycotina

    c) Basidiomycotina **d) Deuteromycotina**

20. Basidiospores are................ in number.
   a) 2 b) **4**
   c) 6 d) 8
21. The book on Fungi and Plant Diseases written by.............
   a) **B.B. Mundakar** b) J.F. Dastur
   c) G Rangaswami d) KC Mehta
22. Reapeating spores produced in rust fungi are ....
   a) Aeciospores b) Basidiospores
   c) Urediospres d) Teleutospores
23. The bacterial colony is known as.............
   a) Spore b) Mycelium
   c) Ooze d) Hyphae
24. *Albugo candida* produces ....
   a) Basidiospores b) Ascospores
   c) Zoospores d) Oospores
25. The symptoms of powdery mildew of pea first appears on.............
   a) Stem **b) Leaves**
   c) Roots d) Flowers
26. Loose smut of wheat is........
   a) Internally seed born b) Externally seed born
   c) Both a and b d) None of these
27. Early blight of potato produces..............
   a) Conidia b) Oidia
   c) Uredia d) Telia
28. Tea rust is caused by...........
   a) Bacteria b) Fungi
   c) Algae d) Virus
29. Citrus greening caused by.........
   a) Fastidious bacteria **b) MLO**
   c) Algae d) Virus
30. Bacterial cell division mainly by............
   a) Binnary fission b) Fragmentation
   c) Budding d) None of these

31. Shape of MLO is.................
   a) Regid b) Circular
   c) Cuboid **d) Polymorphic**
32. Cell wall lack microorganism.................
   a) Bacteria **b) MLO**
   c) Algae d) Virus
33. Teichoic acid found in...........
   a) Gram (+) Bacteria b) Gram(-)Bacteria
   c) Fungi d) Protozoa
34. Father of modern microbiology...............
   a) **Louis Pasteur** b) Kuch
   c) Doi d) Mendel
35. MLO disease transmitted by..........
   a) Leaf hopper b) Aphid
   c) White fly d) Animal
36. Alternate host of black rust is...........
   a) Barberi b) Bajra
   c) Jowar d) Wheat
37. Hot water treatment of seed is useful for control of ....
   a) Loose smut b) Coverd smut
   c) Rust d) Powdery mildew
38. Sterility mosaic disease of Pigeon pea spread by..........
   a) Virus b) Aphid
   c) White fly **d) Mites**
39. Phyllody disease of sesamum spread by..........
   a) Leaf hopper b) Aphid
   c) White fly d) Jassids
40. Fungi inperfecti includes........
   a) Deuteromycotina b) Basidiomycotina
   c) Ascomycotina d) Oomycetes
41. Rust includes in...............
   a) Deuteromycotina **b) Basidiomycotina**
   c) Ascomycotina d) Oomycetes

42. Smut includes in ....
    a) Deuteromycotina **b) Basidiomycotina**
    c) Ascomycotina d) Oomycetes
43. Powdery mildew includes in ....
    a) Deuteromycotina b) Basidiomycotina
    c) Ascomycotina d) Oomycetes
44. Downy mildew includes in................
    a) Deuteromycotina b) Basidiomycotina
    c) Ascomycotina **d) Oomycetes**
45. Father of Indian mycology................
    a) E.J.Butler b) K.C. Mehta
    c) MS Swaminathan d) RS Singh
46. Black heart is disorder of ....
    a) Tomato **b) Potato**
    c) Chilli d) Cabbage
47. Panama wilt is disease of..............
    a) Bamboo b) Mango
    c) Guava **d) Banana**
48. VAM is ....
    a) Bacteria b) MLO
    c) Algae **d) Fungi**
49. Loose smut is controlled by..............
    a) Soil treatment **b) Seed treatment**
    c) Chemical spray d) None of these
50. Little leaf of brinjal is caused by ....
    a) Bacteria **b) MLO**
    c) Algae d) Virus
51. Bacterial diseases are controlled by.............
    a) Kelthanae b) Fingicide
    c) Antibiotics d) Viricids
52. Viruses contain...........
    a) RNA b) DNA
    c) Both **d) Either DNA or RNA**

53. A mature virus particle is known as.......
  a) Viroid **b) Virion**
  c) Capsid d) Nucleocapsid

55. Cauliflower mosaic virus contain..........
  a) RNA **b) DNA**
  c) Both d) Either DNA or RNA

56. Leaf curl of tomato is spread by..........
  a) Leaf hopper b) Aphid
  c) White fly d) Jassids

57. .... is the source of Agar-agar.
  a) Bacteria b) MLO
  c) Algae d) Virus

58. Whiptail disease in Cauliflower is due to deficiency of.........
  a) Copper b) Chlorine
  c) Calcium **d) Molybdenum**

59. Non symbiotic N-fixing bacteria is.............
  a) *Rhizobium* b) *Frankia*
  c) Algae **d) *Azotobacter***

60. Aflatoxicin is produced by............
  a) *Aspergilus flavus* b) *Penicillium*
  c) *Aspergilus niger* d) None of these

61. Bordeaux paste is mixture of..............
  a) $CuSO_4$+lime b) $CuSO_4$+$NaCO_3$
  c) $CuSO_4$+$NaSO_4$ d) $CaSO_4$+$NaCO_3$

62. Citrus canker is caused by............
  a) Bacteria b) Fungi
  c) Algae d) Nematodes

63. Which is a P solubilizing bacteria..............
  a) PSB b) VAM
  c) Clostridium d) Azatobacter

64. Black tip of mango is caused by...............
  a) Bacterium b) Fungus
  c) Virus **d) None of these**

65. Fungicide used for the control of powdery mildew is...........

a) Mancozeb b) Apron

c) Karathane d) Thirum

66. Lichen is an Association of..................

a) Algae and fungus b) Bacteria and fungus

c) Fungus and virus d) Fungus and nematode

67. Fungus used as biological control agent against soil born disease is............

a) *Trichothecium* b) *Sclerothecium*

c) *Alternaria* **d) *Trichoderma***

68. 'Cuscuta' is a parasite on ....

a) Root **b) Stem**

c) Leaf d) Both root and stem.

69. The loose smut disease of wheat is caused by...........

a) *Puccinia graminis* b) *Alternaria tritici*

c) *Ustilago tritici* d) *Urocystia tritici*

70. Khaira disease is associated with which crop............

a) Wheat b) Maize

c) Barley **d) Paddy**

71. Bacteria responsible for nitrogen fixation in Soybean is.........

a) *Rhizobium meliloti* b) *Rhizobium leuminoserum*

c) *Rhizobium trifoli* **d) *Rhizobium japonicum***

72. ELISA test is conducted for detection of.............

a) Bacterium b) Fungus

c) Virus d) Viroid

73. Free living N-fixing bacteria is..............

a) *Rhizobium* **b) *Azospirillum***

c) *Azotobacter* d) All of the above

74. Central Potato Research Institute(CPRI) is lacated at.............

a) Shimla b) Patna

c) Hyderabad d) Lucknow

75. Consider the following processes on host plant occurring during pathogenesis............

1. Landing of inoculum 2. Penetration
3. Germinatiom 4. Recognition
5. Establishment and sporulation

The correct sequence of these processes is

a) 1,2,3,4,5 b) 2,3,1,5,4

c) 1,3,2,4,5 d) 4,1,2,3,5

76. Which microorganism is present in large quantities in soil...........

a) Bacteria b) Fungus

c) Virus d) Protozoa

77. Which is the source of Agar agar.............

a) Bacteria b) Fungus

c) Virus **d) Algae**

78. Which one of the following is a single cell fungi........

a) Yeast b) *Aspergillus*

c) *Penicillium* d) *Alternaria*

79. Most widely used fungicide for smut fungi is.........

a) Vitavax b) Plantvax

c) Bavistin d) Dithane M-45

80. Which one of the following fungicide is not systemic in nature.............

a) Vitavax **b) Thiram**

c) Benlate d) Topsin

81. Yellow mosaic disease of moong spread by......

a) *Bemisia tabaci* b) *Aphis crassivora*

c) *Nephotettixviruscens* d) *Amrascabigulitula.*

82. The fungi which transmit plant viruses belongs to class........

a) Basidiomycetes b) Oomycetes

c) Zygomycetes **d) Plasmodiophoromycetes**

83. *Bacillus poppilae* was discovered by............

a) Beijrink **b) Smith Dutky**

c) R.H.Painter d) Knipling

84. In India the leaf rust of coffee was first time recorded in...........

a) 1856 **b) 1870**

c) 1880 d) 1943

85. Select the nematicides group which are non-fungicide in nature........

a) Methyl bromide b) Nemagon (DBCP)

c) Vapam d) Aldicarb and Phorate

86. In rust cycle the cereal host is infected by...........

a) Uredospores **b) Aeciospores**

c) Teliospores d) Basidiospores

87. Potato Spindle tuber disease is transmitted by.................

a) Mechanically b) Biologiccally

c) Water c) All of above

88. Sucidal germination takes place in..................

a) dodder **b) Striga**

c) Loranthus d) *Dendrophthae falcata*

89. In plant bukling, Puckering and blistering symptoms are produced by.................

a) Bacteria b) Fungus

c) Virus d) Algae

90. Consider the following processes on host plant occurring during pathogenesis............

1. Landing of inoculum 2. Penetration

3. Germinatiom 4. Recognition

5. Establishment and sporulation

The correct sequence of these processes is

a) 1,2,3,4,5 b) 2,3,1,5,4

c) 1,3,2,4,5 d) 4,1,2,3,5

91. Tick out the pair which is not correctly matched

a) Dazomate- Mylone **b) Phorate- Nemachur**

c) Aldecarp-Temik d) Carbofuron-Furadan

92 MLO and spiroplasma are mostly ....

a) Xylem inhibiting **b) Phoem inhibiting**

c) Both a and b d) Stomata inhibiting

93. *Heteroderma avenne* is ....

a) Root knot nematode **b) Cyst nematode**

c) Lesion nematode d) Lance nematode

94. White blister of cruciferous is caused by pathogen...............

a) *Pythium debarynam* **b) *Albugo candida***

c) *Sclerospora sorghi* d) *Plasmophora viticola*

95. Cotton leaf curl virus is transmitted by ....

a) **White fly** b) Aphid

c) Leaf hopper d) Jassids

96. Hatch and slack pathway is found in...............

a) **Maize** b) Wheat

c) Rice d) Soybean

97. Loose smut disease of wheat is an.....................

a) Air born b) Soil born

c) Water born **d) Seed born**

98. NABARD was established in the year............

a) 1980 b) 1981

c) 1982 d) 1983

99. Ufra disease mainly occurs in which crop............

a) Wheat **b) Paddy**

c) Maize d) Braley

100. which of the following bacteria is aerobic and non sumbiotic.......

a) Azospirillum **b) Azatobacter**

c) Rhizobium d) Closteridium

101. Which of the following is the partial stem parasite of mango

a) Cuscutta **b) Loranthus**

c) *Orobanche* sp. d) Striga

102. Which one of the following is odd

a) Ascospores b) Cygospores

c) Clamydospores **d) Oospores**

103. Who developed the 'simple microscope.'

a) Donald b) Knoll & Ruska

c) Robert Hooke **d) A. V. Leewen Hooke**

104. Viruses are reproduced by

a) Budding b) Sexual means

c) Binary fission **d) None of above**

105. Carlous Linnaeus established Latin Bionomial system of nomenclature in his book

a) Species plantarum **b) System nature**

c) Genera plantarum d) All of these

106. Puccnia graminis recondite
   a) Black/stem rust   **b) Brown/leaf rust**
   c) Yellow/ strip rust   d) All of these
107. Bacteria multiply of constant rate & logarithmic number of cells plotted against time is happened in
   a) Stationary phase   b) Lag phase
   c) Declined phase   d) Log phase
108. Bacterial cell wall is made up of
   a) Chitin & cellulose   b) Pectin
   c) Peptidoglycon   d) Lignin
109. Which of the following is the first 'antifungal antibiotic'
   a) Nystatin   b) Tetracydine
   c) Penicillin   d) Streptomycin
110. Which of the following is a phosphate fixer
   a) Bacillus   **c) VAM**
   b) Aspergillus   d) Pencillium

FILL IN THE BLANKS

1. Individual thred of fungus is called **Hyphae**.
2. Group of hyphais is called as **Mycelium**.
3. Cross wall present in mycelium is called as **Septate.**
4. Mycelium with septa is called as **Septate mycelium.**
5. Mycelium without septa is called as **Aseptate mycelium/Coenocytic**.
6. Specialised hyphae up right in growth produced from mycelium is **sporongispore**.
7. A sac like structure or spore fruit containing spore is **Sporangiospore.**
8. Hyphae and thin stem having knob like structure called Sporangia.
9. Root like structure or appendages present on fungal Thallus are called **Rhizoids.**
10. Small sporangium with few spore and without columella is called as **Sporangiole.**
11. Hypha which joins two rhizoids is called **Stolon.**
12. Asexual spore born on hyphae s called **Condium.**
13. Hypha bearing conidium at tip or side tha is called as **Condiospore.**
14. The mycelium grow on epidermal surface of hyphaw called **Ectophytic mycelium**.

15. Special sucking organ of fungus is Haustorium.
16. The hyphae of mycelium grow inside the epidermis is called **Endophytic mycelium**.
17. The mycelium which grows in between two cells called **Intercellular mycelium**
18. The mycelium which grows within the cell of plant called **Intracellular mycelium.**
19. The mycelium which grows in the tissue of plant called **Vesicular mycelium**.
20. The hardened compact mass of hyphae which act as resting body called as **Sclerocium**.
21. The fungi which produce thik cahle like strands made up of hyphae are called as **Rhizomorph.**
22. The thickened or swollen cells of mycelium which contain food material are called **Chlamydospore.**
23. The mycelium hibernating in host tissue to tide over unfavorable condition that mycelium called **dormant mycelium.**
24. The motile spors are called **Zoosporeas/swarmspore**.
25. The nonmotile spors are called as **Aplanospore.**
26. **Spore** is minute reproductive or propogative unit functioning as seed of fungi.
27. The vegetative spors are called as **Arthospore or** Chlamydospore.
28. The spores which formed internally within the enlarged cell or sac is called **Endogenous spore.**
29. The spores which born externally on sporospore are called as **Exogenous spores**.
30. The sac like structure in which ascospores are produced is called as **Ascus**.
31. The thik wall of the spore fruit is called as **Peridium.**
32. The hypa which forms conidospore and erect conidospores collectively called **Coremium.**
33. A spore fruit having cushion shaped stroma covered with the conidia formed inside oozein sticky mass is known as **Sporodochium**.
34. Spherical or oval shaped spore fruit with short conidospore lining inner side is known as **Pycnidium.**
35. Compact mas of hyphae giving rise to short simple, hyaline conidospore closely packed forming cushion like mass is known as **Acervulus.**

36. Little heap like compact mass of sporophores and spores is known as **Sorus.**
37. Inverted cup or bell shped fruiting structure is called as **Aecium.**
38. Flask shaped structure contining pycniosporesand spermatia is known as **Pycnium.**
39. Cleistothecium is closed type of **Ascocarp.**
40. A flask shaped ascocarp with narrow necklike ostiole is known as **Perithecium**.
41. A cup or saucer shape spore fruit with broad opening is **Apothecium.**
42. Puff balls, Bracket fungi and Mushrooms are the examples of **Basidiocarp**.
43. Experession of diseased condition is clled as **Symptom**.
44. **Signs** are experimental or scientific evidence of disease.
45. The transformation of floral part into leaf structure is called as **Phyllody.**
46. Generally steam sterilization in autoclave is done at 15 psi for **15 minutes 121.4 °C**
47. Separation of pathogen from diseased host tissue is called as **Isolation.**
48. **0.1 to1%** $HgCl_2$ is used for surface sterilization.
49. Bacterial cultures are purified by **Streaking** method.
50. Isolation,Inoculation,Reproduction,and Reisolation thease are four steps of **Koch's postulate.**
51. For dry preservation of disease sample **Reiker mount** is used.
52. For wet preservation of diseased specimen **5% formalin** is used.
53. Damping off ,a destructive disease is caused by **Pythium**.
54. Late blight of potato is caused by ***Phytopthora infestans.***
55. White rust in cruciferous caused by ***Albugo candida.***
56. ***Mucor remosissimus*** is most commonly occurring on dead and decaying matter.
57. Wheat rust disease caused by the ***Puccinia graminis tritici.***
58. Coffe rust is caused by ***Hemellela rasatrix.***
59. ***Uromyces pisi*** causes rust of Pea.
60. Sphacelotheca, Ustilago genra causes **Smut disease.**
61. Sclerospora, Plasmopara, perenospora and Bremia causes **downy mildew disease**,
62. **Powdery mildew** disease caused by genera Erisiphae, Phyllactinia, leveillula.

63. Example of **edible fungi**-Agaricus and Pleurotus.
64. **Colletotricum** causes Anthracnose disease.
65. Blast of Paddy is caused by ***Pyricularia oryzae.***
66. Early blight of tomato and potato is caused by ***Alternaria solani.***
67. Leaf spot of rice (Bengal Famine 1942) Caused by ***Helminthosporium Oryzae.***
68. **Tikka disease** of ground nut caused by *Cercospora personata* and *Cercospora arachidicola.*
69. ***Pyricularia grisea*** is imperfect stage of blast of paddy.
70 ***Magnaporthe grisea*** is perfect stage of blast of paddy.
71. In blast of paddy primary and secondary source of infection is by **Conidia.**
72. **3 % Brine solution** treatment is recommended for management of **Blast of paddy.**
73. **Blastisidine** antibiotic is used for management of blast of Paddy.
74. ***Panicum repens*** and ***Brachiarie mutica*** are collateral hosts of Blast of Paddy.
75. **Brown spot of paddy** is the responsible disease for Bengal Famine 1942.
76. Brown spot of paddy is caused by ***Helminthosporium oryzae.***
77. ***Drechslera oryzae*** is perfect stage of Brown spot of paddy.
78. ***Ustilagenoidae virens*** is imperfect or conidial stage of false smut of paddy.
79. ***Claviceps oryzae*** is perfect stage of False smut of paddy.
80. Leaf scald of paddy is caused by ***Ryncosporium oryzae.***
81. ***Sclerotinia sclerotiarum*** causes sheath blight of paddy.
82. Bacterial blight of paddy is caused by ***Xanthomonas campestris pv. oryzae.***
83. **Kresek** is the most destructive phase of Bacterial blight of paddy.
84. **Kresek phase & margin blight** are types of symptoms observed in bacterial blight of paddy.
85. In bacterial blight of paddy primary source of infection is through **seed**.
86. Secondary infection of bacterial blight of paddy is by means of wind & water.
87. Tungro disease of paddy is caused to **RTBV & RTSV**.
88. **RTBV means Rice Tungro Bacillus virus.**

99. **RTSV means Rice Tungro Spherical Virus.**

90. **Iodine test** is recommended for identification of **Tungro disease of paddy.**

91. **Green leaf Hopper (Nephotettix virescene)** is an insect vector responsible for transmission of **Tungro disease of paddy.**

92. **IR 50 & CO 45** are tolerant varieties of paddy for Tungro disease.

93. Grain smut of sorghum is caused by ***Sporisporiun sorghi***.

94. Grain smut of jowar is also called as **covered, kernel or short smut.**

95. **PJ 7K, PJ23K & Nandyal** are resistant varieties of jowar for grain smut.

96. Loose smut of jowar is caused by ***Sporisporiun cruenta.***

97. ***Sporisporiun relianum*** is the causal organism of Head smut of Jowar.

98. Because of the filamentous remnants of the vascular system in the affected earhead Head smut is called as ***Zipari.***

99. Long Smut of jowar is caused by ***Tolyposporium ehrenbargi.***

100. For management of smuts of jowar seed treatment with sulphur @ 4 gm / kg or Thirum @ 3 gm / kg of seed is recommended.

101. Downey mildew of sorghum is caused by ***Perenosclerospora sorghi.***

102. **Shredding of leaves** is the typical symptom observed in **Downey mildew of sorghum.**

103. In Downey mildew of jowar primary source of infection is through **oospores** and secondary infection is by means of **sporangia** disseminated by rain or wind.

104. ***Sphacelia sorgi*** is imperfect stage and ***Claviceps sorghi*** of is sexual stage of Ergot of Jowar.

105. **30% brine solution** treatment is recommended for management of **Ergot of Jowar.**

106. **Jowar Rust** is caused by ***Puccinia purpurea.***

107. ***Oxalis corniculata*** is an alternate host of Jowar rust.

108. Rectangular dark brown leaf spots observed in jowar caused due to ***Cercospora sorghi.***

109. ***Colletotrichum gramanicola*** causes Eye spot or Anthracnose of Jowar.

110. ***Helminthosporium* spp. or *Drechslera* spp.** 9is the cause of tan coloured leaf spots with reddish border in jowar.

111. Sooty stripe of jowar is caused by ***Ramularia sorghi.***
112. ***Gloeocercospora sorhi*** causes Zonate leaf spot in Jowar.
113. Rough leaf spot of Jowar is caused by ***Ascochyta sorghi.***
114. In Charcoal Rot of Jowar ***Rhizoctonia bataticola*** is the sterile stage while ***Macrophomina phaseolina*** is pycnidial stage.
115. Charcoal rot of jowar is locally called as ***Kadkadya.***
116. Grain mould in sorghum is caused by ***Curvularia lunata & Fusarium moniliformae.***
117. **Striga** is **partial root parasite** of Jowar.
118. **Striga** is also called as **Witch weed**.
119. **Striga** is partial root parasite of sugarcane, jowar, maize and other cereals.
120. **Ramkel, Dukri, SAR 1 SAR 2 and BO 1** are resistant varieties of jowar for Striga.
121. **Downey mildew** of Bajra is caused by ***Sclerospora graminicola.***
122. **Downey mildew** of bajra is also called as **Green ear or Witches Broom.**
123. Seed treatment with **Metalaxyl @ 6 gm / kg** seed is recommended for management of **Downey Mildew** of Bajra.
124. **WCC 75, ICMS 7703, RHR 1, RHRBH 8609** and **ICTP 8203** are resistant varieties of bajra for Downey mildew.
125. Ergot of Bajra is caused by ***Claviceps fusiformis.***
126. **Honey Dew** stage of Ergot of bajra contains conidia of the disease.
127. **Sclerotia** of ergot disease contain alkaloid **Ergotoxin or Ergotin** which is responsible for ergot poisoning in animals.
128. **20% Brine solution treatment** is recommended for management of **Ergot of Bajra.**
129. **Sclerotium** is thick, hard, compact mass of mycelium form under adverse condition.
130. **Bajra Rust** is caused by ***Puccinia penniseti.***
131. **Egg Plant (Brinjal)** is an alternate host of Bajra rust.
132. In Bajra rust **Uredial and Telial** stages are observed on Bajra plant while **Pycnial and Aecial** stages are observed on egg plant.
133. In Bajra rust primary infection is through **aeciospores (from Brinjal)** and secondary infection through **uredospores.**
134. **MH 168, 179, 180 and 182** are resistant varieties of bajra for rust.
135. **Bajra smut** is caused by ***Tolyposporium penicillariae.***

136. **RHRBH 8609, WCC 75, ICTP 8203, ICMS 7703** are resistant cultivars of bajra against smut.
137. Downey Mildew of maize is caused by ***Sclerospora maydis.***
138. Primary infection of maize downey mildew of maize is by **oospores present in the soil** while secondary infection is through **sporangia.**
139. Seed Treatment with **Ridomil MZ 72 @ 5–7gm/kg of seed** is recommended for management of **Downey Mildew of Maize.**
140. **Maize smut** is caused by ***Ustilago maydis.***
141. Bacterial stalk and Ear rot of maize is caused by ***Erwinia carotovora.***
142. ***Pseudomonas syringae*** causes bacterial stalk rot of Maize.
143. **Ragi blast** is caused by ***Pyricularia grisa.***
144. Spraying with **Iprobenphos or Edifenphos** are recommended for management of ragi blast.
145. Finger Millet blast is caused by ***Pyricularia setariae.***
146. Leaf spot or Leaf blotch of finger Millet is caused by ***Helminthosporium setariae.***
147. **Black stem rust of wheat** is caused by ***Puccinia graminis tritici.***
148. **Brown rust or leaf rust or orange rust of wheat**is caused by ***Puccinia recondita.***
149. **Yellow rust or Stripe rust of wheat** is caused by ***Puccinia striformis.***
150. ***Barberis vulgaris, Mahonia acauifolia*** are alternate hosts of Black stem rust of wheat.
151. ***Bromus juponicus*** is an alternate host of Yellow or Stripe rust of Wheat.
152. ***Thalictrum polygamum*** is an alternate host of Brown or leaf rust of wheat.
153. In India all three rust perpetuates **through uredospores on self sown wheat crops in hills.**
154. Spraying of Dithiocarbamate @ 0.25% is recommended for management of rusts of wheat.
155. Loose smut of wheat is caused by ***Ustilago tritici.***
156. **Naked rachis in the panicle** is typical symptom of Loose smut of wheat.
157. **Solar heat treatment** is recommended for the management of loose smut of wheat.
158. **Loose smut of wheat** is **internally seed born** disease.
159. In loose smut of wheat mycelium survives in the form of **dormant mycelium** inside the seed.

160. **Kalyan sona 227, PV 18, WG 307, C 302** are resistant varieties of wheat for loose smut disease.
161. Kernal bunt of wheat is caused by ***Neovossia indica.***
162. **Common Bunt** of wheat is caused by ***Neovossia foeitida.***
163. **Kernal Bunt** is also called as **Stinking smut.**
164. Common bunt can be controlled by seed treatment with **carboxin (Vitavax).**
165. Wheat leaf blight is caused by ***Alternaria triticina.***
166. Leaf blight of wheat is **externally as well as internally seed born disease**.
167. Black point of wheat is caused by ***Alternaria, Helminthosporium and Fusarium.***
168. **Whip Smut** of Sugarcane is caused by ***Ustilago scitaminae.***
169. **Formation of whip like out growth covered by white silvery thin membrane** is typical symptom observed in **whip smut of sugarcane.**
170. In **Whip smut of sugarcane infected seed serves as Primary source of infection.**
171. Red rot of sugarcane is caused by ***Colletotrichum falcatum.***
172. ***Glomerella tucumanensis*** is perfect stage of red rot of sugarcane.
173. Infected sett serves as Primary source of infection in red rot of sugarcane.
174. Smut sori contains no of **Chlamydospores.**
175. Sugarcane mosaic is transmitted by **aphids *Melanapsis sacchari & Melanapsis indosacchari.***
176. Grassy shoot of sugarcane is caused by **Mycoplasma Like Organisms.**
177. **Production of numerous tillers at the base of the plant** is the typical symptom of grassy shoot of sugarcane.
178. Grassy shoot of sugarcane is transmitted by **aphids *Aphis maydis, Aphis sacchari and Aphis indosacchari.***
179. **Moist hot air treatment, Areated steam treatment and Hot air Treatments** are recommended for management of **Grassy Shoot of Sugarcane**.
180. Downey mildew of sugarcane is caused by ***Sclerospora sacchari.***
181. Early leaf spot of groundnut is caused by ***Cercospora arachidicol.***
182. ***Cercospora personatum*** causes **late leaf spot of groundnut**.
183. ***Mycospharerella arachidicola*** is **perfect stage** of **early leaf spot of groundnut**.

184. ***Mycospharerella berkeleyii*** is **perfect stage** of **late leaf spot of groundnut**.
185. In Tikka of groundnut **primary and secondary source of infection is through conidia.**
186. Groundnut rust is caused by ***Puccinia arachidis.***
187. Collar rot og groundnut is caused by ***Aspergillus niger.***
188. In **pre emergence collar rot** seeds are attacked by **soil born conidia.**
189. **Stem rot or Collar rot or Sclerotial wilt** of groundnut is caused by ***Sclerotium rolfsi.***
190. **Soil treatment with PCNB** is recommended for management of **stem rot of groundnut.**
191. **PCNB** means **Penta Chloro Nitro Benzene.**
192. **Bud Necrosis of groundnut** is caused by **Tomato Spotted Wilt Virus.**
193. **Bud necrosis virus** perpetuates on weed hosts.
194. **Thrips** transmits **bud necrosis of groundnut**.
195. **Dense planting (15 X 15**) is recommended for management of **bud necrosis of groundnut**.
196. **Downey mildew** of sunflower is caused by ***Plasmopara halstedi.***
197. **Damping off, systemic symptom, local foliar lesion and basal root & stem galls** are different types of symptoms in **Downey mildew of sunflower.**
198. **Oospores i**n the soil serve as primary source of infection in Downey mildew of Sunflower.
199. Sunflower rust is caused by ***Puccinia helianthi.***
200. Sunflower rust is **macrocyclic, autoecious** in nature.
201. **Morden and Surya** are resistant varieties of sunflower for rust.
202. Alternaria leaf blight of sunflower is caused by ***Alternaria helianthi.***
203. Early sowing of sunflower is recommended for management of ***Alternaria* leaf spot.**
204. Sunflower necrosis is caused by **Tobacco Streak Virus.**
205. Tobacco streak virus is transmitted by **sap and thrips.**
206. Leaf spot of Safflower is caused by ***Cercospora carthami.***
207. Safflower leaf blight is caused by ***Alternaria carthami.***
208. **Infected plant debris** serves as **primary source of infection in leaf spot and leaf blight of safflower.**

209. Safflower wilt is caused by ***Fusarium oxysporum*** f. sp. ***Carthami.***

210. Wilt fungus produces **small round microconidia, sickle shaped macro conidia and thick walled chlamydospores.**

211. ***Pseudomonas fluorescence, Trichoderma viridae, Trichoderma harzianum*** seed treatment is recommended for wilt of safflower.

112. Leaf Blotch of turmeric is caused by ***Taphrina maculans.***

213. Spraying of **Bordaux mixture** is recommended for management of leaf blotch of turmeric.

214. ***Colletotrichum capsici*** causes leaf spot of turmeric.

215. Soft rot or Rhizome rot of ginger is caused by ***Pythium myriotylum.***

216. Infected Rhizomes serves as primary source of infection in soft rot.

217. Leaf spot of ginger is caused by ***Ascochyta*** **spp.**

218. For management of soft rot Rhizome treatment with copper fungicide is recommended.

219. **Angular leaf spot** is also called as **Black arm** disease.

220. Angular leaf spot is caused by ***Xanthomonas oxanopodis*** pv ***malvaceraum***.

221. Acid delinting is recommended for management of **Angular leaf spot** of cotton.

222. For acid delinting **concentrated HCL or H_2SO_4** is used.

223. Secondary spread of black arm can be controlled by spraying 100 ppm strptomycine sulphate.

224. Vascular wilt of cotton is caused by ***Fusarium oxysporum*** **f.sp.** ***vasinfectum.***

225. **Cotton wilt** is restricted to black cotton soil with pH **7.6 – 8.00.**

226. **American cotton varieties** are resistant to wilt in India.

227. Grey mildew or Dahiya of cotton is caused by ***Ramularia areola.***

228. ***Mycosphaerella areola*** is perfect stage of grey mildew of cotton.

229. Anthracnose of cotton is caused by ***Colletotrichum gossypii.***

230. ***Glomerella gossypi*** is perfect stage of **Anthracnose of cotton.**

231. Root rot of cotton is caused by ***Rhizoctonia bataticola.***

232. ***Macrophomina phaseolina*** is imperfect stage of root rot of cotton.

233. **Soil mulching** after rain is recommended for management of root rot of cotton.

234. **Crop residue with sclerotia** acts as primary source of infection in root rot of cotton.

235. **Boll rot** is complex fungal disease.

236. Punctures caused by red cotton bug is one of the predisposition **for boll rot** in Cotton.

237. Close spacing and excessive nitrogen application are predisposition conditions for **boll rot in cotton.**

238. Leaf spot or leaf blight is caused by ***Alternaria macrcopora.***

239. Reddening in cotton is due to deficiency of **Magnessium.**

240. Reddening is locally called as ***Lalya.***

241. 2 4 D injury is commonly observed in cotton.

242. Wilt of red gram is caused by ***Fusarium oxysporum* f.sp. *udam.***

243. Tur wilt perpetuates in the soil in the form of **Chlamydospore.**

244. **C 11, BDN 1& BDN 2** are resistant varieties of tur for wilt.

245. **Deep Ploughing** during summer is recommended for management of tur wilt.

246. Sterility mosaic of pigeon pea is transmitted by **Eriophid mite *Aceria cajani.***

247. Gram wilt is caused by ***Fusarium oxysporum* f.sp. *ciceri.***

248. **Vikas, Vishwas** are resistant varieties of grm for **Wilt.**

249. ***Rhictonia bataticola*** is sterile stage of root rot of Bengal gram.

250. ***Macrophomina phaseolina*** is imperfect stage of root rot of Bengal gram.

251. Application of ***Pseudomonas fluorescens @ 10 g /kg*** is recommended for management of root rot of Bengal gram.

252. Stem rot or collar rot of gram is caused by ***Sclerotium rolfsii.***

253. Soil drenching with 0.2% PCNB is recommended for management of Stem rot or collar rot of gram.

254. Ascochyta blight is caused by ***Ascochyta rabiei.***

255. Stunt disease of chick pea is caused by **Chick pea stunt virus CPSV.**

256. Chick pea stunt virus is transmitted by ***Aphis craccivora.***

257. Powdery mildew of green gram and black gram is caused by ***Erysiphae polygoni.***

258. **Clestothecium in infected plant debris** serves as primary source of infection in powdery mildew of green and black gram.

259. Anthracnose of gren and black gram is caused by ***Colletotrichum lindemuthianum.***

260. ***Glomerella lindemuthianum*** is sexual stage of Anthracnose of green and black gram.
261. In anthracnose several spots joins to cause necrotic areas with **Acervuli.**
262. ***Cercospora canescens*** cause leaf spot in green gram and black gram.
263. **Yellow mosaic** is caused by **Virus.**
264. Yellow mosaic is transmitted by white fly ***Bemisia tabaci.***
265. Increase seed rate is recommended for management of yellow mosaic.
266. Leaf curl of green gram and black gram is caused by Tomato spotted wilt virus.
267. Leaf curl of green gram and black gram is transmitted by thrips ***Frankliniella schulzii, thrips tabacci,and Scirtothrips dorsalis.***
268. Soybean rust is caused by ***Phakospora pachyrhizi.***
269. Yield loss as high as 50% is reported in soybean rust.
270. Anthracnose of soybean is caused by ***Colletotrichum truncatum.***
271. Bacterial blight of Soybean is caused ***Pseudomonas syringae*** **pv** ***glycenea.***
272. Bacterial pustule sin soybean is caused by ***Xanthomonas axonopodis.***
273. Seed treatment with **250 ppm streptocycline.**
274. Soybean mosaic virus causes Soybean Mosaic.
275. Soybean mosaic virus is transmitted through **sap and Aphids.**
276. Tobacco mosaic is caused by TMV.
277. TMV is sap transmissible.
278. Leaf curl of tobacco is caused by **Nicotiana virus – 10.**
279. Leaf curl of tobacco is transmitted by **white fly** ***Bemicia tabaci.***
280. ***Orobanche cernua var desertorum*** / **Broom Rape** is complete root parasite on Tobacco.
281. Spraying with allyl alcohol or $CuSO_4$ is recommended for management of ***Orobanche.***
282. Linseed Rust is caused by ***Melampsora lini.***
283. Linseed rust is an **autocious rust.**
284. Linseed wilt is caused by ***Fusarium oxysporum*** **f.so** ***lini.***
285. Linseed wilt is more prominent under **low moisture conditions and light sandy soils.**
286. Castor rust is caused by ***Melampsora ricini.***
287. ***Euphorbia*** **spp.** is an alternate host of castor rust.

288. Leaf blight of castor is caused by ***Alternaria ricini.***

289. ***Jatropha pandurifola & Bridelia hamilatoniana*** are the survival sources of leaf blight fungus in castor.

290. ***Cercospora ricinella*** causes brown leaf spot of castor.

291. ***Cercospora*** in castor survives in the form of dormant myceliumin infected plant debris.

292. Leaf blight of sesamum is caused by ***Alternaria sesami.***

293. ***Cercospora sesami*** causes leaf spot of sesamum.

294. Wilt of sesamun is caused by ***Fusarium oxysporum* f.sp. *sesami.***

295. Dry humid weather and low relative humidity are favourable conditions for powdery mildew of Sesamum.

296. Powdery mildew of sesamum is caused by ***Erysiphae cichoracearum.***

297. ***Xanthomonas campestris pv.sesami & Pseudomonas sesame*** causes bacterial leaf spot.

298. Spraying of **Streptomycine or Oxytrtracycline** is recommended for management of **bacterial leaf spots.**

299. Transformation of floral parts into green leafy structure is called as **Phyllody.**

300. Seasmum phyllody is caused by ***Mycoplasma like organisms.***

301. Sesamum phyllody is transmitted by **Jassids.**

302. **Alternate hosts and weed hosts** are survival sources of Sesamum phyllody.

303. The fungus which completes its life cycle on single host is called as **Autocious.**

304. The fungus which requires more than one host for completion of life cycle is called as **Heterocious fungus.**

305. **Striga** is difficult for management because of its high seed production potential.

306. Typical Offensive alcoholic smell is typical symptom of red rot of sugarcane.

307. Pineapple or sett rot of sugarcane is caused by ***Ceratocystis paradoxa.***

308. Pokkha Boeing of sugarcane is caused by ***Fusarium moniliformae.***

10

Agricultural Entomology

1. Insects are thought to be so very successful because of
   a) Their small size
   b) Ecological diversity
   c) Ability to utilize many food sources
   d) All of the above
2. For their size, insects are much stronger than man because
   a) Their muscles are naturally stronger
   b) They can control muscle response more precisely
   c) They have giant nerve fibers
   d) Of physical properties related to their small size
3. Insects are considered to be beneficial because they are
   a) Effective pollinators
   b) Make useful products
   c) Act as biological control agents
   d) All of above
4. The most important vectors (transmission agents) of human disease would probably be
   a) Moths b) Ants
   c) Beetles **d) Fleas**
5. The most important reason for the success of insects as a group is probably
   a) Parthenogenetic reproduction
   b) Muscle strength to weight ratio
   c) Ability to digest unusual foods
   d) Ability to fly
6. In grasshoppers, the sclerite on the front of the head located between the frons & the labrum is
   a) Clypeus b) Maxilla
   c) Gena d) Vertex

7. The modified hind wings in flies (used for balance) are called
   a) Elytra **b) Halteres**
   c) Hamuli d) Tegmina
8. Another name for an insect walking leg is
   a) Ambulatory b) Fossorial
   c) Cursorial d) Saltatorial
9. A spray that kills insects when they touch it is called
   a) A contact insecticide b) A fumigant
   c) A stomach poison d) A desiccant
10. You find something crawling on your dog that looks like a small flat brown bug; it has eight legs. It is:
    a) An insect b) A flea
    c) A tick d) A brown bug
11. Mosquito males locate females by using:
    a) Scolopophorous sensillae
    b) Campaniform sensillae
    c) Tympanum
    d) Compound eyes
12. The use of X-ray irradiated flies for pest management is an example of:
    a) Sterile male release b) Neoplasia induction
    c) Mutant proliferation d) Environmental hazards
13. What is the mode of action of organophosphate insecticides?
    a) Chitin-synthesis inhibition
    b) Mixed-function oxidase inhibition
    c) Physical suffocation
    d) Changing the ion permeability of membranes
14. More than 500 species of insects are currently resistant to one or more pesticides. How are insects able to resist the toxic action of pesticides?
    a) Cross-resistance
    b) Mixed-function oxidases
    c) Behavioral adaptations
    d) Physiological changes at the level of the target site
    e) All of the above

15. Ants are:
    a) The largest group of social insects (ca. 9,000 described species)
    b) The only social insects in the order Hymenoptera
    c) The only group of insects to be found in the fossil record d. a. and b.
    e) None of the above
16. The greatest threat to biodiversity in terms of the percentage of species affected is:
    a) Habitat degradation b) Disease
    c) Over exploitation **d) Pollution**
17. Mutualisms have evolved between:
    a) Ants and bees (particularly Africanized Honey Bees)
    b) Ants and termites (e.g., the Formosan termite that has invaded Hawaii)
    c) **Ants and plant feeding insects that produce honeydew (e.g., phids and scale insects)**
    d) Ants and plants that provide rewards in the form of food (e.g., extrafloral nectar)
18. The notion that preservation of one species (often a "charismatic" organism that acts as a "flagship species") may aid in the preservation of many others is often called:
    a) A habitat saver b) The umbrella effect
    c) The conservation strategy **d) All of the above**
19. Current uses of genetically modified organisms include:
    a) Glyphosate (Roundup) resistant plants
    b) **Insect resistant plants expressing the Bacillus thuringiensis (Bt) endotoxin gene**
    c) Enhanced microbial pesticides, e.g., baculo viruses expressing scorpion toxin genes
    d) Production of vaccines
    e) All of the above
20. Pathogen derived resistance refers to:
    a) Use of Bacillus thuringiensis endotoxin against Colorado Potato Beetle
    b) Use of genes from a virus to protect a plant from a very similar or homologous virus isolate
    c) Coat protein mediated cross protection
    d) **a and c**
    e) b and c

21. The highest, or most developed, form of sociality among insects is referred to as:
    a) Subsocial
    b) Semisocial
    c) Eusocial
    d) Communal
    e) Quasisocial
22. Some of the evolutionary advantages of social behavior include:
    a) Improved resource acquisition
    b) Improved defense
    c) Improved survival of offspring
    d) Reduced stinging requirements
    e) a, b and c
23. Worker honey bees in a colony:
    a) Are all sterile females
    b) Have the same mother
    c) Are diploid
    d) a, b and c
24. Honey bee caste determination is:
    a) Is age related and regulated genetically and hormonally
    b) Is regulated by photoperiod and temperature
    c) Is regulated by the waggle dance
    d) Is determined by pesticides in the environment
25. Termites differ from honeybees in that they:
    a) Are haplo-diploid
    b) Have no males
    c) Are diploid
    d) c and d
26. Family of the *Droscha magniferae*
    a) Coccidae
    b) Aleurodidae
    c) Aphididae
    d) Pyralidae
27. The two most important structural insect pests in urban situations are:
    a) Moths and butterflies
    b) Spiders and scorpions
    c) Beetles and flies
    d) Termites and ants
28. Family of the *Emmalocera deprcsella*
    a) Chrysomelidae
    b) Pyralidae
    c) Anobiidae
    d) Noctuidae

29. Family of the *Spodoptera litura*:
    a) Chrysomelidae   b) Pyralidae
    c) Anobiidae   **d) Noctuidae**
30. Family of the *Pectinophora gossypiella*:
    a) Tenebrionidae   b) Noctuidae
    c) Gelechiidae   d) Aphididae
31. Approaches to biological control tactics include classical, augmentative and conservation. Classical biological control is the:
    a) Preservation of natural enemies (predators & parasitoids) that are already established in an area
    b) Importation and release of an insect pest to a new area to provide hosts for natural enemies
    c) Culture and release of natural enemies that are already established in the field, but that need a "boost" to effectively control the insect pest species
    d) Importation and release of natural enemies from the native home of an alien insect pest that has invaded a new area
32. Family of the *Bemisia tabaci*:
    a) Apionidae   **b) Aleurodidae**
    c) Pyralidae   d) Pyrrhocoridae
33. An example(s) of a relative method to assess economic threshold levels for an insect pest is:
    a) Number of insects per leaf
    b) Number of insects per plant
    c) Number of insects per twig
    d) a,b and c.
34. Quarantine of an insect pest involves:
    a) Eradication of the pest   **b) Limit the movement of the pest**
    c) Cooperation of the public   d) b and c
35. The equilibrium level in an insect population:
    a) Is the point at which insects can begin to migrate
    b) Refers to fluctuations in the population around a mean
    c) Is important in determining pest status
    d) All of the above e, b and c
36. Which chemicals do insects use to communicate messages at the following three levels, respectively: within the insect body, intra-specifically (between

members of the same species), and inter-specifically (between members of different species)?

a) Hormone, PTTH, and tympanum, respectively.

b) Kairomone, pheromone and hormone, respectively.

c) **Hormone, pheromone and allomone, respectively**.

d) Juvenile hormone, PTTH and luciferin, respectively.

37. The honey bee waggle dance conveys information about the location of nectar sources to other worker bees in the hive. Which of the following senses do worker bees use to interpret the dance?

a) Sight b) Smell

c) Taste d) Touch

38. What is the insect auditory sense structure that detects sound (analogous to the human ear) called?

a) Lek b) Antenna

c) Kairomone **d) Tympanum**

39. Insects can create vibrations that are transmitted through a substrate:

a) That send very specific intraspecific messages, e.g. courtship songs.

b) And used for efficient intraspecific communication over short distances.

c) That represent a secure means of intraspecific communication.

d) And attract mates from great distances, well over a mile.

e) a, b and c

40. The honey bee worker has a "stinger" which

a) Is a modified ovipositor and associated with a poison gland that produces the venom.

b) Has a barb on it which can imbed into the skin and be released by muscles to allow the bee to sting another victim.

c) Has a barb on it which can imbed into the skin of an animal and is left behind to continue injecting venom into the victim.

d) a and c

41. Bubonic plague is:

a) Present in rodent populations along with its efficient louse vector in the Sierra Mountains of California.

b) Present in bear populations along with its efficient flea vector in the Sierra Mountains of California.

c) Present in rodent populations along with its efficient flea vector in the Sierra Mountains of California.

d) **No longer a threat because the flea vector has been eradicated with chemical insecticides in the Sierra Mountains of California.**

42. Examples of some density-independent mortality factors in insect populations are:
    a) Predators, parasitoids, and pathogens.
    b) Predators, chemical insecticides, and intraspecific competition.
    c) Chemical insecticides, hurricanes, and temperature extremes (i.e., hot and cold)
    d) Chemical insecticides, flooding, and intraspecific competition.
43. Which of the following responses occur when predators interact with prey populations?
    a) A numerical response. b) A functional response.
    c) A lag effect **d) a and b only**
44. An example of a biological control against insects is the use of
    a) Herbicides b) Wildlife refuges
    c) Pesticides **d) Sex hormones**
45. As human consumers become less tolerant of insect damage on fruit, the economic thresholds for fruit pests are likely to:
    a) Increase **b) Remain the same**
    c) Decrease d) No way to tell
46. Which of these is NOT considered an insect growth regulator?
    a) Synthetic pyrethroid b) Juvenile hormone analogue
    c) Chitin inhibitor d) Ecdysteroid
47. Organophosphate and carbamate insecticides work by disrupting an insect's:
    a) Digestive system **b) Nervous system**
    c) Respiratory system d) Endocrine system
48. The sterile-male technique would probably not work well for an insect pest whose:
    a) Population is extremely abundant
    b) Individuals are easily mass reared.
    c) Females mate only once in their lifetime
    d) Males are very strong fliers
49. Which of these is an "unbiased" sampling strategy?
    a) Malaise trap b) Light trap
    c) Sticky trap **d) None of these**

50. Breeding nursey stock for higher levels of secondary plant compounds would be an example of:

a) **Antixenosis** b) Xenobiosis

c) Antibiosis d) Tolerance

51. Which of these is likely to be regarded as the most "useful" biological control agent

a) **A beetle that feeds on kudzu**

b) A parasite of lady beetles

c) A predator of robber flies

d) A viral pathogen of lacewings.

52. To which of these groups do insect pathogens belong?

a) Viruses and bacteria b) Protozoa and fungi

c) Bacteria and protozoa **d) All of these**

53. Pest outbreaks tend to occur when:

a) **Crops are planted in monoculture**

b) Natural enemies are imported from abroad.

c) Farmers switch to new crops

d) All of these.

54. Biological control is likely to be most effective when the predator or parasite has a:

a) Long life cycle b) Wide range of preferred hosts

c) **High reproductive rate** d) All of these

55. Which insect orders contain species that are important pests of domestic animals?

a) Siphonaptera and Coleoptera

b) Orthoptera and Hemiptera

c) **Diptera and Phthiraptera**

d) All of these

56. Which control strategy is likely to have the greatest impact on non-target organisms?

a) **Chemical control** b) Cultural control

c) Biological control d) Physical/mechanical control

57. Which insect order is most closely related to Diptera?

a) **Hymenoptera** b) Orthoptera

c) Plecoptera d) Thysanura

58. To which class of arthropods do lobsters and shrimp belong?
    a) Crustacea b) Arachnida
    c) Myriapoda d) Xiphosura
59. The order Hemiptera contains:
    a) Bed bugs and stink bugs
    b) Chewing and sucking lice
    c) Roaches and mantids
    d) Crickets and grasshoppers
60. Which order is not holometabolous?
    a) Siphonaptera b) Hymenoptera
    c) Thysanoptera d) Neuroptera
61. Which order is exclusively herbivorous?
    a) Trichoptera b) Odonata
    c) Phasmatodea d) Thysanoptera
62. Which order is exclusively parasitic?
    a) Diplura **b) Phthiraptera**
    c) Zoraptera d) Diptera
63. Sucking mouthparts are NOT found in:
    a) Fleas b) Lice
    c) Flies **d) Ants**
64. All ametabolous insects are:
    a) Predatory **b) Wingless**
    c) Endognathous d) All of these
65. Immatures of the Neuroptera would be classified as:
    a) Scavengers b) Parasites
    c) Herbivores **d) Predators**
66. What do the orders Mantodea, Dermaptera, and Isoptera have in common?
    a) Winglessness **b) Chewing mouthparts**
    c) Herbivory d) All of these
67. Which insect order is most closely related to Dermaptera?
    a) Hymenoptera b) Orthoptera
    c) Plecoptera **d) Thysanura**
68. Which arthropods have chelicerae?
    a) Spiders b) Millipedes
    c) Shrimp d) All of these

69. The order Orthoptera contains:
   a) Bed bugs and stink bugs b) Chewing and sucking lice
   c) Roaches and mantids **d) Crickets and grasshoppers**
70. Which characteristic would not be found in the Onychophora?
   a) One pair of antennae b) Three tagmata
   c) Jointed legs with claws d) Segmented body
71. Which order is exclusively hematophagous (blood feeders)?
   a) Siphonaptera b) Thysanoptera
   c) Phasmida d) Hymenoptera
72. Which structure is always associated with the Hymenoptera?
   a) Furcula **b) Hamuli**
   c) Collophore d) Elytra
73. Chewing mouthparts never occur in:
   a) Fleas b) Earwigs
   c) Beetles d) Bees
74. All neopterous insects are:
   a) Predatory b) Wingless
   c) Ectognathous d) Hemimetabolous
75. Which developmental stage is found only in the Ephemeroptera?
   a) Prepupa **c) Subimago**
   b) Naiad d) Imago
76. Which orders are most important in the transmission of human disease?
   a) Phasmatodea and Odonata
   b) Hymenoptera and Siphonaptera
   c) Diptera and Phthiraptera
   d) Hemiptera and Thysanoptera
77. A naiad is best described as a(n):
   a) Predatory larva b) Wingless adult
   c) Aquatic nymph d) Scavenger
78. Which order is most closely related to Dermaptera?
   a) Isoptera b) Mecoptera
   c) Psocoptera d) Coleoptera
79. Chelicerate arthropods include:
   a) Millipedes and centipedes b) Lobsters and shrimp
   c) Spiders and ticks d) Lice and fleas

80. Which statement is true for all crustacea?
   a) They live on land
   b) They have chewing mouthparts
   c) They have six walking legs
   d) They are paleopterous
81. Which insect order is never associated with plants?
   a) Hymenoptera b) Thysanoptera
   c) Hemiptera **d) Siphonaptera**
82. Human disease pathogens are transmitted by which order?
   a) Hymenoptera b) Thysanoptera
   c) Diptera d) All of these
83. Odonata and Plecoptera are similar because both have:
   a) Aquatic nymph's b) Endopterygote development
   c) Paleopterous wings d) All of these
84. Which insect order never lives in aquatic environments?
   a) Trichoptera b) Plecoptera
   c) Diptera **d) Orthoptera**
85. Hemiptera and Hymenoptera are similar because both have:
   a) Holometabolous development
   b) Piercing-sucking mouthparts
   c) Neopterous wings
   d) All of these
86. Which insect order is most commonly found in soil litter?
   a) Collembola b) Neuroptera
   c) Lepidoptera d) Phasmatodea
87. In a male insect, which structure would lie below (ventral to) the anus?
   a) Epiproct **b) Aedeagus**
   c) Paraproct d) Furca
88. Which compound would be found in the exocuticle but NOT in the endocuticle?
   a) Chitin b) Protein
   c) Quinone d) Wax
89. To which body segment are the elytra attached?
   a) Mesothorax b) Prothorax
   c) First abdominal d) Metathorax

90. The shell of an insect's egg is called the:
   a) Serosa   **b) Chorion**
   c) Amnion   d) Periplasm

91. Damage symptoms of the *emmalocera depressella*?
   a) Bunchy top   b) Dead harts pulled easily
   c) Spiral glasseries   **d) Dead hearts cannot pulled easily**

92. Which structure is unicellular?
   a) Spine   b) Gland
   c) Seta   d) Pile

93. What is the function of the micropyle in an insect's egg?
   a) Water balance   b) Respiration
   c) Nutrition   **d) Sperm entrance**

94. Which mouthparts lie between the labrum and the maxillae?
   a) Hypopharynx   b) Labium
   c) Mandibles   d) Palps

95. A line of weakness between adjacent sclerites that breaks during molting is called a
   a) Apodeme   **b) Ecdysial suture**
   c) Apophysis   d) Epistomal suture

96. Chitin is most abundant in which part of the exoskeleton?
   a) Epicuticle   b) Cuticulin layer
   c) Procuticle   d) Epidermis

97. In a male insect, which structure would lie above (dorsal to) the anus?
   a) Epiproct   b) Aedeagus
   c) Paraproct   d) Furca

98. What type of chemical monomer forms the backbone of a chitin molecule?
   a) Lipid   b) Sugar
   c) Quinone   **d) Amino Acid**

99. To which body segment are the halters attached?
   a) Mesothorax   b) Prothorax
   c) First abdominal   **d) Metathorax**

100. Which structure lies between the buccal cavity and the salivarium?
   a) Labium   b) Cibarium
   c) Labrum   **d) Hypopharynx**

101. Which structure(s) would be found on an insect's pretarsus?
    a) Trochanter b) Furca
    c) Empodium d) All of these

102. Indirect flight muscles cause wing movement by:
    a) Moving thoracic sclerites
    b) Pulling on axillary sclerites
    c) Exerting hydrostatic pressure
    d) All of these

103. What is the maximum number of ocelli that may be found in an adult insect?
    a) Zero b) Five
    c) Three d) Twenty

104. Which mouthparts lie between the labrum and the maxillae?
    a) Hypopharynx b) Labium
    c) Mandibles d) Palps

105. Which sclerite lies below (ventral to) the frons?
    a) Gena b) Occiput
    c) Clypeus d) Labium

106. A tormogen cell is always associated with a(n):
    a) Spine b) Apodeme
    c) Gland **d) Seta**

107. Chitin is a very important part of the insect's exoskeleton because:
    a) It is impermeable to water
    b) It is rigid and inflexible.
    c) It is not digested by common enzymes
    d) It is flexible and elastic

108. Which structure lies below the frons and above the labrum?
    a) Trochanter **b) Clypeus**
    c) Furca d) Gena

109. Where is the genital opening found on a typical insect?
    a) Just above the epiproct **b) Just below the anus.**
    c) Between the paraprocts d) Inside the tentorium

110. Parapsidal furrows are grooves found on the mesonotum of some parasitic wasps. These grooves would be located:

a) **Above and between the front wings**

b) Under the halteres.

c) On the epimeron

d) No way to tell

111. Which part of the exoskeleton lies between the wax layer and the cement layer?

a) Exocuticle b) Cuticulin layer

c) Endocuticle **d) None of these**

112. Which suture is not found on the head capsule?

a) Pleural suture b) Subgenal suture

c) Epistomal suture d) Frontal suture

113. Which statement about valvulae is incorrect?

a) They are part of the female genitalia

b) They lie just inside the valvifers.

c) They are arranged in three pairs

d) They guide the egg during oviposition

114. The cibarium is best described as:

a) Thoracic muscles that move the wings

b) A structure on the pretarsus.

c) The innermost layer of the epicuticle

d) A muscular pump that sucks food into the mouth

115. Elastic regions of the exoskeleton:

a) Are generally known as sclerites

b) Are found only at the joints.

c) Lack a well-defined exocuticle

d) Contain high concentrations of quinones

116. Which layer(s) of the exoskeleton is(are) secreted by the epidermis?

a) Endocuticle b) Epicuticle

c) Exocuticl **d) All of these**

117. Which structure is not part of the central nervous system?

a) Frontal ganglion **b) Circumesophageal commissure**

c) Tritocerebrum d) Subesophageal ganglion

118. An insect must use both of its compound eyes (simultaneously) in order to perceive:

a) Distance or depth
b) Ultraviolet light
c) Shape or size
d) Polarized light

119. The chemical trail produced by foraging ants would be classified as a(n):

a) Kairomone
b) Allomone
c) Pheromone
d) None of these

120. Which statement about the insect's nervous system is incorrect?

a) The ventral nerve cord controls the heart and gut.
b) The caudal ganglion controls the external genitalia.
c) The brain controls the eyes and antennae.
d) The subesophageal ganglion controls the mouthparts.

121. The deutocerebrum innervates the:

a) Mouthparts
b) Antennae
c) Compound eyes
d) Heart

122. An ommatidium is best defined as a:

a) Subdivision of the ventral nerve cord
b) Functional unit of the compound eye.
c) Mechanoreceptor used for proprioception
d) Ventral lobe of the insect's brain

123. Fly larvae (maggots) move away from a bright source of light. This is an example of a

a) Taxis
b) Reflex
c) Kinesis
d) Transverse orientation

124. A male empiid fly courts a female for 20 minutes and then gives up after he fails to elicit any response. This is an example of:

a) Conditioning
b) Imprinting
c) Habituation
d) Instrumental learning

125. The circumesophageal connective joins the:

a) Deutocerebrum with the tritocerebrum
b) Tritocerebrum with the subesophageal ganglion.
c) Two lobes of the tritocerebrum
d) Frontal ganglion with the hypocerebral ganglion.

126. Compared to most learned behaviors, instinctive (innate) behavior is:
   a) More stereotyped
   b) Less complex
   c) Not subject to evolutionary change
   d) All of these

127. When laying eggs, a female insect returns to her larval host plant, even though she has not fed upon this plant during her adult life. This is an example of:
   a) Conditioning **b) Habituation**
   c) Imprinting d) Instrumental learning

128. In most insects, the sense of smell is localized in the:
   a) Tarsi **b) Antennae**
   c) Maxillary palps d) Frons

129. In insects with dichromatic (2 pigment) color vision, maximum color discrimination is in the range from:
   a) Red to green b) UV to green
   c) Yellow to blue d) Bee violet to bee purple

130. The mandibular gland substance of the queen honey bee inhibits ovarian development among worker bees in the same hive. This is an example of a(n):
   a) Allomone **b) Synomone**
   c) Pheromone d) Kairomone

131. If a nerve impulse started in the tritocerebrum and passed through the stomodeal nervous system until it reached the heart, it would not pass through the:
   a) Recurrent nerve b) Subesophageal ganglion
   c) Frontal nerve **d) Hypocerebral ganglion**

132. An insect's mechanoreceptors would NOT be sensitive to:
   a) Body movement b) Sound vibrations
   c) Wind speed **d) Water vapor**

133. Stridulation is a method of producing sound by:
   a) Vibrating the wings b) Vibrating a resonant membrane.
   c) Striking the substrate d) Rubbing body parts together.

134. In an ant nest, all workers are:
   a) Adult males b) Immature males
   c) Adult females d) Immature females

135. Which pair of structures have the most similar sensory functions?
   a) Chordotonal organs and tympana
   b) Stemmata and pressure receptors
   c) Flex receptors and cerci
   d) Antennae and hair beds
136. A firefly would most likely be classified as a ________ insect.
   a) Crepusular b) Eusocial
   c) Diurnal d) Solitary
137. Female pseudergates may molt into determinant nymphs whenever:
   a) Soldier pheromone is too high
   b) Queen substance is too high
   c) King substance is too high
   d) None of these
138. All insects must communicate in order to:
   a) Find a mate b) Survive the winter
   c) Locate food d) Avoid predation
139. Any chemical used to repel predators would always be classified as a(n):
   a) Pheromone b) Hormone
   c) Kairomone d) Allomone
140. Insects that share a common nest site but do not care for their young are said to be
   a) Quasisocial **b) Semisocial**
   c) Communal d) Solitary
141. Stridulation is a method of producing sound by:
   a) Vibrating the wings b) Vibrating a resonant membrane
   c) Striking the substrate d) Rubbing body parts together
142. Which event might initiate nocturnal behavior in an insect whose activity cycle is under exogenous control?
   a) Sunrise **b) Solar eclipse**
   c) Rainfall d) None of these
143. Which communication signal has low information content, but can be long-lasting in the environment?
   a) Wing color patterns b) Light flashes
   c) Stridulation d) Marking pheromones

144. The sterile-male technique works best when:
   a) The target population is large
   b) Females mate repeatedly.
   c) The pest species can be mass-reared
   d) All of these.

145. If the acute dermal LD-50 of an insect is 50 mg/kg, then:
   a) 50 insects can be killed with 50 mg of the product.
   b) One insect can be killed with 50 mg of the product.
   c) 50% of the insects can be killed with 50 mg of the product.
   d) None of these

146. Anaphylactic shock is best described as an extreme type of:
   a) Entomophibia **b) Allergic reaction**
   c) Parasitosis d) Envenomization

147. *Vibrio cholerae*, the causal aget of cholera, can be carried from one place to another on the feet of flies. This is an example of which type of transmission?
   a) Obligatory b) Mechanical
   c) Transovarial d) Facultative

148. Compared to first generation pesticides, the newer second and third generation compounds are:
   a) More selective and less persistent
   b) More toxic and less selective.
   c) More persistent and less selective
   d) None of these.

149. What is the generally accepted mode of action for organophosphate insecticides?
   a) Chitin inhibitor **b) Cholinesterase inhibitor**
   c) Stomach poison d) Respiratory toxin

150. Which of these denotes a type of host plant resistance characterized by the ability of the plant to outgrow and/or repair damage resulting from an insect attack?
   a) Antibiosi b) Symbiosis
   c) Antixenosis **d) Tolerance**

151. Which of these is a cultural method for controlling insects?
   a) Crop rotation b) Window screens
   c) Quarantine d) Sex pheromone traps

152. Which class of chemical insecticides is characterized by a relatively high degree of environmental persistence?
   a) Carbamates b) Synthetic pyrethroids
   c) Organophosphates **d) Chlorinated hydrocarbons**

153. Which sampling strategy is best suited for insects that live in the soil?
   a) Sex pheromone trap b) Sweeping
   c) Berlese funnel d) Light trap

154. Which common name is incorrectly written?
   a) Horsefly b) Honey bee
   c) Ground beetle **d) Lightningbug**

155. As human consumers become less tolerant of insect damage on fruit, the economic thresholds for fruit pests are likely to:
   a) Increase b) Remain the same
   c) Decrease d) No way to tell

156. Which of these is NOT considered an insect growth regulator?
   a) Synthetic pyrethroid b) Juvenile hormone analogue
   c) Chitin inhibitor d) Ecdysteroid

157. Organophosphate and carbamate insecticides work by disrupting an insect's:
   a) Digestive system **b) Nervous system**
   c) Respiratory system d) Endocrine system

158. The sterile-male technique would probably not work well for an insect pest whose:
   a) Population is extremely abundant
   b) Individuals are easily mass reared.
   c) Females mate only once in their lifetime
   d) Males are very strong fliers

159. Which of these is an "unbiased" sampling strategy?
   a) Malaise trap b) Light trap
   c) Sticky trap **d) None of these**

160. Breeding nursey stock for higher levels of secondary plant compounds would be an example of:
   a) **Antixenosis** b) Xenobiosis
   c) Antibiosis d) Tolerance
161. Which of these is likely to be regarded as the most "useful" biological control agent?
   a) **A beetle that feeds on kudzu**
   b) A parasite of lady beetles.
   c) A predator of robber flies
   d) A viral pathogen of lacewings
162. To which of these groups do insect pathogens belong?
   a) Viruses and bacteria b) Protozoa and fungi
   c) Bacteria and protozoa **d) All of these**
163. Pest outbreaks tend to occur when:
   a) **Crops are planted in monoculture**
   b) Natural enemies are imported from abroad.
   c) Farmers switch to new crops
   d) All of these
164. Biological control is likely to be most effective when the predator or parasite has a(n)
   a) Long life cycle b) Wide range of preferred hosts
   c) High reproductive rate d) All of these
165. Which insect orders contain species that are important pests of domestic animals?
   a) Siphonaptera and Coleoptera
   b) Orthoptera and Hemiptera
   c) Diptera and Phthiraptera
   d) All of these
166. Which control strategy is likely to have the greatest impact on non-target organisms? control?
   a) Chemical control b) Cultural control
   c) Biological control d) Physical/mechanical control
167. The pedicel is the name for the:
   a) 1st leg segment b) 1st antennal segment
   c) 2nd leg segment **d) 2nd antennal segment**

168. Which hormone would NOT be found in adult insects?
   a) Brain hormone (PTTH)   b) Juvenile hormone
   c) Eclosion hormone   **d) All of these**

169. Aquatic immatures of All holometabolous insects are known as:
   a) Nymphs   **b) Larvae**
   c) Naiads   d) Young

170. Suppose you find an interesting arthropod living on the bottom of a fresh water pond. It has eyes, antennae, mandibles, and 5 pairs of legs. You conclude that this organism belongs in the class:
   a) Insecta   **b) Crustacea**
   c) Diplopoda   d) Arachnida

171. "Lumpers" sometimes include Blattodea and Phasmida as suborders of:
   a) Hemiptera   b) Orthoptera
   c) Phthiraptera   d) Neuroptera

172. Chewing mouthparts are not found in:
   a) Thrips   b) Crayfish
   c) Millipedes   d) Bees

173. Which order is exclusively herbivorous?
   a) Hemiptera   b) Odonata
   c) Phasmida   d) Thysanoptera

174. In insect development, the germ band:
   a) Forms the amnionic membrane
   b) Differentiates into three germ layers.
   c) Gives rise to the cleavage and activation centers.
   d) Remains undifferentiated throughout the larval stages

175. Which part of a molt does not occur during apolysis?
   a) Formation of new epicuticle
   b) Resorption of old endocuticle
   c) Formation of new quinone crosslinkages
   d) Activation of molting fluid

176. In larval insects, which hormone inhibits the development of imaginal discs?
   a) Juvenile hormone   b) Eclosion hormone
   c) Brain hormone   d) Ecdysteroids

177. In a normally developing insect, a high titer of juvenile hormone should not be found:
   a) **While it is molting from first to second instar**
   b) Before it becomes a pupa.
   c) When it is a sexually mature adult
   d) In an adult male

178. Which part of a molt does not occur during apolysis?
   a) **Formation of new epicuticle**
   b) Resorption of old endocuticle
   c) Formation of new quinone crosslinkages
   d) Activation of molting fluid

179. In an insect egg, the embryo begins to develop as soon as:
   a) Cells reach the oosome.
   b) **The zygote nucleus starts to divide.**
   c) Hormones are secreted by the activation center.
   d) Yolk contracts from one side of the egg.

180. Which order would a "lumper" NOT include in the Orthoptera?
   a) Mantodea b) Grylloblattodea
   c) Phasmida **d) Isoptera**

181. Which of these characteristics do insects and crustaceans have in common?
   a) Mandibulate mouthparts b) Jointed legs
   c) Open circulatory system **d) All of these**

182. In an obtect pupa:
   a) The insect is surrounded by a silken cocoon
   b) The larval exoskeleton becomes a puparium.
   c) The insect's body forms a chrysalis
   d) **All of these**

183. Which structures would be found in an eruciform larva, but not in a scarabaeiform larva
   a) Prolegs b) Compound eyes
   c) Mandibles d) All of these

184. Which order is most closely related (phylogenetically) to the Neuroptera?
   a) Mecoptera b) Phthiraptera
   c) Blattodea **d) Odonata**

185. Which class is most closely related (phylogenetically) to the Insecta?
    a) Xiphosura   b) Myriapoda
    c) Crustacea   **d) Arachnida**
186. Which group of insects has simple metamorphosis?
    a) Fleas   b) Beetles
    c) Flies   **d) Bugs**
187. Insect blood does not:
    a) Clot   **b) Flow through the wings**
    c) Contain antibodies   d) Transport hormones
188. In insects, the first pair of post-oral appendages are called mandibles. What are these appendages called in Arachnids?
    a) Maxillae   b) Walking legs
    c) Antennae   **d) Chelicerae**
189. Which insects do NOT damage horticultural crops (as immatures)?
    a) Sawflies   b) Whiteflies
    c) Butterflies   **d) Caddisflies**
190. Which insects would be classified as decomposers?
    a) Termites   b) Thrips
    c) Crickets   d) Stoneflies
191. Which sclerite lies below the epistomal suture?
    a) Frons   **b) Clypeus**
    c) Labrum   d) Gena
192. Chewing mouthparts are not found in:
    a) Crickets   **b) Thrips**
    c) Weevils   d) Earwigs
193. Which statement about insect development is correct?
    a) The embryo is nourished by yolk stored in the egg.
    b) The germ band develops inot the embryo.
    c) The serosa forms the yolk sac membrane.
    d) All of these
194 Which part of a molt does not occur during apolysis?
    a) Formation of new epicuticle
    b) Resorption of old endocuticle.
    c) Formation of new quinone crosslinkages
    d) Activation of molting fluid.

195. Which order is both ectognathous and wingless?
   a) Collembola
   b) Phthiraptera
   c) Thysanura
   d) Diplura

196. Why are termites classified as orthopteroids?
   a) They are wingless
   b) They have cerci and chewing mouthparts
   c) They are social insects
   d) All of these

197. A terrestrial arthropod with more than five pairs of legs could not be a(n):
   a) Isopod
   b) Centipede
   c) Arachnid
   d) Symphylan

198. Which group of insects has incomplete metamorphosis?
   a) Fleas
   b) Beetles
   c) Flies
   d) Bugs

199. Which insects do not feed on plants?
   a) Thrips
   b) Whiteflies
   c) Lacewings
   d) Sawflies

200. The recurrent nerve joins:
   a) The two lobes of the tritocerebrum
   b) The tritocerebrum with the subesophageal
   c) The frontal and hypocerebral ganglia
   d) The tritocerebrum with the frontal ganglion

201. If an insect's developmental threshold is 15 degrees F, how many degree-days (DD. does it on a day when the average temperature is 72 degrees F?
   a) 87 DD
   b) 57 DD
   c) 30 DD
   d) No way to tell

202. Broad-spectrum detoxification enzymes are commonly found in:
   a) Blood feeding insects
   b) Polyphagous herbivores
   c) Insect parasitoids
   d) All of these

203. If a population's intrinsic rate of increase ("r") is less than one, then the population is:
   a) Growing rapidly
   b) Stable
   c) Growing slowly
   d) Declining

204. When laying eggs, a female insect returns to her larval host plant, even though she has not fed upon this plant during her adult life. This is an example of:

a) Conditioning **b) Habituation**

c) Imprinting d) Instrumental learning

205. When a newly emerged queen honey bee hears the sound of "piping and quacking" from unemerged queens, she will find and destroy their cells. Apparently, these sounds are an example of:

a) A releaser **b) A transverse orientation**

c) Appetative behavior d) A fixed action pattern

206. Behavior patterns that change drastically over the lifetime of an insect are probably:

a) Learned b) Innate

c) Imprinted d) Afferent

207. What information could NOT be determined from a life table?

a) Significant mortality factors

b) Intrinsic rate of increase

c) Environmental carrying capacity

d) Stage-specific mortality rate

208. A certain insect usually becomes active each day at dusk. If kept in the dark all day, it will still become active around sunset even though it cannot see the sun. This behavior is an example of:

a) A circadian rhythm b) Transverse orientation

c) Diurnal behavior d) Exogenous entrainment

209. Worker ants remember landmarks around their nest entrance & use these as a guide when returning home. This behavior is an example of:

a) Imprinting b) Conditioning

c) Habituation d) Instrumental learning

210. Chemicals released by threatened aphids elicit defensive behavior among the ants that tend these aphids. Such chemicals would be best described as:

a) Allomones b) Hormones

c) Pheromones d) Kairomones

211. Substances in the frass produced by bark beetles attract predators & parasites to trees that are infested by these beetles. Such substance would be best described as

a) Allomones b) Hormones

c) Pheromones **d) Kairomones**

212. When predator changes its search image in response to a change in the density of prey, it exhibits a(n):

a) Conditioned response b) Functional response

c) Numerical responsc d) None of these

213. Which insects are most likely to pollinate foul-smelling flowers?

a) Hover flies b) Honey bees

c) Carrion beetles **d) Stink bugs**

214. If an insect's subesophageal ganglion were paralyzed, it would be unable to:

a) Eat b) See

c) Fly d) Walk

215. Fly larvae (maggots) move directly away from a bright source of light. This is an example of a:

a) Taxis b) Reflex

c) Kinesis d) Transverse orientation

216. Ants remember a food trail by the location of landmarks along the way. This is an example of:

a) Conditioning **b) Imprinting**

c) Habituation d) Instrumental learning

217. A male empiid fly courts a female for 20 minutes and then gives up after he fails to elicit any response. This is an example of:

a) Conditioning b) Imprinting

c) Habituation d) Instrumental learning

218. The central nervous system of an insect controls the:

a) Mandibles and maxillae b) Legs and wings

c) Heart and foregut **d) None of these**

219. The major differences between European and Africanized honey bees are:

a) Physical (size) b) Behavior (agressiveness)

c) Ecological (habitat) **d) All of these**

220. The information content of a sound signal is based on changes in:
   a) Amplitude (loudness) b) Duration (pulsation)
   c) Frequency (pitch) **d) All of these**
221. An ommatidium is the functional unit of the:
   a) Protocerebrum **b) Compound eye**
   c) Subesophageal ganglion d) Male reproductive system
222. Which of these could be an example of an entrainment cue?
   a) Odor of a predator b) Darkness after sunset
   c) Odor of a host plant d) Darkness before sunrise
223. It is possible that an immature insect might imprint on:
   a) Odor of a predator b) Darkness after sunset
   c) Odor of a host plant d) Darkness before sunrise
224. Which of these is a primary ecological event?
   a) Competition b) Parasitism
   c) Immigration d) None of these
225. Which of these is a secondary ecological event?
   a) Emigration b) Mortality
   c) Predation **d) None of these**
226. Which of these is an example of a Mullerian mimic?
   a) A bee that looks like a wasp
   b) A fly that looks like a bee
   c) A katydid that looks like a leaf
   d) A caterpillar that looks like a snake
227. Family of the *Heliothis armigera*
   a) Noctuiidae b) Plutellidae
   c) Chrysomelide d) Pyraustidae
228. Visceral (stomodaeal) Nervous System:
   a) Frontal ganglion b) Hypocerebral ganglion
   c) Recurrent nerve d) Subesophageal ganglion
229. Brain:
   a) Optic lobes
   b) Neurosecretory cells
   c) Circumesophageal commissure
   d) Tritocerebrum

230. The information content of a sound signal is based on changes in:
   a) Amplitude (loudness)   b) Duration (pulsation)
   c) Frequency (pitch)   **d) All of these**
231. An ommatidium is the functional unit of the:
   a) Protocerebrum   **b) Compound eye**
   c) Subesophageal ganglion   d) Male reproductive system
232. Which of these could be an example of an entrainment cue?
   a) Odor of a predator   b) Darkness after sunset
   c) Odor of a host plant   d) Darkness before sunrise
233. It is possible that an immature insect might imprint on:
   a) Odor of a predator   b) Darkness after sunset
   c) Odor of a host plant   d) Darkness before sunrise
234. Which of these is a primary ecological event?
   a) Competition   b) Parasitism
   c) Immigration   d) None of thesc
235. Which of these is a secondary ecological event?
   a) Emigration   b) Mortality
   c) Predation   **d) None of these**
236. Which of these is an example of a Mullerian mimic?
   a) A bee that looks like a wasp
   b) A fly that looks like a bee
   c) A katydid that looks like a leaf
   d) A caterpillar that looks like a snake
237. *Tanymecus indicus* feed on the crop
   a) Paddy   **b) Maize**
   c) Sorghum   d) Mustard
238. Visceral (stomodaeal) Nervous System:
   a) Frontal ganglion   b) Hypocerebral ganglion
   c) Recurrent nerve   d) Subesophageal ganglion
239. Brain:
   a) Optic lobes
   b) Neurosecretory cells
   c) Circumesophageal commissure
   d) Tritocerebrum

240. Chemicals which kill the pests are called.
   a) Insecticides   **b) Pesticides**
   c) Acaricides   d) Avicides
241. Immature stage of beetle is termed as
   a) Larva   b) Caterpillar
   c) Grub   d) Maggot
242. Mites have ____________ pairs of legs and two distinct body regions
   a) 2   **b) 4**
   c) 6   d) 3
243. Predator has __________ type of mouthparts
   a) Sponging   b) Rasping & sucking
   c) Chewing   d) Piercing
244. Instar is ______________________.
   a) Immature of moths   **b) Stage b/w two moults**
   c) A larva   d) Crop pest
245. Cotton jassid belongs to _______________ order of class insecta.
   a) Homoptera   b) Thysanoptera
   c) Coleoptera   d) Orthoptera
246. If an insecticide has 170 ml / acre dose rate and a pack size of 700 ml, how much acre it will spray?
   a) 4   b) 2
   c) Several   d) Single
247. If 500 m^2 sprayed with 16 liter of knapsack sprayer, how much spray volume is used per acre?
   a) 80 liter   b) 128 liter
   c) 150 liter   **d) 130 liter**
248. PB-rope L is _________________________.
   a) Novel insecticide   **b) Sex pheromone**
   c) Carbamate   d) Organophosphate
249. IGR effect
   a) Egg development   b) Pupal development
   c) Larval development   d) Adult emergence
250. _______________ type of nozzle is used for spraying a weedicide.
   a) ULV disc   **b) T-jet**
   c) Hollowcone   d) None of them

251. Active ingredient in Steward is
   a) Chlorphyrifos b) Oxadiazine
   c) Spinosad **d) Indoxacarb**
252. Hollowcone nozzle is used to spray
   a) Weedicide **b) Insecticides**
   c) None of them
253. Pest spectrum of Steward on cotton crop
   a) *Heliothus only*
   b) *Earias & Heliothus*
   c) *Heliothus, Spodoptera, Earias*
   d) *Pectinophora*
254. *Helicoverpa armigera* eggs are
   a) In bunchies under leaf
   b) Scattered mainly 1/3 portion of plant
   c) Not visible without lenses
255. Cotton sticks should be placed ____________ to reduce pink bollworm carry over
   a) Horizontally **b) Vertically**
   c) Inside store
256. PB-rope is a successful IPM tool for ____________________ management.
   a) Army worm b) Americon bollworm
   c) Pink bollworm
257. Pink bollworm take diapause in
   a) Soil b) Unopened boll
   c) Double seed d) All of above
258. Green band is present on fore-wing of moth of
   a) Army worm b) *Earias insulana*
   c) *Earias vitella* d) None of these
259. Rosette flower is attack of
   a) Pink bollworm b) American bollworm
   c) Armyworm d) None of the Above
260. Gurdaspur borer over-winter as
   a) Larva b) Pupa
   c) Adult d) None of these

261. Brinjal fruit borer over-winter as

a) Larva **b) Pupa**

c) Adult d) None of these

262. Maize stem borer damage maize at ________________ stage.

a) Adult **b) Larvae**

c) Both a and b d) Nyphms

263. Rice stem borer hibernate as

a) Larva b) Pupa

c) Adult d) None of these

264. Pesticide ordinance was imposed in

a) 1971 **b) 1973**

c) 1975 d) 1979

265. ETL level of Thrips is

a) 8 / leaf b) 12 / leaf

c) 5 / leaf d) None of these

266. Rice burn is caused by

a) Rice hispa **b) White backed plant hopper**

c) Rice green leaf hopper d) Brown hopper

267. *Chilo partellus* lay eggs on the ________________ .

a) Lower side of leaves b) Middle portion of leaves

c) Upper side of leaves d) None of these

268. *Bracon hebetor* is ________________.

a) Larval parasitoid b) Pupal parasitoid

c) Nymphal parasitoid d) None of these

269. *Epipyrope melanoluca* is ________________.

a) Larval parasitoid b) Pupal parasitoid

c) Nymphal parasitoid d) Adult parasitoid

270. Red pumpkin beetle lay eggs

a) In the soil

b) On upper side of leaves

c) On middle portion of leaves

d) None of these

271. Mango mealy bug has _____________ generations in a year
a) 4 **b) 1**
c) 3 d) 6

272. First insect fossil was found in
a) England b) Russia
c) Scotland d) USA

273. The international code of zoological nomenclature consists of
a) 57 articles b) 67 articles
c) 77 articles **d) 87 articles**

274. Which is the following is not head secleroid
a) Gena b) Frons
c) Epimeron d) Vertex

275. Which is the following is cross vein
a) Costa **b) Radial**
c) Media d) Cubitus

276. In Hymenoptera, the first abdominal segment which is fused with metathorax is called
a) Cornical b) Epiproct
c) Propodium d) Gaster

277. Which is the following is abdominal appendages
a) Gonopore **b) Cerci**
c) Waist d) Apophysis

278. Which of the following muscles are directly related to wings
a) Dorsal muscle **b) Axillary muscle**
c) Basalar muscle d) Sub-alar muscle

279. Economic threshold level of jassid is
a) 1 b) 2
c) 3 d) 4

280. The alimentary canal of insect is derived from
a) Ectoderm **b) Ectoderm & endoderm**
c) Ectoderm & mesoderm d) Ectoderm & mesoderm

281. Most of the caterpillar have legs or abdominal legs on segments
a) 2-5 & 10 **b) 3-6 & 10**
c) 6-10 d) 5-8 & 10

282. Wingless hexapod with six abdominal segments
  a) Diplura b) Thysanura
  c) Collembola d) Protura

283. Monocondylic single mandible is found in
  a) Homoptera **b) Thysanoptera**
  c) Hymenoptera d) Diptera

284. Most of the insects excrete 80-90 % of their nitrogen waste in the form of
  a) Urea **b) Uric acid**
  c) Ammonia d) Ammonium nitrate

285. Which of the following is systemic insecticide
  a) Methamidophos **b) Imidachloprid**
  c) Cypermethrin d) None of these

286. The density of pest population at which control measure should be applied
  a) GEL b) PBL
  c) EIL **d) ETL**

287. The fertilized female of lac insect lays eggs ranging from
  a) 100-200 **b) 200-500**
  c) 500-700 d) Less than 100

288. Which is the following bug is a pest of brinjal
  a) Painted bug b) Plant bug
  c) Lace bug d) Stink bug

289. Sugarcane borer which does not belong to the family pyralidae
  a) *Ammalocera depressella* b) *Chilo infuscatelus*
  c) *Sesamia inferens* d) *Chilo auricilia*

290. Which of the following is neuropteran predators.
  a) Brumus **b) Chrysoperla**
  c) Cryptolaemus d) Apis

291. Chemical name of Proclaim is
  a) Indoxacarb **b) Emmamectan-benzoate**
  c) Cypermethrin d) Bifenthrin

292. Trade name of Spinosad is
  a) Timer b) Denitol
  c) Tracer d) Arrivo

293. Trade name of Difenthioron is
a) Endosulfon b) Carbofuron
c) Polo d) Bestox

294. Chemical present in Mospilon
a) Buprofezin b) Imidacloprid
c) Acetamaprid d) None of these

295. Trade name of Methoxy-fenozide is
a) Runner b) Proaxix
c) Cascade d) None of these

296. ETL level of mites in cotton is ________________.
a) 12-15 b) 8-10
c) 6-7 d) None of these

297. DDT discovered in ____________.
a) 1941 **b) 1939**
c) 1945 d) None of these

298. Which term is used for the movement of coxa towards body
a) Protraction **b) Adduction**
c) Abduction d) Promotion

299. One mesometathoracic & eight abdominal spiracles are functional the respiratory system is called
a) Holoneustic b) Perineustic
c) Hemineustic d) Metaneustic

300. The origin of foregut is
a) Ectodermal b) Mesodermal
c) Endodermal d) None of these

301. Foregut is lined internally by
a) Peritrophic membrane b) Epithelial membrane
c) Intima d) Taenidia

302. The function of peritrophic membrane is
a) Absorption b) Assimilation
c) Protection d) All of these

303. The nervous system of insect is derived from
a) Ectoderm b) Mesoderm
c) Endoderm & mesoderm d) Endoderm

304. Stick insects & leaf insects belongs to the order
 a) Orthoptera b) Embioptera
 c) Phasmida d) Dictyoptera
305. Order Odonata includes
 a) May flies **b) Dragon flies**
 c) Stone flies d) None of these
306. Cotton stainer is ___________.
 a) Pectinophora b) Dytiscus
 c) Helicoverpa **d) Dysdercus**
307. In the formation of cuticle, which of the following layer is secerated first
 a) Exo-cuticle b) Wax layer
 c) Endo-cuticle **d) Cuticulin layer**
308. Moulting fluid is able to digest
 a) Cement layer b) Cuticulin layer
 c) Endo-cutilce d) Exo-cuticle
309. Pheromones are synthesized by
 a) Thoracic glands
 b) Neuro-secretary cells
 c) Glandular epidermal cells
 d) All of the above
310. The gland which produces pheromones in queen honey bee is ___________.
 a) Mandibular glands b) Maxillary glands
 c) Labial glands d) Tharyngial glands
311. Which of the following organs are involved in excretion
 a) Malpighian tubules
 b) Integument
 c) Wall of the alimentary canal
 d) All of these
312. Factors on which penetration of insecticide through insect cuticle does not depend on
 a) Thickness of the cuticle
 b) Chemical nature of the cuticle
 c) Components of the cuticle
 d) Nature of the carriers and solvents

313. In physiological considerations, the resistance to insecticide may be developed due to

a) Conversion of toxicant to non toxic metabolites

b) Excretion of toxicant

c) Storage of the toxicant

d) All of the above

314. Nicotinic effects of organo-phosphatic insecticide result in

a) Giddiness

b) Stiffness of the neck

c) Ataxia

d) None of these

315. Insects feeding on plants of several genera within a family are called

a) Phytopagous b) Polyphagous

c) Oligophagous d) Monophagous

316. Which of the following order comprises phytophagous insects

a) Odonata **b) Phasmida**

c) Siphonoptera d) Mallophaga

317. Which of the following order comprises predacious insect

a) Phasmida **b) Neuroptera**

c) Isoptera d) Lepidoptera

318. Which of the following order comprises parasitic insects

a) Hymenoptera b) Thysanoptera

c) Phasmida d) Lepidoptera

319. Sexual dimorphism is found in ______________.

a) Mango mealy bug b) Aphid

c) Whitefly d) Jassid

320. Which of the following cotton pest belong to family Pyrrhocoridae

a) Dysdercus b) Pectinophora

c) Earias d) Bemisia

321. Which of the following insect belongs to family Dermestidae

a) *Sytophilus oryzae* **b) *Trogoderma granarium***

c) *Tribolium castaneum* d) None of these

322. Which of the following produces more lac, & is important for commercial production
    a) Male **b) Female**
    c) Nymph d) All of the above
323. The fertilized female of mulberry silkworm lays eggs within 24 hours
    a) 100-200 b) 200-300
    c) 300-400 **d) 400-500**
324. In honey bees when the larvae are fed on regular diet of pollen & honey which cast is produced.
    a) Queen **b) Workers**
    c) Drones d) All of these
325. Where the nectar is converted into honey
    a) In the alimentary canal of the queen
    b) In the alimentary canal of the worker
    c) In royal chamber
    d) In special cell of the hive
326. The average locust swarm spread over
    a) 5 km^2 **b) 10 km^2**
    c) 15 km^2 d) 20 km^2
327. Which of the following does not belong to order Lepidoptera
    a) Groundnut leaf minor **b) Pea leaf minor**
    c) Citrus leaf minor d) None of these
328. The type of parthenogenesis where only males are produced is
    a) Arrhenotoky b) Thelytoky
    c) Amphitoky d) None of these
329. Originally, the phytophagous insects were
    a) Monophagous b) Polyphagous
    c) Oligophagous **d) All of these**
330. The minimum period to be given for the assessment of effectiveness of a biocontrol agent is
    a) 2 years b) 3 years
    c) 4 years d) 5 years
331. Vertical resistance is also called
    a) Oligogenic b) Specific
    c) Monogenic **d) All of these**

332. Horizontal resistance is also known as

a) Non-specific b) General

c) Polygenic **d) All of these**

333. The device fitted at the end of the spray-launce & is used for atomization is

a) Hose b) Cut off device

c) Boom **d) Nozzle**

334. In solid cone nozzle, the solid cone of liquid is formed due to

a) Bigger size of the cap

b) Bigger size of the orifice plate

c) Central hole in swirl plate

d) Small size of strainer

335. The nozzle used for producing mist

a) Blast nozzle **b) Rotatory energy nozzle**

c) Kinetic energy nozzle d) Annular nozzle

336. The nozzle used to produce fog

a) Gaseous energy nozzle **b) Thermal energy nozzle**

c) Centrifugal energy nozzle d) Kinetic energy nozzle

337. The greater part of the fat body is made of cell called

a) Haemocytes **b) Trophocytes**

c) Lamphocytes d) Nephrocytes

338. Which of the following is European species

a) *Apis dorsata* **b) *Apis mellifera***

c) *Apis indica* d) *Apis florea*

339. *Bacillus thuringiensis* is most effective at pH

a) 3-6 **b) 9-10**

c) 11-14 d) All of these

340. Environment is sum of ________ factors effecting an organism.

a) Some b) Two

c) All d) None

341. Abiotic environment includes ___________

a) Living organisms

b) Nonliving organisms

c) Weather

d) Weather and all nonliving organisms

342. Micro environment is _______________
   a) Environment very close to an organism
   b) General environment
   c) Environment of a certain area.

343. Macro environment is _____________
   a) Environment very close to an organism
   b) General environment
   c) Overall environment of a certain area.

344. Ecological action is_____________
   a) Effect of various factors on the life on an individual
   b) Effect of temperature and humidity on the life of an individual
   c) Effect of factors other than temperature and humidity on the life of an individual

345. Ecological reaction is ....
   a) Response of an individual to all environmental factors
   b) Rsponse to temperature and humidity by an individual
   c) Rsponse to factors other than temperature and humidity by an individual

346. Plants have _____________ effect on the life of the insects
   a) Useful   b) Harmful
   c) None   **d) Both**

347. _____________features of soil effect the insects
   a) Texture   b) Structure
   c) None   **d) Both**

348. ....is the most important physical factor which effects the life of an insect
   a) Temperature   b) Humidity
   c) Light   d) None of the above.

349. Optimum temperature range for majority of the insects is
   a) 28-30 °C   b) 40-50 °C
   c) 80-90 °C   d) 10-20 °C

350. Absolute humidity is
   a) Actual amount of water in the air
   b) Amount of the water in the air as compared with the amount need to saturate the air
   c) None of above

351. Relative humidity is
   a) Actual amount of water in the air
   b) Amount of the water in the air as compared with the amount need to saturate the air
   c) None of above
352. Directed movement of the insects in response to light are called
   a) Phototaxis b) Photokinesis
   c) Nocturnal d) None of above
353. Non directional movcmcnts of thc insccts in response to light are called
   a) Phototaxis **b) Photokinesis**
   c) Nocturnal d) None of above
354. Insects which are active in the day time are called
   a) Nocturnal **b) Diurnal**
   c) Crepuscular d) None of above
355. Insects which are active in the night time are called
   a) Nocturnal b) Diurnal
   c) Crepuscular d) None of above
356. Insects which are active at dawn or dusk are called as
   a) Nocturnal b) Diurnal
   c) Crepuscular d) None of above
357. Range of the light spectrum which is perceived by the insect is
   a) 2500- 7000°A b) 500-1500°A
   c) 9000-15000°A d) None of these
358. The environment in which a community lives is called as
   a) Biotype b) Biome
   c) Biosphere d) None of these
359. A regional ecosystem is called
   a) Biotype **b) Biome**
   c) Biosphere d) None of these
360. The entire earth having the living organisms is called as
   a) Biotype b) Biome
   c) Biosphere d) None of these
361. 100°C is equal to
   a) 212°F b) 100°F
   c) 300°F d) None of above

362. Freezing point of water is
   a) 32°F
   b) 100ºF
   c) 212ºF
   d) None of these
363. Boiling point of water is
   a) 32ºF
   b) 100ºF
   c) 212°F
   d) None of these
364. Most efficient thermometers used are
   a) Liquid filled thermometers
   b) Gas filled thermometers
   c) Metallic thermometers.
365. Alcohol responds to change in temperature in
   a) 7-8 seconds
   b) 10-20 seconds
   c) 1-2 seconds
366. Mercury filled thermometer responds to the change in temperature in
   a) 25-28 seconds
   b) 35-40 seconds
   c) 7-8 seconds.
367. The study of one or more individuals of a species in relation to environment is called
   a) Autecology
   b) Synecology
   c) None of these
368. The study of community in relation to environment is called
   a) Autecology
   b) Synecology
   c) None of these
369. The competition with in the individual of a species is called
   a) Intra specific competition
   b) Inter specific completion
   c) None
370. The competition between the individual of different species is called
   a) Intra specific competition
   b) Inter specific competition
   c) None
371. The interaction in which at least one species is harmed is called as
   a) Positive interaction
   b) Negative interaction
   c) Commensalisms
   d) None of these

372. The interaction in which at least one species is benefited & other is not harmed is called as

a) **Positive interaction** b) Negative interaction

c) Commensalisms d) None of these

373. The interaction in which both species are benefited is called as

a) Positive interaction b) Negative interaction

c) Commensalisms **d) Symbiosis**

374. The type of interaction in which the food is exchanged between 2 individuals of the same species or different specics is callcd as

a) Trophallaxix b) Positive interaction

c) Negative interaction d) Commensalisms

375. The association in which in the normal situation both species live neutral called as

a) Neutral interaction b) Positive interaction

c) Negative interaction d) Commensalisms

376. Biotic components of an ecosystem are

a) Animals

b) Plants

c) Both animals and plants

d) None of these

377. Natality is_________

a) Birth rate b) Death rate

c) Rate of increase in size d) None of these

378. Mortality is ______________

a) Birth rate **b) Death rate**

c) Rate of increase in size d) None of these

379. Living place of an individual is called

a) Habitat b) Niche.

c) Environment d) None of these

380. Role of an individual in the community is called as

a) Habitat **b) Niche**

c) Environment d) None of these

381. Acarology is study of

a) Mites b) Insects

c) Birds d) None of these

382. Mites and ticks are collectively called
    a) Insects   b) Mammals
    c) Ccari
383. Mites belong to Class
    a) Insecta   **b) Arachnida**
    c) Crustacea
384. Mites are second most diverse group of living organisms after ——————————
    a) Birds   b) Mammals
    c) Insects
385. Mites have generally —————— pairs of walking legs
    a) 2   b) 3
    c) 4   d) Many
386. Mites have ———— pair of antenna
    a) 1 pair   b) 2 pairs
    c) 0 pair
387. In mites the body is divided into —————— regions
    a) 1   **b) 2**
    c) 3   d) 4
388. When head and thorax are fused they are collectively called
    a) Head   b) Thorax
    c) Abdomen   **d) Cephalothorax**
389. Two spotted spider mites belong to family
    a) Tetranychidae   **b) Phytoseiidae**
    c) Cunaxidae   d) Tenuipalpidae
390. Any organism which harms or causes damage to man directly or indirectly called
    a) Insect Pest   **b) Pest**
    c) Agriculture Pest   d) None of above
391. Scutellum is the primary feeding organ the
    a) Larvae   **b) Germinating embryo**
    c) Adults   d) Pupae
392. Insects which are active at night are called
    a) Divrnal Insects   **b) Nocturnal Insects**
    c) Crepuscular Insects   d) None of above

393. Viviparous insects produce
 a) Eggs b) **Young ones**
 c) Nymph d) None of above
394. A free living animal that attacks and feeds on other organisms is called
 a) **Predator** b) Parasite
 c) Parasitoid d) Scavenger
395. The study of insects is called
 a) **Entomology** b) Applied Entomology
 c) Zoology d) None of above
396. Insects which are found every where are called
 a) **Cosmopolitan insects** b) Household Insects
 c) Store grain insects d) None of above
397. The study of form and structure of insects is called
 a) **Insect morphology** b) Insect Physiology
 c) Insect Ecology d) None of above
398. Whiteflies have eggs
 a) Elongate b) Conical
 c) **Stalked** d) Oval
399. Three main parts of antennae
 a) **Scape, Peidcel, Flagellum**
 b) Ring, Funicle, Club
 c) Scape, Club, Flagellum
 d) Pedicel, Scape, Club
400. Antennae are lacking in insect order
 a) **Protura** b) Collembola
 c) Diptera d) Thysanura
401. A material which is used to dilute active material is called
 a) Adjunant b) Adhesive
 c) **Carrier** d) Agitation
402. The food of honey bee queen is called
 a) Gelly b) **Royal gelly**
 c) Bee bread d) Nectar
403. Rearing of silk worm for commercial production of silk is called
 a) **Sericulture** b) Apiculture
 c) Floriculture d) Lac-culture

404. Lac is produced by insects

a) *Bombyx mori* **b) *Laceifera lacca***

c) Apis dorsata d) Apis cerana

405. The ability of a plant by means of which it is less damaged by insects is

a) Tolerance b) Pest avoidance

c) Plant Resistance d) Resistance

406. A population or group of insects composed of a single genotype is called

a) Pilosity **b) Biotype**

c) Genotype d) Phenotype

407. What is most social insect

a) Black ants b) Termites

c) Honey bee d) None of above

408. Which insect have bacteria and protozoa in their digestive system

a) Termites b) Ants

c) Silver fish d) None of above

409. Butterflies have antennae

a) Capetates **b) Clavate**

c) Geniculata fish d) Flabellata

410. Example of monophagous insect is

a) *Helicoverpa armigera* b) Ants

c) Green lace wing **d) None of above**

411. The mixture of active and inert ingredients is called

a) Formulation b) Doze

c) Active ingredient d) None of above

412. What is antidote

a) Treatment given to counteract the effects of a poison

b) Increase the affect of a poison

c) No action against poison

d) None of above

413. The group of pesticide which goes into the system of host and kills pest without harming host is called

a) Systemic b) Contact

c) Selective d) Protectant

414. The parasite which requires only one host for its complete life cycle is called

a) **Monophagous parasite** b) Zeophagous parasite

c) Phytophagous parasite d) Entomophagous parasite

415. The best example of parasites are

a) Ichnenmonids b) *Trichogramma* spp,

c) Cotesia sp **d) All of above**

416. The pesticide which is used for killing or controlling the eggs of insects is

a) Avicide **b) Ovicide**

c) Pesticide d) Fungicide

417. The chemical used of control of insects is called

a) Avicide **b) Insecticide**

c) Pesticide d) Fungicide

418. Cypermethrin, Deltamethrin, Permethrin are example of

a) Organophosphates **b) Pyrethroids**

c) Organochlorine d) Carbamate

419. Desert locust is

a) Migrant pest b) Occasional pest

c) Key pest d) Potential pest

420. Use of living organism to bring down the pest population below economic threshold level is called

a) Biological control b) Cultural control

c) Physical control d) Natural control

421. An egg parasitoid of lepidopterous insect is

a) *Trichogramma* sp. b) *Apanteles* sp

c) Water joint beetle d) Ichnenmon

422. Population prediction of a particular sp with in field is called

a) Forecasting b) Haemo spora

c) Surveillance d) Pest scouting

423. Zinc phosphide is

a) Rodenticide b) Pesticide

c) Insecticide d) Weedicide

424. Insect are

a) Cold blooded animals b) Warm blooded animals

c) None of above

425. Most of insects require
   a) Vitamin A **b) Vitamin B**
   c) Vitamin D d) Vitamin C

426. Which is the strongest animal of the world
   a) Whales b) Elephant
   c) Birds d) Insects

427. The fleas do
   a) Fly **b) Never fly**
   c) May or may not fly

428. Which insect cut the root of the plant
   a) Mole cricket b) Pyrilla
   c) Ground Beetle d) Grylloblatta

429. What is the family of Mosquito
   a) Cullicidae b) Pyralidae
   c) Tineidae d) Bombicidae

430. Photogentic organs are present
   a) Flies **b) Fire files**
   c) Wasps d) Honey bee

431. Insect are
   a) Cold blooded animals b) Warm blooded animals
   c) None of above d) Both a and b

432 In honey bees a flight for mating purpose is called
   a) Nuptial flight b) Straight flight
   c) Tactile flight d) None of above

433. Total or complete resistance against any adverse condition is called
   a) Hmmunilog b) Tolerance
   c) Resistance d) Plant resistance

434. Costal margin of wing of insect is
   a) Frontal margin b) Outer margin
   c) Hinder margin d) Inner margin

435. Apical margin of wing of insect is
   a) Hinder margin b) Frontal margin
   c) Outer margin d) Inner margin

436. Dragonfly and damselfly have type of legs
   a) Frssotial b) Metatorial
   c) Raptorial **d) Basket like**
437. Jumping legs present in grasshopper known as
   a) Saltatorial b) Raptorial
   c) Cursorial d) Natatorial
438. Function of Exo cuticle in insect is
   a) Rigidity of body b) Impermeability of water
   c) Prevent evaporation d) Toughness of flexibility
439. The insect skeleton is composed of series of plates called
   a) Seclerites b) Conjunctivae
   c) Sutures d) Somites
440. Fast acting pharomones are
   a) Primers **b) Releasers**
   c) Semio chemicals d) Allelochemicals
441. Social behaviour is present in
   a) Termites b) Ants bees
   c) Butterflies **d) Termites, ant, Bees**
442. What are productive insects
   a) Silkworms, lac insects, honey bees
   b) Parasites, predators, pollinators
   c) Silkworm, Pollinators, predators
   d) Lac insect, Honey bees, Pollinators
443. The Rapid Reappearance of the pest population in injurions number is called
   a) IPM b) IPC
   c) Pest resurgence d) Pest outbreak
444. Various methods of pest scouting are
   a) Maryo s method b) Diagonal method
   c) Zig zag method **d) All of the above**
445. Potential pest also called
   a) Secondary pest b) Major pest
   c) Minor pest d) Key pest
446. *Aphis lions* are predator of
   a) Aphid b) Jassid
   c) Sugarcane borer d) Pyrilla

447. Pheromone used against the fruitfly is

a) Dichlorvos b) Malathion

c) Carbofuron d) Mancoze

448. The concentration of toxicant that kills 50% of the exposed organism is called

a) LC_{50} b) LD_{50}

c) LC_{25} d) None of above

449. Toxin refers to a

a) Poison b) Prisoner material

c) Both of them d) None of above

450. A substance that is destructive to nerve tissue is called

a) Toxicant **b) Seuath**

c) Aerosol d) Toxin

451. A substance added to a pesticide to improve the qualities of pesticides formulation is called

a) Adjuvant b) Synergist

c) Activator d) Agitator

452. A chemical which inhibits clotting mechanisms of the blood are called

a) Chronic poison b) Bait

c) Defoliate d) Acute poisoning

453. What is antidote of anticongular rodenticide

a) Vitamin k b) Atropine

c) Diazepam d) Earbiturates

454. Diazepam is an antidote of

a) Organophosphate b) Carbamate

c) Organochlorines d) Pyrethorids

455. The pesticide does not allow larval insect pest to moult further is called

a) Insect growth regulator b) Fumigants

c) Sterilant d) Protectant

456. Antecedents prevent pest to cause damage is called

a) Sterilant **b) Pretectant**

c) Systemic d) Contact

457. For safe application of pesticide which things are required

a) Goggles, Respirator b) Overall, gloves

c) Head cores **d) All of above**

458. The ingredient of pesticide formulation responsible for toxic effect is called

a) **Active ingredient** b) Inert ingredient

c) Dose d) Pesticide

459. Mosquitoes, bed bugs are

a) Permanent parasite **b) Intermittent parasite**

c) Transitory parasite d) Obligate parasite

460. Insects that are parasite to other insects are called

a) **Entamophagous parasite**

b) Zoophagous parasites

c) Phytaphagous parasite

461. The control of pest by human controlling activities and laws is called

a) **Regularity method** b) Chemical method

c) Genetic method d) Physical method

462. Cotton bollworms, sugarcane borers are

a) **Major pest** b) Key pest

c) Minor pest d) Secondary pest

463. All the practices used to control the pest population within certain limit are called

a) **Artificial control** b) Natural control

c) Cultural control d) Chemical control

464. The lowest pest population that will cause economic damage is called

a) **Economic injury level** b) Economic threshold level

c) Economic damage d) None of above

465. The pest which damages the crop and causes a loss in quality or such pest is called

a) Insect pest b) Pest

c) **Economic pest** d) None of above

466. The largest insect of the world

a) **Elephant beetle** b) Hairy winged beetle

c) Grosshopper d) Cocas

467. Where the most insects are abundant

a) **Tropical region** b) Sub tropical

c) Temperate region d) None of above

468. Which sex of mosquite bite two human being
   a) Male **b) Female**
   c) Both of sex d) None of above

469. Fire flies are
   a) Flies **b) Beetles**
   c) Fleas d) Wasps

470. Commercial rearing of honey is called
   a) Sericulture **b) Apiculture**
   c) Flopriculture d) Lac culture

471. What is bee bread
   a) Honey and wax b) Pollen and nectar
   c) Honey and pollen

472. The colony of termites is called
   a) Termitorium b) Cage
   c) Hive d) Comb

473. The bees not reared for commercial purpose are called
   a) Domestic bees **b) Child bees**
   c) None of above

474. The show acting pheromones are called
   a) Primers b) Releasers
   c) Semio chemicals d) Allelo chemicals

475. Which enzyme breaks protein
   a) Carbohydrates b) Lipases
   c) Proteage d) Anylase

476. Cocomofian in response to touch
   a) Chemokinensis **b) Stereokinensis**
   c) Hydrokinensis d) Klinokinensis

477. The hearing organs in grasshopper is
   a) Johnshon s organ **b) Tympanal organs**
   c) Chrodotonal organ d) None of above

478. What organ of digestive system prevents the regurgitation
   a) Crop **b) Gizzard**
   c) Esophagous d) Pharynx

479. Which harmone cause moulting in insect

a) **Ecdysone** b) Juvenils

c) Activation hormone d) None of above

480. Metalegs of worker honeybee is

a) **Antenna cleaner** b) Silk secreting

c) Cursorial d) Pollen collecting

481. Grasshopper and Cockroach have type of wings is

a) **Tegmina** b) Hemelytra

c) Stripy d) Membranous

482. Compodeiform is type of

a) Larvae **b) Pupae**

c) Eggs d) Naiad

483. Housefly have mouth parts

a) Sponging type **b) Siphoning type**

c) Rasping type d) Piering sucking type

484. A few species of ants and termites which depend on cultivated plants are

a) **Agricultural insect** b) Insect pest

c) Pest d) None of above

485. Suffering caused in insects due to lack of food is called

a) Aestivation **b) Starvation**

c) Dormancy d) None of above

486. Young ones of fly is

a) Imago **b) Maggot**

c) Grub d) Pupariem

487. Resting stage in endopterygota is called

a) Larva b) Adult

c) Pupae d) Nymph

488. What is T.S.O.

a) **Technical Sales Officer** b) Technical Scientific Officer

c) Tehsil Sales Officer d) None of above

489. The living organisms that usually large, stronger and more intelligent then the parasite is called

a) **Host** b) Prey

c) Predator d) Parasite

490. Termites workers are
   a) **May be a non reproductive male or, non reproductive females**
   b) A non reproductive male
   c) A non reproductive female
   d) None of above

491. Area of each Haemocytometer counting chamber is
   a) 9 mm^2 b) 1mm^2
   c) 6 mm^2 d) None

492. Which solution is used for blood cell counting
   a) Wright stain b) Benedicts reagent
   c) Toisson solution d) All

493. Which are basophilic cells
   a) Prohaemocytes b) Granular Hemocytes
   c) Podocytes d) Oenocytes

494. The blood cells perform the function of coagulation are known as
   a) Prohemocytes **b) Cystocytes**
   c) Podocytes d) Oenocytes

495. Granular Hemocytes are produced from
   a) Prohemocytes b) Cystocytes
   c) Vermiform cell d) All

496. No. of blood cells in one mm^3 is more than
   a) 1,20,000 b) 1,40,000
   c) 1,30,000 **d) 1,00,000**

497. Phagocytosis in the body is done by
   a) Granular hemocytes b) Cystocytes
   c) Oenocytes d) All

498. The function of hemocytopoietic organs is
   a) Destruction of blood cell **b) Production of blood cell**
   c) Cleaning of blood d) All

499. Close packed fibres contains Nuclei in
   a) Central column **b) Periphery**
   c) Longitudinal rows d) At all places

500. The size of tubular muscle fibers is
   a) 10-25 μm b) 10-100 μm
   c) 100 μm-1 mm d) None

501. H. Huxley and A.F Huley gave the model of
   a) Muscle contraction b) Bone movement
   c) Muscle structure d) All

502. Aerodynamics deals with
   a) Motion of liquid **b) Motion of gases**
   c) Motion of wings d) All

503. Upward movement of wing is known as
   a) Lift b) Thrust
   c) Upstroke d) Downstroke

504. Wing Muscle frequency for *Aedes spp.* is
   a) 1000 HZ b) 600 HZ
   c) 100 HZ d) 50 HZ

505. The structure of ecdysone is similar to
   a) Phenolic compound **b) Cholesterol**
   c) Chlorpophyll d) Terpenes

506. The example of lipid related Hormone is
   a) Allatotropin b) Diuretic Hormone
   c) Juvenile Hormone d) All of above

507. Tyrosine is an example of non-essential
   a) Lipid **b) Aminoacid**
   c) Protein d) Hormone

508. Corpora cardiaca produce
   a) Juvenile Hormone
   b) Ecdysone
   c) Prothoracicotropic Hormone
   d) All of above

509. Shedding of old skin is done by
   a) Eclosion hormone b) Ecdysone
   c) Bursicon d) All

510. Bursicon perform the function of
   a) Tanning b) Moulting
   c) Maturity d) All

511. Corpora allata is a
   a) Endocrine glands b) Neurohemal organs
   c) Neurosecretory cells d) Internal organs

512. The concentration of Juvenile Hormone is high at
   a) Egg stage b) Pupal stage
   c) Adult stage d) All
513. Embryo having 3 layer during the development is known as
   a) Gastrula b) Blastula
   c) Germ band d) None
514. When embryo head end moves towards the posterior pole of egg, this movement is known as
   a) Anatrepsis b) Katatrepsis
   c) Posterior closure d) None
515. The eggs of Dermatobia (Diptera. are stimulated to hatch by
   a) Deoxygenated water **b) Warmth**
   c) Radiation d) None
516. Maceration is the process of
   a) Clearing b) Grinding
   c) Boiling d) None
517. The most important tanning agent is
   a) Sclerotin **b) Tyrosine**
   c) Phenole d) All
518. Proventriculus perform the function of
   a) Digestion b) Secretion
   c) Grinding d) Storing
519. Gizzard has four mobile lips with spines on them, for staining in
   a) Fleas b) Beetles
   c) Bees d) Whitefly
520. Goblet cells of Mid gut in Lepidoptera accumulate
   a) Metal and dyes b) Enzymes
   c) Food d) Vitamins
521. The pH of mid gut is
   a) 8 b) 6
   c) 10 d) 9
522 α-amylase act on .
   a) 1,4 α glucosidic linkage
   b) 1,6 α glucosid
   c) 1,2 α glucosidic linkage
   d) All of above

523. Higher termites digest the cellulose with the help of

a) **Protozoa** b) Bacteria

c) Fungus d) Cellulases

524. Hemicellulases can hydrolyze the

a) Cellulose b) Hexosan only

c) Pentosan **d) b & c**

525. Pepsin acts only in

a) Neutral medium b) Basic medium

c) Acidic medium d) All

526. The excretory function of Malpighian tubules is observed by

a) Marcello Malpighi (1669) **b) Herold (1816)**

c) Meckel (1820) d) All

527. The excretory product which is less toxic and insoluble called

a) Ammonia b) Urea

c) Uric acid d) b & c

528. H:N. Ratio in uric acid is

a) 1:1 b) 2:1

c) 3:1 d) None

529. In mosquitoes, the anal lobe can absorb

a) Food **b) Salts**

c) Heat d) All

530. Muscles which are responsible for heart beat in insects are

a) Pulsating muscles **b) Alary muscles**

c) Dorso-ventral muscles d) None

531. In insects, oxygen is delivered by

a) Red blood cells b) White blood cells

c) Tracheal system d) All

532. Pliasma of blood contains

a) 60% H_2O b) 80% H_2O

c) 90% H_2O d) 95% H_2O

533. The neuron that conduct signals away from the central nervous system is known as

a) Afferent neurons **b) Efferent neurons**

c) Internuncial neuron

534. Antennal sensilla is an example
    a) Machanoreceptors b) Chemoreceptors
    c) Photoreceptors
535. Repeatedly firing on Mechanoreceptor as long as stimulus persists known as
    a) Phasic response b) Quick response
    c) Tonic response d) All
536. Pressure receptors give information about depth/height to
    a) Terrestrial insects b) Subterramean insect
    c) Aquatic insects d) All
537. Tympanal organs are present on the front tibia in
    a) Cicadas **b) Crickets**
    c) Moths d) Grasshoppers
538. Chemical substances in gaseous form are detected in insect by
    a) Gustatory receptors **b) Olfactory receptors**
    c) Stretch receptors d) All
539. The type of birth in which insect directly lays young one known as
    a) Oviparity **b) Viviparity**
    c) Parthenogenesis d) None
540. Pupae having appendages free and visible externally is present in
    a) Butterflies **b) Beetles**
    c) Flies d) Moths
541. Study of adverse effects of chemical on living organisms
    a) Drug science **b) Toxicology**
    c) Physiology d) None
542. Any agent that is capable of producing a deleterious response in biological systems producing death.
    a) Poison b) Drug
    c) Biochemical agent
543. Toxicity of chemical depends on
    a) Time b) Concentration
    c) Route of administration **d) All**
544. When the action of one chemical reduce the other chemical known as
    a) Antogonism b) Synergism
    c) Potentiation d) Additive effect

545. Effects produced by the ingestion of caustic substances or of irritant material

a) **Local toxicity** b) Systemic toxicity

c) Immediate toxicity d) Delayed toxicity

546. The time required to kill 50% test animal is

a) LD_{50} **b) LT_{50}**

c) LC_{50} d) a & b

547. Margin of safety

a) LD_1/ED_{99} b) LD_{99}/ED_1

c) LD_{50}/ED_{50} d) None

548. Toxicity of insecticide by administration of single lethal dose for a short period of time is

a) Acute b) Chronic

c) Sub chronic d) None of these

549. Acaricides are used to kill

a) Algae b) Fungi

c) Mites d) None

550. Chemical used to kill birds.

a) Onicides b) Predicides

c) Avicides d) Silricides

551. Chemical used to kill fish

a) Piscicide b) Predicides

c) Siluicides d) Avicides

552. Chemical used to destroy or inactive harmful micro-organisms

a) Desiccant **b) Disinfectant**

c) Defsliants d) None

553. Poisons cause unconsciousness in insects and are fat soluble

a) Narcotic poisons **b) Nerve poisons**

c) Physical poison d) Miscellaneous

554. Poisons inhibits the acetylcholinerase resulting build up of Acetylcholine

a) Axonic poison **b) Synaptic poison**

c) Nerve poison d) Muscle poisons

555. Insecticide which block the insect spiracles are

a) Muscle poison **b) Physical poisons**

c) Narcotic d) None

556. Sodium arsenate is a
   a) Inorganic b) Organic
   c) Element d) None
557. Nereistoxin is a compound having origin
   a) Plant **b) Animal**
   c) Natural organic d) None
558. Rotenone is a compound having origin
   a) Plant b) Animal
   c) Natural organic d) None
559. Strobane belong to group
   a) Organo chlorine b) Organophosphate
   c) Carbamate d) None
560. Acetphate belong to group
   a) Organochlorine **b) Organophosphate**
   c) Carbamate d) None
561. Aldicarb belong to group
   a) Organochlorine b) Organophosphate
   c) Carbamate d) None
562. Diafenthuron belongs to group
   a) Organochlorine **b) Thiourea**
   c) Pyrethriods d) Carbamate
563. Imidacloprid is a
   a) Fumigante **b) Nicotinyl insecticides**
   c) Ropellent d) None
564. Methyl bromide is a
   a) Fumigant b) Repellent
   c) Attractant d) None
565. Fenvalerate belongs to family
   a) Pyrethroid b) Carbamate
   c) Thiourea d) None
566. Dicofol is a
   a) Insecticide **b) Acaricides**
   c) Rotentiicda d) Fungicides

567. Benzyl benzoate repel the
a) Flies **b) Mosquitoes**
c) Mites d) All

568. Carbamates have same mode of action as
a) Organochlorine **b) Organophosphate**
c) Pyrethroids d) None

569. Reduction is a phase metabolism
a) I b) II
c) I & II d) None

570. Carboxylesterares is metabolism of class
a) I b) II
c) I & II d) None

571. Extent of toxicity depends on
a) Time of exposure
b) Concentration
c) Route of administration
d) All

572. Toxin is produced by
a) Living organisms b) Only plants
c) Only microbes d) Only animals

573. Toxin produced by microbes
a) Endotoxin b) Mycotoxin
c) Aphlatoxin d) Phytotoxin

574. Toxin is injected by sting/bite is
a) Zootoxin **b) Venom**
c) Bacterial toxin d) None

575. Branch of toxicology that is hybrid of analytic chemistry and fundamental toxicological principles
a) Chemical toxicology **b) Forensic toxicology**
c) Environmental toxicology d) None

576. Ethyl alcohol have LD_{50} value (mg/kg)
a) 1 b) 5
c) 1,000 **d) 10,000**

577. The chemical is more toxic if LD_{50} is
a) Low b) High
c) Moderate d) None

578. Nephrotoxic is chemical toxic to
   a) Liver **b) Kidney**
   c) Blood d) Eyes
579. Ototoxic is chemical toxic to
   a) Liver **b Ear**
   c) Eyes d) Kidney
580. Exposure of chemical refers to repeated exposure to chemical for 1 month or less is
   a) Sub-chronic **b) Sub acute**
   c) Chronic d) Acute
581. The compounds with ability to cause birth deformities
   a) Carcinogenic b) Mutagenic
   c) Teratogenic
582. Have more half life
   a) Pyrethroids b) Carbamates
   c) Organophosphate **d) Organochlorine**
583. When two chemical control balance each other by producing opposite effect on the same physiological function is
   a) Chemical antagonism b) Inactivation
   c) Functional antagonism d) None
584. Which formulation has less active ingredient quantity
   a) EC b) SC
   c) Dusts d) WP
585. Methyl Eugenol is
   a) Attractant b) Repellent
   c) Insecticide **d) Sex pheromone**
586. Chemical used in the treatment in moth and timber proofing against
   a) Impreganting material b) Poisons bait
   c) Slow released insecticide d) None
587. The minimal effective dose of any chemical that evopres a stated all or none response is called
   a) TD b) ED
   c) LD d) None
588. Ability to give maximum response of a chemical is
   a) Potency **b) Efficacy**
   c) Concentration d) Effective dose

589. Highly extracted chemical have clearance between

a) **0.7-1** b) 0.5-0.7

c) 0.1-0.5 d) Zero

590. Kairomone have utility for

a) Emitter **b) Receiver**

c) Both d) None

591. The study of insects is called

a) **Entomology** b) Anthropology

c) Zoology d) Pathology

e) Parasitology

592. Any organism which harms or causes damage to man directly or indirectly is called

a) **Pest** b) Insect

c) Insect Pest d) Agriculture Pest

593. Insects belong to the class

a) **Insecta** b) Pauropoda

c) Symplyla d) Crustacea

594. The practice of dining one's own species

a) **Cannabolism** b) Parasitism

c) Diapause d) Aestivation

595. Insects in which young ones pass through complex or complete metamorphosis are said to be:

a) **Holometabola** b) Ametabola

c) Hemimetabola d) Hyper metamorphosis

596. The young ones of holometabolus insects are called

a) **Larvae** b) Nymph

c) Naiad d) Maggots

597. Insects which develop their wings externally belong to the class

a) **Exopterygota** b) Endopterygota

c) Apterygota d) None of them

598. The resting stage of Endopterygot insects is

a) **Pupa** b) Larva

c) Adult d) Nymph

599. The young ones of hemimetabola those are terrestrial in habitat are

a) **Nymphs** b) Naiads

c) Larvae d) Pupae

600. Larvae of beetles are known as
   a) Grubs b) Maggots
   c) Imago d) Instars
601. Young ones of fly are
   a) Maggots b) Grubs
   c) Imago d) All above
602. The form of insect after complete metamorphosis
   a) Imago b) Puparium
   c) Stadium d) Pupa
603. The type of diapause which occur in winter
   a) Hibernation b) Aestivation
   c) Dormancy d) Starvation
604. Suffering caused in insect due to lack of food
   a) Starvation b) Aestivation
   c) Dormancy d) Diapause
605. Insects that feed on one type of food
   a) Monophagous b) Oligophagous
   c) Omnivorous d) Phytophagous
606. Insects which feed other insects are to be known as
   a) Entomophagous b) Cannibalism
   c) Parasitism d) Predatism
607. Aphids is an example of
   a) Viviparous b) Oviparous
   c) Parthenogenesis d) All above
608. Insects that active at night are
   a) Nocturnal b) Diurnal
   c) Crepuscular d) None of them
609. Insects which are active during morning or evening twilight
   a) Crepuscular b) Diurnal
   c) Nocturnal d) Predator
610. In insect ganglion is a part of
   a) Nervous system b) Respiratory System
   c) Reproductive System d) Muscular system
611. Insects that found everywhere are
   a) Cosmopolitan insects b) Household insects
   c) Stored grain insects d) None of above

612. Male, female mosquitoes have antennae
   a) **Plumose, Pilose** b) Aristase, Plumose
   c) Pectinate, Plumose d) Pectinate pilose
613. House flies antennae are
   a) **Aristate** b) Stylate
   c) Ensiform d) Capitate
614. The dorsal sclerotized region of insect body is
   a) **Tergum** b) Pleuron
   c) Sternum d) None of above
615. The lateral sclerotized portion is
   a) **Pleuron** b) Tergum
   c) Sternum d) All above
616. The main body region of insects are
   a) **Tagmosis** b) Antecosta
   c) Acrotergite d) Symphyta
617. Grasshopper and cricket have mouth parts
   a) **Biting chewing type** b) Piercing sucking
   c) Chewing lapping d) Biting and sponging
618. Costal margin of wing of insect is
   a) **Frontal margin** b) Anal margin
   c) Outer margin d) Inner margin
619. Campodeiform is type of
   a) **Larva** b) Egg
   c) Naiad d) Nymph
620. Type of pupae with appendages are free and not glued to the body is
   a) **Exarate** b) Obtect
   c) Coarctate d) Vermiform
621. Hind wings of true flies are modified into tiny knobbed structure
   a) **Halteres** b) Pseudohaltere
   c) Filohaltere d) Membranous
622. Beetles & weevils have fore wing very thick and hard
   a) **Elytra** b) Hemelytra
   c) Strippy d) Filohaltere
623. Dragonfly and damselfly have type of legs
   a) **Basket forming** b) Fossorial
   c) Cursorial d) Netatorial

624. Tentorium is
a) **Endoskeleton of head** b) Exoskeleton of head
c) All above d) None of above

625. Function of exo-cuticle is
a) **Rigidity of body parts** b) Impermeability of water
c) Prevention d) Toughness

626. Insect body divided into external grooves called as
a) **Suture** b) Sclerite
c) Somites d) Acron

627. Which hormone cause moulting
a) **Ecdysome** b) Ecdysis
c) Exuvium d) Moulting

628. What enzymes break protein
a) **Protease** b) CH_2O
c) Lipases d) Amylase

629. Type of reproduction in which young ones produced from unfertilized eggs
a) **Parthenogenesis** b) Viviparity
c) Polyembryony d) Oviparity

630. The hearing organ in grasshopper is
a) **Tympanal organ** b) Johastan organ
c) Chorodontonal organ d) All of above

631. Locomotion in response to odour
a) **Stereokinesis** b) Chemokinesis
c) Taxis d) Kinesis

632. Fast acting pheromones
a) **Releasers** b) Primers
c) Somio chemical d) Allelo chemical

633. Social behaviour is present in
a) **Termites** b) Butterflies
c) Moths d) Flies

634. The ability of plant by which it is less damaged by insect
a) **Tolerance** b) Avoidance
c) Immunity d) Resistance

635. Complete resistance against adverse conditions is
a) **Immunity** b) Resistance
c) Tolerance d) Avoidance

636. The identical food of queen is
a) **Royal jelly** b) Water
c) Honey d) Nectar

637. Lac is produced by insect
a) ***Laccifer lacca*** b) *Bombyx mori*
c) *Apis cerana* d) *Apis dorsata*

638. Commercial rearing of honey is
a) **Apiculture** b) Sericulture
c) Lac culture d) All above

639. Silk is produced by insect
a) ***Bombyx mori*** b) *Gryllus* sp.
c) *Apis cerana* d) *Apis mellifera*

640. Fire flies are
a) **Beetles** b) Flies
c) Fleas d) Wasps

641. The largest insect of the world is
a) **Elephant beetle** b) Winged beetle
c) Locust d) Grasshopper

642. Where the insects are abundant
a) **Tropical region** b) Sub-tropical region
c) Temperate region d) None of the above

643. Which insect cut the root of the plant
a) **Mole Cricket** b) Ground beetle
c) Pyrilla d) Grylloblatid

644. The rapid reappearance of the pest population in injurious number is
a) **Pest resurgence** b) Pest outbreak
c) Pest resistance d) IPM

645. The amount of pest induced injury level to the crop which will justify the cost of artificial control measure
a) **Economic damage** b) Economic threshold
c) Economic injury level d) None of the above

646. Proventriculus is a part of

a) **Digestive system** b) Reproductive System
c) Respiratory System d) Nervous System d.

647. The family of desert locust is

a) **Acrididae** b) Gryllidae
c) Tetrigidae d) Gryllotelpidae

648. Curclionidae is the family of

a) **Weevils** b) Beetles
c) Flies d) Borers

649. Subimaginal moulting occure in

a) **Mayflies** b) Stoneflies
c) Fireflies d) Scorpionflies

650. Secondary Male genitalia present in

a) **Odonata** b) Plecoptera
c) Blatteria d) Mentodia

651. Anal fold in the wing developed for the first time in

a) **Plecoptera** b) Orthoptera
c) Lepidoptera d) Hemiptera

652. Tegmina presents in

a) **Orthoptera** b) Diptera
c) Homoptera d) Collembola

653. Telson tail present in

a) **Protura** b) Diplura
c) Thysanura d) Strepsiptra

654. Six segmented abdomen present in

a) **Collembola** b) Diplura
c) Dictyoptera d) Coleoptera

655. Mouth parts Asymmetrical in

a) **Thysanoptera** b) Neuroptera
c) Mecoptera d) Hymenoptera

656. Division of labor present in

a) **Honeybees** b) Flies
c) Cockroaches d) Lice

657. Sexual dimorphism occur in
   a) **Mango mealybug** b) Grasshopper
   c) Human louse d) Cricket
658. When the immature ones capable to produce young ones called
   a) **Paedogensis** b) Parthenogensis
   c) Anamorphism d) Oviparity
659. When all spiracles are functional in insect respiration called
   a) **Holopneustic** b) Apneustic
   c) Oligopneistic d) Amphipneustic
660. Nodus and pterostigma present in the wing of
   a) **Odonates** b) Fire brates
   c) Ants d) Stylopids
661. All members are parasitic in nature in the insect order
   a) **Strepsiptera** b) Hymenoptera
   c) Lepidoptera d) Coleoptera
662. Jugum in insect is a part of
   a) **Wing** b) Leg
   c) Antenna d) Abdomen
663. Hamuli on the wing present in
   a) **Hymenopterous insects**
   b) Lepidopterous insects
   c) Dipterous insects
   d) Mecopterous insects
664. Egg laying capability in insect is known as
   a) **Fecundity** b) Reproductive potential
   c) Biological potential d) Natality
665. Utilization of all the resources in the present area by an insect species community called
   a) **Niche** b) Habitat
   c) Agro-eco-system d) Ecological race
666. A living place of an insect population is known as
   a) **Habitat** b) Environment
   c) Ecology d) Niche
667. Branching of food chain into various directions
   a) **Food web** b) Food links
   c) Trophic association d) Energy pyramid

668. Halteres present in the insect order
   a) **Diptera** b) Embioptera
   c) Hemiptera d) Mallophaga
669. Cerci asymmetrical in
   a) **Web spinner** b) Ear wig
   c) Grouse locust d) Thrips
670. Binomial nomenclature introduced by
   a) **Linnaeus** b) Fabricious
   c) Uvarov d) Kirby
671. Ontogeny repeats phylogeny deals to
   a) **Biogenetic Law** b) Darwin law
   c) Law of priority d) Law of segregation
672. Systema Naturae is a publication of
   a) **Linnaeus** b) Darwin
   c) Aristotle d) Lamarck
673. Flacheri is a disease of
   a) **Silkworm** b) Honeybees
   c) Grasshoppers d) Beetles
674. American foul brood is a disease of
   a) **Honeybees** b) Lac insects
   c) *Bombyx mori* d) *Embia* spp.
675. On the land mounds are formed by
   a) **Termite** b) Ants
   c) Psocids d) Wasps
676. Antennae are absent in
   a) **Telson tail insects** b) Spring tail insects
   c) Double tail insects d) None of above
677. Raptorial type of legs are found in
   a) **Praying mantis** b) Dragonflies
   c) Crickets d) Flies
678. Dead hearts in sugarcane is caused by
   a) **Borers** b) Pyrilla
   c) Black Bug d) Mole cricket

679. Bunchy top in sugarcane is found due to

a) **Top borers** b) Stem borers

c) Root borers d) Gurdaspur borer

680. Roset flowers in cotton are found due to

a) **Pink bollworm** b) Spotted bollworm

c) American bollworm d) Army worm

681. Parasite of maize borere is

a) ***Epipyrops*** b) *Apenteles*

c) *Cotesia* d) *Trichogramma*

682. Aphid lion is called

a) ***Chrysopa*** b) Ladybird beetle

c) Assassin bug d) Pirate bug

683. Cornicles are presents in

a) **Aphids** b) Whiteflies

c) Jassids d) Scale insects

684. Acaricides are the chemicals used to kill

a) **Mites** b) Insects

c) Scorpion d) Mice

685. Myiasis is a disease caused by

a) **Flies** b) Mites

c) Ticks d) Caterpillar

686. Scabies is the problem caused by

a) **Mites** b) Ticks

c) Flies d) Maggots

687. Leishmaniasis is disease caused by

a) **Sand flies** b) Stoneflies

c) House flies d) Horse flies

688. Sleeping sickness is caused by

a) Tsetse flies b) Black flies

c) Flash flies d) Face flies

689. Dengue fever is transmitted by

a) **Mosquito** b) Flies

c) Caterpillar d) Ants

690. Epidemic Typhus is transmitted by

a) **Human Louse** b) Chicken louse

c) Mite d) Tick

691. *Trogoderma granarium* (Everts) belongs to family——————

a) **Dermestidae** b) Bostrichidae
c) Curculionidae d) Gelichidae

692. —————— normally attacks on upper layer of stored wheat.

a) **Khapra beetle** b) *Tribolium castaneum*
c) Lesser grain borer d) Rice Weevil

693. Damage is only caused by only grub stage of the ——————

a) Red flour beetle **b) Khapra beetle**
c) Saw toothed beetle d) Dhora beetle

694. *Sitophilus oryzae* belongs to family ——————

a) Gelichidae **b) Curculionidae**
c) Tenebrionidae d) None of all

695. Reddish hair are present on the body of the larvae of——————

a) *Rhyzopertha dominica* b) *Tribolium castaneum*
c) *Sitotroga cerealella* **d) *Trogoderma granarium***

696. —————— is shown by the Khapra beetle

a) Phototropism b) Geotropism
c) Thigmotropism d) None of all

697. Benzequinone is secreted by the dermal glands of ——————

a) *Rhyzopertha dominica* **b) *Tribolium castaneum***
c) *Sitotroga cerealella* d) *Trogoderma granarium*

698. Prothorax of *Oryzophilus surinamensis* L. has—————— toothed like projection along each side.

a) 9 b) 5
c) 6 d) 3

699. *Oryzophilus surinamensis* L. overwinter as ——————

a) Adult **b) Larvae**
c) Pupa d) Egg

700. Pectinate antennae are present in adult of ——————

a) Khapra beetle b) Red flour beetle
c) Dhora beetle **d) Lesser grain borer**

701. *Sitotroga cerealella* is commonly known as Angoumois Grain moth as it was first described from the ——————Province Angoumois in 1736.

a) French b) German
c) Brazilian d) Dutch

702. *Corcyra cephalonica* is a serious pest of stored ___________

a) Wheat **b) Rice**

c) Gram d) Oat

703. Optimum temperature require for the best growth of stored insect pests is ___________

a) 36-40 °C **b) 28-32 °C**

c) 20-25 °C d) 16-20 °C

704. Before storage, moisture contents of the commodity should be___________

a) 15-20% b) 20%

c) 10% d) 14%

705. ___________ attack the whole grains both before and after harvest.

a) Secondary Pests **b) Primary Pest**

c) Tertiary Pest d) None of All

706. ___________attack the damaged or broken grain or flour

a) Secondary Pests b) Primary Pest

c) Tertiary Pest d) None of All

707. ___________ is a period in the life cycle when metabolism is reduced to a minimum due to unfavorable conditions.

a) Diapause b) Thigmotropism

c) Resistance d) Metamorphosis

708. At ___________ moisture contents the rates of development of stored grain insect populations are slow

a) High b) Optimum

c) Low d) All of them

709. Family of Indian meal moth is ___________

a) Pyralidae b) Gelichidae

c) Dermestidae d) None of all

710. Pygidium is not covered by the elytra of___________

a) Kharpa b) Red flour beetle

c) Dhora d) None of all

711. Eggs of___________ are used for the rearing of various biological control agents

a) Indian meal moth b) Dhora

c) Angoumois grain moth **d) Rice Moth**

712. ——————diapause is only expressed when conditions are unfavorable.

a) Obligate **b) Facultative**

c) Temporary d) None of all

713. Unavoidable diapause is ——————

a) Facultative **b) Obligate**

c) Temporary d) All of them

714. If there is more moisture contents in the stored commodity, ———— will grow on it

a) Fungi b) Nematodes

c) Algae d) Bacteria

715. Adult of ——————have well developed rostrum

a) *Callosbruchus chinensis* b) *Tribolium castaneum*

c) *Sitophilus oryzae* d) *Trogoderma granarium*

716. Maximum of stored grain insect pests belong to order——————

a) Homoptera **b) Coleoptera**

c) Diptera d) Lepidoptera

717. Irregular wholes present in the damaged grains is the identification mark of the damage of ——————

a) Khapra beetle **b) Lesser grain borer**

c) Rice weevil d) Angoumois grain moth

718. ——————gas is produced from agtoxin® tablets

a) Ethylene b) Methane

c) Phosphine d) None of all

719. Deltamethrin is a ——————

a) Grain fumigant **b) Grain Protectant**

c) Repellent d) All of them

720. Recommended dose of deltamethrin to be applied in a storage structure is

a) 50 L per 100 L of water **b) 1 L per 100 L of water**

c) 5 L per 50 L of water d) 10 L. per 100 L of water

721. Recommended dose of Aluminum phosphide to be applied per tone is

a) 10 tablets **b) 2-3 tablets**

c) 5 tablets d) 20 tablets

722. Bostrichidae is the family of
a) **Lesser grain borer** b) Red flour beetle
c) Rice Weevil d) Angoumois grain moth

723. *Azadirachtin* is found in
a) Motia b) Citrus
c) Neem d) Sweet flag

724. Botanical name of Sweet Flag is
a) ***Acorus calamus*** b) *Azadirachta indica*
c) *Mangefera indica* d) None of all

725. A secondary pest is a
a) Khapra beetle **b) Red Flour Beetle**
c) Rice Weevil d) Lesser Grain Weevil

726. The outer most layer of pericarp or fruit coat is ——————
a) Endodermis **b) Epidermis**
c) Mesodermis d) None of all

727. Method of Expressing moisture in grain:
a) Wet Weight basis b) Dry weight basis
c) Both a and b d) None of all

728. A high polymer with non-identical repeating units of amino acids:
a) Carbohydrates **b) Proteins**
c) Lipids d) Vitamins

729. A curve describing the equilibrium relationship of sorbed water and vapor pressure (or relative humidity) at a given temperature is
a) Isotherm b) Parabola
c) Both a. and b d) None of All

730. The power of insects to reproduce is
a) Diapause **b) Fecundity**
c) Natality d) None of all

731. In insects, the organ involved in fertilization to receive & store the sperms after copulation
a) Accessory gland **b) Spermatheca**
c) Oviduct d) Pedicel

732. Formula of Phosphine is
a) PH_4 **b) PH_3**
c) PH_2 d) None of all

733. Concentration of phosphine to be maintained in a storage structure:
a) 600 ppm b) 800 ppm
c) 100 ppm **d) 200 ppm**

734. Plant characteristics that lead insects away from a particular host:
a) Preference **b) Non preference**
c) Antibiotics d) None of all

735. Antixenosis is a ————word means against or expelling guest.
a) Greek b) Japanese
c) Italian d) French

736. Semiochemicals which promote communication between members of the same species:
a) Allelochemicals b) Kairomones
c) Pheromones d) None of all

737. Defensive chemicals producing negative responses in insects are
a) Pheromones **b) Allomones**
c) Kairomones d) Allelochemicals

738. ————are advantageous to an insect, promoting host finding, Oviposition and feeding
a) Pheromones b) Allomones
c) Allelochemicals **d) Kairomones**

739. Type of non preference present in spotted cucumber beetle is
a) Allelochemical nonpreference
b) Morphological nonpreference
c) Both a. and b
d) None of all

740. Factors involved in antibiosis are related to:
a) Plants b) Insects
c) Both plants & insects d) All of them

741. DIMBOA, a cyclic hydroxamic acid is an allelochemic associated with antibiosis is found in
a) Cotton b) Wheat
c) Corn **d) Sugarcane**

742. Gossypols are present in
a) Wheat **b) Cotton**
c) Maize d) None of all

743. Larry P. Pedigo is author of famous book

a) Introductory Entomology

b) Applied Entomology

c) Entomology and Pest Management

d) None of All

744. Lack of insect infestation, or injury to the host plant because of transitory circumstances such as incomplete infestation is referred as

a) Host Evasion **b) Escape**

c) Induced Resistance d) None of all

745. Under some circumstances a host may pass through the most susceptible stage quickly or at a time when insect numbers are reduced. Such type of psuedoresistance is known as:

a) Escape **b) Host Evasion**

c) Susceptibility d) All of them

746. The term used for temporary increased resistance resulting from some condition of plant or environment is known as:

a) Induced Resistance b) Escape

c) Host evasion d) None of all

747. A variety which a specific insect never consume or injure under any known condition is a ————————variety

a) Resistant **b) Immune**

c) Susceptible d) Highly resistant

748. Level of resistance which cause a variety to show less damage or infestation by an insect than the average for the crop under consideration is:

a) High Level of resistance **b) Low level of resistance**

c) Moderate Resistance d) None of all

749. A variety which shows average or more than average damage by an insect is a................variety.

a) Immune **b) Susceptible**

c) Resistant d) None of all

750. The relative amount of heritable qualities possessed by the plant which influence the ultimate degree of damage done by the insect is known as

a) Immunity **b) Resistance**

c) Susceptibility d) None of All

751. ——————is a basis of resistance in which the plant shows an ability to grow and reproduce itself or to repair injury to a marked degree in spite of supporting a population approximately equal to that damaging a susceptible host.

a) **Tolerance** b) Preference

c) Nonpreference d) Resistance

752. Death of young immatures, reduced growth rate, shortened adult life span etc. are the symptoms of insect affected by ——————

a) **Antibiosis** b) Tolerance

c) Non preference d) All of them

753. Phenolic compounds produced by plants when they become diseased or are attacked by insects:

a) **Phytoalexins** b) Semiochemicals

c) Allomones d) Kairomones

754. The resistance which depends on environmental conditions is

a) Host Evasion

b) Enviromental resistance

c) **Morphological resistance**

d) None of all

755. Different populations of an insect specie that vary in their virulence to a cultivar are referred to as:

a) Pathotype b) **Biotype**

c) Paratype d) All of them

756. A gene which allows a pest species to overcome resistance and once more attack a plant is

a) **Virulent gene** b) Resistant gene

c) Susceptible gene d) All of them

757. ....recognize two types of resistance vertical and horizontal resistance.

a) **J.E. Van der Plank** b) Pedigo

c) Atwal d) None of all

758. The type of resistance which describes cultivars that express resistance against a broad range of genotypes of insects is

a) Vertical resistance b) **Horizontal resistance**

c) Morphological resistance d) None of all

759. The type of resistance which describes cultivars that express resistance against a one or a few genotypes of insects is

a) Vertical resistance **b) Horizontal resistance**

c) Morphological resistance d) None of all

760. Oligogenic resistance is also called ——————

a) Major gene resistance b) Minor gene resistance

c) Both (a and b) d) None of all

761. The resistance which is conferred by one or only a few gene is

a) Polygenic resistance **b) Oligogenic resistance**

c) Both (a and b) d) None of all

762. Polygenic resistance is also called——————

a) Major gene resistance **b) Minor gene resistance**

c) Both (a and b) d) None of all

763. The resistance which is conferred by many genes, each contributing to the resistance effect is

a) Polygenic resistance b) Oligogenic resistance

c) Both (a and b) d) None of all

764. Resistance which is conferred by mutable substances in cell cytoplasm is

a) Oligogenic resistance b) Polygenic

c) Cytoplasmic resistance d) All of them

765. Cytoplasmic inheritance is due to the cytoplasm of the zygote comes from the ———

a) Sperms **b) Ovum**

c) Both (a and b) c) None of All

766. Any technique that utilizes living organisms, or substances from those organisms to make or modify a product to improve plants or animals or to develop microorganisms for specific uses is known as

a) Biotechnology b) Molecular technology

c) Both a and b d) None of all

767. The dose of a toxicant that will kill 50 percent of the test to whish it is administered

a) LC_{50} **b) LD_{50}**

c) LT_{50} d) None of All

768. Economic threshold level of insect pest in IPM of stored grains is

a) 5 **b) 0**

c) 4 d) All of them

769. *Callosobruchus chinensis* L. is the zoological name of :

a) Gram Dhora b) Moong Dhora

c) Saw toothe beetle d) None of all

770. *Oryzophilus surinamensis* L. belongs to family:

a) Bruchidae **b) Silvanidae**

c) Curculionidae d) Tenebrionidae

771. Rodents damage to stored food is of

a) Three fold b) Five fold

c) Seven fold c) Two fold

772. Life span of rodents is

a) 4-5 years **b) 1-2 years**

c) 6-7 years d) None of all

773. Breeding season in rodents is

a) Jan-April b) May-August

c) Through out the year d) Septemer-December

774. Warfarin is an

a) Anticoagulant b) Acute Poison

c) Chronic poison d) None of all

775. *Rattus meltada* is

a) Soft furred field rat b) Indian Gerbil

c) House rat d) Norway Rat

776. *Lepisma sacharina* is the zoological name of

a) Silverfish b) Firebrat

c) House cricket d) None of all

777. Adult of silverfish has ——————caudal filaments.

a) 5 b) 7

c) 3 d) 4

778. ——————feeds on glue and starchy materials with its chewing mouthparts.

a) Cockroach b) Mosquito

c) Crickets **d) Silverfish**

779. House cricket belong to family——

a) Grylidae b) Lepismatidae

c) Blattidae d) None of all

780. American cockroach is known as————

a) ***Periplanata americana*** b) *Acheta domestica*

c) *Lepisma sacharina* d) None of all

781. Soldier caste is present in

a) Honey bee **b) Termites**

c) House fly d) None of all

782. *Psocus lineatus* is

a) Bird louse **b) Book louse**

c) Mammal louse d) None of all

783. Liposcelidae is the family of———

a) Bird louse **b) Book louse**

c) Mammal louse d) None of all

784. There are ————nymphal instars

a) 2 b) 7

c) 5 d) 1

785. Carpet beetle belongs to family:

a) Dermestidae b) Cimicidae

c) Pediculidae d) None of all

786. *Lyctus africanus* is the zoological name of

a) Carpet beetle **b) Powder Post Beetle**

c) Bed Bug d) Human Louse

787. Human flea belongs to order

a) Siphonaptera b) Coleoptera

c) Diptera d) None of all

788. *Aspergillus flavipus* produces ————

a) Sterigmatocystin **b) Aflatoxin**

c) Ochratoxin d) None of all

789. A type of apparent host plant resistance in which a particular plant condition or environmental state makes a plant more resistant to pests that under other circumstances.

a) Induced resistance b) True resistance

c) Susceptibility d) None of all

790. Asexual life cycle of *plasmodium* is called

a) Schizogony b) Sporogony

c) Both a and b d) None of all

791. Erythrocytic cycle of *plasmodium* occurs inside the
   a) White Blood Cell b) Red Blood Cell
   c) Platelets d) None of all
792. *Musca domestica*'s larvae are known as
   a) Grubs **b) Maggots**
   c) Caterpillars d) All of them
793. *Tinea pellionella* is commonly known as
   a) Cloth Moth b) Carpet Moth
   c) House fly d) Bed Bug
794. Ants belong to family:
   a) Formicidae b) Dermestidae
   c) Antidae d) None of all
795. Sperms enters the egg through an opening in the egg covering called as
   a) Micropyle b) Hypocotile
   c) Endoderm d) None of all
796. Three layered embryo is called__________
   a) Blastula **b) Gastrula**
   c) Morula d) All of them
797. In parasitic Hymenoptera, more than one embryo are formed through asexual division. The process is know as
   a) Polyendry **b) Polyembryony**
   c) Polyploidy d) None of them
798 The act of the larvae leaving the egg is called__________________
   a) Eclosion b) Enclosion
   c) Ecdyson d) None of all
799. Juvinle Hormone is produced by glands accessory to brain known as
   a) Corpora cardiaca **b) Corpora allata**
   b) Prothoracic gland d) None of all
800. The_____________cycle refers to a single generation each year
   a) Univoltine b) Only voltine
   c) Monovoltine d) None of all
801. The orientation of head where the mouthparts are in a continuous series with legs
   a) Prognathous **b) Hypognathous**
   c) Opisthognathous d) None of above

802. The orientation of head where the mouthparts are projected forward along the horizontal axis of body

a) Prognathous b) Hypognathous

c) Opisthognathous d) Opisthosynchous

803. The orientation of head where the mouthparts are projected backward

a) Prognathous **b) Opisthosynchous**

c) Hypognathous d) None of above

804. Groove making the line of fusion b/w distinct plates of the head capsule

a) Sulcus **b) Suture**

c) Furca d) Ostia

805. A ridge giving strength against the strain imposed on the head capsule

a) Sulcus b) Furca

c) Suture d) None of above

806. Internal skelton of head for the attachment of Muscle

a) Tentorial pits b) Furca

c) Epiproct **d) Suture**

807. The roots of the tentorial arms which appear as depressions

a) Tentorium **b) Tentorium pits**

c) Funca d) Suture

808. Just after harvesting the silkworm cocoon having living pupa

a) Blue cocoon b) White cocoon

c) Green cocoon d) Yellow cocoon

809. The phenomenon where the pest is repeatedly parasitised by the same species of parasite

a) Super parasitism b) Hyper parasitism

c) Multi parasitism d) None of above

810. The phenomenon where a pest is parasitized by another parasite

a) Hyper parasitism b) Multi parasitism

c) Super parasitism d) None of above

811. Leaving the pest below the Economic threshold level for survival of natural enemies during insecticidal application

a) Terminal residue b) Residue

c) Pest residue d) None of above

812. The density of pest at which control measure should be applied to prevent it form reaching the Economic injury level

a) **Economic threshold level**

b) General equilibrium level

c) Toxicity level

d) None of above

813. The average population density of an insect population over a long period of time.

a) Toxicity level b) Economic threshold level

c) Economic injury level **d) None of above**

814. The Muscle which are directly associated with the wing but more the wings as a result of distortion which they produce in the shape of thorax

a) Direct Muscle b) Control Muscle

c) Depress Muscles **d) Indirect Muscle**

815. The 11th abdominal segment is often represented by a dorsal triangular or shield shaped Fergal plate

a) Epiproct b) Apolysis

c) Suture d) Sulcus

816. The outerlaye of insect body comprising epidermis and cuticle

a) Ecdysis **b) Integument**

c) Apolysis d) Hydrolysis

817. Separation of old cuticle from underlying epidermis

a) Hydrolysis b) Ecdysis

c) Apolysis d) None of above

818. The shedding of remnants of the old cuticle

a) Endocytosis b) Apolysis

c) Diastasis **d) Ecdysis**

819. Endosulfan Insecticide belongs to the group

a) Phenolic b) Organophosphate

c) Carbamate **d) Chlorinated hydrocarbons**

820. Aldicarb belongs to the group.

a) Phenolic b) Organophosphate

c) Carbamate d) Chlorinated hydrocarbon

821. Poisoning symptoms of parathian.

a) Inactiveness **b) Restlessness**

c) Fanning movement d) Jitters

822. Poisoning symptoms of Rotenone.

a) Inactiveness b) Restlessness
c) Fanning movement d) Jitters

823. Poisoning symptoms of BHC insecticides.

a) Inactiveness b) Restlessness
c) Fanning movement d) Jitters

824. Poisoning symptoms of DDT insecticide

a) Inactiveness b) Restlessness
c) Fanning movement **d) Jitters**

825. Site of action of organophosphate insecticide

a) Post synaptic membrane b) Axonic membrane
c) Synaptic junction d) Pre synaptic membrane

826. Site of action of Nicotine insecticide

a) Post synaptic membrane
b) Axonic membrane
c) Post synaptic membrane
d) Pre synaptic membrane

827. Site of action of cylodines insecticide

a) Post synaptic membrane b) Axonic membrane
c) Synaptic junction **d) Pre synaptic membrane**

828. Common name of the *Chilo sacchariphagous*

a) Internode bores b) Gurdaspur bores
c) Root borer d) Top borer

829. Nature of action of Phostoxin insecticides

a) Chitin inhibitor **b) Fumigant**
c) Contact d) Systemic

830. Nature of action of Diflubenzuron insecticide

a) Chitin inhibitor b) Fumigant
c) Contact d) Systemic

831. Nature of action of Chlorthion insecticide.

a) Chitin inhibitor b) Fumigant
c) Contact d) Systemic

832. Nature of action of Thiodemeton insecticide

a) Chitin inhibitor b) Fumigant
c) Contact **d) Systemic**

833. Mechanoreceptors gives response

a) Light b) Humidity

c) Body movements d) Pressure

834. In mantids the pincers are formed by apposition of tibia and ______ to catch hold the prey

a) Tibia b) Coxa

c) Tarsus **d) Femur**

835. The peritrophic membrane is absent in Hemiptera and adult

a) Lepidoptera b) Coleoptra

c) Hymenoptera d) Diptera

836. The ________ are the opening in the wall of the heart

a) Femur b) Tibia

c) Ostia d) Coxa

837. In nymph/larvae maximum sclerotization is found in

a) Maxilla b) Labrum

c) Labium **d) Mandible**

838. Maximum sclerotization is found in ______________of adult insect.

a) Mesonstum b) Metanolum

c) Pronotum d) None of above

839. The ______________ of caterpillars are hollow, cylindrical outgrowth of the body wall the lumen of which is continuous with hacmocoel.

a) Hypopharynt b) Thorax

c) Abdomen **d) Prolog**

840. The johnstons organ is situated in the _________ segment of the antenna

a) First **b) Second**

c) Third d) Fourth

841. Most of insect excrete 80 to 90 % of their nitrogen waste in the form of

a) Uric acid b) Ammonia

c) Urea d) None of above

842. Insect living in fresh water or extremely moist environment excrete their nitrogen waste in the form of

a) Nitric Acid **b) Ammonia**

c) Nitrogen d) Uric acid

843. Sclerotization is a process by which the cuticle become

a) Soft b) Dark

c) Hard d) None of above

844. Melanization is process by which the cuticle become

a) Black & White b) Hard

c) Soft d) Dark

845. Normally nersc axons have a resting potential of about

a) - 60 mv b) - 65 mv

c) - 75 mv **d) -70 mv**

846. Damage symptoms of the *Bissetia steniellus*

a) Bunchy top b) Dead harts pulled easily

c) Spiral galleries d) Dead hearts can not pulled easily

847. Damage symptoms of the *Scirpophaga nivilla*

a) Bunchy top b) Dead hearts pulled easily

c) Spiral galleries d) Dead hearts can not pulled easily

848. Damage symptoms of the *Chilo infuscatellus*

a) Bunchy top **b) Dead hearts pulled easily**

c) Spiral galleries d) Dead hearts can not pulled easily

849. Causal organism of the maggot disease

a) Virus b) *Bacillus thuringiensis*

c) *Nosema bombycis* **d) *Trichlyga sorbillans***

850. Causal organism of the Bacterial intoxication

a) Virus **b) *Bacillus thuringiensis***

c) *Nosema bombycis* d) *Trichlyga sorbillans*

851. Host plant of the Mulberry silkworm

a) *Ricinus communis* **b) *Morus* sp.**

c) *Terminalia arjuna* d) *Machilus bombyciana*

852. Host of the *Entomophthora muscae*

a) Lepidopterous caterpillars **b) Husefly**

c) Grasshoppers d) Aphid

853. *Serratia marcessens* belongs to the group

a) Fungi **b) Bacteria**

c) Virus d) Nematode

854. NPV pathogen belongs to the group

a) Fungi b) Bacteria

c) Virus d) Nematode

855. *Neoplectana* pathogen belongs to the group
   a) Fungi b) Bacteria
   c) Virus **d) Nematode**
856. *Menochilus* belongs to the family
   a) Coccinellidae b) Pentatomidae
   c) Reduviidae d) Chrysopidae
857. *Chysoperla* predator belongs to the family
   a) Coccinellidae b) Pentatomidae
   c) Reduviidae **d) Chrysopide**
858. Antennae of the moth
   a) Aristate **b) Pectinate**
   c) Serrate d) Monilform
859. Antennae of the Thrips
   a) Aristate b) Pectinate
   c) Serrate **d) Monilform**
860. Antennae of the Housefly
   a) Aristate b) Pectinate
   c) Serrate d) Monilform
861. Bi-pectinate antennae is found in
   a) Mosquito **b) Silkworm**
   c) Butterfly d) Honeybee
862. Plumose antennae is found in
   a) Mosquito b) Silkworm
   c) Butterfly d) Honeybee
863. Geniculate antennae is found in
   a) Mosquito b) Silkworm
   c) Butterfly **d) Honeybee**
864. Clavate antennae is found in
   a) Mosquito b) Silkworm
   c) Butterfly d) Honeybee
865. *Thrips tabaci* have mouth parts
   a) Biting and chewing b) Piercing and sucking
   c) Rasping and Sucking d) Sponging

866. *Musca domestica* have mouthparts

a) Biting and chewing b) Piercing and sucking
c) Rasping and Sucking **d) Sponging**

867. What type of legs found in mantid

a) Jumping b) Grooming
c) Grasping d) Digging

868. What type of legs found in Honeybee

a) Jumping **b) Grooming**
c) Grasping d) Digging

869. Pro-preoreceptros give response

a) Light b) Humidity
c) Body movement **d) Pressure**

870. Hygroreceptors give response

a) Light b) Humidity
c) Body movement **d) Pressure**

871. Photoreceptors give response

a) Light b) Humidity
c) Body movement d) Pressure

872. If the description of new species is based on single specimen of type series.

a) Holotype b) Paratype
c) Syntype d) Hetrotype

873. All the specimen of the series, when there is no holotype

a) Holotype b) Paratype
c) Syntype **d) Hetrotype**

874. After the holotypc is labeled , Each specimen of the remaining of the types

a) Paratype b) Holotype
c) Syntpe d) Hetrotype

875. Phytophagous insects feeding on plants of one or few closely related species with in a genus

a) Oligophayous **b) Moniphagous**
c) Polyphayous d) Diphagous

876. Phytophagous insects feeding on plants of several genra with in a family

a) Monophayous b) Polyphagous
c) Oligophagous d) Diphagous

877. Biodiversity of insects depends upon the_________ conditions of the environment.

a) Geographical & Physical b) Chemical & Biological

c) None of above **d) All of above**

878. Adult insects are categorized with the response of light are foll.

a) The diurnal species b) The nocturnal species

c) The crepuscular species **d) All of above**

879. The sweep net consists of a nylon cloth with a mouth about ______cm in diameter.

a) 20 cm **b) 30 cm**

c) 40 cm d) None of above

880. Pit-fall tray contains a container such as a ____________________.

a) Jar b) Tube

c) Funnel d) None

881. In Berles's funnel, the top of the funnel extends into a jar of_________% alcohol.

a) 60 % **b) 70%**

c) 80% d) None

882. The adults of Aphidoidea are preserved in __________ tubes.

a) 75% alcohol b) 85% alcohol

c) 95% alcohol d) None

883. The class insecta is divided into ___________subclasses.

a) 2 b) 3

c) 4 d) None

884. The subclass Ametabola is divided into ________ orders.

a) 2 b) 3

c) 4 d) None

885. The family lepismatidae belongs to the suborder _________________.

a) Microcoryphia **b) Zygentoma**

c) Dicellurata d) None

886. The *Japyx* sp. belongs to the order ____________________

a) Thysanura b) Protura

c) Diplura d) None

887. Acerentomidae is the important family of order ______________

a) Thysanura b) Diplura
c) Protura d) None

888. The process of increasing 3 abdominal segments during the post embryonic development is called ________________

a) Metamorphosis **b) Anamarphosis**
c) Mitosis d) None

889. In Protura, first pair of __________ perform the function of antemae.

a) Wings **b) Legs**
c) Abdomen d) None

890. In Collembola, abdomen is ______________ segmented.

a) 5 **b) 6**
c) 7 d) None

891. In Collembola, hook like structure is present on abdominal segment 3 that is known as.

a) Collophore **b) Retinaculum**
c) Furcula d) None

892. The family Neelidae belongs to the sub-order __________ of the order Collembola

a) Arthropleona **b) Symphyleona**
c) Filipalpia d) None

893. In _______________ the mouthparts are of chewing type but vestigial.

a) House fly b) Butterfly
c) Mayfly d) None

894. In Ephemeroptera the sub-imaginal moulting is _________

a) Present b) Absent
c) Present or absent d) None

895. Ephemeros means ___________________

a) Short lived b) Long lived
c) Short or long lived d) None

896. The nymphs of _________________ are aquatic and called naiads.

a) Drangonflies b) Damselflies
c) Mayflies d) None

897. The family caenidae belongs to the super family __________

a) Ephemeroibea **b) Baetoidea**
c) Heptagenioidea d) None

898. The family ________________ belongs to the super family Baetoidea.
 a) Ephemerellidae b) Ephemeridae
 c) Heptageniidae d) None

899. O*dontos* means ___________
 a) Bristle b) Hook
 c) Tooth d) None

900. The members of Odonata are commonly called ____________
 a) Mayflies and damselflies
 b) Mayflies and dragonflies.
 c) Dragonflies and damselflies
 d) None

901. An elongate nodus is present on ___________in Odonata.
 a) Wings b) Legs
 c) Abdomen d) None

902. Dragonflies belong to the suborder __________
 a) Anisoptera b) Zygoptera
 c) Anisozygoptera d) None

903. *Pantala* spp. belong to the family______________
 a) Libellulidae b) Aeshnidae
 c) Gomphidae d) None

904. ________________are the families of suborder Zygoptera
 a) Gomphidae and Aeshnidae
 b) Litbellulidae and Cordulgasteridae
 c) Coenagrionidae and Agrionidae
 d) None

905. Damselflies belong to the suborder ______________________
 a) Anisoptera **b) Zygoptera**
 c) Anisozygoptera d) None

906. In plecoptera, the anal lobe of the hind wing is folded on the wing during ________
 a) Flight **b) Rest**
 c) Flight & rest d) None

907. Plecoptra is divided into ________________ sub-orders
 a) 2 **b) 3**
 c) 4 d) None

908. In _______________ the maxillary palpi are seta like.

a) *Perla* sp. b) *Anex* sp.

c) *Podorous* sp. d) None

909. Locusts belong to the order

a) Plecoptera **b) Orthoptera**

c) Embioptera d) None

910. In orthoptera, speialized _______ organs are present.

a) Auditory

b) Stridulatory

c) Auditory and stridulatory

d) None

911. Orthoptera is divided into suborder.

a) 2 b) 3

c) 4 d) None

912. Suborder ensifera belongs to the order _______________

a) Plecoptera **b) Orthoptera**

c) Homoptera d) None

913. Mole cricket belongs to the family ____________________

a) Gryllidae **b) Gryllotalpidae**

c) Tridactylidae d) Trigonidiidae

914. Acrididae belongs to the suborder ________________

a) Ensifera **b) Caelifera**

c) Blattaria d) None

915. Ak grasshopper belongs to the family ______________________

a) Acrididae b) Tetrigidae

c) Pamphigidae **d) Pyrogomorphidae**

916. Phasma means _____________

a) A host **b) A ghost**

c) A host and ghost d) None

917. Leaf insects and stick insects belong to the order _______________

a) Grylloblatodea

b) Phasmida

c) Grylloblatodea and Phasmida

d) None

918. Leaf insects belong to the family____________________

a) Phasmidae **b) Phylliidea**

c) Neelidae d) Agrionidae

919. *Derma* means ______________

a) Dress b) Wool

c) Skin d) None

920. Earwig belongs to the order ______________

a) Zoraptera **b) Dermaptera**

c) Phasmida d) None

921. Forficulidae belongs to the order ____________

a) Zoraptera b) Orthoptera

c) Dermaptera d) None

922. Labiidae belongs to the order______________

a) Grylloblattodea b) Orthoptera

c) Dermaptera d) None

923. *Embios* means ________________

a) Lively b) Deadly

c) Lively and deadly d) None

924. The members of the order ______________ are commonly called cockroaches and preying mentids

a) Ephemeroptera b) Plecoptera

c) Embioptera **d) Dictyoptera**

925. Dictyoptera is divided into ______________ suborders

a) 2 b) 3

c) 4 d) 5

926. In____________ head is concealed under the pronotal shield

a) Orthoptera b) Homoptera

c) Dictyoptera d) Neuroptera

927. *Periplanata americana* belongs to the suborder__________

a) Blattaria b) Mantodea

c) Caelifera d) None

928. In Isoptera, *"iso"* means ______________

a) Unequal **b) Equal**

c) Larger d) Smaller

929. Termitorium is a ___________ where all members of the colony exist

a) Room
b) Loan
c) House
d) None

930. *Odontotermis obesus* belongs to the family______________

a) Rhinotermitidae
b) Termitidae
c) Kalotermitidae
d) Hodotermitidae

931. Termites can be collected from the __________________

a) Soil
b) Water
c) Paper
d) Wood

932. "*zor*" means _________________

a) Lively
b) Deadly
c) Purely
d) None

933. "*psoco*" means ___________________

a) To eat
b) To gnaw
c) To drink
d) None

934. Liposcelidae family belongs to the order_____________

a) Orthoptera
b) Zoraptera
c) Psocoptera
d) Lepidoptera

935. *Liposcelis* sp. belongs to the order_______________

a) Lepidoptera
b) Neuroptera
c) Coleoptera
d) Psocoptera

936. Chicken louse belongs to the order__________________

a) Siphunculata
b) Dermaptera
c) Mallophaga
d) None

937. Philopteridae belongs to the order__________________

a) Phasmida
b) Siphunculata
c) Mallophaga
d) None

938. "*siphunos*" means ________________

a) Glass
b) Rubber
c) Tube
d) Jar

939. In ______________________ head is broader than prothorax.

a) Chicken louse
b) Human louse
c) Chicken louse and human louse
d) None

940. Phthiriidae family belongs to the order________________________

a) Phasmida b) Protura

c) Thysanoptera **d) Siphunculata**

941. Sucking lice of horses belong to the family ___________________

a) Pediculidae b) Phthiriidae

c) Haematopinidae d) Monoponidae

942. "*hemi*" means ____

a) Hole **b) Half**

c) Hear d) Hair

943. Bugs belong to the order ________________________

a) Homoptera **b) Hemiptera**

c) Hymenoptera d) None

944. Terrestrial bugs belong to the suborder______________________

a) Cryptocerata **b) Gymnocerata**

c) Adephaga d) None

945. Water bugs belong to the sub order ________________________

a) Cryptocerata b) Gymnocerata

c) Adephaga d) None

946. Shield bugs belong to the family ________________

a) Lygaeidae **b) Pentatomidae**

c) Cimicidae d) Tingidae

947. Giant water bugs belong to the family ___________________________

a) Corixidae b) Nepidae

c) Hydrometridae **d) Belostomatidae**

948. Sugarcane leafhopper belongs to the order ________________________

a) Hemiptera **b) Homoptera**

c) Hymenoptera d) None

949. In whiteflies the last nymphal instars is very inactive and look like a pupa. It is to be called __________ pupal stage.

a) True **b) False**

c) Complete d) Incomplete

950. Mango mealy bugs belong to the order ___________________________.

a) Mallophaga b) Hemiptera

c)) Homoptera d) Hymenoptera

951. Homoptera is divided into __________suborders

a) 2 b) 3

c) 4 d) 5

952. Lanternflies belong to the order ___________________________

a) Diptera b) Lepidoptera

c) Homoptera d) Hemiptera

953. *Pyrilla perpusilla* belongs to the family _______________

a) Psyllidae **b) Lophopidae**

c) Pentatomidae d) Peridae

954. Diaspididae family belongs to the order _________________________.

a) Dermaptera b) Hemiptera

c) Homoptera d) Lepidoptera

955. Lac insects belong to the order ___________________

a) Lepidoptera b) Hymenoptera

c) Homoptera d) None

956. Lacciferidae belongs to the order ____________________________

a) Lepidoptera b) Coleoptera

c) Homoptera d) Hymenoptera

957. In Thysanoptera, the mouthparts are ___________________________

a) Symmetrical **b) Asymmetrical**

c) Chewing d) None

958. Thysanoptera is further divided into _____________________________ suborders.

a) 2 b) 3

c) 4 d) 5

959. In terebrantia the end of abdomen is _________________

a) Tube like **b) Blumtly roumded**

c) Elongate d) None

960. Tubulifera belongs to the order __________________________

a) Trichoptera b) Thysanura

c) Thysanoptera d) None

961. Family Thripidae belongs to the order ____________
   a) Thysanura   **b) Thysanoptera**
   c) Trichoptera   d) None

962. Holometabola is also known as ____________
   a) Hemimetabola   b) Exopterygota
   c) Endopterygota   d) None

963. "*neuro*" means ____________
   a) A neck   b) A net
   c) A nerve   d) A needle

964. Green lacewing belongs to the family
   a) Nemapteridae   b) Gomphidae
   c) Ascalaphidae   **d) Chrysopidae**

965. Antlion belongs to the order ____________
   a) Hymenoptera   **b) Neuroptera**
   c) Isoptera   d) Thysanoptera

966. Antlion belongs to the family ____________
   a) Ascalaphidae   **b) Myrmeleontidae**.
   c) Nemopteridae   d) None

967. Rove beetle belongs to the family ____________
   a) Geotrupidae   b) Silphidae
   c) Stephylinidae   d) None

968. Firefly belongs to the family ____________
   a) Silphidae   **b) Lampyridae**
   c) Histeridae   d) None

969. Powder post beetle belongs to the family ____________
   a) Anobiidae   b) Bostrichidae
   c) Lyctidae   d) None

970. Human flea belongs to the order ____________
   a) Mallophaga   b) Siphunculata
   c) Siphonaptera   d) Strepsiptera

971. Horse flies belong to the order ____________
   a) Dermaptera   **b) Diptera**
   c) Lepidoptera   d) None

972. Robber flies belong to the family ____________

a) Asilidae b) Tabanidae

c) Culicidae d) None

973. Cabbage butterflies belong to the family ____________

a) Muscidae b) Cecidomyiidae

c) Pieridae d) Pyralidae

974. Wood wasps belong to the family ____________

a) Vespidae **b) xiphydriidae**

c) Tenthredinidae d) None

975. Honey bees belong to the family ____________

a) Apidae b) Vespidae

c) Formicidae d) Scoliidae

976. Butterflies belong to the order ____________

a) Diptera **b) Lepidoptera**

c) Hymenoptera d) None

977. Insect whose larvae are quite unlike the adult along with the presence of pupul instar

a) Hopometabolous b) Hemi-metabolus

c) Hemimetaboluos d) Hetrometabolous

978. Insects having no metamorphosis

a) Hopometabolous **b) Ametabolous**

c) Hemimetabolous d) Hetrometabolous

979. Self sufficient and self regulated habit where biotic and abiotic components intract together for exchange of energy in a continous cycle

a) Community **b) Ecosystem**

c) Habitat d) Environment

980. A complex unit formed by all the population of that area

a) Community b) Ecosystem

c) Environment d) Habitat

981. The transfer of food energy from the plants through a series of organisms with repeated eating and being eaten

a) Food Chain b) Food web

c) Biotic Potential d) None of above

982. The interlocking pattern of food chain with all sorts of short aa cuits & connections

a) Food chain **b) Food web**

c) Biotic potential d) Antibiosis

983. Conversion of 6-carbon chain glucose molecule into two molecules of 3-carban chain pyrusic acid

a) Glycolysis b) Kerbcycle

c) Transition d) Antibiosis

984. Series of reaction in mitochondrion that brings about oxidation of actyle residues to CO_2 liberating H_2 and forming water

a) Glyclysis **b) Kerbscycle**

c) Transition d) Antibiosis

985. Organelles where protein synthesis take place

a) Mitochondia **b) Aibosome**

c) Cell membrane d) DNA

986. Chemical which give adaptive advantage to the producer

a) Allomones b) Kiaromones

c) Attractants d) Repellents

987. Chemical which give adaptive advantage to the reseiver

a) Allomones **b) Kairomones**

c) Attractants d) Repellents

988. Chemcials which inhibit feeding or piercing

a) Supressants b) Deterrents

c) Attractants d) Repellents

989. Chemicals which prevent maintenance of feeding or oviposition

a) Supressants **b) Deterrents**

c) Attractants d) Repellents

990. Chemical which orient insects towards the host

a) Attractants b) Repellents

c) Supressants d) Deterrents

991. Chemical which orient insects away from the host

a) Attractants **b) Repellent**

c) Supressants d) Deterrents

992. The study of economic poisons, their effects, mechanism of action and metabolism of toxicant

a) Entomology b) Embryology

c) Toxicology d) Botany

993. Ability of a chemical to bring about changes in the biological system of the target animal

a) Acute toxicity b) Chronic toxicity

c) Toxicity d) Poisoning

994. Acute stage of poisoning due to the application of a single dose

a) Toxicity **b) Acute toxicity**

c) Chronic toxicity d) None of above

995. Condition of toxicity which lasts for the entire life of the target animal and has the accumulating effect of small repeated doses.

a) Toxicity b) Acute toxicity

c) Chronic toxicity d) Hazards

996. The probability of being harmed due to the use exposon/handling of the toxic substances

a) Hazard b) Toxicity

c) Risk d) Acute toxicity

997. The concentration of a toxicant residue in or on a food when first offered for consumption.

a) Acceptable daily intake **b) Maximum residual limit**

c) Biomagnification d) None of above

998. The amount of initially laid down insecticidal chemical on the surface

a) Biomagnification b) Acceptable daily intake

c) Maximum residul limit **d) Toxicity deposit**

999. Family of ht *Chilo partellus*

a) Muscidae b) Scarabaeidae

c) Arctiidae **d) Crambidae**

1000. Family of the *Sitotroga cerelalella*

a) Coccidae **b) Aleurodidae**

c) Aphididae d) Pyralidae

1001. The word thysanura is derived from thysan and ura in which the ura means.

a) Bristle **b) Tail**

c) Tube d) None

1002. Which common name is incorrectly written?

a) Horsefly b) Honey bee

c) Ground beetle d) Lightningbug

11

Breeding of Field and Horticultural Crops

1. International Rice Research Institute is located at
   a) Mexico **b) Philippines**
   c) Nigeria d) Columbia
2. Use of combining ability as a measure of gene action was first suggested by
   a) Wright (1921) b) Griffing (1956)
   c) Sprague and Tatum (1942) d) Hayman (1954)
3. In India first Gamma garden was started at
   a) Calcutta b) Bangalore
   c) Delhi d) Coimbatore
4. Chromosome number of rice is
   a) 2n= 14 **b) 2n= 24**
   c) 2n = 20 d) 2n= 16
5. Botanical name of mung bean is
   a) *Vigna radiata* b) *Vigna mungo*
   c) *Glycine max* d) *Cajanus cajan*
6. The term vertical resistance and horizontal resistance were coined by
   a) Robinson (1971) b) Russell (1978)
   c) Van der Plank (1963) d) Nelson (1973)
7. Cotton crop belongs to family
   a) Leguminosae b) Gramineae
   c) Malvaceae d) Liliaceae
8. Colchicine is used for inducing
   a) Mutation **b) Polyploidy**
   c) Sterility d) Dormancy

9. ICPH 8 is the hybrid of crop

a) Cotton b) Safflower

c) Tur d) Sunflower

10. Which of the following is not interspecific hybrid

a) H-6 b) NHH 44

c) DCH 32 d) AHH 468

11. NBPGR is located at

a) Karnal **b) New Delhi**

c) Hyderabad d) Kanpur

12. The concept of pure line theory was developed with

a) Maize **b) Princess Bean**

c) Garden pea d) Wheat

13. Multiline is a mixture of several

a) Pure lines b) Inbred lines

c) Isogenic lines d) Clones

14. An open pollinated variety is used as a tester in

a) Simple RS **b) RS for GCA**

c) RS for SCA d) Reciprocal RS

15. The formula F1 – F2/F 1 x 100 is used for estimation of

a) Useful Heterosis b) Heterobeltiosis

c) Average Heterosis **d) Inbreeding depression**

16. The use of synthetic varieties was first suggested by

a) Mc Gill **b) Hays and Garber**

c) Jenkins d) Shull

17. Muller first used X rays for induction of mutation in

a) Drosophila b) Corn

c) Barley d) Datura

18. In half diallel total crosses among parents are equal to

a) P (P-1)/2 b) P (P+1)/2

c) P (P-1) d) P (P+1)

19. Which of the following stability analysis model is most commonly used in plant Breeding

    a) Finlay and Wilkinson model **b) Eberhart and Russell model**

    c) Perkins and Jinks model d) Freeman and Perkins model

20. Gene for gene hypothesis was proposed by

    a) Nelson **b) Flor**

    c) Van der Plank d) Robinson

21. In maize resistance to European Corn borer is associated with

    a) Waxiness of leaves b) High

    c) High DIMBOA in leaves d) High silica content in leaves

22. The term ideotype was coined by

    a) **Donald** b) Finlay

    c) Jennings d) Watson

12

Seed Technology

1. Genetic principles of seed production were given by
   - a) Feistritzer (1975)
   - **b) Kadam (1942)**
   - c) Kadam (1936)
   - d) Swaminathan (1970)
2. Objectionable weed seed in wheat seed production is
   - **a) Chandvel**
   - b) Johnsoon grass
   - c) Sudan grass
   - d) Wild rice
3. The objectives of seed certification was given by
   - a) Kadam (1942)
   - **b) Douglas ((1971)**
   - c) Agrawal (1950)
   - d) Mendel (1866)
4. Seed stratification means
   - a) Exposure of seed to chemical treatment
   - b) Exposure of seed to physical treatment
   - **c) Exposure of seed to temperature treatment**
   - d) Exposure of seed to X-ray treatment
5. In essential structure of seedling in dicot plants have
   - a) One cotyledon
   - **b) Two cotyledons**
   - c) Three cotyledons
   - d) None of these
6. Electrophoresis test is utilized for
   - **a) Identity of protein banding pattern**
   - b) Seed viability
   - c) Identity of chromosome complement
   - d) Seed germination

7. Maximum permissible limit of seed borne disease in wheat for foundation seed is

a) **0.10 %** b) 0.40 %

c) 0.50 % d) 0.30 %

8. The genetic purity are genuineness of variety is tested by

a) Viability test b) Germination test

c) **Grow out test** d) Phenol test

9. Foundation seed is the progeny of

a) Certified seed b) Nucleus seed

c) **Breeder seed** d) Truthful seed

10. Maharashtra State Seeds Corporation was established in

a) May 2004 b) **April 1976**

c) April 1970 d) June 1980

11. The legally sanctioned system for quality seed multiplication and production of notified released variety is

a) Seed production b) Seed testing

c) Seed processing d) **Seed Certification**

12. The synchrony in flowering of male and female parents in hybrid seed production is called as

a) Staggering b) **Synchronization**

c) Nicking d) None of these

13. In Jowar / Bajara hybrid seed production the male sterility exploited is

a) **Cytoplasmic genetic male sterility**

b) Genetic male sterility

c) Cytoplasmic male sterility

d) None of these.

14. In seed viability test the chemical used is

a) Sodium chloride b) **Tetrazolium**

c) Hydrogen peroxide d) None of these

15. Single shield shaped cotyledon is present in

 a) Groundnut **b) Maize**

 c) Castor d) All of these

16. Removal of off types from seed production plot is known as

 a) Rogueing b) Shattering

 c) Harvesting d) None of these

17. The headquarter of MSSC is located at

 a) Pune b) Parbhani

 c) Rahuri **d) Akola**

18. State seed certification agency is meant for

 a) Seed production **b) Seed certification**

 c) Seed processing d) Seed testing

19. The rapid seed multiplication is a goal of

 a) Seed production b) Seed technology

 c) Seed certification d) None of these

13

Seed Production

1. The nucleus seed in cereals is produced by

   a) Ear to Row method b) Plant selection

   c) Progeny selection d) Head selection

2. Foundation seed is the progeny of

   a) Truthfully Labeled seed b) Foundation seed stage I

   c) Nucleus seed **d) Breeder seed**

3. In India NSC started its function during

   a) 1963 b) 1965

   c) 1947 d) 1962

4. The breeding tool for cotton hybrid seed production is

   a) Cytoplasmic male sterility **b) Emasculation and dusting**

   c) Self incompatibility d) Geneic male sterility

5. The breeding tool utilized for redgram hybrid seed production is

   a) CMS b) CGMS

   c) GMS d) Emasculation

6. Block system is adopted for the hybrid seed production in

   a) Cotton b) Maize

   c) Sorghum d) Castor

7. The seed replacement rate of hybrids

   a) 40% b) 75%

   c) 50% **d) 100%**

8. Breeder seed is the progeny of

   a) Foundation seed b) Breeder seed

   c) Nucleus seed d) Certified acid

9. The acid used for cotton delinting
   a) Citric acid b) Acetic acid
   c) Nitric acid **d) Sulphuric acid**
10. The chemical used for dormancy breaking in sunflower
   a) GA b) Kinetin
   c) Ethrel d) Coumarin
11. Two line breeding system could be adopted for hybrid seed production
   a) Sorghum b) Cotton
   c) Paddy d) Tomato
12. Metaxenia is the symptom of deterioration in
   a) Physical purity b) Physiological quality
   c) Genetic purity d) All
13. Supplementary pollination is practiced to enhance seed set in
   a) Castor b) Redgram
   c) Chillies **d) Sunflower**
14. In verticilium wilt the vascular tissue will be
   a) Black colour **b) Pink colour**
   c) Brown colour d) Brown and black
15. In fusarium wilt the vascualr tissue will be
   a) Black colour b) Pink colour
   c) Brown colour **d) Brown and black**
16. Bt-cotton is the transgenic crop promoted against
   a) Sucking pest **b) Boll worm infestation**
   c) Storage pest d) Sitophelus
17. *Aspergillsu* spp. Is the common
   a) Field fungi **b) Storage fungi**
   c) Designated disease d) Contaminating agent
18. The widely used bio-control agent against macrophomina infection
   a) Tricoderma b) Bacillus
   c) Rhizopus d) Pseudomonas

19. The widely used nutrient as foliar spray to increase seed set in pulses
    a) NAA b) MH
    c) Ethrel **d) DAP**
20. National organization involved in seed production is
    a) NSC b) ISTA
    c) ISST d) ICAR
21. A cotton variety with colored lint
    a) Coconadal b) MCU8
    c) Sujatha d) Anjali
22. Rope pulling is practiced for good seed set in hybrid seed production of
    a) Sorghum **b) Rice**
    c) Sunflower d) Castor
23. The hybrid seed production method adopted in paddy is
    a) PGMS b) CMS
    c) TGMS **d) All**
24. Staggered sowing is practiced for
    a) Good field establishment b) Tolerate to pest and diseases
    c) Uniform flowering d) Easy processing
25. Jerking is the practice adopted in hybrid seed production of
    a) Sorghum b) Tomato
    c) Paddy **d) Bajra**
26. Occurrence of tip sterility is common in
    a) Rice b) Sorghum
    c) Barley **d) Pearlmillet**
27. Doak's method is adopted in hybrid seed production of
    a) Cotton b) Redgram
    c) Paddy d) Castor
28. Ear to row progeny method is adopted in production of
    a) Breeder seed **b) Nucleus seed**
    c) Foundation seed d) Certified seed

29. Darkened plumule occurs in

    a) Bajra **b) Groundnut**

    c) Sorghum d) Redgram

30. Darkened plumule in groundnut is occurs due to the deficiency of

    a) Boron b) Calcium

    c) Iron d) Zinc

31. Pustovit model is followed in

    a) Castor b) Cotton

    c) Cluster bean **d) Sunflower**

32. Isolation could be modified based on the number of border rows in

    a) Maize b) Sorghum

    c) Pearlmillet d) Castor

33. Temperature dependent pistillate lines are used for hybrid seed production in

    a) Redgram b) Maize

    c) Sorghum **d) Castor**

34. Inseparable other crop seed in wheat is

    a) Oat b) Rye

    c) Barley **d) All**

35. The best method for seed extraction in tomato is

    a) Acid method b) Alkali method

    c) Fermentation method d) All

36. Gibberelic acid sprayed to Hybrid Rice seed production plots for

    a) Delayed flowering b) Enhanced flowering

    c) To induce flowering **d) Complete exertion of panicle**

37. Genetic purity in the field is controlled through

    a) Seed Testing b) Seed sampling

    c) Field Inspection **d) Rogueing**

38. Synchronized flowering between parental lines of bajra is achieved by

    a) Detasseling **b) Jerking**

    c) Rope pulling d) GA spray

39. In seed production, mechanical admixtures in a seed lot affect the
    a) Physical purity b) Genetic purity
    c) Keeping quality of the seed d) Physiological quality
40. The objectionable weed in rice is
    a) *Oryza sativa V. fatua* b) Circium arvense
    c) Sorghum halopanse d) Cuscuta spp.
41. Seed plot technique is used in
    a) Cotton hybrid seed production b) Rice seed production
    c) Potato seed production d) Tomato seed production
42. The propagules of garlic is called as
    a) Rhizome **b) Bulb**
    c) Corm d) Cloves
43. Grow out test is usually conducted for
    a) Cotton b) Rice
    c) Pulses d) Sorghum
44. A male sterile line in hybrid seed production is
    a) 'B' line b) 'R' line
    c) A' line d) Maintainer line
45. Male line in hybrid seed production is called as
    a) R line b) Maintainer line
    c) Restorer line **d) a and c**
46. Maintainer line in hybrid seed production plot is called as
    a) R line **b) B line**
    c) Restore/ line d) a and c
47. Hybrid rice production is carried out by
    a) Two line b) Three line
    c) Four line **d) Multi line system**
48. Seed year was celebrated during
    a) 1968 b) 1966
    c) 1993 d) 1961
49. Type of flowers in coconut is
    a) Monoecious **b) Dioecious**
    c) Bisexual d) None

50. The pollination behavior of palm trees
    a) Self pollinated
    b) Cross pollination
    c) Often cross pollination
    d) Self and cross pollination
51. Seed production using polyploids is common in
    a) Sugarcane
    b) Sorghum
    c) Beetroot
    d) Turmeric
52. Savitha is a hybrid of
    a) Cotton
    b) Bhendi
    c) Chillies
    d) Sorghum
53. In Cotton Varalaxmi is a hybrid of
    a) Interspecific
    b) Intraspecific
    c) Both
    d) None
54. Hemp is a
    a) Pulse crop
    b) Fiber crop
    c) Fruit crop
    d) Vegetable
55. An alternate crop to sugarcane is
    a) Beetroot
    b) Sweet sorghum
    c) Sugarbeet
    d) None
56. Presence of mericarp is common feature of
    a) Anacardiaceae
    b) Umbelliferae
    c) Solanaceae
    d) Labitae
57. Heterosis is
    a) Genetic vigour
    b) Physical vigour
    c) Physiological vigour
    d) None
58. Designated inseparable other crop seed in barley is
    a) Oat
    b) Paddy
    c) Wheat
    d) a & c
59. Pollinating agent of cabbage is
    a) Insects
    b) Wind
    c) Water
    d) Ants
60. Volunteer plants are
    a) Produced by hard seeds
    b) Seed shedding
    c) Indehiscent fruits
    d) All

61. Over wintering is essential for flowering in
    a) Bhendi
    b) Onion
    c) Chow Chow
    d) Cauliflower
62. Male sterility is first identified in
    a) Onion
    b) Chillies
    c) Tomato
    d) Bittergourd
63. Detasseling is the technique used for hybrid seed production in
    a) Castor
    b) Cotton
    c) Maize
    d) Tomato
64. COTH-1 is a hybrid of
    a) Tomato
    b) Bhendi
    c) Brinjal
    d) Potato
65. The volunteer plants are
    a) Weeds
    b) Diseased plants
    c) Low vigor plants
    d) Plants of previous season
66. Downward bending of plants is called as
    a) Hyponasty
    b) Epinasty
    c) Chemostasis
    d) None
67. Epimerals are plants having
    a) Short life cycle
    b) Biennials
    c) Long life cycle
    d) All
68. Isolation distance required for tomato (variety) certified seed production
    a) 400m
    b) 100m
    c) 250m
    d) 300m
69. Folding of plant organs upon drying is called
    a) Hydrochory
    b) Autochory
    c) Xerochory
    d) Telechory
70. Adherence of seed with soil is termed as
    a) Metaspermy
    b) Myxospermy
    c) Zoospermy
    d) Biospermy
71. Plants which produces fruits beneath the soil surface is called as
    a) Bicarpic
    b) Geocarpic
    c) Epicarpic
    d) Hypocarpic

72. Example for hysterogeocarpic fruit

a) Carrot b) Potato

c) Groundnut d) Beetroot

73. Formation of fruits under the soil through gynophore is called

a) Geocarpic **b) Hysterogeocarpic**

c) Hypocarpic d) Epicarpic

74. Both fruit and flowers are borne under the soil is called

a) Hysterogeocarpic **b) Protogeocarpic**

c) Geocarpic d) None

75. Breeding tool utilized for onion hybrid seed production

a) GMS b) CMS

c) CGMS d) Emasculation & dusting

76. Heterpstyled flowers are present in

a) Potato b) Onion

c) Brinjal d) Chillies

77. Minimum Isolation Distance required for bittergourd foundation seed production

a) 800 m **b) 1000 m**

c) 400 m d) 500 m

78. Isolation distance recommended for foundation seed production in cole crops

a) 1000 mt **b) 1600 m**

c) 800 m d) 1200 m

79. A cross between parents differing in a single gene is

a) Double hybrid **b) Mono hybrid**

c) Single cross hybrid d) None

80. Author of Book on Seed Technology

a) R.L. Agrawal b) P.K. Agrawal

c) M. Bhaskaran d) Tyagi

81. The environmental factor, which influences the wheat grain dormancy, is

a) Temperature b) Relative Humidity

c) Rainfall d) All

82. The temperature which causes seed dormancy in wheat is
    a) 15-20°C b) 20-30°C
    c) 25-35°C **d) 10-20°C**
83. Pre-harvest sprouting occurs in wheat at
    a) 20-28°C b) 20-30°C
    c) 25-35°C d) 15-20°C
84. The seeds of wheat are non dormant when it develops in
    a) 5-10°C **b) 20-28°C**
    c) 10-15°C d) 15-20°C
85. Central Rice Research Institute is located in
    a) Cuttack b) Aduthurai
    c) Karnal d) Hyderabad
86. International Research Centre for Potato is located in
    a) Cali, Columbia b) Manila, Philippines
    c) Limer, Peru d) Elbaton, Mexico
87. Passport data of a seed is
    a) Seed health status
    b) Germination
    c) Purity
    d) Complete Information about the seed
88. Wonder Rice
    a) CR 20 b) IR 20
    c) IR 8 d) ADRRH-1
89. The seed obtained from single plant in a breeding programme
    a) Nucleus seed **b) Primordial seed**
    c) Basic seed d) Stock seed
90. An Autogamous oilseed
    a) Castor b) Gingelly
    c) Sunflower **d) Groundnut**
91. An Allogamous oilseed
    a) Sunflower b) Groundnut
    c) safflower d) mustard

92. An Alloautogamous oilseed
    a) Safflower
    b) Groundnut
    c) **Sesame**
    d) Mustard

93. An Autogamous cereal
    a) Rice
    b) Sorghum
    c) Bajra
    d) Ragi

94. An Allogamous cereal
    a) Ragi
    b) Rice
    c) Maize
    d) Wheat

95. An Alloautogamous cereal
    a) Sorghum
    b) Rice
    c) Ragi
    d) Wheat

96. For synchronized maturation of somatic embryos it requires
    a) GA
    b) Cytokinin
    c) Auxin
    d) ABA

97. An Autogamous pulse
    a) Cowpea
    b) Redgram
    c) Greengram
    d) None

98. An Allogamous pulse
    a) Cowpea
    b) Redgram
    c) Green gram
    d) None

99. An Alloautogamous pulse
    a) Pigeon pea
    b) Blackgram
    c) Green gram
    d) Cowpea

100. Intermediate between allo and autogamous crop
    a) Jute
    b) Cotton
    c) Rice
    d) Sorghum

101. Nature of Polyembryonic seedling
    a) 100 percent paternal
    b) 100 percent maternal
    c) Equal contribution of both percent
    d) 75 % maternal and 25 % paternal

102. Objectionable weed of rice

a) Oat b) Abelmoschos

c) Wheat **d) *Oryza sativa var. fatua***

103. Public sector organization involved in seed production is

a) ISST b) TDC

c) TUCAS **d) NSC**

104. Adaptive Research Trial is performed

a) To test the existing variety b) After releasing a variety

c) Before releasing a variety d) None

105. The gametocyde used in sorghum is

a) Colchicin b) Ethrel

c) FW 450 d) All

106. Spraying of gametocvdes induce the production of

a) Male flowers **b) Female flowers**

c) Bisexual flowers d) None

107. Top cross is otherwise known as

a) Inbred variety cross b) Single cross

c) Double cross d) Triple cross

108. Predominantly self-pollinated but often cross-pollinated crops are termed as

a) Alloautogamous b) Allogamous

c) Cleistogamous d) Autogamous

109. King of Indian forest is

a) Neem b) Rose wood

c) Casuarina **d) Teak**

110. Matured tomato fruit is accumulated with

a) Chromoplast b) Carotenoids

c) Acids d) Chlorophyll

111. During fruit maturation in tomato, chlorophyll converted into

a) Anthocyanin b) Phytochrome

c) Carotenoid **d) Chromoplast**

112. Femaie sterility in sorghum is influenced by
    a) Relative huumidity
    b) Temperature
    c) Rainfall
    d) Micro nutrient
113. Flowering from tip to bottom is
    a) Basipetal
    b) Centripetal
    c) Acropetal
    d) None
114. Flowering from centre to both sides
    a) Basipetal
    b) Centripetal
    c) Acropetal
    d) None
115. Flowering from bottom to top
    a) Acropetal
    b) Basipetal
    c) Centripetal
    d) None
116. An acropetal flowering crop
    a) Cumbu
    b) Gingelly
    c) Sorghum
    d) Rice
117. Ccentripetal flowering is seen in
    a) Pearl millet
    b) Sorghum
    c) Maize
    d) Rice
118. Example for basipetal flowering
    a) Pearlmillet
    b) Sorghum
    c) Maize
    d) Rice
119. Nature of male sterility in mustard is
    a) Nuclear
    b) Geneic
    c) Cytoplasmic
    d) Environmental
120. Monocarpic plant
    a) Bamboo
    b) Teak
    c) Rose wood
    d) Sandal
121. Among Solanaceous vegetables Sprouting is common problem in
    a) Tomato
    b) Potato
    c) Chillies
    d) Brinjal
122. The chemical which arrests the potato sprouting is
    a) CCC
    b) Methyl bromide
    c) Maleic hydrazide
    d) All

123. King of coarse grain
   a) Cumbu **b) Jowar**
   c) Ragi d) Maize

124. Chemical used as osmoregulator in synthetic seed production is
   a) ABA b) Cytokinin
   c) IAA d) GA

125. An annual cross pollinated vegetable crop
   a) Amaranthus b) Tomato
   c) Carrot d) Cauliflower

126. Fruit of rose is called as
   a) Drupe b) Achene
   c) Hip d) Done

127. The element involved in pollen grain germination
   a) Carbon b) Sulphur
   c) Boron d) Molybdenum

128. Seed multiplication ratio for potato is
   a) 1:4 b) 1:8
   c) 1:12 **d) 1:16**

129. Ideal temperature for bolting in cabbage is
   a) 10-15^{0}C b) 4-7^{0}C
   c) 3-5^{0}C d) None

130. The headquarters of ISTA is located in
   a) Holland **b) Switzerland**
   c) Copenhagen d) Washington

131. Reproduction by sexual and as well as by apomixis
   a) Facultative apomixis b) Obligate apomixes
   c) Adventitive apomixes d) None

132. Type of flowers present in banana
   a) Monoecy b) Diocecy
   c) Bisexual d) None

133. The extent of varietal contamination depends on
   a) Natural crossing b) Population of weed plants
   c) Population of diseased plants d) None

134. Varietal purity is checked by

a) **Grow out test**
b) Field plot test
c) Accelerated ageing test
d) Tetrazolium test

135. Presence of B line in A line in sunflower hybrid seed production plot is called

a) Off type
b) **Pollen shedder**
c) Rogue
d) Weed

136. Pollinator of maize

a) Bees
b) Beetles
c) Water
d) **Wind**

137. Genetic purity of seed crop is maintained by

a) Rogueing
b) Authenticated seed source
c) Isolation between fields
d) **All**

138. Seed replacement rate for maize hybrid is

a) 25 %
b) 78%
c) 69%
d) **100%**

139. In synthetic seed, the following part is the natural

a) Endosperm
b) Seed coat
c) **Embryo**
d) None

140. The following families, seeds possessed hard seed coat

a) Asteracea
b) Poacea
c) **Leguminaceae**
d) Euphorbiacea

141. During seed production hard seed causes

a) **Volunteer plants**
b) Diseased plants
c) Weed plants
d) All

142. An albuminous dicot seed

a) **Castor**
b) Peas
c) Beans
d) Mango

143. Natural inhibitor present in seeds

a) Cytokinin
b) IAA
c) **ABA**
d) GA

144. Seedless fruits are developed as a result of

a) **Parthenocarpy**
b) Sporophytic Apomixes
c) Obligate apomixes
d) Gametophytic apomixis

145. Glumes are persistent in

a) Sorghum
b) Paddy
c) **Fodder Sorghum**
d) Cumbu

146. An example for triploid endosperm is

a) Pear
b) Apple
c) **Seedless grapes**
d) Plum

147. Ganga 5 is a hybrid of

a) **Maize**
b) Sorghum
c) Bajra
d) Rice

148. Ganga 5, the hybrid maize is a product of

a) Triple cross
b) Single cross
c) **Double cross**
d) Double top cross

149. The isolation distance recommended to avoid contamination with Johnson grass in hybrid sorghum is

a) 200 m
b) 100 m
c) **400 m**
d) 50 m

150. The isolation distance in meters to avoid contamination with forage sorghum with high tillering and grassy panicle in hybrid sorghum is

a) 200 m
b) 100 m
c) **400 m**
d) 50 m

151. Differential blooming dates for modifying isolation distance are permitted in

a) Sorghum
b) Paddy
c) Wheat
d) **Maize**

152. Occurrence of Sorghum halapense in sorghum CSH5 hybrid seed production is known as

a) Pollen shedder
b) **Off type**
c) Rogue
d) Objectionable weed

153. The number of border rows required for production of certified seed class of sorghum hybrid is

a) 6
b) 5
c) **4**
d) 2

154. Normally marker plants are used to identify the following

a) Male rows
b) Female rows
c) Border row
d) Hybrid

155. The male inflorescence of maize is

a) Tassel
b) Silk
c) Cyme
d) Recemose

156. After harvest, the cobs are sorted out for

a) Off textured
b) Off colored
c) Malformed
d) All

157. The popular double cross hybrid of maize is

a) Deccan
b) Ganga 5
c) CORH1
d) CORH 2

158. The herbicide used for maize seed production is

a) Atrazine
b) Basaline
c) Glyphosate
d) All mentioned

159. In French bean seeds are produced by

a) Self pollination
b) Cross pollination
c) Often cross pollination
d) Self in compatibility

160. In seed production, the selection of land should be primarily free from

a) Off types
b) Rogues
c) Volunteer plants
d) Weeds

161. The flower colour of safflower

a) Red
b) Yellow
c) Orange
d) White

162. Seed multiplication ratio of cotton is

a) 28
b) 46
c) 52
d) 23

163. Knee bent is common in seedlings of

a) Potato
b) Tomato
c) Onion
d) Chillies

164. A biennial self fertile cross pollinated crop

a) Carrot b) Cabbage

c) Knol khol d) Cauliflower

165. Seed multiplication ratio of groundnut is

a) 1:36 **b) 1:8**

c) 1:22 d) 1:30

166. Physiological maturity symptom of ribbed gourd is

a) Complete drying of fruit b) Change of fruit color to red

c) Turn of fruit color to yellow d) Change of fruit color tc black

167. Pollen viability period of cotton flower is

a) 36 hour **b) 24 hour**

c) 22 hour d) 30 hour

168. In cauliflower optimum temperature required for curd formation is

a) Below 5°C **b) 6.5 to 11°C**

c) 10 to 15°C d) 0 to 5°C

169. Seed multiplication ratio of ragi is

a) 1:420 **b) 1:200**

c) 1:300 d) 1:100

170. Seed renewal period for bajra variety is

a) 2 year b) 1 year

c) 3 year d) 6 months

171. The physiological maturation symptom of bhendi is

a) Mellowing of fruit **b) Hairline crack in fruits**

c) Hardening of fruits d) Change of seed color into black

172. Objectionable weed plant of cucumber is

a) *Cucumis hardwickii* b) *Ciirullus lanatus*

c) *Cucumis sativus* d) *Citrullus colosynthis*

173. Kamnganni cotton is

a) *G. arboreum* b) *G. Herbaasum*

c) *G. barbadense* d) *G. hirsiitum*

174. The rattle sound during shaking of fruit is the symptom of proper drying in

a) Bhendi **b) Groundnut**

c) Bittergourd d) Cotton

175. Mottled Seed coat is seen in

a) Castor b) Greengram

c) Bengalgram d) Blackgram

176. Planting ratio for bajra hybrid seed production is

a) 2:5 b) 2:6

c) 2:8 d) 2:4

177. The number of border rows for hybrid seed production of bajra is

a) 6 **b) 8**

c) 10 d) 4

178. Planting ratio for sorghum hybrid sccd production is

a) 2:4 b) 2:6

c) 2:8 d) 2:5

179. The number of border rows recommended for hybrid seed production of sunflower is

a) 8 b) 6

c) 10 **d) 4**

180. Planting ratio recommended for sunflower hybrid seed production is

a) 3:1 b) 3:2

c) 2:3 d) 3:3

181. Pusa synthetic is a hybrid of

a) Cabbage **b) Cauliflower**

c) Knol-khol d) Carrot

182. International Cotton Advisory Committee is located at

a) Paris b) Rome

c) Washington d) Mumbai

183. Optimum temperature required for cauliflower seed production is

a) 25 to 28°C b) 5 to 10°C

c) 12 to 18°C d) 18 to 25°C

184. The inflorescence of maize tassel is
   a) Spike b) Panicle
   c) Branched panicle d) Spadix
185. The duration required for complete opening of staminate flowers in maize
   a) 14 days b) One week
   c) 2 days d) 20 days
186. The commercial uses of maize is prominent in
   a) Dextrose industry b) Brewery industry
   c) Alcohol industry **d) All**
187. Objectionable weed of water
   a) *Cucumis hardwickii* b) *Cucumis sativus*
   c) *Citrullus lanatus* **d) *Citrulhis colosynthis***
188. In single cross hybrid seed production, the pedigree involved is
   a) A x B
   b) (A x B) x C
   c) (A x B) x open pollinated variety
   d) (A x B) x (C x D)
189. In three way cross hybrid seed production, the pedigree involved is
   a) A x B
   b) (A x B) xC
   c) (A x B) x open pollinated variety
   d) (AxB) x (C xD)
190. A dioecious annual vegetable crop
   a) Spinach b) Knoll-khol
   c) Radish d) Turnip
191. Often cross pollinated hermaphrodite annual crop
   a) Amaranthus b) Spinach
   c) Bnendi d) Water melon
192. Self incompatible vegetable crop
   a) Carrot b) Onion
   c) Spinach **d) Cabbage**
193. DSR (Directorate of Seed Research) is located at
   a) Mau b) Delhi
   c) Coimbatore d) Hyderabad

194. PPV and FRA denote
    a) Protection of Plant Varieties and Farmers Right Act
    b) Patenting of Plant Varieties and Farmers Right Act
    c) Patenting of Protected Varieties and Farmers Right Act
    d) Protection of Plant Varieties and Farmers Representation Act
195. PPV and FR was implemented in India from
    a) January 1, 2005 b) July 1, 1991
    c) October 2, 1969 d) December 29, 1966
196. The first transgenic crop cleared by GEAC
    a) Bt cotton b) Bt corn
    c) Bt cauliflower d) Bt Brinjal
197. The Golden rice is rich in
    a) Vitamin A b) β-carotene
    c) Protein d) Vitamin C
198. The transgenic golden rice was developed by
    a) IRRI, Manila b) IPS, Switzerland
    c) IARI, Delhi **d) a and b**
199. The gene responsible for creation of bt toxin in seeds is
    a) Cry gene b) VIP gene
    c) Protein d) TRYPSIN
200. VIP stands for
    a) Vegetative Insecticidal Protein
    b) Vigour improvement programme
    c) Viability identification project
    d) Vegetative improvement programme
201. The plant originated insecticidal protein
    a) Trypsin inhibitase b) Lactin
    c) Chiitinase **d) All**
202. The advanced technology responsible for introduction of specific genes into seeds is
    a) Recombinant gene technology
    b) QTL
    c) RFLP
    d) PCR

203. Gossypium hirsutum has 2n number of

a) 52 b) 26

c) 32 d) 13

204. The cotton variety suitable for rice fallow under Tamil Nadu Condition is

a) TCHB213 b) MCU8

c) MCU 7 d) MCU12

205. In Cotton, MCU stands for

a) Madras Combodia Uganda b) Madurai Cotton Union

c) Madras Cotton Uganda d) Madurai Combodia Uganda

206. TMC stands for

a) Techniques of Multiple Cotton

b) Technology Mission on Cotton

c) Technology of Modem Cotton

d) Techniques for Multiplication of Cotton

207. Example of naked seed cotton variety

a) Suvin b) MCU7

c) LRA5166 d) ANJALI

208. Cotton variety developed by genie male sterility is

a) Surabhi b) Suvin

c) Suguna d) Shruthi

209. Example of interspecific cotton (G. hirsutum x G.barbadense) hybrid

a) Varalakshmi b) AAH-1

c) CICRH1 d) Lakshmi

210. The cotton hybrid having a special character of presence of genetic markers

a) CICRH1 b) TCHB213

c) TM1312 d) DCH-32

211. The only cotton variety adaptable to different environmental conditions

a) LRA5166 b) Anjali

c) Arogya d) MCU10

212. Uppam cotton is

a) *Gossypium arboretum* **b) *Gossypium herbaceum***

c) *Gossypium barbadense* d) *Gossypmm hirsutum*

213. Upland cotton is

a) *Gossypium arboreum* b) *Gossypium barbadense*

c) *Gossypium barbadense* **d) *Gossypium hirsutum***

214. The cotton variety resistant to verticilium wilt is

a) TCHB213 b) SVPR1

c) MCU-5VT d) MCU5

215. Bt cotton varieties developed by MAHYCO company under commercial cultivation are

a) MECH 12 b) MECH 22

c) MECH 32 d) MECH 42

216. Mosaic disease of Urd bean is first reported during 1963 from

a) IARI b) MAU

c) HAU d) TNAU

217. Seedling blight of maize is

a) Soil and seed borne b) Seed borne

c) Wind borne d) Soil borne

218. In cotton, leaf / boll shedding can be reduced by spraying of

a) CCC **b) NAA**

c) $ZnSO_4$ d) $MgSO_4$

219. In cotton, Tirak disorder refers to

a) Zn deficiency b) Mg deficiency

c) Bad opening of bolls d) N_2 deficiency

220. In cotton, topping can be done by spraying of

a) Urea b) NAA

c) CCC d) DAP

221. Gypsum is applied during earthing up for better pod formation in

a) Redgram **b) Groundnut**

c) Gingelly d) Greengram

222. Breeder seed is the progeny of

a) Nucleus seed b) Registered seed

c) Foundation seed d) Certified seed

223. Avicinnia seeds are dispersed by

a) Animals b) Wind

c) Ants d) Water

224. The temperature range which aggravate the seedling blight of maize

a) 18-26°C b) 20-25°C
c) 10-15°C d) 15-20°C

225. Tag color of Breeder seed is

a) Opal green **b) Golden yellow**
c) White d) Blue

226. Isolation distance for foundation seed production of sun flower

a) 400 **b) 600**
c) 800 d) 1000

227. The chemical used for enclosing the synthetic seed is

a) EDTA **b) Sodium alginate**
c) PEG d) Calcium oxy chloride

228. Acid recommended for breaking physical dormancy is

a) Sulphuric acid b) HC1
c) HNO_3 d) Gibberellic acid

229. Convenient method of seed collection in teak is

a) Crown collection b) Climbing by trees
c) Ground collection d) Shooting down branches

230. Example for Monocarpic plant is

a) Bamboo b) Casuarinas
c) Pine d) Terminalia

231. The species which required after ripening period for dormancy breaking is

a) Jamun b) Avicennia
c) Gmelina **d) Ginkgo**

232. Best suited season for planting TPS.

a) April-May b) May-June
c) June-July d) July-August

233. The fruits which passed through the animal intestine and aids in seed dispersal is called as

a) Ectozoochory b) Mimichory
c) Animochory **d) Endozoochory**

234. Isolation distance for foundation seed production of onion is

a) 400 m
b) 1000 m
c) 500 m
d) 800 m

235. In fodder sorghum, grain dormancy is influenced by

a) Provenance
b) Nutrient
c) Moisture stress
d) Environment

236. Optimum season of planting onion bulbs for seed production is

a) Nov-Dec
b) June-July
c) May-June
d) Aug-Sep

237. Colored pigment present in immatured cotton seed is

a) Gossypol
b) Anthocyanine
c) Carotenoids
d) Xanthophyll

238. Progeny of nucleus seed

a) Breeder seed
b) Foundation seed
c) Registered seed
d) Certified seed

239. Seed Village concept is adopted in

a) Andhra Pradesh
b) Karnataka
c) Bihar
d) Both a & b

240. The tool utilized for hybrid seed production in brinjal

a) CMS
b) GMS
c) CGMS
d) Manual modification

241. MCU-5vt cotton is a

a) Hybrid
b) Essentially derived variety
c) Special purpose variety
d) Independently derived variety

242. The headquarters of Central Institute for Cotton Research (CICR), is located at

a) Coimbatore
b) Mumbai
c) Nagpur
d) Delhi

243. The breeding tool utilized for hybrid seed production in redgram

a) Self incompatibility
b) CMS
c) GMS
d) Hand emasculation and dusting

244. A pseudocereal crop

a) Ragi
b) Jowar
c) Maize
d) Amaranthus

245. Maize crop is highly respensive to this micro nutrient

a) Boron b) Ferrous

c) Zinc d) Manganeses

246. The designated disease of wheat is

a) Grain smut b) Karnal bunt

c) Head smut **d) Loose smut**

247. The inflorescence of onion

a) Panicle b) Spike

c) Cormbose **d) Umbel**

248. Presence of Embryoless seed is common feature in

a) Fennel b) Fenugreek

c) Carrot d) Potato

249. The orchid seeds are germinated in

a) Sand medium b) Roll towel

c) Nutrient agar medium d) All

250. The examples for the seeds without nutritive tissue (endosperm)

a) Amaranthus b) Panicum grass seed

c) Orchid seed d) Onion

251. Seed is defined as

a) Matured ovule b) Embryo enclosed in a seed coat

c) Any propagative material **d) All**

252. The amino acid which have symmetric carbon atom

a) Alanine b) Methienine

c) Valine **d) Alycine**

253. The plant pigment responsible for seed dormancy and seed germination is

a) Xanthophyll b) Chlorophyll

c) Anthocyanin **d) Phytochrome**

254. The dormancy present in seeds of crops belonging to Fabaceae family is

a) Morphological dormancy b) Physiological dormancy

c) Physical dormancy d) Combined dormancy

255. The characteristic feature of morphological dormancy I the presence of

a) **Under developed embryo** b) Hard seed coat

c) Inhibitors d) No endosperm

256. The eminent feature that differentiate Angiosperm and Gymnospern seed is

a) **Seed coat** b) Embryo

c) Endosperm d) Cotyledon

257. The synthetic seed is

a) Fluid drilled seed b) Seed without seed coat

c) Seed tablet d) **Artificial seed**

258. Sucrose is a

a) Monosaccharide b) **Oligosaccharide**

c) Trisaccharide d) Polysaccharide

259. The modern techniques for varietal identification is

a) **Electrophoresis** b) Growout test

c) Phenol test d) Peroxidase test

260. The enzyme responsible for prediction of viability through Tetrazolium test is

a) Peroxidase b) Amylase

c) Super oxide dismutase d) **Dehydrogenase**

261. The book on Seed Viability was written by

a) R.N. Basu b) Ellies

c) Frederic Nobbe d) **E.H. Roberts**

262. Lettuce seed exhibits dormancy of

a) **Photodormancy** b) Innate dormancy

c) Induced dormancy d) Physiological dormancy

263. A trisaccharide

a) Sucrose b) **Raffinose**

c) Glucose d) Maltose

264. A non-sugar carbohydrate

a) Sucrose b) Maltose

c) **Starch** d) Raffinose

265. Cotyledon of monocot is
   a) Coleorhiza
   b) Aleuron layer
   c) Scutellum
   d) Coleoptile
266. The aleuron layer of monocot seed is
   a) Dead
   b) Viable
   c) Non-viable
   d) None
267. Cotyledon is the storage tissue in
   a) Castor
   b) Sorghum
   c) Cluster bean
   d) Ragi
268. The special feature of bajra flower that favours cross pollination is
   a) Self incompatibility
   b) Protogyny
   c) Prtoandry
   d) Heterostyly
269. Caruncle is a type of
   a) Aril
   b) Fuzz
   c) Lint
   d) Elaiosome
270. An Alloautogamous oilseed is
   a) Safflower
   b) Groundnut
   c) Sesame
   d) Mustard
271. Disintegration of parts of seed during abscission
   a) Rhenolysis
   b) Schizolysis
   c) Histolysis
   d) None
271. The ecological suicide of the crop seeds occur at field due to accumulation of
   a) HCN
   b) Ethylene
   c) Carbon monoxide
   d) Carbon disulphide
272. Malachite green test used to identify
   a) Germination %
   b) Viability
   c) Vigour
   d) Mechanical damage
273. Tetrazolium test is used for evaluation of
   a) Dormancy
   b) Viability
   c) Vigour
   d) Mechanical damage
274. The seeds of castor has the following appendage
   a) Awn
   b) Bridle
   c) Wing
   d) Caruncle

275. Multi and monogerm seeds are available in

a) **Beet root** b) Carrot
c) Coriander d) Onion

276. Seed to solution ratio is less in this seed treatment

a) **Hardening** b) Fortification
c) Dormancy breaking d) Mid storage correction

277. The final product of the TZ test is

a) Dehydrogenase b) TZ chloride
c) **Triphenyl Formosan** d) All

278. The color of Formosan in TZ test is

a) **Pink** b) Yellow
c) Colorless d) White

279. TZ test is otherwise called as

a) Vigor test b) **Quick viability test**
c) Germination test d) Seedling evaluation test

280. Vigor loss

a) Proceeds viability lossy
b) **Preceeds viability loss**
c) Simultaneously occur with viability loss
d) 2°C

281. G A is

a) Cell division factor b) **Cell elongation factor**
c) Root initiation factor d) Short initiation factor

282. The chemical which cause seed dormancy in Coriander is

a) Phenol b) ABA
c) CCC d) **Coumarine**

283. Parthenocarpy means

a) Viable seed b) Non-viable seed
c) **Without zygote formation** d) None

284. In seed, inner membranous layer is called

a) Testa b) **Tegmin**
c) Integument d) Hilum

285. Aril is a seed structure which is present in
   a) Castor   b) Coconut
   c) Nutmeg   d) Oil palm
286. In dicots food materials are stored in
   a) Endosperm   b) Embryo
   c) Cotyledons   d) None
287. Nucellus of the embryosac after fertilization is used for development of
   a) Endosperm   b) Perisperm
   c) Seed coat   d) Embryo
288. Food material is supplied to embryo in monocot through
   a) Scutellum   b) Plumule
   c) Radicle   d) Coleoptile
289. Shield shaped cotyledon present in monocot is called
   a) Embryonic axis   b) Coleorhiza
   c) Scutellum   d) Tegmen
290. Maturation of male and female parts of flowers at different time is called
   a) Herkogamy   **b) Dichogamy**
   c) Syngamy   d) Autogamy
291. Allogamy favours
   a) Self pollination   **b) Cross pollination**
   c) Self incompatibility   d) Parthenocarpy
292. Cleistogamous favours
   a) Self pollination   b) Cross pollination
   c) Self incompatibility   d) Parthenocarpy
293. Herkogamy means male and female flowers
   a) Matured at different time   b) Matured at same time
   c) Have a barrier   d) None
294. Endospermic dicot seed
   a) Chickpea   b) Bean
   c) Groundnut   **d) Fenugreek**
295. Strophiole controls
   a) Respiration   b) Transpiration
   c) Photosynthesis   **d) Imbibitions of water**

296. In an embryo, embryonic root is

a) Radicel b) Plumule
c) Hypocotyl d) Coleoptile

297. Caryopsis is the fruit of

a) Leguminaceae b) Labitae
c) Malvaceae **d) Poaceae**

298. Single seeded fruit which have fused fruit and seed wall is

a) Schizocarp b) Nut
c) Achene **d) Caryopsis**

299. The perisperm is present in

a) Coconut **b) Coffee**
c) Maize d) Cucurbit seeds

300. Hypo-epigeal germination is seen in

a) Groundnut b) Lettuce
c) Peperomia peruviana d) Castor

301. Monocot seed which has epigeal germination is

a) Maize b) Barley
c) Oats **d) Onion**

302. Beta vulgaris is a

a) Monogerm seed b) Multi germ seed
c) Viviparous seeds **d) 1 & 2**

303. Palenology is deals with

a) Study of seed b) Study of flower
c) Study of pollen d) Study on seed pests

304. Zoophyllous means pollination by

a) Animals b) Birds
c) Water d) Wind

305. Albuminous proteins are

a) Soluble in water b) Soluble in air
c) Soluble in acid d) Soluble in alcohol

306. Storage protein present in wheat is

a) Glutelin b) Prolamin
c) Albumin d) Globulin

307. Storage protein of paddy is

a) Glutelin b) Prolamin

c) Albumin d) Globulin

308. Storage protein of barley is

a) VIscin b) Zein

c) Hordem d) Albumin

309. Eminent prolamin in wheat is

a) Zein b) Hordein

c) Glaiden d) Globulin

310. Eminent prolamin present in maize is

a) Zein b) Hordein

c) Glaiden d) Globulin

311. Paddy seeds lack in

a) Zein b) Albumin

c) Globulin **d) Prolamin**

312. Legume proteins are

a) Visilins b) Legumins

c) 1 & 2 d) None

313. Mostly Dicot seeds are absent in

a) Albumin b) Prolamin

c) Glutelin d) Globulin

314. Protein is present in seeds in the form of

a) Crystallin b) Metallic

c) Non-metallic d) None

315. The proteins present in peanut is

a) Arachin and Conarachim b) Arachidinic

c) Fabain d) Viscin

316. The protein present in soybean is

a) Glycine b) Arachin

c) Zein d) Conarchin

317. The protein present in hemp is

a) Edestin b) Zein

c) Hordein **d) Glaiden**

318. The protein present in peas is

a) **Vicilin** b) Zein
c) Glycine d) Glutelin

319. In Gymnospermous seeds, the food is stored in

a) Cotyledon b) Seed coat
c) Embryo **d) Megagametophyte**

320. The composition of glycoprotein is presence of

a) Natural sugars and glucose **b) Protein with carbohydrate**
c) Protein with iron, d) Simple protein

321. Heterogenity is less in

a) Enzyme protein **b) Non-enzyme protein**
c) Storage protein d) Haemoprotein

322. Heterogeneity is more in

a) Enzyme protein b) Non-enzyme protein
c) Storage protein d) Haemoprotein

323. Seed coat impermeability in Sida spinosa is due to

a) Hard cells b) Phenols
c) Lignins d) None

324. The type of germination in Pisum is

a) Epigeal **b) Hypogeal**
c) Both d) Hypo- epigeal

325. In Fagus, the type of Germination is

a) Epigeal b) Hypogeal
c) Both d) Hypo- epigeal

326. In Robina, the type of Germination is

a) Epigeal b) Hypogeal
c) Both d) Hypo- epigeal

327. In Juglans, the type of Germination is

a) Epigeal **b) Hypogeal**
c) Both d) Hypo- epigeal

328. Allelopathic chemical which present in Juglans is

a) Viscin **b) Juglone**
c) Cyanidin d) Quinone

329. The allelopathic chemical which present in Eucalyptus is
  a) Terpene b) Cyanidin
  c) Quinone d) Viscin

330. The hard seed which possess viviparous germination is
  a) Medicago b) Delonix
  c) Cassia **d) Acacia**

331. Differences in vigor between two seed lots of same hybrid is
  a) Genetic vigour b) Physical vigour
  c) Physiological vigour d) None

332. Electrical Conductivity of seed steep water is negatively correlated with
  a) Seed moisture content b) Seed viability
  c) Seed vigour d) Seed health

333. More number of glycosidic linkages are seen in
  a) Oligosaccharides **b) Polysaccharides**
  c) Monosaccharides d) Disccharides

334. The seed coat of apple is Impermeable to
  a) Water **b) Gas**
  c) Light d) All

335. Sporophytic self incompatibility is seen in
  a) Cruciferae b) Leguminacae
  c) Cucurbitaceae d) Umbelliferae

336. The Mn deficiency in onion leads to
  a) Black plumule b) Gmmative seeds
  c) Shrivelled seed **d) Reduced germination**

337. High Electrical Conductivity of seed leachate indicates the
  a) High respiration rate **b) Membrane weakness**
  c) Loss of food reserve d) All

338. The living bodies which present in a cell is collectively called as
  a) Cell inclusions b) Protoplasm
  c) Nucleus **d) Cell organelles**

339. The non- living bodies which present in a cell is collectively called as
  a) Cell inclusions b) Protoplasm
  c) Nucleus d) Cell organelles

340. Leaf like cotyledons are present in
a) Cucurbits
b) Cruciferae
c) Solanaceae
d) Pepporomia

341. Mitochondria which present in a cell is a
a) Cell inclusions
b) Living
c) Cell organelles
d) Both b & c

342. Lysosomes are called as
a) Power house of cell
b) Suicidal bag of cells
c) Respiration site
d) Site of glycolysis

343. Endoplasmic reticulum is a
a) Cell inclusions
b) Living
c) Cell organelles
d) Both b & c

344. Endoplasmic reticulum is placed between
a) Plasma membrane and nucleus
b) Plasma membrane and mitochondria
c) Plasma membrane and golgi bodies
d) Vacuoles and nucleus t

345. Mechanical tearing of abscission tissue during seed dispersal is called as
a) Rhenolysis
b) Schizolysis
c) Histolysis
d) None

346. Name of the fatty acid which present in Elaiosome is
a) Erucic
b) Ricinolic
c) Linoleic
d) Arachidinic

347. The nature of fatty acid in elaiosome is
a) Saturated
b) Unsaturated
c) Poly unsaturated
d) Poly saturated

348. Ricinolic acid is present in
a) Cucurbits
b) Maize
c) Castor
d) Rape seed

349. Site of Cell wall synthesis
a) Lysosomes
b) Lomosomes
c) Golgi bodies
d) Vacuole

350. Desiccation of germinating seed is prevented by presence
a) Seed coat
b) Endosperm
c) Mucilage
d) Perisperm

351. Bio-safety regulation were first prepared in the year

a) 1996 **b) 1990**

c) 1998 d) 2003

352. In a dormant seed, embryo growth is

a) Arrested b) Prevented

c) Inhibited d) Induced

353. Suspension of germination by unfavorable environmental conditions is called

a) Physical Dormancy b) Embryo dormancy

c) Quiescence d) Mechanical dormancy

354. Suspension of seed germination

a) Dormancy b) Dead

c) Hard d) All

355. Precursor for ethylene synthesis is

a) Methionine and b-alanine **b) Tryptaphene**

c) Phytiri d) Glutaline

356. The wavelength of 700 to 800 nm carries

a) Plant pfr b) Fungal pfr

c) Algal pfr d) Bacterial pfr

357. The wavelength of 400 to 510 nm in plants causes

a) Stomatal opening b) Stomatal closure

c) Rosetting of leaves **d) Internodal elongation**

358. Example for varied depth of dormancy in single fruit is

a) Accacia spp b) Terminalia spp.

c) Bidens bipinnat d) Tectonu grandis

359. Phytochrome has close association with

a) Starch **b) Protein**

c) Fats d) Vitamins

360. Phytochrome associated proteins are called as

a) Glutalines b) Phytins

c) Prolamines **d) Chromographic proteins**

361. The color of the phytochrome is

a) Green b) Red

c) Blue d) Blue-green

362. Oxygen pressure which favors germination is

a) 0.05 atm
b) 0.08 atm
c) 0.01 atm
d) 0.10 atm

363. Dormant seed of Agrostrema githago is broken under

a) High oxygen content
b) High nitrogen content
c) High water content
d) High carbon-di-oxide concentration

364. State of seed dormancy under particular temperature and the non dormancy of same seed at another temperature is termed as

a) Relative dormancy
b) Photodormancy
c) Skotodormancy
d) Thermodormancy

365. Pre cursor of lignin

a) Phenol
b) Tannin
c) Carotein
d) Chlorogenic acid

366. Most common form of transportable carbon imported into seeds is

a) Nitrogen
b) Ammonia
c) Sucrose
d) None

367. In cantor calvin cycle enzymes are found in

a) Choloroplast
b) Cell wall
c) Nucleus
d) None

368. Carbon source for synthesis of lipid is

a) Sucrose
b) Fatty acids
c) Aminoacids
d) None

369. Phospholipids are present in

a) Deteriorated cells
b) Non-living cells
c) Living cells
d) All

370. Sterols are soluble in

a) Water
b) Acid
c) Alcohol
d) Fat solvents

371. Diosgenin which is present in Dioescoria sp is a

a) Steroid
b) Alkaloid
c) Hormone
d) Terpene

372. Carotenoids contain

a) **Oxygen** b) Nitrogen
c) Hydrogen d) Helium

373. Carotenoids absence of oxygen is

a) Xanthophyll **b) Carotenes**
c) Both d) None

374. In Greek "Protein" means

a) Gram b) Rich food
c) Prime food **d) First rank**

375. Example for carotenoid which contain oxygen is

a) Xanthophyll b) Carotenes
c) Both d) None

376. Free super oxide radical is

a) Mutant **b) Cytotoxic**
c) Promoter d) All

377. Lipoprotein is a

a) Simple protein b) Conjucated protein
c) Derived protein d) All

378. The major auxin in developing seed is

a) Cytokinin **b) IAA**
c) Kinetin d) All

379. Pre cursor for 1AA is

a) Acetyl Co-A b) Trypsin
c) Tryptophan d) None

380. Commonly used synthetic Gibberellin is

a) GA_3 b) GA_5
c) GA_7 d) GA_{21}

381. During seed storage, free super oxide radical is generated by

a) Mutation b) Growth of microorganisms
c) Enzyme oxidation d) None

382. Tocopherol is

a) Vitamin E b) Growth regulator
c) Insecticide d) Herbicide

383. H_2O_2 in aged seeds is removed by the enzyme
   a) Catalase b) Super oxide dismutase
   c) Peroxidase d) Amylases
384. Site of rRNA genes are
   a) Mitochondria b) Golgi bodies
   c) Nucleolus d) Vacuoles
385. The damage in rRNA can be
   a) Irreparable **b) Repairable**
   c) Compensate by rRNA d) None
386. Nucleotidyl transferase is
   a) An enzyme b) A compensator of rRNA
   c) An antioxidant d) None
387. Nucleotidyl transferase rapairs the damage in
   a) mRNA b) RRNA
   c) tRNA d) DNA
388. Dormancy influenced by seed color
   a) Red gram b) Cowpea
   c) Salsola volvensii d) Casurina
389. Color of non-dormant seeds of salsola are
   a) Brown **b) Green**
   c) Black d) Grey color
390. The colour of dormant seeds of salsola are
   a) Black b) Green
   c) Brown **d) Grey**
391. Differential dormancy in Bidens is due to
   a) Environment
   b) Genetic
   c) Interaction of environment and genetic
   d) Edaphic
392. Hordeum exhibits the dormancy of
   a) Physical b) Physiological
   c) Chemical **d) Both a & c**
393. The dormant seed part of hordeum is
   a) Embryo b) Endosperm
   c) Seed coat d) All

394. In Synopsis, the type of dormancy is
a) Morphological
b) Physiological
c) Physical
d) Both a & c

395. Sprouted cereal grains are rich in
a) Alpha amylase
b) GA
c) Beta amylase
d) Starch

396. In synthetic seed production Auxin and cytokinin induces
a) Proliferation of somatic embryos
b) Somaclonal variation
c) Microbial growth
d) Darkening of the media

397. Alkaloids are rich in
a) Hydrogen
b) Nitrogen
c) Oxygen
d) Hydrocarbons

398. Gossypol is a type of
a) Alcohol
b) Alkaloid
c) Aldehyde
d) Chlorophyll

399. Color of gossypol pigment is
a) Yellow
b) Green
c) Pink
d) Red

400. Gossypol is present in the seeds of
a) Blackgram
b) Cotton
c) Sunflower
d) Maize

401. Protochlorophyll is a
a) Alkaloid
b) Pigment
c) Aldehyde
d) Alcohol

402. Protochlorophyll is present in
a) Cucurbits
b) Crucifers
c) Pulses
d) Oil seeds

403. The color of amylase on exposure to iodine solution
a) Yellow
b) Green
c) Blue
d) Purple red

404. The color of amylopectin when exposed to iodine solution is
a) Yellow
b) Blue
c) Green
d) Purple red

405. Amylose percentage in a starch grain is
a) **20-25%** b) 10-15%
c) 15-20% d) 25-30%

406. Amylopectin percentage in starch grain is
a) 30-35% b) 25-30%
c) 50-75% d) 35-40%

407. Glycolysis takes place in
a) Mitochondria **b) Cytoplasm**
c) Endoplasmic reticulum d) Nucleus

408. The phase after imbibition and before radicle protrusion during germination
a) Lag phase b) Log phase
c) Both d) None

409. Albumins are coagulated by
a) Cooling b) Pasturization
c) Heating d) None

410. Leucosins are
a) Fatty acid b) Pigments
c) Alkaloids **d) Protein**

411. Albumins are soluble in
a) Alcohol b) Acid
c) Water d) Saline solution

412. Globulins are soluble in
a) Water **b) Saline solution**
c) Acid d) Alcohol

413. Metabolically non active substance
a) Glutalins b) Globulin
c) Albumin d) Leucosin

414. Oryzenin of rice is a
a) Globulin **b) Glutalin**
c) Albumin d) Leucosin

415. Legumin of peas are
a) Leucosin b) Glutalin
c) Albumin **d) Globulin**

416. Protein which is much useful in varietal identification is
a) Albumin
b) Glutaline
c) Prolamine
d) All

417. Trypsin is
a) An inhibitor
b) A promoter
c) A growth hormone
d) An enzyme

418. Trypsin is present in
a) Rice
b) Cowpea
c) Soybean
d) Wheat

419. Morphine is
a) Protein
b) An alkaloid
c) An amino acid
d) A phenolic compound

420. Morphine is present in
a) Coffee beans
b) Poppy seed
c) Nut meg
d) Cinnamomum

421. Nitrate along with ethylene promotes
a) Vigour
b) Dormancy
c) Viability
d) Germination

422. Dark germination of chenopodium album is promoted by
a) KNO_3
b) Ethylene
c) KNO_3 with ethylene
d) GA

423. Ethylene production is favored in soil at
a) Low pH
b) High pH
c) Neutral pH
d) No change in ethylene production due to varying soil pH

424. The seed which produces ethylene is
a) Xanthium
b) Chenopodium
c) Neerium
d) Calotropis

425. Ethylene production is more is
a) Non dormant seeds
b) Dormant seed
c) Hard seed
d) All

426. A germination inhibiting alkaloid is
a) Coumarin
b) Abisinthin
c) Phenol
d) Tannin

427. Abisinthin is a germination inhibiting alkaloid present in
 a) *Santalum album* **b) *Artemesia abisinthium***
 c) *Bauhinia varigata* d) *Pongamia pinnata*
428. Synthesis of hydrolytic enzymes in germinating cereal grain starts from
 a) Embryo b) Endosperm
 c) Aleuron layer d) Seed coat
429. Synthesis of enzymes in germinating seed is controlled by
 a) Gibberellins b) Ethylene
 c) IAA d) Kinetin
430. Stimulation of alpha amylase synthesis by GA is enhanced
 a) Kinetin b) Ethylene
 C) IAA **d) Cytokinin**
431. For synthesis of alpha amylase, cytokinins are released from
 a) Aleurone layer **b) Endosperm**
 c) Embryo d) All
432. The seed structure essential for synthesis of hydrolyzing enzymes
 a) Embry **b) Wndosperm**
 c) Test d) Tegmen
433. In rice epithelium layer of scutellum is the source for
 a) GA b) Cytokinin
 c) Alpha and beta amylase d) All
434. Early source of alpha amylase during maize seed germination is
 a) Endosperm **b) Scutellum**
 c) Aluerone layer d) Embryo
435. In seeds energy mobilization is enhanced by the enzyme
 a) Lyases b) Catalases
 c) Aluerone layer d) Embryo
436. Energy mobilization in squash seed is enhanced by
 a) Catalase **b) Iso citrate lyase**
 c) Amylases d) All
437. Pulse proteins are deficient in
 a) Cytein b) Cystine
 c) Methionine d) All

438. Nucleic acid metabolism is enhanced by
a) ABA
b) GA
c) Ethylene
d) IAA

439. Protein metabolism increases with the higher concentration of
a) GA
b) Ethylene
c) ABA
d) IAA

440. Type of dormancy in *Terminalia* spp.
a) Mechanical dormancy
b) Physical dormancy
c) Physiological dormancy
d) Combined dormancy

441. In synthetic seed production, methylation causes
a) Callus formation
b) Somaclonal variation
c) Embryogenesis
d) None

442. The product of lipolysis
a) Glucose
b) Glycerol and Free Fatty Acid
c) Amino acids
d) Free radicals

443. Sequential removal of one carbon atom from fatty acids
a) Beta oxidation
b) Autooxidation
c) Alpha oxidation
d) None

444. b -oxidation is directly coupled with
a) Glycolisis
b) Kreb cycle
c) Glycosylate cycle
d) Calvin cycle

445. The Free Fatty Acid production from fat is due to
a) Anabolism
b) Condensation
c) Hydrolysis
d) None

446. Hydrolysis of fat takes place in
a) Amyloplast
b) Starch grains
c) Oleosomes
d) Protein bodies

447. Oxidation of fatty acid takes placeman
a) Golgi apparatus
b) Glyoxysomes
c) Lysosomes
d) Endoplasmic reticulum

448. Conversion of malate to succinate takes place in
a) Nucleus
b) Lysosomes
c) Mitochondria
d) Golgi bodies

449. Conversion of malate to sucrose takes place in

a) **Cytosol** b) Mitochondria

c) Lysosomes d) Nucleus

450. Conversion of glycerol into sucrose is the process of

a) Starch degradation **b) Fat degradation**

c) Protein degradation d) None

451. Cleavation of internal peptide bonds is carried by enzymes

a) Endopeptidases b) Ectopepciidases

c) Proteases d) Amino peptidases

452. Enzyme responsible for elevation of terminal amino acids is

a) Carboxy peptidases b) Endopeptidases

c) Exopepdidases **d) Aminopeptidases**

453. Sequential hydrolyzing of single amino acid is activated

a) Aminopeptidases **b) Carboxy peptidases**

c) Endopeptidases d) Ectopepdidases

454. In legumes, major transportable form of amino acid is

a) Glutelin **b) Asparagine**

c) Globulin d) Methionine

455. In peas, major transportable form of amino acid is

a) Methionine b) Asparagines

c) Hemoserine d) Trypsin

456. In castor, major transportable form of amino acid is

a) Globulin **b) Glutarnine**

c) Hemoserine d) Asparagine

457. Source of phosphate in dry grains

a) Pyruvic acid b) Phytic acid

c) Phytin d) None

458. In cereals, phytin is stored in

a) Aleurone layer b) Endosperm

c) Scutellum d) Embryo

459. Special cells between macroscleroids and parenchymatous cells of seed coat

a) Scleronchyma b) Colenchyma

c) Osteoscleroids d) None

460. Osteoscleroids are present in

a) Embryo **b) Seed coat**
c) Endosperm d) Radical

461. Osteoscleroids are present in these crops

a) Legumes b) Cereals
c) Oil seeds d) All

462. Naturally occurring plant hormone

a) GA b) IAA
c) Cytokinin d) None

463. Benzyl Adenine is a

a) Gibberelin b) Auxin
c) Cytokinin d) None

464. Amygdasin is a

a) Glucoside b) Peptin
c) Hormone d) Enzyme

465. Seeds with amygdasin is

a) Pista b) Cashew nut
c) Almond d) Acroot

466. Sinignin I, the amino acid s present in

a) Black mustard b) Gingelly
c) Mustard d) Groundnut

467. Hollow style is common in

a) Maize b) Cotton
c) Groundnut d) Blackgram

468. The vitamin which involved in respiration is

a) Vitamin E b) Thiamine
c) Ascorbic acid d) Vitamin d

469. Alpha tocopherol is a

a) Hormone b) Glucoside
c) Enzyme **d) Anti oxidant**

470. During seed germination synthesis of these enzymes broken down the stored food reserves.

a) Oxidative enzymes **b) Hydrolytic enzyme**
c) Respiratory enzymes d) All

471. Corn endosperm development is due to more of
a) Pectin
b) Amylose
c) Amylopectin
d) None

472. The fatty acid represented as 20 :1 is
a) Oleic
b) Stearic
c) Palmitic
d) Linoleic

473. In absence of GA, alpha amylase synthesis
a) Nil
b) High
c) Low
d) Equal

474. G A along with cytokinin leads to
a) More alpha amylase synthesis
b) Arrests the alpha amylase
c) Low synthesis
d) Beta amylase synthesis

475. During germination energy mobilization in castor is enhanced by
a) Protease
b) Lipase
c) Alpha amylase
d) Phosphorelase

476. During germination energy mobilization in dwarf bean is enhanced by
a) Lipase
b) Protease
c) Alpha amylase
d) Catalase

477. Protein mobilization in mung bean is enhanced by the enzyme
a) Catalase
b) Protease
c) Lipase
d) Asparagine synthase

478. In cucumber, fatty acid oxidation is by
a) Protease
b) Molecular oxygen
c) Lipase
d) Catalase

479. In cotton, lipase activity is largely depends on the presence or
a) Endosperm
b) Cotyledon
c) Seed coat
d) Embryonic Axis

480. Axis in lettuce play a major role in
a) b-mannanase synthesis
b) Protease
c) Lipase
d) Catalase

481. In groundnut, amylolytic activity is in
a) Cotyledon
b) Embryonic Axis
c) Testa
d) All

482. In lettuce, alpha galactosidase activity is promoted by

a) Cotyledon **b) Embryonic Axis**

c) Testa d) Endosperm

483. In lettuce, mobility enzymes are present in

a) Seed coat b) Embryo

c) Cotyledon **d) Endosperm**

484. In lettuce, light induces the action of

a) Embryonic Axis b) Endosperm

c) Cotyledon d) Seed coat

485. In presence of light, embryonic axis of lettuce seed produces

a) GA b) IAA

c) Cytokinin d) Alpha amylse

486. Oxidation of fat is inhibited by

a) Addition of sucrose b) Activity of GA

c) Fatty acids d) Protein

487. Accumulation of Leucine in cotyledon affects

a) Sucrose synthesis b) Protein synthesis

c) Fat synthesis **d) Aminopeptidase activity**

488. Phenylalanine accumulation in cotyledon affects

a) Protein degradation b) Protein synthesis

c) Fat synthesis d) Sucrose synthesis

489. In germinating cucumber seed the sink is

a) Axis b) Endosperm

c) Seed coat d) Cotyledon

490. Inactive form of precursor of alpha amylase is

a) Cytokinin b) GA

c) Zymogen d) Zeatin

491. In seeds production of alpha amylase is

a) de-novo b) Direct

c) Indirect d) 1&2

492. Dicot seed which has hypogeal germination is

a) Mung bean b) Urd bean

c) Peas d) Groundnut

493. De-novo synthesis of alpha amylase requires

a) Amino acids b) Fat

c) Carbohydtarate d) DNA

494. Mobilization of stored reserve is takes place during

a) Radicle protrusion **b) Lag phase**

c) Post germination d) Pre germination

495. Galactomannan is a

a) Hemicelluiose b) Cellulose

c) Tannin d) None

496. Galactomannan is a component of

a) Nucleus **b) Cell wall**

c) Mitochondria d) RNA

497. Native starch grain is

a) Amylose and Amylopectin b) Cellulose and hemicelluloses

c) Cutin and chitin d) Glucose and sucrose

498. Native starch grains are hydrolysed by

a) Alpha amylase b) Catalase

c) Protease d) Lipase

499. Small integument outgrowth is called as

a) Caruncle **b) Aril**

c) Hairs d) Elaeiosome

500. Phosphorylase activity is negligible in

a) Pulses b) Cereals

c) Oilseeds d) Cotton

14

Seed Processing

1. Decorticator is used for shelling pods in

   a) Bhendi b) Maize

   c) Groundnut d) Sunflower

2. Debearders are used in processing of

   a) Barley **b) Oats**

   c) Wheat d) Rice

3. Blending is permitted in case of

   a) Different varieties of same species

   b) Same varieties

   c) Composites

   d) All

4. The temperature limit for heated air drying is

   a) 110° F b) 65° F

   c) 87° F d) 168° F

5. First phase of processing is

   a) Conditioning and cleaning

   b) Drying

   c) Seed treatment

   d) Storage

6. Conditioning and pre cleaning improves

   a) Genetic purity b) Seed health

   c) Physical purity d) Vigour

7. In processing the role of scalper is
   a) Scarification b) Debeardeing
   c) Dewiniging **d) Rough cleaning**
8. Scalper favours the cleaning of seeds which contain
   a) Bristles b) Wings
   c) High trash d) Less trash
9. Indent cylinder separator, separates the seeds based on
   a) Shape b) Breadth
   c) Surface texture **d) Color**
10. Basic grading is separation of seeds based on
   a) Size b) Shape
   c) Surface texture d) Color
11. Specific gravity separator separates seeds based on seeds differing in
   a) Density b) Breadth
   c) Color d) Shape
12. Seed differing in size can be separated using
   a) Pre-cleaner b) Aspirator
   c) Seed grader d) Debearders
13. Hard seed coat can be smoothened by using
   a) Hammer mill **b) Scarifier**
   c) Debearder d) Draper belt
14. Round and flat seeds in a seed lot can be separated by
   a) Draper belt b) Indent cylinder separator
   c) Specific gravity separator d) Debearder
15. Dodder mill separates seeds based on
   a) Colour b) Shape
   c) Surface texture d) Size
16. Seeds which differ in color can be separated by
   a) Electronic color sorter b) Draper belt
   c) Dodder mill d) Magnetic separator
17. Magnetic separator separates seeds based on their
   a) Color b) Surface texture
   c) Shape **d) Affinity towards liquid**

18. Excessive glumes in forage seeds can be removed by
    a) Dodder mill b) Draper belt
    c) Debearder d) Magnetic separator
19. Electrostatic separator, separates seeds based on their
    a) Shape b) Affinity towards liquid
    c) Surface texture **d) Difference in electrical conductivity**
20. Clusters of seeds can be separated by
    a) Magnetic separator b) Debearder
    c) Huller d) Decorticator
21. Troublesome seed appendages can be removed by
    a) Debearder **b) Hammer mills**
    c) Magnetic separator d) Decorticator
22. Barley awns are removed by using
    a) Debearder b) Hammer mills
    c) Magnetic separator d) Decorticator
23. In air screen cleaner fast shaking of sieves will help in removal of
    a) Heavier seeds b) Stones
    c) Nematode galls **d) Cleaning chaffy seeds**
24. Low shake speed in a air screen cleaner is used to process
    a) Flat seeds **b) Round shape seeds**
    c) Oblong seeds d) Oval
25. Seeds differing in length can be separated by
    a) Magnetic separator **b) Indent cylinder separator**
    c) hammer mill d) Electrostatic separator
26. In an air screen cleaner top screen does the function of
    a) Cleaning **b) Scalping**
    c) Removes awns d) Removes appendages
27. In an air screen cleaner middle screen does the function of
    a) Cleaning b) Scalping
    c) Grading d) Removes awns
28. Seeds from serotinus cones are extracted by
    a) Scorching b) Beating
    c) Wet d) Acid

29. The first step of seed processing is
    a) Basic cleaning b) Grading
    c) Sieving d) Upgrading
30. Gmelina seeds can be extracted by
    a) Fermentation b) Abrasion
    c) Maceration d) Acid method
31. Normally seed extraction is not applicable to
    a) Pterocarpus b) Conifers
    c) Serotinous fruits **d) Dipterocarpus**
32. The ideal location for placing scalper in a processing complex is
    a) Entry b) At the end
    c) Nearby grader d) Any where
33. From pinus cones seeds are removed using
    a) Thumbler b) Thresher
    c) Stone bearder d) Sheller
34. During processing the genetic purity assessment is taken
    a) Maize b) Rice
    c) Sorghum d) Bajra
35. During processing care should be taken to avoid
    a) Mechanical damage b) Heat damage
    c) Frost damage d) Thrashing injury
36. Empty seeds of Emblica officinalis can be removed by
    a) Shape grading b) Size grading
    c) Specific gravity grading d) Color grading
37. The seeds are not extracted from fruits during processing in
    a) Ber **b) Teak**
    c) Jamun d) Neem
38. Color grading could be adapted to separate good seeds in
    a) *Acacia mellifera* b) *Acacia nilotica*
    c) *Cassia fistula* d) *Cassia hybrida*
39. Wet extraction is the common practice of extraction in
    a) Chillies b) Bhendi
    c) Onion **d) Bitter gourd**

40. Wet extraction is the common practice of extraction in

 a) **Sandal** b) Neem

 c) Jamun d) All

41. The temperature limit for heated air drying is

 a) **110° F** b) 65° F

 c) 87° F d) 168° F

42. Clusters of seeds can be separated by

 a) Magnetic separator b) Debearder

 c) **Huller** d) Decorticator

43. Cuscuta seeds are removed from Lucerne using

 a) Color sorter b) **Magnetic separator**

 c) Spiral separator d) Inclined belt

44. Following is an upgrading operation in the processing sequence

 a) Pre cleaning b) Size grading

 c) Aspiration d) **Specific gravity grading**

45. Iron powder is used in separartion of good seeds in

 a) **Peas** b) Redgram

 c) Cowpea d) Horsegram

46. Mirror is used in separation of good seeds in

 a) Incline belt b) Magnetic separator

 c) Spiral separator d) **Electronic color sortor**

47. Threshing of sorghum ear heads adopting the following method is harmful

 a) Hand shelling b) Mechanical thresher

 c) Beating with sticks d) **Tractor trading**

48. Following helps in separation of seed from gymnosperms

 a) **Kiln drying** b) Sun drying

 c) Over drying d) Scorching

49. Round and flat seeds of peas can be separated by using

 a) Incline belt b) Magnetic separator

 c) **Spiral separator** d) Electronic color sortor

50. The book on "Seed Processing" was written by

 a) Modi B.M. b) N.P. Neema

 c) Gregg d) **S.S. Atwal**

14.1. Seed Storage and Seed Treatment

1. Storage life of seed is influenced by
   a) Storage environment b) Genetic make up of seed
   c) Moisture content of seed **d) All**
2. Darkening of seed coat during storage is due to
   a) Oxidaton of Phenol b) Cellulose
   c) Hemi cellulose d) Fructose
3. The desiccant used for storage of seed is
   a) Silicagel b) Wood ash
   c) Activated clay d) Calcium, carbonate
4. The chemical used for Mid-storage correction
   a) KC1 b) ABA
   c) PEG **d) KH_2 PO_4**
5. The pesticide widely recommended for pre harvest sanitation spray
   a) Nuvan b) Endosulphon
   c) Monocrotophos **d) Malathion**
6 . Bruchid is a
   a) Field pest b) Storage pest
   c) Parasite **d) Field carryover storage pest**
7. Liquid Nitrogen is used in
   a) Cryopteservatidn b) Ultra dry storage
   c) Control storage d) *In-situ* storage
8. The safe moisture content for storage of paddy seeds under ambient condition is
   a) 6% b) 8%
   c) 13% d) 10%
9. For safe storage the best-suited storage place will have
   a) High temperature b) Low temperature
   c) High humid **d) Cool and dry atmosphere**
10. Coimbatore is classified as
   a) Poor storage place **b) Fair storage place**
   c) Good storage place d) Best storage place
11. Best storage place in India is
   a) Jaipur **b) Mumbai**
   c) Simla d) Agra

12. Nomograph is useful to predict
    a) Germination percentage **b) Seed viability period**
    c) Seed vigour d) Seed storage pest
13. Deterioration is more in
    a) Non dormant seed b) Dormant hard seed
    c) Non dormant hard seed d) Dormant normal seed
14. Electrical Conductivity of seed steep Water indicates
    a) Germinability b) Viability
    c) Field planting value **d) Membrane integrity**
15. OH proper seed storage seed quality is
    a) Deteriorated b) Improved
    c) Maintained d) None
16. Size of base collection of heterogenous material to store in a gene bank is
    a) 12,000 seeds b) 10,000 seeds
    c) 5000 seeds d) 15,000 seeds
17. Size of base collection of homogenous material to store in the gene bank is
    a) 1000 seeds b) 2000 seeds
    c) 4000 seeds d) 500 seeds
18. Thumb rule for safe seed storage has been developed by
    a) Thompson **b) Harrington**
    c) Bass d) Justis
19. Liquid nitrogen is used for
    a) Germplasm storage b) Cold storage
    c) Cryogenic storage d) All
20. Long term preservation of seed under low temperature is termed as
    a) Cryogenic b) A long term preservation
    c) old storage **d) All**
21. Dr. Basu, the Seed technologist specialized in
    a) Mid storage correction b) Seed hardening
    c) Pelleting d) Seed Coating
22. The chemical used for seed hardening
    a) KCl b) Water
    c) KNO_3 d) KH_2PO_4

23. Storage life of seed is influenced by
    a) Temperature & Relative Humidity
    b) Season of production
    c) Structure of seed
    d) Color of seed
24. The book on seed viability was written by
    a) R.N. Basu b) Ellies
    c) Frederic Nobbe **d) E.H. Roberts**
25. Normal storage unit of Melia is
    a) Pyrene b) Drupe
    c) Berry d) Seed
26. Seed hardening is
    a) Pre-sowing seed treatment
    b) Pre-storage seed treatmen
    c) Mid-storage seed treatment
    d) None
27. Hardened seed performed well in
    a) Marginal lands b) Wet lands
    c) Rainfed sowing d) Garden land
28. N-trichloromethyl thio-4 cyclohexene-1,2 di carboximide is
    a) Captan **b) Thiram**
    c) Malathion d) Bavistin
29. Polyethylene Glycol is useful in
    a) Priming b) Hydropriming
    c) Osmotic priming d) None
30. Priming is much suited pre sowing seed treatment for
    a) Sub optimal condition b) Dry lands
    c) Optimum condition d) All
31. Stratification is the treatment given to break
    a) Immature embryo dormancy
    b) Mechanical dormancy
    c) Physical dormancy
    d) All

32. Physiological dormancy is due to
    a) Absence of PGR b) Hard seed
    c) Insufficient space d) Presence of inhibitors
33. Dormancy of apple seeds is broken by
    a) Scarification **b) Cold stratification**
    c) Growth regulator d) All
34. Seed pelleting is
    a) Pre-sowing seed treatment
    b) Pre-storage seed treatment
    c) Mid-storage seed treatment
    d) None
35. Infusion of Plant Growth Regulator into the seed through organic solvent
    a) Dry permeation b) Hydration-dehydration
    c) Hardening d) Priming
36. Panchagavya is
    a) Biocontrol agent b) Botanic used for seed treatment
    c) Bio pesticide **d) Bio product used for multipurpose**
37. During dry permeation the seed moisture content is
    a) Reduced b) Increased
    c) No change d) None
38. Seed treatment chemical against loose smut of wheat is
    a) Thiram b) Bavistin
    c) Carboxin d) Mancozed
39. The priming agent, which does not penetrate the cell wall is
    a) PEG b) Mannitol
    c) Halogens d) D-mannitol
40. The priming agent which penetrate the cell wall is
    a) PEG **b) Mannitol**
    c) Halogens d) D-mannitol

15

Seed Health

1. Hallow heart in pea occurs due to
   a) Calcium deficiency
   b) Molybdenum deficiency
   c) Boron deficiency
   d) Zinc deficiency
2. Presence of pathogen on the surface of the seed is termed as
   a) Admixture
   b) Infestation
   c) Infection
   d) Contamination
3. Presence of pathogen inside the seed is termed as
   a) Admixture
   b) Infestation
   c) Infection
   d) Contamination
4. Presence of sclerotia or galls is termed as
   a) Admixture
   b) Infestation
   c) Infection
   d) Contamination
5. Concomitant contaminant of seed is
   a) Infestation
   b) Infection
   c) Admixture
   d) None
6. Externally seed borne pathogen is
   a) *Tilletia* spp.
   b) *Alternaria* spp
   c) ***Cercospora kikuchii***
   d) Diplodia zeae
7. In Sorghum, Mycelium of Fusarium monliforme is present in
   a) Endosperm
   b) Embryo
   c) Inner seed coat
   d) Surface of the seed coat
8. The causal organism of downy mildew in maize is present in
   a) Endsoperm
   b) Scutellum
   c) Upper part of the plumule
   d) Coleoptile

9. Brown spot in rice is transmitted through
   a) Seed b) Soil
   c) Wind d) Water
10. Fusarium is a
   a) Field fungi b) Storage fungi
   c) Both d) None
11. Lesser grain borer is the storage pest of
   a) Rice b) Sorghum
   c) Spices d) Pulses
12. Musty odour and dust in seed storage godown indicates presence of
   a) Indian meal moth **b) Khapra beetle**
   c) Mites d) Pulse beetle
13. The storage pest of wheat is
   a) Khapra beetle b) Cigarette beetle
   c) Pulse beetle **d) Lesser grain borer**
14. Objectionable disease in sesame is
   a) Downey mildew b) Powdery mildew
   c) Cercospora leaf spot d) Septoria leaf blight
15. Scale is the objectionable insect pest of
   a) Potato **b) Tapioca**
   c) Cowpea d) Tomato
16. PCNB media is most useful in detection of fungal species
   a) *Aspergillus* spp. b) *Phythium* spp.
   c) *Penicillium* spp. d) *Fusarium* spp.
17. Bacterial pathogen associated with seed is detected through
   a) ELISA b) Electropherosis
   c) HPLC d) RAPD
18. Karnal bunt of wheat can be identified by
   a) NaOH soaking test b) Blotter method
   c) PCNB d) Agar plate method
19. Double diffusion test is used for the deduction of
   a) Seed borne bacteria **b) Seed borne nematodes**
   c) Seed borne viruses d) None

20. Black color discoloration in wheat seed is due to the infection of
    a) *Tilletia indica* spp. b) *Alternaria* spp.
    c) *Cercospora* spp. d) *Aspergillus* spp.
21. Collateral host of pearl millet ergot is
    a) Cenchrus b) Paddy
    c) Wheat d) Barley
22. *Ephestia cautella* in brinjal is a
    a) Primary pest b) Field pest
    c) Secondary pest d) Storage pest
23. Ascophyta blight of bean is caused by
    a) *Ascochyta phasolorun* b) *Macrosiphum pisi*
    c) *Xanthomonas* spp. d) *Colletotrichum lindemuthuinum*
24. Cautella larvae is attacked by
    a) Bracon hebetor b) Plodia
    c) Trichoderma d) NPV
25. Scientific name of lesser grain borer
    a) *Exerohilium oryzae* b) *Triboloium castaneum*
    c) *Bruchids* **d) *Rhizopertha dominica***
26. *Rhizopertha dominica* is a
    a) Feeder of germ b) External feeder
    c) Internal feeder d) Feeds on storage tissues
27. In rice seeds Curvularia causes
    a) Black discoloration **b) Eye shaped discoloration**
    c) Brown discoloration d) Round shape discoloration
28. Exerohilium oryzae in rice causes
    a) Black discoloration b) Eye shaped discoloration
    c) Brown discoloration d) Round shape discoloration
29. Light pink/discoloration in seeds is due to
    a) *Colletotrichum capsici* b) *Alternaria alternate*
    c) *Fusarium monliforme* d) *Exerohilium oryzae*
30. Presence of dark brown spot in seed is due to
    a) *Fusarium monliforme* **b) *Alternaria alternate***
    c) *Colletotrichum capsici* d) *Exerohilium oryzae*

31. Fruit rot of chilli is caused by
    a) *Alternaria alternate* b) *Fusarium monliforme*
    c) *Colletotrichum capsici* d) *Exerohilium oryzae*
32. Fruit rot disease of chilli is
    a) Air borne b) Soil borne
    c) Seed borne d) Water borne
33. Brine solution is
    a) 30% sugar solution b) 20% sugar solution
    c) Jaggery solution **d) Common salt solution**
34. Brine solution is recommended against
    a) Seed infection b) Seed deterioration
    c) Seed infestation d) All
35. As per schedule of Plant Quarantine Regulation 1981, the quarantine pest of mango is
    a) Seed weevil b) Mango slug
    c) Red ant d) Tea mosquito bug
36. Leakage of organic metabolites from seed induces the
    a) Growth of microorganisms
    b) Ageing
    c) Vigor lose
    d) All
37. Death of a plant part due to pest attack
    a) Chlorosis b) Yellowing
    c) Necrosis d) None
38. Plant Quarantine Regulation was proposed during the year
    a) 1981 b) 1966
    c) 1969 d) 1983
39. Wheat variety which is susceptible to loose smut is
    a) Kalian sona b) Arjun
    c) NP830 **d) Sonalika**
40. Brown spot of rice is caused by
    a) *Fusarium monliforme* b) *Helminthosporium oryzae*
    c) *Pyricularia oryzae* d) *Cercospora* sp.

41. The viability period of pea pod spot pathogen is

a) 6 months **b) 6 years**

c) 6 weeks d) 6 days

42. Black rot of cabbage is caused by

a) Fungi **b) Bacteria**

c) Virus d) Nematode

43. A sudden broke down of bacterial blight of rice was occurred red from Bihar during

a) 1972 **b) 1962**

c) 1968 d) 1980

44. Seedling blight of maize was first observed in India during

a) 1957 b) 1975

c) 1960 d) 1963

45. Allium seeds are given with phytosanitary certificate for the disease

a) Smut b) Bulb rot

c) Silver shoot d) All

46. Uricystis cepulae causes

a) Onion smut b) Blackleg

c) Leaf spot d) Soft rot

47. Without phytosanitary certificate for smut disease the onion seeds cannot be exported to

a) Thailand b) Malaysia

c) Singapore **d) Pakistan**

48. Presence of pathogen on the surface of the seed is termed as

a) Admixture b) Infestation

c) Infection **d) Contamination**

49. Storage pest of Shorea robust a is

a) Sitophilus b) Bruchids

c) Agathiphaga d) Caryedon

50. Designated diseases of Tomato

a) Leaf blight and mosaic **b) Early blight and leaf spot**

c) Leaf spot and little leaf d) Little leaf and Early blight

16

Seed Certification and Quality Control

1. In bhendi field, the permissible limits for wild bhendi for Foundation and certified seed production is

   a) 0.10, 1.00 b) 0.05, 0.10

   c) 0.1, 1.5 **d) None**

2. Weed seed, other crop seed and inert matter are the fractions of

   a) Purity analysis b) Germination

   c) Seed viability test d) All

3. In seed quality control system golden yellow tag is given to indicate

   a) Nucleus seed **b) Breeder seed**

   c) Foundation seed d) Certified seed

4. The color of seed tag for Foundation seeds

   a) Blue color b) Golden yellow

   c) Green color **d) White color**

5. As per seed certification procedures the tag should be accompanied with

   a) Producer label b) Processing report

   c) Seed test results d) Seed standards

6. In India , the total number of State Farm Corporations operated are

   a) Ten b) Eleven

   c) Two d) One

7. The seed control order emphasizing the need for

   a) Certification

   b) Seed Testing

   c) License for sale of seed

   d) Notification

8. The New Seed Policy was introduced in seed industry during

   a) 1988 b) 1999

   c) 1969 d) 2001

9. In India Seed certification is
   a) Compulsory **b) Voluntary**
   c) Tentative d) Statuary
10. Indian seed certification rules are based on the rules pro-posed by
   a) ISTA b) ISST
   c) OECD d) AOSA
11. Certified seed is the progeny of
   a) Breeder seed **b) Foundation seed**
   c) Nucleus seed d) Truth fully labeled seed
12. Azar blue e color tag is enclosed with the seed bag of
   a) Certified seed b) Foundation seed
   c) Breeder seed d) Nucleus seed
13. The designated disease of wheat
   a) Karnal Bunt b) Head smut
   c) Leaf spot d) Ergot
14. Dodder is the objectionable weed plant in
   a) Rice b) Bhendi
   c) Mustard **d) Lucerne**
15. The media used for bitter gourd seed germination test
   a) Sand b) Paper
   c) Blotter paper d) Soil
16. Days for first and final count for paddy seed germination test
   a) 4,10 b) 4,21
   c) 4,7 **d) 5,14**
17. Certification could be done only for
   a) Released varieties **b) Notified varieties**
   c) Private varieties d) Central varieties
18. Seed Act was formulated and enacted during
   a) 1966 and 1969 b) 1966 and 1968
   c) 1963 and 1966 d) 1988 and 1990
19. Seeds less than half size, during purity analysis is considered as
   a) Other crop seed **b) Inert matter**
   c) Pure seed d) Weed seed

20. Diaphonoscope is used in
    a) Purity analysis b) Seedling evaluation
    c) Varietal identification d) Seed health
21. The submitted sample size for both groundnut kernal and pods for purity analysis
    a) 250gm b) 100 gm
    c) 1000gm d) 600 gm
22. Phenol color test is used for identification of
    a) Purity analysis b) Mechanical damage
    c) Varietal identification d) Seed health
23. Grow out test is practiced to ensure
    a) Field emergence b) Seedling vigor
    c) Physical purity **d) Genetic purity**
24. ISTA was established during
    a) 1968 b) 1966
    c) 1924 d) 1997
25. Fusrium wilt in Cicer orietanum is spread through
    a) Seed b) Soil
    c) Wind d) Water
26. KOH bleach test in sorghum is useful to assess
    a) Viability b) Mechanical damage
    c) Varietal purity d) Vigor
27. Sodium hydroxide test for wheat is useful in assessing
    a) Vigor b) Viability
    c) Mechanical damage **d) Varietal purity**
28. Peroxidase test for soybean is useful to assess
    a) Viability **b) Varietal purity**
    c) Vigor d) Mechanical damage
29. Phenol test for wheat is useful to assess
    a) Varietal purity b) Mechanical damage
    c) Viability d) Vigor
30. Nobbe trier is useful in
    a) Sampling b) Dividing
    c) Weighing d) Purity analysis

31. In cotton number of plants / count in field inspection

a) 100 b) 1000
c) 500 d) 250

32. The minimum germination percentage for ground nut as per Minimum Seed Certification Standards

a) 60 b) 65
c) 70 d) 75

33. The submitted sample size for paddy is

a) 100g b) 40g
c) 400g d) 10g

34. The RH required in a germination room is

a) 70 b) 85
c) 95% d) 75

35. Electrophoresis is a test useful for

a) Differentiating Varieties
b) High and low vigour seeds
c) Viable and non- viable seeds
d) Dormant seeds

36. Minimum weight of submitted sample for Moisture estimation in paddy is

a) 75g b) 100g
c) 25g **d) 50g**

37. Boerner divider is otherwise called ad

a) Gamete divider b) Soil divider
c) Conical divider d) Centrifuge divider

38. Number of primary sample to be taken from the paddy seeds stored in 35 containers

a) 7 **b) 10**
c) 35 d) 5

39. Number of primary sample to be taken from 4500 kg of sorghum seeds stored in bulk

a) 9 b) 10
c) 4 **d) 7**

40. The working sample size for tomato is

a) 10 g b) 100 g
c) 40 g **d) 7 g**

41. Submitted sample size for maize is
    a) 400gm b) 500 gm
    c) 800 gm **d) 1000 gm**
42. Working sample size for groundnut pods
    a) 100gm b) 500 gm
    c) 750 gm **d) 1000 gm**
43. In Coniferae seed without seed coat is considered as
    a) Pure seed b) Weed seed
    c) inert matter d) None
44. Genetic monogerm cultivars of beet are considered as
    a) Caryopsis **b) Mericarp**
    c) Achenes d) Nut
45. Number of seeds to be tested for assessing germination percentage as per ISTA is
    a) 100 **b) 400**
    c) 200 d) 240
46. In estimation of moisture content the container used for seed packing should be
    a) Moisture pervious b) Moisture resistant
    c) Moisture impervious **d) Moisture vapour proof**
47. Brick gravel test is a
    a) Vigour test b) Viability test
    c) Varietal identification test d) None
48. Brick gravel test is used to measure
    a) Physical status **b) Physiological stamina**
    c) Biochemical activity d) Chemical property
49. Speed of germination is
    a) Physical vigour test **b) Physiological vigor test**
    c) Biochemical vigor test d) Chemical
50. Tetrazoliumn test is also a
    a) Physical vigour test b) Physiological vigor test
    c) Biochemical vigor test d) None
51. Number of counts required for a maize field of 5 ha
    a) 5 **b) 9**
    c) 7 d) 8

52. Designated disease of mustard
    a) Leaf Spot b) Downey mildew
    c) Powdery mildew **d) Alternaria**
53. Central Seed Testing Laboratory was established during
    a) 1960 b) 1966
    c) 1968 d) 1969
54. Validity period of fresh seeds as per certification standards
    a) 6 months **b) 9 months**
    c) 12 months d) 10 months
55. International Seed Network Initiative was created by
    a) FIS b) OECD
    c) ISTA d) WTO
56. International Seed Network Initiative was started during
    a) June 1999 b) June 2000
    c) June 1998 d) June 1996
57. Section5of Seeds Act (1966) deals with
    a) Notification b) Central Seed Committee
    c) Appellate Authority d) Definition of Seeds
58. The size of the certification tag is
    a) 15 X 7.5 cm b) 10 X 11cm
    c) 15 Xl0cm d) 15 X 15cm
59. Important seed borne disease accounted in seed certification of wheat is
    a) Common bunt **b) Loose smut**
    c) Kernel bunt d) Downey mildew
60. Grow out test is must for hybrids of
    a) Maize **b) Cotton**
    c) Rice d) All
61. Seecls (control) order is proposed during
    a) 1983 b) 1955
    c) 1966 d) 1968
62. Designated disease of Knol khol
    a) Black leg b) Leaf spot
    c) Black bunt d) All

63. Minimum germination required for cauliflower seed as per Minimum Seed Certification Standard

a) 65 b) 90
c) 85 d) 80

64. A test to determine field emergence potential is

a) Brick gravel test b) Grow out test
c) Field plot test d) Phenol color reaction test

65. This class of seed is certified by the Seed Certification Agency

a) Breeder seed b) Primordial seed
c) Foundation seed d) Labelled seed

66. DUS testing fetches importance under

a) Protection of Plant Varieties and Farmers Right act
b) Seed Act
c) Essential Commodity Act
d) Seed control order

67. Minimum germination percentage recommended by Minimum Seed Certification Standards for tomato is

a) 65 **b) 70**
c) 80 d) 75

68. Seed Act was implemented in India from

a) 1st Jan, 2005 b) 2nd December, 1966
c) 2nd October, 1969 **d) 29th December, 1966**

69. Seed rule was implemented in India from

a) 1st Jan, 2005 b) 5th October, 1969
c) 2nd October, 1969 d) 29th December, 1966

70. Plant quarantine act was passed during the year

a) 1981 **b) 1976**
c) 1967 d) 1966

71. Phytosanitay certificate assures that the seed is free from

a) Weed seed b) Other crop seeds
c) Inert matter **d) Pathogens**

72. Plaint Quarantine regulations was passed during the year

a) 1981 b) 1976
c) 1967 d) 1966

73. Minimum germination standard for paddy foundation seed
a) 80 b) 100
c) 65 d) 98

74. The pure seed fraction recommended for groundnut is
a) 99% b) 98%
c) 96% d) 97%

75. In Seed Testing Laboratory dividers are used to obtain
a) Composite sample b) Primary sample
c) Submitted sample **d) Working sample**

76. The isolation distance recommended in meters to avoid contamination with Johnson grass in hybrid sorghum is
a) 200 b) 100
c) 400 d) 5

77. Pearson square law is adopted for
a) Blending b) Testing
c) Dividing d) Sampling

78. Objectionable weed plant of cucumber is
a) *Cucumis hardwickii* b) *Citrullus lanatus*
c) *Cucumis sativus* d) *Citrullus colosynthis*

79. Maximum size of seed lot of onion in Kg.
a) 40,000 b) 10,000
c) 20,000 **d) 5,000**

80. Without phytosanitary certificate for smut disease the onion seeds cannot be exported to
a) Thailand b) Malaysia
c) Singapore **d) Pakistan**

81. Isolation distance for foundation seed production of onion is
a) 400 m **b) 1000 m**
c) 500 m d) 800 m

82. In certification, the number of counts to be taken from 6 to 10 acres
a) 6 b) 7
c) 8 d) 9

83. In seed testing, permitted deviation from the standard is called
a) Objection **b) Tolerance**
c) Deviation d) Critical difference

84. The designated diseases of sorghum
    a) Loose smut **b) Grain smut**
    c) Green ear d) Alternaria blight
85. Pod verification is done in
    a) Groundnut b) Blackgram
    c) Cowpea d) Redgram
86. The sample taken at one point in a seed lot
    a) Primary sample b) Composite sample
    c) Submitted sample, d) Working sample
87. Cob sorting is done to identify
    a) Diseased cob b) Matured cob
    c) Big sized cob **d) Off type cob**
88. Designated disease of brinjal
    a) Leaf spot **b) Little leaf**
    c) Leaf blight d) All
89. The seed samples sent for analyses by the seed inspector
    a) Certified sample **b) Official sample**
    c) Service sample d) Bulk sample
90. As per ISTA the germination test has to be conducted with
    a) Pure seed fraction b) Whole submitted sample
    c) Whole working sample d) Submitted sample
91. Notification is done under seed act to bring the variety
    a) For national level cultivation
    b) For state level cultivation,
    c) For quality seed production
    d) To bring under purview of seed certification
92. Seed sampling in cotton is done using
    a) Stick trier b) Nobbe trier
    c) Spoon method **d) Hand sampling**
93. The submitted sample size for amaranthus
    a) 1 g b) 10 g
    c) 20 g d) 100 g
94. Seed testing is the science of evaluating seed for its
    a) Planting value b) Vigour
    c) Contamination of seed lot d) Health status

95. Referee testing of seeds is being conducted at
    a) State seed testing lab
    b) Private seed testing lab
    c) Accredited seed testing lab
    d) Central seed testing lab

96. In rice KOH, test is useful for
    a) Varietal identification b) Viability testing
    c) Assessing vigour potential d) Mechanical damage

97. As per ISTA working sample should contain a minimum
    a) 2500 seeds b) 4000 seeds
    c) 250 seeds d) 400 seeds

98. In tetrazolium test the viability of the seed is assessed by the development of pink color on
    a) Embryo b) Endosperm
    c) Cotyledon **d) All living parts**

99. The maximum area could be registered for seed certification is
    a) 4 ac b) 5 ac
    c) 4 ha **d) 10 ha**

100. Image analysis of seed for varietal identification is based on
    a) Morphological features
    b) Physiological features
    c) Biochemical characteristics of seeds
    d) Histological features of seeds

101. Validation for a seed lot can be obtained for
    a) Two times b) Three times
    c) Any number of times d) None

102. To provide alternate temperature in a germination test, the high temperature is to be followed for
    a) 8 hr b) 10 hr
    c) 9 hr d) 12 hr

103. The light intensity required for germination of non- dormant seed in lux
    a) 150 b) 450
    c) 250 d) 350

104. Seed testing is to be done under

a) **Controlled condition** b) Ambient condition

c) Cold atmosphere d) At field condition

105. Germination test results are to be reported in

a) One decimal places **b) Whole number**

c) Two decimals d) Three decimals

106. Labelling of seed packages under Seed Act is

a) Voluntary **b) Compulsory**

c) Need based d) None

107. Orange certificate is

a) Phytosariitary certificate **b) Seed sample certificate**

c) Seed lot certificate d) Seed passport

108. Test weight is decided based on weight of

a) 100 seeds b) 2500 seeds

c) 1000 seeds d) 2000 seeds

109. Soil dividers are used for

a) Mixing b) Dividing

c) Sampling **d) (a) and (b)**

110. Boerner divider work on the principle of

a) Specific gravity **b) Gravitational force**

c) Centrifugal force d) Seed morphology

111. In purity analysis wings is considered as

a) Pure seed **b) Inert matter**

c) Other crop seed d) Damaged seed

112. Samaras without true seed in purity analysis is known as

a) Pure seed b) Inert matter

c) Other crop seed d) Fruit

113. The standard method for moisture estimation is

a) Oven dry method b) Digital Moisture meter

c) Infrared moisture meter d) Toluene method

114. Blotter test is recommended by ISTA for analyzing

a) Seed germination b) Seed vigor

c) Seed health d) Mechanical damage

115. The concept of seed vigour was first proposed by

a) Roberts, 1969 b) Delouche, 1969

c) Isloy 1951 d) TcKrony, 1976

116. The pure seed fraction recommended for mustard is

a) 97% b) 98%

c) 99% d) 96%

117. The pure seed fraction recommended for maize inbred/ composite/ synthetic is

a) 99% b) 98%

c) 99% d) 97%

118. The pure seed fraction recommended for maize single cross and hybrids are

a) 96% **b) 98%**

c) 99% d) 97%

119. The pure seed fraction recommended for cereals is

a) 98% **b) 96%**

c) 99% d) 97%

120. Father of Seed Testing

a) Roberts b) Mc Donald

c) Frederick Nobbe d) R.N. Basu

121. The first terminology used by Nobbe to explain seed vigor is

a) Shooting strength b) Energy

c) Stamina d) Tolerance ability

122. The earliest vigor test

a) NH_4CI **b) Brick gravel**

c) Mannitol d) Paper piercing

123. The light intensity which favours the seed germination is

a) 700 to 780 nm b) 600 to 660 nm

c) 310 to 450 nm d) 280 to 300 nm

124. The wavelength of 280 nm and below is

a) Lethal to plants

b) Enhance photosynthesis

c) Favourable for plant growth

d) Enhances metabolic cycles

125. Number of notified Seed Testing Laboratory at Tamil Nadu
   a) 2   b) 4
   c) 8   d) 5
126. All gymnosperms show
   a) Mixer of both   b) Hypogeal germination
   c) Epigeal germination   d) None
127. During germination, rate of imbibition increases with
   a) Increased temperature   b) Low water content
   c) Low RH   d) Low temperature
128. When compared to laboratory germination test, rate of imbibition in soil is
   a) High   b) Low
   c) Equal   **d) High or equal**
129. Imbibition is a
   a) Physical process   b) Chemical process
   c) Biochemical process   d) All
130. Phenol test is conducted in
   a) Paddy   **b) Wheat**
   c) Maize   d) Pearl millet
131. KOH test is conducted to identify the
   a) Viability   b) Mechanical damage
   c) Varieties   d) Vigour
132. GAD A test was formulated by
   a) Roberts, 1969   b) Woodstock, 1976
   c) Hiltner, 1969   **d) Linko, 1961**
133. The instrument used for measuring the respiration rate of seeds
   a) Hygrometer   **b) Manometer**
   c) Lactometer   d) Psychrometer
134. The compound associated with tetrazolium test is
   a) Alkaloid   b) Phenol
   c) Formazon   d) Tannin
135. The enzyme associated with tetrazolium test is
   a) Catalase   b) Super oxide dismutase
   c) Dehydrogenases   d) Amylases

136. Cold test is considered as best method of estimating vigour in

a) Corn b) Paddy

c) Wheat d) Soybean

137. Cool termination test is a vigour test for

a) Cotton b) Mustard

c) Corn d) Soybean

138. The type of germination in onion is

a) Hypogeal **b) Epigeal**

c) Semi hypogeal d) None

139. The headquarters of ISTA is located in

a) Tharanxndt, Germany b) Connecticut, USA

c) Zurich, Switzerland d) New Delhi, India

140. Mechanical damage can be identified by

a) Ferric chloride test b) Sulphuric acid test

c) KOH test d) Phenol test

141. VCU test stands for

a) Value for cultivation and use

b) Variety for cultivation and use

c) Variety for common use

d) Variety for commercial use

142. The scientist closely associated with speed of germination

a) Maguire b) Woodstock

c) Roberts d) Ellies

143. The scientist closely associated with mobilization efficiency test

a) Maquire **b) Shrivastva and Sareen**

c) Roberts d) Ellies

144. The scientists closely associated with vigour index calculation

a) Abdulbaki and Anderson

b) Shrivastva and Sareen

c) Roberts

d) Ellies

145. The scientist closely associated with exhaustion test is

a) Maguire **b) Germ**

c) Roberts d) Ellies

146. The scientist closely associated with X-ray test is

a) Simek and Gustefsson b) Germ

c) Roberts d) Ellies

147. Nobbe coined the word 'triebkraft' during the year

a) 1876 b) 1963

c) 1758 d) 1966

148. Hiltner and Hussion proposed brick gravel as vigour test during the year

a) 1876 b) 1963

c) 1758 **d) 1911**

149. Paper piercing technique was suggested as vigour test by

a) Fritz, 1965 b) Roberts, 1969

c) Hiltner, 1969 d) Woodstock, 1966

150. Tetrazolium test was first formulated by

a) Lakon, 1942 b) Roberts, 1969

c) Hiltner, 1969 d) Woodstock, 1976

17

Agricultural Economics

1. ______ an application of the accounting principles to the business of farming.

   a) Farm planning b) Farm budgeting

   c) Farm accounting d) Marketing

2. 'Beef' and 'hides' are examples of:

   a) Independent enterprise **b) Joint enterprise**

   c) Supplementary enterprise d) Compitative enterprise

3. 'Indian Farming' is published by:

   a) Ministry of Agriculture Government of India

   b) ICAR

   c) National Seed Corporation of India

   d) None of these

4. "Rent is the price paid for the use of land" who said it ?

   a) Ricardo **b) Carver**

   c) Keynes d) None of these

5. "Under free and perfect competition there could not be any involuntary unemployment amongest wage earners in the labour market." This theory was established by :

   a) Prof. J.B. Say **b) Prof. Pigou**

   c) Prof. Keynes d) None of these

6. Per capita land available in India

   a) 1/3ha b) 1/6 ha

   c) 1/4 ha **d) 1/7 ha**

7. A consumer spends his income according to the law of:
   a) Diminishing marginal utility
   b) Increasing cost
   c) Equi-marginal utility
   d) Least cost

8. A crop loan over Rs. 1,00,000 will require
   a) Equitable mortage b) Registered mortage of land
   c) Personal security d) None of these

9. A farmer having less than one hectare of irrigated land, is known as:
   a) Small farmers **b) Marginal farmers**
   c) Big farmers d) None of these

10. A group of technical units are known as:
   a) Farm firm **b) Plant**
   c) Economic unit d) All above

11. A market structure with large number of firms selling homogeneous products is known as
   a) Monopoly market **b) Monopolistic competition**
   c) Perfect competition d) None of these

12. A holding which allow to a man a chance of producing sufficient to support himself and his family in resonable comfort after paying his necessary expenses is called
   a) Basic holding b) Optimum holding
   c) Operational holding **d) Economic holding**

13. A market in which the purchase and sale is a commodity takes place at time 't' but the exchange of the commodity takes after 't+1' time, the market is known as
   a) Spot b) Cash market
   c) Forward market d) General market

14. A statement which shows the financial condition and stability of the business at a particular point of time is known as
   a) Net worth statement
   b) Business statement
   c) Physical efficiency measures
   d) None of the above

15. A table is a

a) Material good b) Non-material good

c) Free good d) None of the above

16. About 70% farmers have less than _____ hactare of land in India :

a) 5 **b) 2**

c) 4 d) 1

17. Absence of interaction between resources and activities in the process of production is called

a) Linearity **b) Non-linearity**

c) Quasi-non-linearity d) Quasi-linearity

18. According to the Directorate of marketing and Inspection ______ per cent may be taken as the average marketing margin for all surplus food grains in India.

a) 15 b) 20

c) 25 d) 35

19. Agricultural Development Banks are sponsored by

a) Reserve Bank of India **b) State Bank of India**

c) Nationalized Banks d) Co-operative Banks

20. Agricultural price commission was established in

a) 1964 b) 1966

c) 1965 d) 1967

21. Air is

a) Economic goods **b) Free goods**

c) Transferable goods d) All above

22. Agricultural Refinance and Development Corporation (ARDC) was set up in

a) 1963 b) 1975

c) 1952 d) 1967

23. As income increase the expenditure on light, fuel and rent generally

a) Increases b) Decreases

c) Remains the same d) None of the above

24. At present, the farming system of India has become

a) Export oriented b) Technology oriented

c) Market oriented d) Domestic need oriented

25. Average fixed cost is equal to :
    a) Total fixed cost/100 b) Total fixed cost/total variable cost
    c) Total fixed cost/output d) Total fixed cost/input
26. Basic fundamental law of agriculture is :
    a) Law of diminishing return
    b) Law of equimarginal return
    c) Law of substitution
    d) Law of demand and supply
27. Who was the first economist to have evolved the technique of Indifference Curve Analysis?
    a) David Ricardo b) Bohm Bawerk
    c) F. Y. Edgeworth d) C. Pigou
28. Break-even point is determined by
    a) MC=MR b) MC=AVC
    c) MC=AC=AR **d) TR=TC**
29. Building, machinery and implements are examples of:
    a) Variable resources **b) Fixed resources**
    c) Flow resources d) None of the above
30. By preparing chairs the wood creates :
    a) Form utility b) Time utility
    c) Place utility d) Knowledge utility
31. Capital market deals with
    a) Cotton b) Wheat
    c) Raw material **d) Bonds & Shares**
32. Central cooperative bank operates normally at
    a) District level b) Village level
    c) National level d) None of these
33. Central government finance the RRB's the extent of
    a) 35% b) 17%
    c) 50% d) 40%
34. Chairman of Planning Commission is
    a) Prime Minister
    b) President
    c) Appointed by Prime Minister
    d) Appointed by President

35. Common Area Development Programme (CADP) were started in :
    a) 1974 b) 1962
    c) 1976 d) 1979
36. Commodity market deals with
    a) Bonds b) Shares
    c) Wheat d) None of these
37. Co-operative farming, Collective farming, Capilistic farming, State farming and Peasant farming are
    a) Types of farming **b) Systems of farming**
    c) Both these d) None of these
38. Co-operatives for tribes are called as
    a) Camp co-operative societies
    b) Multi-purpose societies
    c) Lead Bank
    d) Savita
39. Creation of utility by way of marketing is known as
    a) Consumption **b) Production**
    c) Distribution d) Exchange
41. Crop farming & milk production is an example of
    a) Competitive enterprise
    b) Complementary enterprise
    c) Supplementary enterprise
    d) None of them
42. Dairy farming, poultry farming, crop farming and pig farming are
    a) Type of farming b) Systems of farming
    c) Both a & b d) None of them
43. Decrease in demand means
    a) Demand change due to change in price
    b) Demand changes not due to the change in price but due to income
    c) Both a & b
    d) None of these
44. Demand for necessary goods is
    a) Elastic **b) Inelastic**
    c) Perfectly elastic d) None of the above

45. The marginal productivity theory is based on the assumption of
   a) Imperfect competition   b) Monopolistic competition
   c) Perfect competition   **d) Elastic competition**
46. Economic laws are not ascertain as
   a) Physical law   b) Moral law
   c) Government law   d) All above
47. Economics is a :
   a) Social science   b) Political science
   c) Natural science   d) None of these
48. Economics is a an
   a) Art   b) Science
   c) Art & science   d) None of these
49. Economy of an developing country is marked by
   a) Predominance of agriculture
   b) Predominance of industry
   c) Predominance of transportation
   d) None of them
50. Enterprise budgeting deals with input-output relationship of
   a) A set of different enterprises
   b) A single enterprises of the farm
   c) Both of the above
   d) None of the above
51. Expenditure on fertilizers is called
   a) Fixed cost   **b) Variable cost**
   c) Marginal cost   d) Total cost
52. Export-Import Bank of India was set up of 1st January
   a) 1980   **b) 1982**
   c) 1981   d) 1983
53. Extent of land under forest in India is
   a) 21%   b) 20%
   c) 27%   d) 16%

54. Farm credit may be defined as lending
   a) For the development of land & labour
   b) For more yield
   c) For the development of Agriculture
   d) For the development of forestry, poultry, piggery etc.

55. Farm management deals with
   a) Judicious decision
   b) Use of scare resources
   c) Profit maximization & family satisfaction
   d) All these

56. Farm planning involves
   a) Preparing farm budget in advance
   b) Selecting and adopting best package of practices
   c) Both of these
   d) None of these

57. First land Mortagage Bank was set up in Madras in the year
   a) 1929 b) 1951
   c) 1934 d) 1921

58. Food Corporation of India (FCI) was established in January :
   a) 1963 b) 1966
   c) 1964 **d) 1965**

59. For purchasing of seeds, fertilizers etc., the loan distributed is called :
   a) Short term loan b) Long term loan
   c) Medium term loan d) All of the above

60. Gross return plus charge in inventory minus total cost is equal to
   a) Farm income b) Family income
   c) Tax d) None of the above

61. Oligopoly is a market situation which is characterized by the existence of
   a) One firm b) Two firms
   c) Several firms **d) Few firms**

62. How many plots of one hectare area can be farmed from one square km area?
   a) 10 b) 50
   c) 100 d) 1000

63. How much farmers have land holding more than 10 hectares?
   a) 15% b) 8%
   c) 10% **d) 4%**

64. Human wants are generally
   a) Static **b) Recurring**
   c) Non-recurring d) Limited

65. If change in price is 1% and change in demand is 1% demand will be called
   a) Elastic **b) Praportionate elastic**
   c) Inelastic d) None of the above

66. If more and more capital and labour are applied to a fixed piece of land, the system of cultivation or farming is known as
   a) Intensive cultivation b) Extensive cultivation
   c) Co-operative farming d) Large scale farming

67. If substitution ratio is equal to price ratio then cost will be
   a) Minimum b) Increasing
   c) Maximum d) Decreasing

68. If the income elasticity of demand is greater than one, the commodity is
   a) A necessity **b) A luxury**
   c) An inferior good d) A essentiality

69. In classical production function, rational zone is always
   a) First zone **b) Second zone**
   c) Third zone d) None of the above

70. In a market situation, when there is only one seller of a commodity, it is
   a) Duopoly Market b) Oligopoly Market
   c) Monopoly Market d) None of the above

71. In a manufacturing industry generally applies law of
   a) Constant return b) Increasing return
   c) Decreasing return d) All of the above

72. If two items are supplementry then demand of one item will decrease against the ______ in price of another item
   a) Increase b) Maximum
   c) Decrease d) Minimum

73. If two items are complementry then demand of one item will increase for __________ in price of another item

a) **Increase** b) Decrease

c) No effect d) Not known

74. If the quantity of commodity demand remains unchanged as its price changes, the coefficient of price elasticity of demond is

a) Greater than one b) Zero

c) Smaller than one **d) Equal to one**

75. If the quantity of a commodity demanded does not change when its price, the demand curve is

a) Negatively sloped b) Positively sloped

c) Verticaly sloped d) None of these

76. In law of supply the relationship between price and quantity supplied is

a) Direct b) Indirect

c) Both a and b d) None of the above

77. Who wrote the book, 'The Theory of Monopolistic Competition?

a) Joan Robinson **b) E. H. Chamberlin**

c) A.C. Pigou d) Frederic Benham

78. In perfect competition, there are

a) Large no of buyers & few no of sellers in the market

b) Large no sellers & few no of buyers in the market

c) Number of buyers & sellers are large and nearly equal

d) All of above

79. In the short run, Average Cost, Average Variable Cost and Marginal cost Curves are 'U' shaped due to the operation of

a) Law of equimarginal returns

b) Substitution between two factor inputs

c) Law of variable proportion

d) Time comparison principle

80. In which planning period profit rule says that gross return should cover variable cost

a) Long run **b) Short run**

c) Both a & b d) None of the above

81. A boom is marked by

a) Full employment
b) Under employment
c) Overfull employment
d) None of the above

82. Income tax is a

a) Direct tax
b) Indirect tax
c) Both a & b
d) None of these

83. Land Development Banks are parts of

a) Co-operative Banks
b) Nationalized Banks
c) Agricultural Development Bank
d) Regional Rural Banks

84. Level of output of a particular commodity depends upon the quantities of inputs used for its production. This relationship is known as

a) Production process
b) Product mix
c) Production function
d) Cost function

85. Long term loans is given for the period of

a) More than 5 years
b) 2 to 5 years
c) 4 years
d) All of the above

86. Man's wants are

a) Limited
b) Unlimited
c) Countable
d) Scarce

87. Major 14 banks were nationalized in the year

a) 1970
b) 1969
c) 1975
d) 1973

88. Marginal cost is equal to

a) Change in total cost /change in output
b) Change in total cost + 100
c) Average fixed cost
d) None of the above

89. Marginal farmers are those farmers having land holding :

a) Less than 5 acres
b) Less than 2 acres
c) Less than 1 acre
d) All of those

90. Market demand curve is faced by

a) Monopolist
b) Competitive firm
c) Joint firm
d) Oligopoly firm

91. Marshall defines economics as

a) **The study of mankind in the ordinary business of life**

b) The study of human behavior as a relationship between end and scarce means which have alternative uses

c) An enquiry into the nature and causes of the wealth of nations

d) Fundamentally a science of scarcity

92. Means to satisfy human wants are

a) Unlimited b) Limited

c) Both a & b d) None of the above

93. NABARD Act was passed in ________ , 1979.

a) January b) February

c) March d) April

94. NABARD came into existence on July 12,

a) 1980 b) 1981

c) 1982 d) 1983

95. Name the market in which permanent or durable commodities are traded?

a) Long period market b) Short period market

c) Secular market d) Bullion market

96. Net capital ratio is equal to :

a) Total assets/Total liabilities

b) Total liabilities /Total assets

c) Total assets/Current liabilities

d) None of the above

97. Net return per hectare is :

a) Over all efficiency measure

b) Partial efficiency measure

c) Specific efficiency measure

d) None of the above

98. Optimizing the use of farm resources on an individual farm level. It is a :

a) Farm management b) Production Economics

c) Agricultural marketing d) Macro economics

99. Payment made to labour for its assistance to production, is called :

a) Rent **b) Wage**

c) Interest d) None of the above

100. Per Quintal calculated cost is known as :

a) Cost of cultivation **b) Cost of production**

c) Cost of farming d) None of the above

18

Agricultural Statistics

1. "Statistics is a science of calculations and averages", the definition was given by :
   a) R.A. Fisher
   b) Boddington
   c) Bowley
   d) Anderson
2. "Statistics is a study of population, variation and methods of data reduction" is the definition of statistics according to:
   a) A.L. Bowley
   b) R.A. Fisher
   c) Boddington
   d) None of these
3. The character which cannot be measured numerically is known as ______ variable.
   a) **Qualitative**
   b) Quantitative
   c) Continuous
   d) None of these
4. The word "statistics" is used as:
   a) Singular
   b) Plural
   c) Both a and b
   d) None of these
5. Father of statistics is :
   a) Bowley
   b) R.A. Fisher
   c) Boddington
   d) Anderson
6. "When the principles of statistics are applied on living thing or organisms, the science is called:
   a) Bioinformatics
   b) Statistics
   c) Biometry
   d) None of these
7. Qualitative characteristics of an individual which shows variability is known
   a) **Attribute**
   b) Quantitative variable
   c) Continuous variable
   d) None of these
8. The word statistics means quantitative data, when it is used as:
   a) **Plural**
   b) Singular
   c) Both (a) & (b)
   d) None of these

9. Statistics deals only with _______ characters.
   a) Quantitative b) Qualitative
   c) Both a & b d) None of these
10. The author for book entitle “A Hand book of Agricultural Statistics” is:
   a) Rangaswamy **b) R.S. Chandel**
   c) B.L. Agaeawal d) None of these
11. The author for book entitle “A text book of Agricultural Statistics” is:
   a) Rangaswamy b) R.S. Chandel
   c) B.L. Agaeawal d) None of these

Unit 2: Frequency Distribution and Frequency Curves

1. _________ means number of items occurs in a class
   a) Frequency b) Proportion
   c) Percentage d) None of these
2. With the help of histogram we can prepare
   a) Frequency polygon b) Frequency curve
   c) Frequency distribution **d) All of these**
3. If the mean and variance of ‘A” series and ‘B’ series are as Mean(A)=20 and Variance (A)=25 and Mean(B)=16 and variance(B)=16 which of the two series is more consistent.
   a) Series A
   b) Series B
   c) Series A and B are equally consistent
   d) None of these
4. When classification of data is made on the basis of time is known as:
   a) Geographical **b) Chronological**
   c) District wise d) None of these
5. Histogram is a
   a) Line chart b) Polygon
   c) Bardiagram d) None of these
6. The value of median can be decided graphically from:
   a) Frequency curve **b) Ogive**
   c) Histogram d) None of these
7. Frequency of a variable is always :
   a) An integer b) In percentage
   c) A fraction d) None of these

8. In case of open ended series, ________ is not possible to calculate :
   a) **Mean** b) Median
   c) Mode d) None of these
9. Data classified on the basis of area is called________
   a) Chronological classification
   b) Geographical classification
   c) Qualitative classification
   d) None of these
10. Data classified on the basis of time is called________
   a) Chronological classification
   b) Geographical classification
   c) Qualitative classification
   d) None of these
11. _________ is the lowest and highest values of the distribution that can be included in the class
   a) **Class limit** b) Class midpoint
   c) Class interval d) None of these

Unit 3: Measures of Central Tendency

1. Median and mode of a series 5, 3, 7, 4, 9, 7 and 6 are respectively:
   a) 5 and 7 b) 4 and 9
   c) 6 and 7 d) None of these
2. If a constant 5 is added to each observation of a data series having mean 5 then, the new mean is
   a) 0 b) 5
   c) 25 **d) 10**
3. Sum of squares of deviations is minimum when it taken from :
   a) Mode b) Median
   c) Arithmetic mean d) None of these
4. If 25,34 and 43 are the mid-class values of classes then, the first class is:
   a) 25-34 **b) 20.5-29.5**
   c) 24.5-34.5 d) None of these
5. _______ is an ideal measure of central tendency.
   a) Standard deviation b) Mode
   c) Median **d) Arithmetic mean**

6. AM = GM = HM, when all observations of a series are:

   a) Different **b) Same**
   c) Even d) Odd

7. _______ means extent of scatterness of observations around measure of central tendency.

   a) Dispersion b) Skewness
   c) Kurtosis d) None of these

8. _________ is an ideal measure of central tendency.

   a) Arithmetic mean b) Mode
   c) Median d) Standard deviation

9. The principle of making use of greater homogeneity within block is known as:

   a) Randomization **b) Local control**
   c) Replication d) None of these

10. ______ is most affected by extreme values

    a) Arithmetic mean b) Mode
    c) Median d) Weighted mean

11. Median is _______ type of average.

    a) Algebraic **b) Positional**
    c) Commercial d) None of these

12. If the mean of five observations X, X+2, X+4, X+6, X+8 is 11, then the mean of first four observations is:

    a) 9 b) 9.5
    c) 10 d) 10.5

13. The most suitable measures of central tendency for qualitative data is

    a) Mean **b) Median**
    c) Mode d) None of these

14. The Mean Deviation can never be :

    a) Zero **b) Negative**
    c) Positive d) None of these

15. As an average the mode is :

    a) Positional average b) Mathematical average
    c) Commercial average d) None of these

16. " (X_i % 20) = 0, then $X =$ ______

    a) 0 b) -20
    c) 20 d) None of these

Unit 4: Measures of Dispersion

1. If a constant 10 is subtracted from each observation of a set, then the new variance is:
   a) Unaltered b) Reduced by 25
   c) Reduced by 5 d) Increased by 25
2. Unitless measure of dispersion is :
   a) Variance b) Standard deviation
   c) Coefficient of variation d) Range
3. Standard deviation of a series 6, 6, 6, 6, 6 and 6 is ______
   a) 12 b) 36
   c) 6 **d) 0**
4. If sample variance is 64 , number of observation = 16 and mean = 10, then S.Em. will be;
   a) 4 **b) 2**
   c) 8 d) 80
5. Which is the simple measure of dispersion:
   a) Mean deviation b) Standard deviation
   c) Range d) Variance
6. Variance is square of
   a) Range **b) Standard deviation**
   c) Quartile Deviation d) Mean deviation
7. If each value of a series is divided by 10, then the C.V.% is:
   a) Unaltered b) Reduced by 10
   c) Reduced by 100 d) Increased by 10
8. The Coefficient of variation is always express in:
   a) Percent b) Proportion
   c) Ratio d) None of these
9. If $0.2X_{max} = 2X_{min} = 20$, then the range is:
   a) 10 b) 100
   c) 90 d) 50
10. If 0.2AM = 2SD, then the C.V.% is:
    a) 10 b) 100
    c) 90 d) 50
11. $S^2 > S$ when:
    a) **$S>1$** b) $S = 1$
    c) $0<S<1$ d) None of these

12. ____________ is relative measure of dispersion
    a) S.D. b) Variance
    c) C.V.% d) None of these

Unit 5: Probability distribution

1. Probability can takes value from:
    a) -1 to 1 b) - to 1
    c) -to **d) 0 to 1**
2. If A & B are mutually exclusive event. then P(A?B) is equal to :
    a) P(A)+P(B) b) P(A) P(B)
    c) P(A)+P(B) P(A B) d) P(A)+P(B) + P(A B)
3. If A and B are two events which have no points in common, the events A and B are:
    a) Mutually exclusive b) Independent
    c) Complimentary to each d) None of these other
4. Probability is expressed as
    a) Ratio b) Percentage
    c) Proportion **d) All the above**
5. If A & B are Independent Events, then P(AB) is:
    a) P(A)×P(B) b) P(A) + P(B)
    c) P(A)+P(B)-P(AnB) d) P(A)+P(B) + P(AnB)
6. Classical probability is possible in case of :
    a) Equilikely outcomes b) Unequilikely outcomes
    c) both (a) and (b) d) All of above
7. The probability of all possible outcomes of a random experiment is always equal to :
    a) One b) Zero
    c) Infinity d) None of these

Unit 6: Normal distribution

1. The curve of normal distribution is :
    a) Symptotic curve **b) Asymptotic curve**
    c) Both a & b d) None of these

3. The shape of curve of normal distribution at the centre towards the X-axis is :

a) Convex **b) Concave**

c) Both a & b d) None of these

3. The coefficient of skewness of normal distribution is :

a) **0** b) 3

c) 6 d) 8

5. The coefficient of Kurtosis of normal distribution is :

a) 0 **b) 3**

c) 6 d) 8

6. $\mu \pm 2\sigma$ covers area under normal curve is: (a) (b (c) (d)

a) 50% b) 68%

c) **95%** d) 99%

7. Normal distribution is given by _________

a) De Moivre b) Bernoulli

c) S D Poisson d) R A Fisher

Unit 7: Statistical Inference and testing of hypothesis

1. The χ^2 test was given by :

a) Spearman b) W.S. Gossett

c) R. A. Fisher **d) Karl Pearson**

2. The error committed by accepting true null hypothesis is :

a) Type-I error b) Type-II error

c) Both a & b **d) None of these**

3. Which one is non-parametric test?

a) F–test **b) ?2 -test**

c) Z-test d) t-test

4. The test used to compare two different population with respect to their variances is

a) **F-test** b) Z-test

c) t-test

5. In a 2 x 2 contingency table, R_1=100, C_1=30, C_2=120, the expected frequency of E_{22} is ___

a) 20 b) 150

c) 40 d) None of these

6. "Number of student in the university" is an example of ________ population.

   a) Real b) Hypothetic
   c) Infinite d) None of these

7. If cal F > table F $_{(0.01)\,(10\ edf)}$, then result is said to be;

   a) Significant b) Non-significant
   c) Highly significant d) None of these

8. The probability of committing type-I error denoted by :

   a) α b) β
   c) γ d) None of these

9. t-test is given by:

   a) Boddington **b) W S Gossett**
   c) R A Fisher d) Spearman

10. Whether test is one tailed or two tailed depends on

    a) **Alternate hypothesis** b) Null hypothesis
    c) Composite hypothesis d) Simple hypothesis

11. Paired t-test is applicable when the observations are

    a) Paired b) Equal in number
    c) Dependent **d) All of these**

12. The hypothesis of no difference between different population parametric values from which samples are drawn is called :

    a) Hypothesis **b) Null hypothesis**
    c) Alternate hypothesis d) None of these

13. The error committed by rejecting true null hypothesis is

    a) **Type-I error** b) Type-II error
    c) Both a & b d) None of these

14. The test of significance for n<30 is known as ;

    a) Z test **b) t- test**
    c) F test

15. The test(s) used to compare two different population with respect to their means is/are ;

    a) $?^2$ -test b) Z-test
    c) t-test **d) Both b & c**

16. If rank correlation is 1, means that ______________
    a) The ranks awarded by
    b) There is perfect association two judges are same between the ranks awarded by two judges
    c) All differences are zero
    d) All of these

Unit 8: Correlation analysis

1. Range of correlation coefficient is :
    a) **-1 to +1** b) 0 to 100
    c) -2 to 20 d) None of these
2. When both variables are varying in the same direction then it is the case of ___ correlation.
    a) **Positive** b) Negative
    c) Multiple d) None of these
3. The correlation between pressure and volume of gas is :
    a) Perfect +ve **b) Perfect -ve**
    c) Imperfect -ve d) Imperfect +ve
4. Algebraic method for studying correlation between two variable is given by:
    a) W S Gossett b) Spearman
    c) R A Fisher **d) Karl Pearson**
5. The unit of correlation coefficient is
    a) Kg/cc **b) Unitless**
    c) Per cent d) None of these
6. _____ coefficient is unit free.
    a) Correlation b) Regression
    c) Both (a) and (b) d) None
7. When two variables are studied simultaneously in a population then it is said to be:
    a) **Bivariate population** b) Univariate population
    c) Both (a) and (b) d) None

Unit 9: Regression analysis

1. ________ analysis works out functional relationship between two variables

   a) Regression b) Correlation
   c) Both a & b d) None of these

2. Rate of change in dependent variable is measured as :

   a) Coefficient of variation **b) Regression coefficient**
   c) Correlation coefficient d) None of these

3. _______ test is used to test significance of regression coefficient.

   a) F–test b) Z-test
   c) T-test d) ?2 –test

4. The rate of change in dependent variable(y) with unit change in independent variable(x) is known as

   a) $\mathbf{b_{yx}}$ b) r_{yx}
   c) b_{xy} d) None of these

5. IIf one regression coefficient is greater than unity then the other must be

   a) Greater than unity b) Equal to unity
   c) Less than unity d) None of these

6. _____ coefficient is independent of origin but not of scale.

   a) Regression b) Correlation
   c) Both (a) and (b) d) None of these

Unit 10: Sampling

1. "Number of star in the sky" is an example of ________ population.

   a) Finite b) Hypothetic
   c) Infinite d) None of these

2. Any number estimated from sample is known as :

   a) Parameter **b) Value**
   c) Statistic d) None of these

3. The nature of relationship between sample size and sampling error is:

   a) Positive **b) Negative**
   c) Zero d) Constant

4. When each unit has an equal chance of being selection, then ___ method of sampling is to be used.

   a) Stratified   **b) Simple random**

   c) Cluster   d) Systematic

5. If the members of population does not exist in reality then the population is called :

   a) Hypothetical   b) Real

   c) Finite   d)

6. The sampling error decreases as the size of sample :

   a) Remain constant   b) Decreases

   c) **Increases**   d) None of these

Unit 11: Experimental Design

1. Error d.f. in LSD

   a) **(t-1)(t-2)**   b) r(t-1)

   c) (r-1) (t-1)   d) None of these

2. Repetition of the treatment in an experiment is known as:

   a) Randomization   b) Local control

   c) Replication   d) None of these

3. In RBD, number of treament =10, replication=4, treatment SS=54, then what will be treatment MS (MST)?

   a) 5   b) 9

   c) 6   d) 5.4

4. It is a mathematical process of partitioning the total sum of square into various recognized sources of variation.

   a) MS   **b) ANOVA**

   c) EMS   d) None of these

5. Random allotment of treatment within block is known as:

   a) **Randomization**   b) Replication

   c) Local control   d) None of these

6. When fertility gradient in two way direction __ design is used.

   a) CRD   **b) LSD**

   c) RBD   d) None of these

7. An experimental unit in a research work is
   a) A field plot
   b) A group of insects
   c) An animal
   d) All of these
8. The factor like spacing, date of sowing and varieties are often used as
   a) Treatment
   b) Replication
   c) Experimental unit
   d) None of these
9. In a CRD with 9 treatments and 5 repetition, error degree of freedom are
   a) 36
   b) 49
   c) 45
   d) 40
10. When experimental materials are homogenous then __ design is to be used.
   a) RBD
   b) CRD
   c) LSD
   d) None of these
11. Local control is absent in __ design.
   a) RBD
   b) CRD
   c) LSD
   d) None of these
12. An experimental design is :
   a) A map
   b) An architect
   c) A plan of expt
   d) All of above
13. Randomization is a process of allotting treatments to the experimental units :
   a) With equal probability
   b) In a sequence
   c) As per the will of investigator
   d) None of these
14. Experimental error is due to :
   a) Variation in treatment effects
   b) Extraneous factors
   c) Experimenter's mistakes
   d) None of these
15. Local control of error is a device to maintain :
   a) Homogeneity within blocks
   b) Homogeneity between blocks
   c) Both (a) and (b)
   d) None of these

16. The maximum error degree of freedom can be provided for same numbers of treatment and replication of a experiment by:

a) RBD b) **CRD**

c) LSD d) None of these

19

Agricultural Extension

1. .... is the study of human relationship in rural environment.
   a) Sociology **b) Rural sociology**
   c) Indian sociology d) None of the above
2. Journal of Extension is published from ....
   a) UK **b) USA**
   c) Germany d) Holland
3. Father of Sociology..............
   a) Auguste Compte b) J.P. Legan
   c) J.B. Chitamber d) None of the above
4. Trustworthiness & competency are elements of ....
   a) Credibility b) Fidelity
   c) Empathy d) None of the above
5. Extension method classified as individual, group and mass contact according to...........
   a) Form **b) Use**
   c) Periodicity d) Number of people contacted
6. The .... population is more homogenous in nature.
   a) Rural b) Urban
   c) Social d) None of the above
7. The technique used for projects involving activities of non -repetitive nature is ....
   a) CPM b) WBS
   c) PERT d) PRA
8. There is definite procedure of functioning in ....
   a) Primary group b) Secondary group
   c) Horizontal group d) None of the above

9. ....is the arrangement of individuals or groups of people into hierarchically arranged in a community?

a) Social group **b) Social stratification**

c) Social organization d) None of the above

10. It is most rigid and clearly graded type of social stratification and has been often referred to as the extreme form of closed ....system.

a) Class **b) Caste**

c) Social d) None of the above

11. The term caste was derived from the Portuguese word '................'

a) Caste b) breed

c) Race **d) None of the above**

12. ....is the patterns of learned behavior.

a) Culture b) Rituals

c) Folkways d) None of the above

13. Violation of ....viewed very seriously.

a) Folkways b) Mores

c) Taboos d) None of the above

14. ....are not innate.

a) Attitude b) Value

c) Cultural lag d) None of the above

15. .... is an organized system of social relationships which embodies certain common values and procedures and meets certain basic needs of society.

a) Social institution b) Social organization

c) Social value d) None of the above

16. The audible range of sound waves for human beings is between ....

a) 20 & 30000 Hertz b) 20 & 10000 Hertz

c) 10 & 30000 Hertz **d) 20 & 20000 Hertz**

17. Guttman scale is basically a ....

a) Summanted rating scale b) Equal appearing interval scale

c) Cumulative scale d) None of the above

18. The family is the most basic ....

a) Social institution b) Social organization

c) Social value d) None of the above

19. The difference between what is and what ought to be is **..........**

a) Need **b) Aim**

c) Goal d) Objective

20. A blue print for action is ....

a) Plan b) Programme

c) Objective d) Project

21. Lab to Land programmed is associated with ICARs ....

a) Golden jubilee b) Silver jubilee

c) Diamond jubilee d) Platinum jubilee

22. The president of ICAR is ....

a) Prime Minister **b) Union Agricultural Minister**

c) Director General d) Finance Minister

23. The book entitled 'Agricultural Extension' was written by ....

a) A Reddy b) R Chambers

c) Van Den Ban d) R M Rogers

24. Extension is considered as a ....

a) Hard Science b) Conceptual Science

c) Pure Social Science d) Decision Oriented Science

25. ATMA is a component of ....

a) NAIP **b) NATP**

c) ICT d) SREP

26. .... is a belief in super natural powers.

a) Religion b) Family

c) Education d) None of the above

27. .... involves alteration in the structure and function of society.

a) Social value **b) Social change**

c) Social control d) None of the above

28. They arise out of the political system.

a) MLA b) MP

c) Chief Minister **d) All above**

29. The Psychology was derived from .... word 'Psyche' meaning is soul or Atman.

a) Greek b) Latin

c) French d) English

30. MBO was developed in ....
    a) 1948 **b) 1954**
    c) 1923 d) 1936
31. The term Extension Education was first coined in ....
    a) USA b) UK
    c) Netherland d) India
32. Father of University Extension ....
    a) James Staurt b) Van Den
    c) Paul Leagan d) Robert Chambers
33. A recognizable working imitation or replication of the original ....
    a) Model b) Specimen
    c) Objects d) Mock-up
34. .... French psychologist evolved good tests on intelligence.
    a) Alfred Binet b) Brown
    c) Thorndike d) None of the above
35. I.Q is determined .... % by the heredity and ....% by environment.
    a) 68%, 32% b) 32%, 68%
    c) 20%, 80% d) 20%, 20%
36. Personality comes from the ....'Persona' which means the mask worn by players in the theater.
    a) Greek **b) Latin**
    c) French d) English
37. In SWOT Analysis 'T' stands for__.
    a) Team **b) Threats**
    c) Targets d) Troubleshoot
38. According to the I.Q. formula a child with an M.A. of 10 and C.A. 10, so what is I.Q.? Level of Child.
    a) Normal b) Abnormal
    c) Border line d) Superior
39. The term Sociology was coined by__.
    a) Auguste Comte b) Sing S.N.
    c) Raddy S.V. d) Bhatnagar
40. Long Form of KVM.
    a) Krushi Vidnyan Mandal b) Krushi Vidnyan Mohostav
    c) Krushi Vasant Mohostav d) Krushi Vidhyarti Mandal

41. Father of Sociology.
    a) Auguste Comte b) Sing S.N.
    c) Raddy S.V. d) Bhatnagar

42. IN Word Extension, 'Ex' meaning ___.
    a) Out b) Outstanding
    c) Out off d) Stretching

43. ______ is a positive or negative feeling one has towards any psychological object.
    a) Attitude b) Objective
    c) Principle d) Psychology

44. Example of Professional leader.
    a) Sarpanch b) Gramsevek
    c) Cast leader **d) President**

45. .... are the customary ways of behaving in the society.
    a) Folkways b) Rituals
    c) Traditions d) None of the above

46. .... are the negative action envisaging what ought not to be done, e.g. not smoking in front of elders.
    a) Rituals b) Tradition
    c) Folkways **d) Taboos**

47. S-M-C-R-E model developed by__.
    a) Aristotles b) Shannon-Weaver
    c) Leagans **d) Rogger & Shoomaker**

48. OHP is a ____.
    a) Indirected Projector b) Directed Projector
    c) Reflected Projector **d) Reflected & Indirected Projector**

49. Learning by Doing is a Principle of__.
    a) Method Demonstration b) Result Demonstration
    c) Group Discussion **d) Method & Result Demonstration**

50. Seeing is believing is a Principle of__.
    a) Method Demonstration **b) Result Demonstration**
    c) Group Discussion d) Method & Result Demonstration

51. ____ is the Bridge between communicator and learner.
    a) Speaker b) Message
    c) Channel d) Feed Back

52. Farm science center is a synonym of
   a) FTC b) DGC
   c) KVK d) Teleclub
53. NAEP is implemented in the year ....
   a) 1980 **b) 1982**
   c) 1986 d) 1984
54. The ATMA operates at ....
   a) State level **b) District level**
   c) National level d) Block level
55. The new name of VLW is ....
   a) VDO b) VEO
   c) CDO d) VDW
56. Logic is a science of ....
   a) Reality b) Foam
   c) Truth **d) Reasoning**
57. The first transfer of technology project of ICAR was ....
   a) LLP b) ORP
   c) AICPND d) KVK
58. The NAARM training for freshly recruited ARS trainees falls under.........
   a) Pre-training **b) Induction training**
   c) Orientation training d) Refresher training
59. Attitude scale are used to measure............
   a) Opinion b) Judgment
   c) Fact d) None of the above
60. The medium that does not disturb normal work much.........
   a) Television **b) News paper**
   c) Radio d) Video
61. Desert Development Programme was launched on...........
   a) 1977-78 b) 1968-69
   c) 1971- 72 d) 1956-57
62. While reading any visual, human eye moves normally in a ....
   a) 'Y' like Pattern b) 'c' like Pattern
   c) 'W' like Pattern **d) 'Z' like Pattern**

63. The optimum number of flash card is ....

a) 10-12 b) 12-14

c) 14-16 d) 16-18

64. International women's day is celebrated on ....

a) 8th March b) 16th October

c) 1st November d) 22nd December

65. The basic unit of development under IRDP is ....

a) District b) Family

c) Village d) CD block

66. Poster is most effective at which stage.................

a) Awareness b) Evaluation

c) Testing d) Persuasion

67. An agricultural innovator is a ....

a) Traditional leader b) Opinion leader

c) Functional leader d) Formal leader

68. The term 'Management' was derived from ....

a) Latin b) French

c) Greek d) Sanskrit

69. 'POSCORB' as management function was developed by ....

a) Gullick & Urwick b) Urwick

c) L. Gullick d) H. Fayol

70. Brainstorming method was developed by ....

a) Alex Osborn b) Gorden

c) Andrews d) Kolb

71. Training is basically a ....

a) Product **b) Process**

c) Activity d) Programme

72. The basic aim of science is ....

a) Theory **b) Prediction**

c) Control d) None of the above

73. 'covedale' methodology of training is the characteristic methodology followed in ....

a) IARI b) MANAGE

c) IIM d) SIETI

74. National Service Scheme was started in ....
    a) 1966 b) 1967
    c) 1953 **d) 1969**
75. The most commonly used method in a social survey is ....
    a) Observation b) Interview
    c) Questionnaire d) Case study
76. Age is classified under ....
    a) Discontinuous variable b) Discrete variable
    c) Continuous variable d) Intervening variable
77. The S in the SMART objective refers to ....
    a) Simple **b) Specific**
    c) Sincere d) Secure
78. Modernization must start from..........
    a) Man b) Individual
    c) Group **d) Society**
79. Linkert scale for measurement of attitude falls under ....
    a) Nominal level **b) Ordinal**
    c) Interval d) Ratio
80. The word logic has its root in ....
    a) Greek b) Latin
    c) French d) Persian
81. The unit of correlation coefficient is.........
    a) Kg/cc b) Per cent
    c) No unit d) None of the above
82. The science that deals with adult learning is ....
    a) Androgogy b) Pedagogy
    c) Penology d) Edaphology
83. Who is considered as the father of extension education.......
    a) Adivi Reddy b) O.P Dahama
    c) K.N Singh d) J B Chaitamber
84. Administration is ....
    a) Policy making
    b) Execution of policy
    c) Giving direction to things
    d) None of the above

85. Entrepreneur is people who take ....

a) **High risk** b) Low risk
c) No risk d) Moderate risk

86. LCD expands to ....

a) Laizer Crystal Display b) Laizer Crystal Digital
c) Liquid Crystal Digital **d) Liquid Crystal Display**

87. The concept of five year plan was adopted from ....

a) China **b) Russia**
c) Britain d) America

88. The third tire of Panchayat Raj is.........

a) Zilla Parishad b) District
c) Panchayat Samiti d) Block

89. Micro lab exercise in a training programme is conducted at its.............

a) Beginning b) Middle
c) End d) Any time

90. The T & V system was sponsored by ....

a) WHO **b) World Bank**
c) USAID d) IMF

91-95 Match the pairs ....

a) Seminar	1) Presentation of research under expert guidance
b) Symposium	2) Papers covers different sub division of a topic
c) Workshop	3) Emphasis on small working groups
d) Conference	4) Pooling of experience among expert group
e) Syndicate	5) Primary study groups from among representatives

96-100 Match the pairs ....

f) IRDP	**1) 1978**
g) IAAP	**2) 1964**
h) NAEP	**3) 1983**
i) IADP	**4) 1966**
j) HYVP	**5) 1960**

1. Use of demonstration in extension work was first made by

   a) Dr. A.T. Mosher b) Dr. John Tuley

   c) Dr. Seaman Knapp d) Dr. A.W. Van Den Ban

2. Which Extension approach is more used by NGOs than Government Extension Organizations?

   a) Authoritarian approach **b) Participatory approach**

   c) Coercive approach d) Non-participatory approach

3. A registered society of key stakeholders involved in agricultural activities for sustainable agricultural development of the district is known as

   a) NGO b) FIAC

   c) ATMA d) DRDA

4. Extension education is a type of

   a) Formal education **b) Non formal education**

   c) Informal education d) None of these

5. Last step in extension teaching is

   a) Satisfaction b) Conviction

   c) Action by the learner d) Desire

6. Single sheet of paper folded to make four pages of printed material is called as

   a) Folder **b) Leaflet**

   c) Booklet d) Bulletin

7. I.C.A.R. was established in the year

   a) 1929 b) 1934

   c) 1904 d) 1937

8. Extension education should develop the programmes

   a) On the directions of Extension Agents.

   b) According to the needs of farmers.

   c) With the directions of Gram Sevak.

   d) With all of them.

9. A rural reconstruction institute was established at Shriniketan in the year

   a) 1908 **b) 1921**

   c) 1912 d) 1935

10. 'Krishi Vigyan Kendras' are sponsored by
    a) U.G.C. b) I.A.R.I.
    c) I.C.A.R. d) State Government
11. Bulletins, leaflets, circular letter, posters, fairs, exhibitions, radio and television are the media of
    a) Individual Communication b) Official Communication
    c) Group Communication **d) Mass Communication**
12. A,B,C of journalism stands for
    a) Accuracy, Brevity and Clarity
    b) Attractive, Brief and Clear
    c) Accuracy, Brief and Clarity
    d) None of these
13. Which are the devices used to create system in which communication takes place between the instructor and the learner ?
    a) Learning theories **b) Teaching Methods**
    c) Teaching aids d) None of these
14. Gurgaon Experiment was started by
    a) F.L.Brayne. b) Albert Mayer
    c) M.K.Gandhi. d) Spencer Hatch
15. National Extension Service in India was established in
    a) 1950 b) 1952
    c) 1951 **d) 1953**
16. Indirect Projection Technique is used in
    a) Slide Projector **b) Overhead Projector**
    c) Opaque Projector d) None of these
17. In Tape Recorder the plastic or paper tape is coated with a very finely ground of
    a) Copper oxide material b) Sliver oxide material
    c) Iron Oxide material d) Iron + Silver Oxide material
18. Use of 5 'W's and 'H' is a guide in writing the
    a) Circular letter b) Personal letter
    c) News story d) Folder
19. Who is supposed to be the father of sociology?
    a) F.Stuart b) Sorokin
    c) Zimmerman **d) Auguste comte**

20. The book"Rural sociology in India" is authored by
    a) Sanderson **b) Desai A.R.**
    c) Smith T.L. d) Sorokin P.A.
21. Temporary collection of people reacting to a stimulus is known as
    a) Mob **b) Crowd**
    c) Audience d) Mass
22. Panchayat Samiti is guided by
    a) Zilla Parishad
    b) V.L.W.
    c) BDO and his extension officers
    d) None of these
23. The purpose of introducing agricultural universities in India is to improve the agriculture through
    a) Extension and Research
    b) Extension
    c) Extension, teaching and research
    d) Teaching
24. The basic village institutions are
    a) Panchayat, Hospital and School
    b) Panchayat, Co-operative and School
    c) Youth club, School and Co-operative
    d) Family, Mahila Mandal & School
25. "Panchayat Raj" was started in the year
    a) 1953 **b) 1959**
    c) 1955 d) 1952
26. Panchayat Raj was first time introduced in which of the following states?
    a) Andhra Pradesh b) Rajasthan
    c) Pubjab d) Orissa
27. Which of the following indicates the quality of individual's total behaviour ?
    a) Characteristics **b) Personality**
    c) Attitude d) Trait
28. Maximum number of members in Gram Panchayat is
    a) 15 **b) 17**
    c) 19 d) 13

29. Who is the First Citizen of a village ?

a) Gramsevak | b) **Sarpanch**
c) Talathi | d) Police Patil

30. The Service Co-operatives provide the long term loan for

a) Crop production | b) Purchase of implements
c) Construction of well | d) **Purchase of tractor**

31. I. Q. level of Genius person is

a) 141-180 | b) **181 & above**
c) 91-100 | d) None of these

32. The tendency to consider one's own culture as the best is termed as

a) Cultural ego. | b) Cultural pride
c) Cultural bias | **d) Ethnocentrism**

33. It is an error- correcting mechanism that can overcome noise.

a) Encoder | **b) Feed back**
c) Diffusion | d) Communication

34. It is discriminatory response of an organism to stimulus.

a) Communication | b) Diffusion
c) Innovation | d) Feed back

35. The ability to project ourselves into others personalities is called

a) Apathy | b) Sympathy
c) Empathy | d) Non of these

36. Channels used for communication to large number of people.

a) Mass media | b) Interpersonal
c) Intrapersonal | d) None of these

37. Action-reaction interdependence in the process of communication is called

a) Diffusion | b) Transmission
c) Feed back | d) None of these

38. These are physical bridges between the sender and the receiver of message.

a) Message | **b) Channels**
c) Communication | d) Link

39. Leagan's model of communication has number of elements

a) Four
b) Five
c) Six
d) Seven

40. It is the degree to which communication sources are perceived as trustworthy and competent by the receiver.

a) Compatibility
b) Observability
c) Credibility
d) Communicability

41. The flow of information from top to bottom in the organisation is called

a) Cross communication
b) Downward Communication
c) Upward communication
d) Diagonal communication

42. It is the mutual and reciprocal influencing of each others behavior.

a) Feed back
b) Communication
c) Interaction
d) Diffusion

43. National Institute of Agricultural Extension Management is known as

a) NAARM
b) CRIDA
c) MANAGE
d) NIRD

44. STEP means

a) Satellite Telephone Exchange Process
b) Satellite Training and Education Programme
c) Satellite Telecommunication Experiments Project
d) Seed Testing Experiment Programme

45. Who are traditional and the last to adopt an innovation?

a) Laggards
b) Late majority
c) Innovators
d) Early adopter

46. The University Grants Commission has started the programme of students engaged in higher studies and the educated public at large.

a) INSAT-1A
b) INSAT- 1B
c) INSAT-1C
d) INSAT-1D

47. Is the degree to which an Individual acts as an opinion leader for variety of topics?

a) Monomorphism
b) Polymorphism
c) Triomorphism
d) Heterophily

48. It is the degree to which an innovation may be experimented with on a limited basis called as

a) Compatibility
b) Communicability
c) Trialability
d) Relative advantage

49. An innovation is a

a) Perceived newness of these three
b) New practice
c) New object
d) New idea

50. Number of adopter categories are

a) Four
b) Five
c) Six
d) Three

20

Fundamentals of Horticulture

1. Pomology word is derived from a————————

   a) Greek word b) Latin word

   c) English word d) None of these

2. Deficiency of ——————vitamin causes scurvy.

   a) A b) B

   c) C d) D

3. Diseased free plants in micro propagation can be achieved through ————

   a) Meristem culture b) Leaf culture

   c) Stem culture d) Root culture

4. Flower thinning in grapes is done with—————— hormone.

   a) GA3 b) IBA

   c) IAA d) CPA

5. Fruit thinning growth regulator is——————

   a) NAA b) Ethylene

   c) 4-CPA d) IAA

6. Scientific names are written in—————— language.

   a) Latin b) English

   c) Roman d) Italian

7. Hot water treatment of hard coat seed for coat permeability is called———.

   a) Verbalization b) Scarification

   c) Stratification d) None of these

8. Agricultural and Processed Food Products Export Development Authority (APEDA) was established——————

   a) 1980 **b) 1986**

   c) 1985 d) 1990

9. Maximum number of plants can be planted in the orchard by the system———

a) Diagonal **b) Hexagonal**

c) Square d) Rectangular

10. Mallika is a cross between——————— ———————

a) Dashehari & Langra **b) Neelum & Dashehari**

c) Neelum & Langra d) Banganapalli & Alphanso

11. Bunchy top is a disease of ————————————

a) Banana b) Citrus

c) Guava d) Pine apple

12. In budding & grafting the union between stock & scion takes place through——

a) Phloem b) Cortex

c) Cambium d) Xylem

13. In grafting lower part of plant is known as ————————

a) Bud b) Apical

c) Stock d) Scion

14. Which is most suitable C/N ratio for growth and fruiting is concerned———

a) CC/NN **b) CCC/NN**

c) CCC/N d) CC/NNN

15. L-49 is selection from Allahabad Safeda made during 1927 by Dr. G. S. Cheema at—

a) Pune b) Allahabad

c) Lucknow d) New Delhi

16. Mango fruit can be best stored at ————————————

a) 4 °C **b) 8 °C**

c) 16 °C d) None of these

17. Modified stem of banana is called as ——————————.

a) Sword suckers **b) Rhizome**

c) Water sucker d) Corm

18. The nutrient element which improves quality of fruit is———————

a) K b) Zn

c) P d) Ca

19. Iron deficiency in plant is characterized by ———————————
    a) Intervenial chlorosis of old leaves
    b) Little leaf
    c) Yellowing of new leaves
    d) Molting of leaf
20. Among fruits the highest vitamin 'A' content is in mango and it is about— ———
    a) 200 IU/ 100 g b) 1500 IU/ 100 g
    c) 4000 IU/ 100 g d) 300IU/ 100g
21. Ber is commercially propagated by———————————
    a) Seed **b) Budding**
    c) Inarching d) Layering
22. Pomology is defined as science of cultivation of ———————————-
    a) Fruits b) Vegetables
    c) Flowers d) None of these
23. Which of the following is a ripening hormone———————————
    a) G A3 b) Cytokinin
    c) Eethylene d) Abscisic acid
24. A plant which completes its life cycle within one season is called as—— ——————
    a) Annual b) Biennial
    c) Perennial d) None of these
25. Acta horticulture is a publication of———————————
    a) ASHS, USA **b) ISHS, Belgium**
    c) JSHS, Japan d) HIS, India
26. Fig belongs to the family ———————————
    a) Moraceae b) Arecaceae
    c) Annonaceae d) Lauraceae
27. Lalit is an improved variety of———————————-
    a) Guava b) Papaya
    c) Grape d) Pineapple
28. Micro grafting is used to produce plants free from ———————————
    a) Viruses b) Fungus
    c) Bacteria d) Nematode

29. Wind break for protecting orchards from strong wind is planted on —————— direction of the orchard.
    a) South-west b) North-East
    c) South-East **d) North-West**
30. ——————is an intensive type of vegetable gardening
    a) Truck garden **b) Market garden**
    c) Kitchen garden d) Floating vegetable garden
31. Physiological disorder 'stony fruit' is observed in——————fruit crop.
    a) Banana b) Citrus
    c) Guava **d) Custard apple**
32. Application of fertilizers through drip system of irrigation is known as———————.
    a) Fertigation b) Drip irrigation
    c) Fustigation d) Fertilizer application
33. For ripening, fruits are treated with ——————.
    a) Cycocel **b) Ethylene**
    c) GA d) IAA
34. Seed treatment of breaking hard seed coat by mechanical means is called as ————.
    a) Scarification b) Stratification
    c) Abrazing d) Grading
35. —————— is generally used for rooting of cuttings.
    a) NAA b) GA
    c) IBA d) Cytokinin
36. Guava belongs to family ——————
    a) Caricaceae **b) Myrtaceae**
    c) Anacaridiaceae d) Moraceae
37. —————— is regular bearer mango cultivar.
    a) Neelum b) Dashahari
    c) Kesar d) Alphanso
38. —————— system of training is followed in mango.
    a) Open center b) Bower system
    c) Central lea **d) Modified leader**
39. —————— of the following plants is propagated vegetatively.
    a) *Luffa cylindrical* **b) *Coccinia indica***
    c) *Luffa acutangula* d) *Cucurbita pepo*

40. Phule Raja is a hybrid of ———————-

a) Okra **b) Tomato**

c) Brinjal d) Cucumber

41. Kalipatti is variety of ——————————— crop.

a) Pomegranate b) Kagzi lime

c) Sapota d) Mango

42. Hexagonal system of planting accommodate -—————— % of more no. of plants than square system.

a) 20 **b) 15**

c) 10 d) 25

43. The angle made by the attachment of a branch to the trunk or another branch is called as

a) Spur **b) Crotch**

c) Sprout d) Scaffold

44. In grafting the upper part of plant is known as ——————————— .

a) Scion b) Branch

c) Stock d) Shoot

45. Vellai Collumban a Polyembryonic root stock is used in grafting operation for ———

a) Citrus b) Sapota

c) Custard apple **d) Mango**

46. Kagzi lime is commercially propagated by ———————

a) Budding b) Layering

c) Cutting **d) Seed**

47. In micro propagation the plant part used is known as ———————

a) Explant b) Shoot

c) Organ d) Bud

48. The herbicides which kill the entire vegetation of the treated area is ——————————.

a) Non- selective herbicide

b) Selective herbicide

c) Translocated herbicide

d) Contact herbicide

49. Alternate bearing in mango is not observed in ——————.

a) Alphanso b) Pairi

c) Totapuri d) Kesar

50. The development of fruit in the absence of fertilization, the phenomenon is known as ——————

a) Pollination b) Misfertilization

c) Parthenocarpy d) None

51. Popular thorn less rootstock of rose is

a) Grandgala b) Marcedes

c) Motera d) All

52. Off sets are mainly used to propagate

a) Agave b) Pandanus

c) Aloe **d) All**

53. Bottom heating technique is useful is propagation of

a) Coleus **b) Bougainvillea**

c) Ara caria d) Rose

54. .... is a form of repair grafting

a) Bridge grafting b) Top working

c) Both d) None

55. Oldest propagation method of mango is

a) Stone grafting **b) Inarching**

c) Veneer grafting d) Bridge grafting

56. For rooting of cutting which of the following growth regular is mostly used

a) GA_3 b) IAA

c) IBA d) NAA

57. Best method of vegetative propagation in pomegranate is

a) Veneer grafting b) Patch budding

c) Chip budding **d) Air layering**

58. Villaicolamban is a root stock used in

a) Mango b) Tamarind

c) Sapota d) Guava

59. Khirni is used as root stock for

a) Sapota b) Longan

c) Mango d) Jamun

60. Stooling is commercial method of propagation
    a) Apple   b) Litchi
    c) Guava   d) Citrus
61. Example of non endospermic seed is————
    a) Orchid   b) Coconut
    c) Mango   d) None of these
62. Edible portion of coconut is ————
    a) Thalamus   **b) Endosperm**
    c) Placenta   d) None of these
63. Success of a graft union is mostly depends upon ————
    a) Union of bark   **b) Union of cambium**
    c) Union of xylem   d) None of these
64. Commercially Strawberry is propagated by ————
    a) Bulbs   **b) Runners**
    c) Tubers   d) Corms
65. Costliest cladding material for protected structures is...............
    a) Poythene   b) **Polycarbonate**
    c) Polyethylene   d) Carbon paper
66. Salt tolerant tootstock in mango is ————
    a) Alphonso   **b) Kurukkan**
    c) Villaicolamban   d) None of these
67. Polyembrony is observed in ————
    a) Litchi   **b) Jamun**
    c) Guava   d) None of these
68. Phylloxera is a problem of............
    a) Grape   b) Coconut
    c) Mango   d) None of these
69. Callus is a group of———— tissue
    a) Parenchymatous   b) Scheleronchymatous
    c) Both a) and b)   d) None of these
70. Dog ridge is a rootstock of————
    a) Rose   b) Coconut
    c) Grape   d) None of these

71. Grafting is possible in ——————

a) Arecanut b) Oil palm

c) Coconut **d) None of these**

72. *Canna indica* is propagated by——————-

a) Rhizomes b) Suckers

c) Tubers d) None of these

73. Dahlias are propagated by——————

a) Tubers b) Seed

c) Both a) and b) d) Corm

74. Thiourea is used as ——————

a) Vase solution b) Rooting hormone

c) Dormancy breaker d) Weedicide

75. 2-4-D is an example of ——————

a) Weedicide b) Auxin

c) Both a) and b) d) None of these

76. —————— is a thornless rootstock of rose

a) BHR 41 **b) BHR 4**

c) IARI 4 d) IARI 41

77. Rose seeds are extracted from——————

a) Thalamus b) Balusta

c) Hips d) Etario

78. Virus free plants can be produced from shoot tips due to high levels of endogenous ———

a) Auxins b) Beta carotenoids

c) Absiccic acid d) None of these

79. 4-chlorofurone (CPPU) is an example of ——————

a) Growth retardant **b) Cytokinin**

c) Auxin d) None of these

80. ……….. is responsible for downward flow of water and nutrients in plants

a) Xylem b) Meristem

c) Phloem d) None of these

81. Tongue layering is commercially followed in————

a) Strawberry b) Mangosteen

c) Guava d) Apple

82. *Wadelia lobata* is propagated by————

a) Cutting b) Eye budding

c) Ring budding d) Micro grafting

83. Somaclonal variation has now became a problem in ————

a) Banana b) Citrus

c) Litchi d) Apple

84. Apomixes is closely related to……..

a) Nucellus b) Cambium

c) Xylem d) None of these

85. Genetic ability of a cell to regenerate in to whole plant is called as ————

a) Phytogenesis **b) Totiopotency**

c) Hippoglycemis d) Vernalization

86. Scarification is a term related to ————

a) Bud dormancy **b) Seed dormancy**

c) Rejuvenation d) All of these

87. Commercially ixora is propagated by————

a) Cleft grafting b) Seed

c) Air layering d) Eye budding

88. Rejuvenation of old trees is possible through————

a) Bridge grafting b) Chip budding

c) Tissue culture d) Compounding

89. ———— rootstock is suitable for HDP in apple

a) M999 **b) M9**

c) W9 d) M99

90. EMCA series of rootstock of Apple is resistant to ————.

a) Viruses b) Bacteria

c) Fungi d) Mycoplasma

91. ——————— test is used to measure viability of seed.

a) ELISA **b) Tetrazolium**

c) Germination d) Sulphuric acid

92. The commonly employed rootstock for propagation of pear is ————

a) Temple b) 1613

c) Kainth d) Seedling

93. ——————— is a dwarfing rootstock of pear.

a) Quince b) Quince A

c) Quince D **d) Quince C**

94. ——————— rootstock of peach is resistant to root knot nematode.

a) Nemaguard b) Dogridge

b) Seedling d) Mahua

95. Myrobalan is a vigorous rootstock of ———————

a) Apricot b) Cherry

c) Plum d) Pear

96. *Anacardium pumilum* is a dwarf rootstock of ——————.

a) Mango **b) Cashew nut**

c) Mangosteen d) Walnut

97. Papaya is commercially propagated by ——————

a) Seed b) Cutting

c) Soft wood grafting d) Hard wood cutting

98. Bud union is most susceptible to ——————— than any other part of Rose.

a) Low Moisture b) Low humidity

c) Low temperatue d) High Humidity

99. ——————— rootstock of Citrus is resistant to Greening.

a) Adajamir b) Troyer citrange

c) Rough lemon d) Rangpur lime

100. ………….. is a world's largest selling potted plant

a) Acalypha **b) Poinsettia**

c) Tithonia c) Gaillardia

21

Fruit Science

1. __________________ work for grape fruit setting.
   a) Alar
   b) IAA
   c) Cytokinin
   d) Abscissic acid
2. A fruits that develops from a hollow pear-shaped fleshy receptacle (hypanthodium) which encloses a number of minute male and female flowers in known as :
   a) Aggregate fruit
   b) Hesperidium
   c) Pome fruit
   d) Syconus fruit
3. A perfect jelly have pectin of :
   a) 1.5 %
   b) 1.0 %
   c) 11.25 %
   d) 2.0 %
4. Air layering is most common in :
   a) Rose
   b) Litchi
   c) Grape
   d) Guava
5. Allahabad Safeda is the variety of :
   a) Mango
   b) Guava
   c) Loquat
   d) Grapes
6. An apple tree will give the fruits after __________ of planting
   a) 5 years
   b) 3 years
   c) 2 years
   d) 8 years
7. Artificial ripening is very difficult in :
   a) Lemon
   b) Papaya
   c) Persimon
   d) Plums
8. Asepsis mean :
   a) Exclusive of air
   b) Exclusion of moisture/water
   c) Exclusion of dust and spray
   d) Exclusion of micro-organism

9. Branch of science that deals with study of principles of propogation and production of vegetables is called:
   a) Olericulture b) Floriculture
   c) Pomology d) None of these
10. Canning is a method of
   a) Heat processing b) Non heat processing
   c) Sterilization d) Any other
11. Citrus fruits can be preserved for a few weeks at room temperature by :
   a) Submerging them in cold water and then drying
   b) Keeping them in well ventilated room
   c) Putting them in an atmosphere rich in CO_2
   d) By wrapping individual fruit in HDP envelopes
12. Culcutta Early seedless and Rose scented are the varieties of :
   a) Guava b) Papaya
   c) Mango **d) Lithchi**
13. Cutting from broad leaved evergreen tress are usually taken in :
   a) Early summer b) Early winter
   c) Late summer d) None of the above
14. Die back of citrus can be controlled with the application of :
   a) Bordeaux mixture b) Endosulfan
   c) Zinc sulphate d) B.H.C
15. Fastenning vines to a upright support of a tree called panagara (*Erithrina indica*) known as :
   a) Kniffen system b) Head system
   c) Single stake system d) Cordon system
16. Fin in India is grown in :
   a) Madhya Pradesh b) Punjab
   c) Kerala **d) Gujrat**
17. For jelly making the best fruit is :
   a) Sour apple b) Ripe banana
   c) Ripe mango **d) Ber**
18. For jelly preparation very important fruit is :
   a) Guava b) Mango
   c) Apple d) Grapes

19. GA_3 _______ spray can increase the size of grape.
    a) 20 ppm b) 1000ppm
    c) 1 ppm d) 2 ppm
20. Grapevine will start fruiting after ____of planting.
    a) 4 years b) 5 years
    c) 1.5 years d) 2.5 years
21. Grapes are generally dried in :
    a) Sun b) Dehydrator
    c) Spray drier d) Vaccum drier
22. Grapes are pruned only once in northern india while they are pruned twice in southern India. This difference is due to the face that grapes :
    a) Shed leaves in winter in northern India while they remain evergreen in southern India
    b) Are early in bearing in northern India while they bear late in southern India
    c) Bear lightly in northern India while they bear heavily in southern
    d) Are less prone to diseases in southern India
23. Grapes contain which of the following acids ?
    a) Malic acid **b) Tartaric acid**
    c) Hydrocyanic acid d) Glutonic acid
24. Ground layering is most layering is most common in :
    a) Rose b) Litchi
    c) Begonia d) Pomegranate
25. Guava tree will give the fruits after ________ of planting.
    a) 4 years b) 2 years
    c) 7 years d) 10 years
26. Guava is a native of :
    a) Tropical south-east Asia b) Tropical Africa
    c) Tropical America d) Sub-tropical India
27. Hard-wood cutting is a propagating material used in :
    a) Date b) Fig
    c) Grape d) Begonia
28. Himrod and Perlette are the varieties of :
    a) Grape b) Mango
    c) Papaya d) Guava

29. Ideal pH for orchard crops is :

a) 6-8 b) 5-7

c) 4-6 d) 9-13

30. In apple small, narrow and mottled leaves are primarily because of the deficiency of :

a) Zinc b) Iron

c) Potassium d) Iodine

31. In budding the length of scion bud should be :

a) 1.0" to 2.0" b) 2.0" ti 2.5"

c) 0.5" to 1.12" d) None of these

32. In cutting ________ inches long part of one year age should be used.

a) 6-9 b) 12-16

c) 1-2 d) 15-20

33. In grafting lower part of plant is known as :

a) Stock b) T-Shield

c) Both of them d) None of them

34. In grafting upper part of stem is called :

a) Stock **b) Scion**

c) Bud d) Apical

35. In hexagonal method of tree planting, about ________ percent more trees can be planted than triangular method.

a) 25 b) 40

c) 10 **d) 15**

36. In hilly area which system of fruit planting should be used :

a) Contour b) Strip cropping

c) Wind strip cropping d) None of these

37. In orchard layout smallest area should be allocated under :

a) Irrigation channels **b) Road and path**

c) Manures pit d) Farm building

38. Jam is prepared with :

a) Fruit pectin and pulp b) Fruit pulp alone

c) Fruit pectin alone d) Pectin, pulp seed and skin mix

39. Kohir Safed and Safed jam are the varieties of :

a) Pomegrante **b) Guava**

c) Date palm d) Mango

40. Lemon squash is preserved for a longer period without discolouration by the use of :
   a) Malic acid and potassium metabisulphite
   b) Citric acid and Potassium
   c) Benzoic acid and citric acid
   d) Potassium metabisulphite

41. Litchi does not flower in south Indian plateau in winter months :
   a) For want of sufficient low temperature in winter months
   b) Because of the high temperature prevlent at the time of flower formation
   c) Because of high relative humidity present at the time of flower formation
   d) Because of excessive light stimulus present at the time of flowering formation

42. Litchi was introduced to India from :
   a) Indonesia b) Japan
   c) China d) Malaya

43. Maximum number of fruit plants can be planted in the orchard by the system :
   a) Digonal system b) Square system
   c) Hexagonal system d) Rectangular system

44. Muscat Red is a variety of :
   a) Grapes **b) Pomegranate**
   c) Plums d) Apple

45. Name the fruit crop which is used as hedge :
   a) Durentta plumeri **b) Karonda**
   c) Kikar d) Ticoma stans

46. Out of following which fruit plants need 'Bahar' treatment :
   a) Litch and loquat **b) Guava and pomegranate**
   c) Ber and datepalm d) Grape and anola

47. Planting distance of individual fruit species provides the following advantages :
   a) Uniform growth
   b) Allows easy orchard operation
   c) Improper utilization of orchard space
   d) Proper supervision

48. Plants not suitable for wind break in orchard is :

a) *Casurina equisetifolia* **b)** ***Prosopis juliflora***

c) *Dulbergia siso* d) *Sizygium cuminii*

49. Pollination of the fig flower by the blastophage wasp taked place through :

a) Fasciation b) Parthenogenesis

c) Caprification d) Apomixis

50. Pomegranate, fig, olive and grape have been placed in ________ salt tolerant group of fruit trees.

a) High b) Low

c) Medium d) Very high

51. Popular method of orchard planting is :

a) Square system b) Degonal system

c) Hexagonal system d) Rectangular system

52. Quincunx in horticulture refers to :

a) Alphonso and Banganpalli b) Neelum and Langra

c) Neelum and Alphonso d) Dashehari and Neelum

53. Rcmoval of undesirable leaves from the tree is known as :

a) Disbudding **b) Defoliation**

c) Defruiting c) Deblossoming

54. Removal of undesirable branches by picking auxiliary buds is known as :

a) Clipping **b) Nipping**

c) Budding d) Topping

55. Richest source of vitamin C is :

a) Lemon b) Orange

c) Cucumber **d) Anola**

56. Root cutting for propagation are used in :

a) Dog wood b) balck berry

c) Fig **d) Apple**

57. Root cutting is a material used for propagation in :

a) Pomegrante b) Lime

c) Pummelo d) Grape

58. Seedlesssness in grape is due to :

a) Embroyo abortion b) Parthnocarpy

c) Aneuploidy d) Lack of pollination

59. Square method of planting is most common in :
    a) Mango b) Litchi
    c) Citrus fruits **b) All of above**

60. Temperate fruits like apple, peach, pear and plum should be planted in the month of :
    a) March-April **b) December-January**
    c) July-August d) September-October

61. The edible part of pomegranate fruit is :
    a) Testa of fruits b) Endosperm of seed
    c) Fleshy ovary d) Juicy embryo

62. The ideal time for cutting evergreen trees is :
    a) Rainy season b) Winter
    c) Late spring d) None of the above

63. The main objective of growing intercrops with the main fruits crop is to :
    a) Help the fruit crop to grow better
    b) Improve the soil fertility
    c) Check soil erosion
    d) None of the above

64. The most widely used plant growth substances in grape culture for reducing compactness of bunches and improving berry size is :
    a) N.A.A **b) GA_3**
    c) I.A.A d) 2,4 D

65. The number in as unit area becomes almost double of square system in :
    a) Rectangular b) Triangular
    c) Quincunx system d) Contour system

66. Which of the following heterostyly conditions is found ?
    a) Litchi b) Date
    c) Fig d) Walnut

67. Which of the following is not a self pollinated fruit crop ?
    a) Guava **b) Grape**
    c) Peach d) None of them

68. Which of the following is not a auxin ?
    a) GA_2 b) NAA
    c) 2,4 D d) IAA

69. Which of the following is not a cross pollinated fruits crop?
 a) Mango b) Litchi
 c) Apple **d) None of them**

70. Which of the following is not a cross pollinated fruits crop?
 a) Papaya b) Jackfruit
 c) Cherry **d) None of them**

71. Which of the following is not a growth promoter ?
 a) Auxin b) Gibberellin
 c) Abscissic acid d) Cytokinin

72. Which of the following is not a kind of detached grafting?
 a) Wedge, Splice b) Saddle, Tongue
 c) Side, Crown **d) None of them**

73. Which of the following is not a method of tree planting ?
 a) Square method b) Triangular method
 c) Hexagonal method **d) None of them**

74. Which of the following is not a self incompatible fruit crop ?
 a) Pear b) Almond
 c) Apple **d) Guava**

75. Which of the following is not a sub-tropical fruit crop ?
 a) Litchi **b) Peach**
 c) Loquat d) Papaya

76. Which of the following is not a sub-tropical fruit crop ?
 a) Phalsa b) Grape
 c) Loquat **d) Papaya**

77. Which of the following is not a tropical fruit crop ?
 a) Banana b) Cashewnut
 c) Fig d) Mango

78. Which of the following is not a variety of apple ?
 a) Beauty of bath **b) Roma**
 c) Rome beauty d) Winter banana

79. Which of the following is not a variety of apple ?
 a) Red delicious **b) Blood red**
 c) Golden delicious d) None of the above

80. Which of the following not the kind of budding ?

a) Ring b) Flute

c) Chip **d) None of above**

81. Which of the following not the kind of budding?

a) Patch b) Shield

c) Ring **d) All of above**

82. Which of the following is the kind of detached grafting?

a) Veneer b) Saddle

c) Tongue **d) All of above**

83. Which of the following chemical is used for the preservation of fruit products :

a) Potassium sulphate b) Potassium maganate

c) Potassium metabisulphide **d) Postassium metabisulphite**

84. Which one of the following fruits contains more fat than the rest ?

a) Apple b) Guava

c) Avocado d) Jackfruit

85. Which one of the following fruits will be most useful in human diet for avoiding scurry disease ?

a) Mandarin Orange b) Guava

c) Aonla d) Apple

86. Which one of the following genetic factors is responsible for poor fruit set in custard apple ?

a) Heterostyly **b) Dioecious nature**

c) Dichogamy d) Self-incompatibility

87. Which one of the following groups of crops is most suitable and recommended for inter-cropping in the young orchards?

a) Short duration fodders b) Short duration fruit crops

c) Popular and Eucalyptus **d) Short duration legume vegetables**

88. In grape __________ is phylloxera resistant rootstock

a) 1616 b) Dogridge

c) Salt Creek **d) St. George**

89. In grape commercially used PGR is __________

a) GA3 b) IBA

c) Cytokinin d) Ethrel

90. In grape cultivation among which of the technique is followed for improving fruit yield & quality
   a) Crop regulation
   b) Girdling and Growth regulators
   c) Thining of flower bud and berry
   d) All of above
91. The family of litchi is _______
   a) Sapindaceae b) Anacordiacea
   c) Rutaceae d) None of these
92. In apple ______ is vigorous rootstock
   a) M 12 b) MM 111
   c) M 20 d) M 9
93. Almond Kernel contains a cyanogenic glucoside ________
   a) Cytocin **b) Amygadalin**
   c) 1 d) None of these
94. The scientific name of Walnut is _________
   a) *Juglans ugla L* b) *Prunus dulcis*
   c) *Litchi scemsis* d) None of the above
95. Bitter pit is the physiological disorder observed in _______
   a) Pomegranate b) Mango
   c) Apple d) Alomond
96. In Pomegranate oily spot disease is caused due to _______
   a) Bacteria b) Fungi
   c) Virus d) Nematode
97. Konkan Bahadoli is the cultivar of _________
   a) Jaomun b) Mango
   c) Pomegrante d) None of these
98. Plum belongs to _______family
   a) Rosaceae b) Rutaceae
   c) Punicaceae d) None of these
99. In strawberry ______ is the aroma containing compound
   a) Ethyl hexanoate b) Ethyl butanoate
   c) Linatool **d) All of these**

100. The cultivated strawberry having diploid chromosome number Zn = __________

a) 28 **b) 14**

c) 30 d) 20

101. Which year is celebrated as the United Nations Decade on Biodiversity?

a) 2001-2010 **b) 2011-2020**

c) 2021-2030 d) 2031-2040

102. The term biological diversity was used first by

a) Savina Virk b) Hurrington

c) Raymond F. Dasmann d) Alexander

203. Who coined the term "Hotspots"

a) Savina Virk b) Hurrington

c) Raymond F. Dasmann d) Alexander

104. Centers of origin concept was first given by

a) L.B. Singh b) J.G. Hawkes

c) K.V. Peter **d) N.I.Vavilove**

105. Crop plants evolved from wild species in the area showing maximum diversity are termed as

a) Primary centre of origin

b) Secondary centre of origin

c) Microcenter

d) Centre of origin

106. The cultivated areas, where crop plants show considerable diversity but they do not originate from there are called as

a) Primary centre of origin **b) Secondary centre of origin**

c) Microcenter d) Centre of origin

107. The area which are important for plant collection as well as for an experimental study are called as

a) Primary centre of origin b) Secondary centre of origin

c) Microcenter d) Centre of origin

108. "Law of homologous series" is stated by

a) N.I.Vavilove b) J.G. Hawkes

c) L.B. Singh d) K.V. Peter

109. The collection which are used for long term storage are called as

a) Base collection b) Active collection

c) Working collection d) Core collection

110. The collection which are used for medium term storage are called as
a) Base collection **b) Active collection**
c) Working collection d) Core collection

111. The collection which are used for short term storage are called as
a) Base collection b) Active collection
c) Working collection d) Core collection

112. The collection which are derived from base collection to represent the genetic spectrum are called as
a) Base collection b) Active collection
c) Working collection **d) Core collection**

113. The trips arranged for the collection of germplasm from different areas are called as
a) Introduction b) Selection
c) Exploration d) Collection

114. Sum total of hereditary material present in a crop species and its wild relatives are called as
a) Germplasm b) Exploration
c) Conservation d) Heredity

115. The varieties which has evolve without a systematic and sustained plant breeding effort are called as
a) Land races b) Absolute varieties
c) Varieties in cultivation d) Breeding lines

116. The varieties were developed by systematic breeding effort are called as
a) Land races **b) Absolute varieties**
c) Varieties in cultivation d) Breeding lines

117. The varieties which are good sources of genes for yield and quality are called as
a) Land races b) Absolute varieties
c) Varieties in cultivation d) Breeding lines

118. The populations often contain valuable gene combinations are called as
a) Land races b) Absolute varieties
c) Varieties in cultivation **d) Breeding lines**

119. The wild species from which crop species were directly derived and they are easy to cross with the concern crop species are called as
a) Wild forms b) Wild relatives
c) Land races d) Absolute varieties

120. The wild species from which crop species were not directly derived and they are difficult to cross with the concern crop species are called as

a) Wild forms **b) Wild relatives**

c) Land races d) Absolute varieties

121. Conservation of genetic resources within their natural habitat are called as

a) *In-situ* Conservation b) *Ex - situ* Conservation

c) Preservation d) Documentation

122. Conservation of genetic resources outside their natural habitat are called as

a) *In-situ* Conservation **b) *Ex - situ* Conservation**

c) Preservation d) Documentation

123. Which Conservation is mainly used for cultivated plants multiplied by seeds?

a) *In-situ* Conservation **b) *Ex-situ* Conservation**

c) Field gene bank d) Cryopreservation

124. Seeds which are dried to a moisture content of 5 % or less without lowering their viability are called as

a) Orthodox seeds b) Recalcitrant seeds

c) Preserved seeds d) Moist seeds

125. The viability of seeds drops drastically if their moisture content is reduced below 12-13% are called as

a) Orthodox seeds **b) Recalcitrant seeds**

c) Preserved seeds d) Moist seeds

126. The storage of biological samples (tissues) in viable condition at ultra low temperature of liquid nitrogen at -150° C to -196° C are called as

a) *In-vitro* Conservation b) *In-situ* Conservation

c) *Ex-situ* Conservation **d) Cryopreservation**

127. Those area of land in which germplasm of recalcitrant crop species is maintained in the form of plants are called as

a) Seed gene bank **b) Field gene bank**

c) Shoot tip gene bank d) DNA gene bank

128. Protected area of great genetic diversity under natural condition i.e. *In-situ* conservation are called as

a) Extinction b) *In-situ* Conservation

c) Gene sanctuaries d) Plant genetic resources

129. The germplasm which is collected within the country are called as
a) Absolute cultivars b) Modern cultivars
c) Indigenous collection d) Exotic collection

130. The germplasm which is collected from the other country are called as
a) Exotic collection b) Indigenous collection
c) Absolute cultivars d) Modern cultivars

131. The gene pool in which intermating is easy and leads to production of fertile hybrids are called as
a) Gene Pool **b) Primary gene pool**
c) Secondary gene pool d) Tertiary gene pool

132. The genetic material that leads to partial fertility on crossing with primary gene pool are called as
a) Primary gene pool **b) Secondary gene pool**
c) Tertiary gene pool d) Gene Pool

133. The genetic material which leads to production of sterile hybrid on crossing with primary gene pool are called as
a) Gene Pool b) Primary gene pool
c) Secondary gene pool **d) Tertiary gene pool**

134. Improved varieties of recent past are know as
a) Absolute cultivars b) Modern cultivars
c) Primitive cultivars d) Wild forms

135. The currently cultivated high yielding varieties are known as
a) Absolute cultivars **b) Modern cultivars**
c) Primitive cultivars d) Wild forms

136. Yellow fertilizing dust found in flowers are called as
a) Androecium b) Gynoecium
c) Pollen d) Seed

137. Part of a plant from which another plant can grow are called as
a) Androecium b) Gynoecium
c) Pollen **d) Seed**

138. Making a list of goods are called as
a) Inventory b) Conservation
c) Storage d) Documentation

139. Who pointed out that easiest and least expensive way of preserving plants genetic resources is by seed storage

a) Shibukawa b) Alexander

c) Harrington d) Ganeshan

140. The process of compilation, analysis, classification, storage and distribution of information are called as

a) Characterization b) Conservation

c) Evaluation **d) Documentation**

141. The prophylactic measures that is used to prevent the entry of new diseases, insects and weeds from other country are called as

a) Quarantine b) Cryopreservation

c) *In-vitro* conservation d) Eradication

142. Botanical name of mandarin is

a) *Citrus sinensis* b) *Citrus aurantifolia*

c) *Citrus limonia* **d) *Citrus reticulate***

143. Botanical name of sweet orange is

a) *Citrus sinensis* b) *Citrus aurantifolia*

c) *Citrus limonia* d) *Citrus reticulate*

144. Botanical name of acid lime is

a) *Citrus sinensis* **b) *Citrus aurantifolia***

c) *Citrus limonia* d) *Citrus reticulate*

145. Mango belongs to the family

a) Rutaceae **b) Anacardiaceae**

c) Vitaceae d) Moraceae

146. Citrus belongs to the family

a) Rutaceae b) Anacardiaceae

c) Vitaceae d) Moraceae

147. Grape belongs to the family

a) Rutaceae b) Anacardiaceae

c) Vitaceae d) Moraceae

148. Jackfruit belongs to the family

a) Rutaceae b) Anacardiaceae

c) Vitaceae **d) Moraceae**

149. Guava belongs to the family

a) Annonaceae b) Rhamnaceae

c) Myrtaceae d) Musaceae

150. Banana belongs to the family

a) Annonaceae b) Rhamnaceae

c) Myrtaceae **d) Musaceae**

151. Custard apple belongs to the family

a) Annonaceae b) Rhamnaceae

c) Myrtaceae d) Musaceae

152. Ber belongs to the family

a) Annonaceae **b) Rhamnaceae**

c) Myrtaceae d) Musaceae

153. Sapota belongs to the family

a) Sapotaceae b) Caricaceae

c) Rosaceae d) Euphorbiaceae

154. Papaya belongs to the family

a) Sapotaceae **b) Caricaceae**

c) Rosaceae d) Euphorbiaceae

155. Apple belongs to the family

a) Sapotaceae b) Caricaceae

c) Rosaceae d) Euphorbiaceae

156. Aonla belongs to the family

a) Sapotaceae b) Caricaceae

c) Rosaceae **d) Euphorbiaceae**

157. Litchi belongs to the family

a) Rubiaceae **b) Sapindaceae**

c) Camillaceae d) Palmae

158. Coconut belongs to the family

a) Rubiaceae b) Sapindaceae

c) Camillaceae **d) Palmae**

159. Coffee belongs to the family

a) Rubiaceae b) Sapindaceae

c) Camillaceae d) Palmae

160. Tea belongs to the family

a) Rubiaceae b) Sapindaceae

c) Camillaceae d) Palmae

161. Botanical name of Guava is

a) *Psidium guajava* b) *Vitis vinifera*

c) *Musa paradisica* d) *Zizyphus mauritiana*

162. Botanical name of grape is

a) *Psidium guajava* **b) *Vitis vinifera***

c) *Musa paradisica* d) *Zizyphus mauritiana*

163. Botanical name of ber is

a) *Psidium guajava* b) *Vitis vinifera*

c) *Musa paradisica* **d) *Zizyphus mauritiana***

164. Botanical name of Banana is

a) *Psidium guajava* b) *Vitis vinifera*

c) *Musa paradisica* d) *Zizyphus mauritiana*

165. Origin of mango is

a) Central America **b) Indo-Burma**

c) China d) Tropical America

166. Origin of Mandarin is

a) Central America b) Indo-Burma

c) China d) Tropical America

167. Origin of Papaya is

a) Central America b) Indo-Burma

c) China **d) Tropical America**

168. Origin of Sapota is

a) Central America b) Indo-Burma

c) China d) Tropical America

169. Botanical name of Cashewnut is

a) *Theobroma cacao* b) *Areca catechu*

c) *Elaeis guineensis* **d) *Anacardium occidentale***

170. Botanical name of Cocoa is

a) *Theobroma cacao* b) *Areca catechu*

c) *Elaeis guineensis* d) *Anacardium occidentale*

171. Botanical name of Oil Palm is

a) *Theobroma cacao* b) *Areca catechu*

c) *Elaeis guineensis* d) *Anacardium occidentale*

172. Botanical name of Arecanut is

a) *Theobroma cacao* **b) *Areca catechu***

c) *Elaeis guineensis* d) *Anacardium occidentale*

173. Origin of Rubber is

a) Brazil b) Indonesia

c) Phillipines d) Africa

174. Origin of Arecanut is

a) Brazil b) Indonesia

c) Phillipines d) Africa

175. Origin of Coconut is

a) Brazil **b) Indonesia**

c) Phillipines d) Africa

176. Origin of Oil Palm is

a) Brazil b) Indonesia

c) Phillipines **d) Africa**

177. Betelvine belongs to the family

a) Piperaceae b) Bromeliaceae

c) Lauraceae d) Tilliaceae

178. Avocado belongs to the family

a) Piperaceae b) Bromeliaceae

c) Lauraceae d) Tilliaceae

179. Pineapple belongs to the family

a) Piperaceae **b) Bromeliaceae**

c) Lauraceae d) Tilliaceae

180. Phalsa belongs to the family

a) Piperaceae b) Bromeliaceae

c) Lauraceae **d) Tilliaceae**

181. Botanical name of Bael is

a) *Aegle marmelos* b) *Grewia asiatica*

c) *Syzygium cumini* d) *Prunus amygdalus*

182. Botanical name of Almond is

a) *Aegle marmelos* b) *Grewia asiatica*

c) *Syzygium cumini* **d) *Prunus amygdalus***

183. Botanical name of Phalsa is

a) *Syzygium cumini* b) *Aegle marmelos*

c) *Prunus amygdalus* **d) *Grewia asiatica***

184. Botanical name of Jamun is

a) *Prunus amygdalus* **b) *Syzygium cumini***

c) *Grewia asiatica* d) *Aegle marmelos*

185. Karonda belongs to the family

a) Apocynaceae b) Oleaceae

c) Leguminaceae d) Actinidaceae

186. Kiwi fruit belongs to the family

a) Apocynaceae b) Oleaceae

c) Leguminaceae **d) Actinidaceae**

187. Tamarind belongs to the family

a) Apocynaceae b) Oleaceae

c) Leguminaceae d) Actinidaceae

188. Olive belongs to the family

a) Apocynaceae **b) Oleaceae**

c) Leguminaceae d) Actinidaceae

189. State the origin of Pomegranate

a) Iran b) Irak

c) Egypt d) India

190. State the origin of litchi

a) South China b) Brazil

c) Africa d) Phillipines

191. Give the native of guava

a) Iran **b) Tropical America**

c) Tropical Africa d) Maxico

192. Write Botanical name of Woodapple

a) *Actinida deliciosa* b) *Prunus persica*

c) *Feronia limonia* d) *Morus alba*

193. Write cultivated species of Jackfruit.

a) *Jugalans regia* b) *Ananas comosus*

c) *Malus domestica* **d) *Artocarpus heterophyllus***

194. Botanical name of grape fruit is

a) *Citrus grandis* b) *Citrus paradisi*

c) *Citrus madurensis* d) *Citrus latifolia*

195. Botanical name of Pummelo is

a) *Citrus paradisi* b) *Citrus reticulata*

c) *Citrus limoni* **d) *Citrus grandis***

196. State the commercially cultivated species of Cashewnut

a) *Anacardium occidentale*

b) *Mangifera indica*

c) *Cocus nucifera*

d) *Persia americana*

197. Dinkar is the popular variety of

a) Aonla b) Ber

c) Fig d) Tamarind

198. Kanchan is the popular variety of

a) Aonla b) Fig

c) Tamarind d) Ber

199. Phule Sharbati is the variety of

a) Sweet orange b) Mandarin

c) Acid lime d) Seedless lime

200. Guava belongs to the family

a) Rutaceae b) Vitaceae

c) Moraceae **d) Myrtaceae**

201. State the commercial rootstock used in *citrus sinensis*

a) Khirni b) Rayon

c) Rangpur lime d) Cleopatra mandarin

202. State the commercial rootstock used in *Achras zapota*

a) *Citrus limonia* b) *Citrus jambhiri*

c) *Vitis vinifera* **d) *Manilkaria hexandra***

203. Hen and chicken disorder is found in

a) Mango b) Sapota

c) Grape d) Fig

204. Guava is commercially propagated by
    a) Air layering **b) Tongue layering**
    c) Inarching d) Soft wood grafting
205. All Prunus species belongs to the family
    a) Moraceae b) Rutaceae
    c) Rosaceae d) Myrtaceae
206. Amrapali is cross between
    a) **Dasheri x Neelum** b) Dasheri x Totapuri
    c) Neelum x Chausa d) Bombay x Kalapady
207. Mallika is across between
    a) Bombay x Kalapady b) Alphanso x Neelum
    c) **Neelum x Dasheri** d) Neelum x Langra
208. Polygamous plants are those plants that produce
    a) **Male, female and hermaphrodite flowers**
    b) Male flowers only
    c) Female flowers only
    d) Hermaphrodite flowers
209. Citrus fruit belong to family
    a) Myrtaceae b) **Rutaceae**
    c) Anacardeaceae d) Sapindaceae
210. Apple belongs to family
    a) **Rosaceae** b) Caricaceae
    c) Myrtaceae d) None
211. Diploid varities of apple are
    a) Self unfruitful b) **Self fruitful**
    c) both a and b d) None
212. Olour is polyembryonic variety of
    a) Guava b) Citrus
    c) Jamun d) **Mango**
213. Kinnow is a cross between
    a) **King and Willow leaf** b) Mandarin and sweet orange
    c) Willow leaf and Wilking d) King and Wilking
214. Seedlessness in grapes is due to
    a) Lack of pollination b) Parthinocarpy
    c) Aneuploidy d) **Embryo abortion**

215. Name the fruit plant which bears fruits only once in its life time
   a) **Banana** b) Plum
   c) Arecanut d) Custard apple
216. Latest mango hybrid variety released from Maharashtra is
   a) Nileshwar dwarf b) **Suvarna**
   c) Amrapali d) Mallika
217. Male gamete carries ————chromosome number
   a) n b) 2n
   c) 3n d) 3n-1
218. Mango fruit is a
   a) Pome b) Pepo
   c) Berry d) **Drupe**
219. Method of breeding can be used for studying ancestral charactaristics
   a) Pure line b) Mass selection
   c) **Pedigree** d) None of these
220. Progeny of a hybrid plant
   a) Breds true b) Resembles maternal plant
   c) Resembles paternal plant d) **Segregation**
221. Poliination taking place between the flowers borne by the same parent (plant) is called
   a) **Geitonogamy** b) Alogamy
   c) Xenogamy d) None of the above
222. Sterility/ incompability of distant crosses can be overcome to produce hybrid by
   a) Pollen culture b) Anther culture
   c) Explant culture d) **Embryoculture**
224. The evolutionary histry of a species is refered as
   a) Phylogeny b) Progeny
   c) Organic evolution d) Natural selection
225. The fleshy edible part of mango fruit is
   a) Endocarp b) **Mesocarp**
   c) Epicarp d) Pericarp
226. The inflorescence of banana is known as
   a) Catkin b) Receme
   c) Spike d) **Spadix**

227. The physical basis of heredity is termed as

a) Gene pool	b) gene frequency
c) Germplasm	d) None of the above

228. When only one fruit developes from single overy of aflower it is said to be

a) Aggregate fruit	b) **Simple fruit**
c) Multiple fruit	d) Composite fruit

229. Which of the following leads to the cross pollination

a) Unisexuality	b) Dichogamy
c) Heterostyly	**d) All the above**

230. A dwarf rootstock of pear is

a) Kainth	b) Quince A
c) Quince B	d) **Quince C**

231. A dwarf rootstock of apple is

a) **M-9**	b) M-13
c) M-12	d) M25

232. A seedless grape hybrid developed at IIHR Bangalore is

a) **Arkavati**	b) Arka Hans
c) Arka sham	d) None of above

233. Abortion of the embryo before maturation is problem in improvement of which crop

a) Mango	b) Guava
c) **Grape**	d) Litchi

234. According to flowering habbit Datepalm is

a) Monocious	b) **Diocious**
c) Hermaphrodite	d) Andromonocious

235. A spur type apple cultivar is

a) Cox Orange pippin	b) **Red spur**
c) Golden Delicious	d) Rich-e-Red

236. Resistant source for mosaic/leaf curl virus in papaya breeding

a) *Carica califlora*	b) *Carica pentagona*
c) *Carica candemacrensis*	d) *Carica microcarpa*

237. Ratna x Alphanso are parents of

a) Mallika	b) **Sindhu**
c) Amrapali	d) None of above

238. Red Sitaphal a variety of Annona evolved by
   a) Mutation
   b) Introduction
   c) **Chance seedling selection**
   d) Hybridization

239. Punjab Gold is the variety of
   a) **Pear** b) Apple
   c) Peach d) Strawberry

240. Pusa giant papaya cultivar is
   a) Gynomonocious b) Monocious
   c) **Diocious** d) Gynodiocious

241. Rosica is mutant cultivar of
   a) Ber b) **Mango**
   c) Apple d) Aonla

242. Salt resistant rootstock of grape
   a) **Salt Creek** b) 1613
   c) Dogridge d) All the above

243. Seedlessness in most grape varieties is due to
   a) Parthinocarpy b) **Stenospermocarpy**
   c) Polyembryony d) Apomixis

244. Self sterile varieties of grapes are
   a) Angoor Kalam b) Hur
   c) Banque Abyad d) **All of these**

245. Solo is the variety of
   a) Mango b) Apple
   c) **Papaya** d) Banana

246. Stenospermocarpy in mango is observed in which variety
   a) Neelum b) Alphanso
   c) Bombay Green d) **Sindhu**

247. Swarna Roopa is the variety of
   a) Aonla b) **Litchi**
   c) Apple d) Mango

248. Tahiti lime is
   a) **Triploid** b) Diploid
   c) Pentaploid d) Haploid

249. Test cross is crossing F_1 with which of the following

a) Dominant parent | b) **Recessive parent**
c) Either of the parent | d) None of these

250. Basic chromosome number of mango is

a 20 | b 18
c 40 | d **10**

251. The chromosome number (2n) of aonla is

a 16 | b 22
c **28** | d 24

252. The chromosome number (2n) of peach is

a **12** | b 16
c 24 | d 28

253. The chromosome number (2n) of guava is

a 26 | b 16
c 24 | d **22**

254. The highest papain yielding variety of papaya is

a CO_1 | b CO_2
c **CO_6** | d CO_4

255. The inflorescence of pear is

a Panicle | b Spadix
c Raceme | d **Corymb**

256. The main insect responsible for pollination in mango

a **House fly** | b honey bee
c Midge fly | d Over fly

257. The most cold hardycitrus rootstock is

a Lemon | b Mosambi
c **Trifoliage orange** | d Lime

258. The plants which can not set fruits with their own pollen are called

a **Self–unfruitful** | b Un fruitful
c Cross mating | d Cross fruitful

259. The ploidy level of commercial strawberry is

a Tetraploid | b Diploid
c **Octaploid** | d Triploid

260. Pusa Majesty variety of papaya is
   a) **Gynodiocious** **b)** Diocious
   c) Hermaphrodite d) Gynomonocious
261. The type of infloresscene in ber is
   a) Raceme b) Solitary
   c) Umbel d) **Cyme**
262. Chromosome number (2n) of pine apple is
   a) 45 b) 32
   c) **50** d) 75
263. NDUAT Faizabad developed varieties of which fruit crop
   a) **Aonla** b) Guava
   c) Mango d) Litchi
264. Which is not the cultivar of grape
   a) Arka Kanchan b) Arka Hans
   c) Arka Trishna d) **Arka Mridula**
265. Embryo culture technique has important role in
   a) Haploid production b) Shortening of breeding cycle
   c) Rapid seed viability test d) **All of these**
266. Flesh colour of Lalit guava is
   a) White b) Yellow
   c) **Pink** d) None of these
267. Pomegranate Ganesh and G-137 are developed through
   a) Introduction b) **Selection**
   c) Hybridization d) Mutation
268. Pomegranate Mridula is developed through
   a) Introduction b) Selection
   c) **Hybridization** d) Mutation
269. Sabour Madhu and Sabour Priya are the hybrids of
   a) Mango b) Guava
   c) Aonla d) **Litchi**
270. The first coconut hybrid in the world was produced by
   a) R.V. Pillai b) S.C. Harland
   c) **J.S. Patel** d) S.N. Ghosh

271. Pineapple produces how many fruits in its life
 a) Two b) Four
 c) **One** d) Many
272. Pine apple plant flower at the age of
 a) **11-12 months** b) 3-4 months
 c) 6-7 months d) None of these
273. Jamun belong to family
 a) Anacardiaceae b) **Myrtaceae**
 c) Apocynaceae d) Vitaceae
274. Andromonocious condition is found in
 a) Guava b) Sapota
 c) Citrus d) **Mango**
275. Clestogamy condition is found in
 a) Mango b) Guava
 c) **Sapota** d) Jamun
276. Unisexuality mechanizm ofthe flower facilitate
 a) **Cross pollination** b) Selfpollination
 c) Both a and b d) None ofthese
277. Polyethelene glycol is (PEG) used as
 a) Molecular marker b) Mutagen
 c) **Fusagenic agent** d) Selflife improver
278. Gene for improving self life of apple
 a) ACC synthase b) Attacin esterase
 c) Polygalacturonase d) **All of these**
279. The induced mutant variety of mango is
 a) Davis Haden b) Rosica
 c) Both a and b c) **None of these**
280. Banana is
 a) **Monocoteledonous** b) Dinocoteledonous
 c) Both a and b d) None of these
281. If the somatic chromosome number is not exact multiple of the basic number it is known as
 a) Euploid b) **Anuploid**
 c) Diploid c) None of these

282. The gynodiocios cultivar of papaya produces
   a) **Both female and hermaphrodite flowers on same plant**
   b) Both male and hermaphrodite flower son same plant
   c) Male and female flowers separately on different plants
   d) Male and female flowers on same plants
283. Cashew nut is
   a) Self pollinated crop **b) Cross pollinated crop**
   c) Both a and b d) None of these
284. Cashew apple which false fruit is swollen
   a) Calyx b) Corolla
   c) **Pedicel** d) Embryo
285. Hathijhool variety of aonla is also known as
   a) **Francis** b) Chakaiya
   c) Krishna d) NA-6
286. L-49 variety of guava is also known as
   a) Allahabad Safeda b) Lalit
   c) Sweta d) **Sardar**
287. Breba is parthenocarpically produced crop of
   a) **San pedro fig** b) Capri fig
   c) common fig d) Both b & c
288. Pusa Nanha variety of papaya is developed by using
   a) Beta rays **b) Gamma rays**
   c) Alpha rays d) X rays
289. Time of fruit bud differentiation in in aonla is
   a) **March- April** b) February-March
   c) January February d) April-May
290. Chance seedling of Chakaiya suitable for processing is
   a) NA7 (Amrit) b) NA5 (Krishna)
   c) NA9 (Neelum) d) **NA4 (Kanchan)**
291. Ber variety tolerant against salinity & alkalinity
   a) **Gola** b) Seb
   c) Umran d) Banarasi
292. Bangalore blue is the cross between
   a) Ontario x Sultania b) Vinifera x Sultania
   c) **Vinifera xLabrusca** d) Sultania xLabrusca

293. Pollination of fig flower by the blastophaga wasp is known as
   a) Fasciation b) Parthenogenesis
   c) Apomixis d) **Caprification**

294. Which of the following mango variety is off season growing
   a) Rosica b) Neelum
   c) Niranjan d) Langra

295. Which of the following reproductive mechanism of plants is asexual
   a) Amphimixis b) **Apomixis**
   c) Both of these d) None of these

296. Which of following statement is correct about inheritance pattern of apple
   a) **Red colour is dominant over red**
   b) Yellow colour is dominant over green
   c) Colour is co-dominant inherited
   d) None of these

297. Which of the following technique is used for detection of virus
   a) **ELISA** b) AFLP
   c) RFLP d) RAPD

298. Which of the following fruit is known as balausta
   a) Litchi b) Fig
   c) Mango d) **Pomegranate**

299. Which the following is male sterile cultivar of peach
   a) **JH Hale** b) Flordasum
   c) Sharball d) Red heaven

300. Which one of the following belongs to a genera other than that of other three
   a) Plum b) Almond
   c) **Pear** d) Peach

301. Which of the following is botanically not fruit
   a) Woodapple b) **Cashewapple**
   c) Custardapple d) Jackfruit

302. Which one of the following fruit is syconus
   a) Fig b) Pineapple
   c) Jackfruit d) Strawberry

303. Which pairs is monocious
   a) Hazelnut, Datepalm **b) Coconut, Aonla**
   c) Papaya, Pistachionut d) Date, Chinese gooseberry

304. Winter banana is the variety of

a) Litchi b) Banana

c) **Apple** d) Pineapple

305. Dashehari 51 differs from Dashehari because

a) It is tolerant to mango hopper

b) **It is resistant to powedery mildew**

c) Tolerant to antracnose

d) All above

306. In the case of horizontal resistant the rate of reproduction of pathogen is

a) Zero b) **> 0 but < 1**

c) >1 d) None of these

307. Dormancy due to presence of ABA is found in ____________ fruit crops.

a) Tempertae b) Tropical

c) Dryland d) Subtropical

308. Seeds remain viable for long time at low temperature known as __________ seed.

a) Recalcitrant b) Viable

c) Orthodox d) None of these

309. Seeds don't remain viable for long time at low temperature known as __________ seed.

a) Recalcitrant b) Viable

c) Orthodox d) None of these

310. In cryopreservation seed stored in ______ at -196^{0}C temperature or liquid CO_2 at -43^{0}C temperature.

a) N_2 b) H_2O_2

c) H_2SO_4 d) None of these

311. Glycerol, Dimethyl sulphoxide are used as ____________ .

a) Cryoprotactants b) Cryopreservatives

c) Antitransparent d) None of these

312. __________ is a growth inhibitor which acts as "Stress harmone".

a) Gibberellins **b) Abiscissic acid**

c) Cycocel d) Auxins

313. Irreversible increase in size, weight, or volume of a cell, organ or plant known as ____________

a) Differentiation b) Development

c) Growth c) None of these

314. __________ means any situation in which meristematic cells gives rise to two or more types of cells, tissues or organs which are qualitative different from each other.

a) Development b) Growth

c) Differentiation d) Callus

315. $\frac{\text{Total leaf area per plant or leaf}}{\text{Area of land occupied by plant}}$ ________ =

a) Leaf area ratio b) Net assimilation rate

c) Leaf area index d) Relative crop growth rate

316. ________________ = Leaf area ratio x Net assimilation ratio.

a) Leaf area ratio b) Net assimilation rate

c) Leaf area index **d) Relative crop growth rate**

317. ____________ indicates the efficiency of plant to grow.

a) Leaf area b) Growth rate

c) Relative crop growth rate d) None of these

318. ___________ is/are the level/levels of differentiation in plants.

a) Organ b) Tissue

c) Cell **d) Organ, Tissue and Cell**

319. Morning glory, Strawberry and Amaranthus are _______________

a) Obligatory short day plants

b) Obligatory long day plants

c) Facultative short day plants

d) Facultative long day plants

320. Carnation, Spinach and radish are _______________

a) Obligatory short day plants

b) Obligatory long day plants

c) Facultative short day plants

d) Facultative long day plants

321. Cosmos and Salvia are _______________

a) Obligatory short day plants

b) Obligatory long day plants

c) Facultative short day plants

d) Facultative long day plants

322. Beet, turnip and petunia are ______________
a) Obligatory short day plants
b) Obligatory long day plants
c) Facultative short day plants
d) Facultative long day plants

323. *Trifolium ripens* is ____________
a) Short day-long day plants
b) Obligatory long day plants
c) Facultative short day plants
d) Long day-short day plants

324. Bryophyllum and *Cistrus nodrunum* are ______________
a) Obligatory long day plants
b) Facultative short day plants
c) Short day-long day plants
d) Long day-short day plants

325. Mango, brinjal, citrus and okra are ______________
a) Obligatory long day plants
b) Facultative short day plants
c) Day neutral plants
d) Long day-short day plants

326. Sequence of light and dark in 24 hours is known as _________
a) Photoinductive cycle **b) Photoperiodic cycle**
c) Non Photoinductive cycle d) After effect

327. An appropriate photoperiodic cycle that induces flowering is known as
a) Photoinductive cycle b) Critical day length
c) Non Photoinductive cycle d) Photoperiodic cycle

328. Beet needs _________ photoinductive cycles for flowering.
a) 1 **b) 15**
c) 17 d) 7

329. Salvia needs _______ photoinductive cycles for flowering.
a) 17 b) 4
c) 2 d) 10

330. Vernalization is a phenomenon in which flowering is conditioned by _____ temperature.
a) Low b) High
c) Intermediate d) None of these

331. Semi permeable membranes are active when water content is ________ %.

a) 10 **b) >17**

c) 5 d) None of these

332. Seeds of amaranthus and some varieties of tomato are ____________

a) + vely photoblastic b) – vely photoblastic

c) Neutral d) None of these

333. Onion seed is ________

a) + vely photoblastic **b) – vely photoblastic**

c) Neutral d) None of these

334. The seed in which germination is promoted by light is known as __________

a) Neutral **b) + vely photoblastic**

c) – vely photoblastic d) None of these

335. In ___________ seed where germination is inhibited by light.

a) Neutral b) + vely photoblastic

c) – vely photoblastic d) None of these

336. Positively photoblastic seed, after imbibition if are exposed to prolonged dark period, they fails to germinate which is known as ___________.

a) Photo Dormancy **b) Skoto Dormancy**

c) Seed coat Dormancy d) None of these

337. If after imbibition the –vely photoblastic seeds exposed to prolonged light fails to germinate is known as ______

a) Photo Dormancy b) Skoto Dormancy

c) True Dormancy d) None of these

338. _________ is a natural inhibitor and mainly responsible for dormancy.

a) IBA **b) Abscisic acid (ABA)**

c) 2,4 D d) GA

339. Development of fruit without fertilization known as ___________

a) Parthenocarpy b) Sternospermocarpy

c) Parthenogenesis d) none of these

340. ________ is phenomenon where development of seed without fertilization occurs.

a) Parthenocarpy b) Sternospermocarpy

c) Parthenogenesis d) None of these

341. ________ is special type seedlessness.
   a) Ginko b) Parthenocarpy
   c) Sternospermocarpy d) None of these

342. Single sigmoid curve of fruit growth pattern is observed in _____ fruit(s).
   a) Apple b) Pineapple
   c) Strawberry **d) All of these**

343. Double sigmoid curve of fruit growth pattern is observed in _____ fruit(s).
   a) Peach b) Apricot
   c) Plum **d) All of these**

344. Qualitative transformation of a matured fruit is termed as _________ .
   a) Senescence **b) Ripening**
   c) Maturation d) None of these

345. ___________ are very high potency gibberellins.
   a) GA-2, GA-6 and GA-9 b) GA-11, GA-12 and GA-14
   c) GA-3, GA-7 and GA-32 d) GA-10, GA-15 and GA-120

346. Hemicelluloses are more important in banana which decreases from ____ % at maturity to 1-2% at ripening.
   a) 9 b) 7
   c) 5 d) 4

347. ________ is a climacteric fruit.
   a) Grape and Pepper **b) Fig and Apple**
   c) Pomegranate and Citrus d) Pineapple

348. Methionine is the precursor of ________.
   a) Ethylene b) Gibberellins
   c) Cytonins d) Auxins

349. ________ is a non climacteric fruit.
   a) Apple b) Guava
   c) Pomegranate d) Pear

350. ________ is a non climacteric fruit.
   a) Apple **b) Pepper**
   c) Papaya d) Tomato

351. ___________ is colouring pigment of peach and guava.
   a) Anthocyanin b) Xanthophyll
   c) Lycopene **d) Carotene**

352. ________ is colouring pigment of Jamun, Grape and Phalsa.
   a) Anthocyanin b) Xanthophyll
   c) Lycopene d) Carotenoid
353. _________ is colouring pigment of citrus.
   a) Xanthophyll b) Anthocyanin
   c) Lycopene **d) Carotenoid**
354. Carotene and xanthophylls are colouring pigments of _________.
   a) Banana b) Guava
   c) Tomato d) Strawberry
355. __________ is commercially used to induce flowering in pineapple.
   a) Cycocel b) Abscisic acid
   c) Auxin d) Gibberellins
356. Senescence is a _________ process which naturally terminate functional life of organ or organism or any live life.
   a) Constructive **b) Deteriorative**
   c) Neutral d) None of these
357. Pollination of the fig flower by the blastophage takes place through ______________.
   a) Fasciation b) Parthenogenesis
   c) Caprification d) Apomixes
358. Pusa Delicious a gynodioecious variety of papaya has which of the following sex forms.
   a) Pistillate and Hermaphrodite
   b) Pistillate
   c) Staminate
   d) None of these
359. Parthenocarpy is seen in case of ____________
   a) Custard apple b) Chiku
   c) Banana d) Pomegranate
360. Seed which is having live embryo is known as ___________.
   a) Seed maturity b) Seed class
   c) Seed viability **d) Seed viability**
361. Manjari Naveen is a variety of __________ fruit crop.
   a) Guava **b) Grape**
   c) Pineapple d) Custard apple

362. Pusa Pratibha, Pusa Shreshtha and Pusa Pitambar are the hybrids of .... fruit crop.

a) Papaya b) Apple
c) Banana **d) Mango**

363. Thar Sevika hybrid of ber is cross between ____________

a) Seb x Katha b) Katha x Seb
c) Umran x Katha d) None of these

364. Ratna variety of mango is a cross between ____________.

a) Alphonso & Benganapalli **b) Neelum & Alphonso**
c) Neelum &Langra d) Dasheri & Neelum

365. ____________ is rootstock used for importing dwarfness in Allahabad Safeda.

a) Pusa Srijan b) *Psiclium cattleianum*
c) Vineland 4 d) Geneva 65

366. Furete is improved variety of avocado is a cross between __________

a) Mexican & Guatamalan type
b) Guatamalan & West Indies type
c) Mexican & West indies type
d) None of these

367. Which one of the following is a monoembryonic citrus?

a) Sweet orange **b) Pummelo**
c) Acid lime d) Mandarin

368. Sai-sharbati, the cultivar of acid lime is ____________.

a) Hybrid cultivar b) Introduction
c) Clonal selection d) None of these

369. National Research Centre for Citrus is located at __________.

a) Pune b) New Delhi
c) Nagpur c) Banglore

370. *Annona atemoya* (Island gem) x *Annona squamosa*(Mammoth) are the parentage of ____________

a) Atemoya b) Balanagar
c) African pride **d) Arka sahan**

371. Indicator plant for tristeza virus in citrus is ____________________.

a) C. *reticulatla* **b) *C. aurantifolia***
c) *C. paradisi* d) *C. limettoides*

372. ________________ is the gene responsible for improving shelf life in, banana.

a) PG inhibitor protein b) SAM transferase

c) Acc synthesis d) None of these

373. Phalsa belongs to the family______________

a) Euphorbiaceae **b) Tiliaceae**

c) Rosaceae d) Rutaceae

374. Red Sitaphal, a variety of Annona was evolved as ______________

a) Chance seedling b) Mutation

c) Hybridization d) Introduction

375. Which of the following fruit crops is amphidiploid_______________.

a) Mango b) Strawberry

c) Banana d) Kiwifruit

376. Rayan is commonly used as rootstock in the propagation of which one of the following fruit crops?

a) Mango b) Custard apple

c) Tamarind **d) Sapota**

377. Konkan prolific is the variety of _____________ .

a) Jackfruit b) Mango

c) Cashewnut d) Coconut

378. Which one of the following variety of mangoes is developed by clonal selection and bears fruit regularly?

a) Niranjan b) Manajira

c) Dashehar-51i d) Arka Neelkiran

379. Olmo H. D. is a well-known ___________ breeder.

a) Grape b) Mango

c) Banana d) Persimon

380. Tangors are the hybrids of _______________.

a) Mandarin x Grape fruit b) Mandarin x Sweet orange

c) Lime x Lemon d) Tangelos x sweet orange

381. Swaran roopa early, non cracking and seedless variety of _________.

a) Litchi b) bael

c) Phalsa c) Cracking

382. Katol gold is the variety of _______________ .

a) Sweet orange b) Mandarin orange

c) Acid lime d) Lemon

383. Which one of the following conditions is the reason for the seedlessness in "Thompson seedless" grapes?

a) Incomplete flower b) Non-viable pollen

c) Parthenocarpy **d) Stenopermoycarpy**

384. Which of the following types of flowers are present in mango panicles?

a) Male and hermaphrodite

b) Female only

c) Male and female

d) Male and neutral

385. Temple rootstock of grape is resistant for ______________ .

a) Nematode **b) Pierce's disease**

c) Salt d) None of these

386. Which one of the following is a polyembryonic mango?

a) Alphonso b) Neelum

b) olur **d) Dasheri**

387. Ganesh x Gul-a-Shah red = _____________

a) Jyothi **b) Mridula**

c) Ruby d) None of these

388. Seedless mango "Sindhu" is a result of backcross between _______________.

a) Alphonso x Benganpalli **b) Ratna x Alphonso**

d) Ratna x Neelum d) Neelum x Dashehari

389. Mallika is a cross between ___________

a) Dashehari x Langra b) Neelum x Langra

c) Neelum x Dashehari d) Banganpalli x Alphanso

390. Seedlessness of Behat coconut a variety of guava is due to ___________

a) Parthenicarpy **b) Triploidy**

c) Self incompatibility d) Parthenogenesis

391. Colt is rootstock of __________

a) Cherry b) Pear

c) plum d) Apple

392. Dwarfness in Papaya is a desirable character which is _____________ about its inheritance.

a) recessive b) Dominant

c) Epistatic d) None of these

393. Which one of the following is the gynodioecious cultivar of papaya
a) Ranchi b) Pusa Dwarf
c) Pusa Giant **d) Pusa Majesty**

394. Which one of the following is a regular bearing variety of mango ?
a) Langara b) Samar Bahista Chausa
c) Amarpali d) Aplhonso

395. Laksha Ganga is an hybrid of ____________
a) Arecanut **b) Coconut**
c) Walnut d) pecan nut

396. Homozygosis in early generation is fast due to ______________.
a) Selfing b) Back crossing
c) Sib-mating d) Hybridization

397. Pusa delicious and Pusa majesty varieties of papaya are __________
a) Andrmonoecious **b) Gynodioecious**
c) Dioecious d) None of these

398. Edible banana is seedless because of _______________.
a) Embryo abortion
b) Absence of ovule
c) Vegetative parthenocarpy
d) Stimulated parthenocarpy

399. According to flowering habit datepalm is ______________.
a) Monoecious b) Andromonoecious
c) Dioecious d) Hermaphrodite

400. Dogridge is a salt tolerant rootstock of ________________.
a) Citrus b) Apple
c) Grape d) Sapota

401. "Arka Shyam " is a hybrid variety of ___________________.
a) Jamun b) Pomegranate
c) Grape d) Mulberry

402. Genomic classification of banana was given by
a) Simmond & Shephard b) Decandole
c) Swingle d) Carl Linnaeus

403. Femaleness in papaya is controlled by genotype __________
a) M_1M b) M_2M
c) M_1M_2 **d) mm**

404. Resistance source for mosaic/leaf curl virus in papaya breeding is ________________.

a) ***Carica cauliflora*** b) *Carica pentagona*

c) *Carica candamarcensis* d) *Carica microcarpa*

405. Which portion of the plant is considered to be free from vitruses?

a) Xylem **b) Meristem**

c) Cambium d) Embryo

406. Seedlessness in grape is controlled by ___________________.

a) Recessive polygenic b) Dominant gene

c) Cytoplasmic d) None of these

407. Long form of HACCP is.............

a) Hazard Analysis Critical Control Point

b) Hazard Anatomical Citric Cyclic Percent

c) Hydrous Ammonia Catalyst Critical Point

d) None of these

408. IFOAM meaning ____________

a) International Federation of Orange Agro Movement

b) International Federation of Olympic Athletic Movement

c) International Federation of Organic Agriculture Movement

d) None of these

409. Tropical soils are generally low in ——

a) Organic matter b) Phosphorus

c) Potash d) All a to c

410. Organic Horticulture means____________.

a) Maintaining a living soil

b) Making available the essential nutrients

c) Organic mulching for soil conservation

d) All above

411. The disadvantage of organic manures is _________.

a) All nutrients are not available

b) Will not maintain C:N ratio

c) Nutrients available in limited quantity

d) None of these

412. Heap method, pit method and NADEP method are for____________

a) Composting b) Green manuring

c) FYM d) All of these

413. Water hyacinth weed is rich in ____________

a) N and K b) N and P

c) N and S d) N and Ca

414. The fungus __________ decompose the coir pith within 20 days which is very valuable biomass.

a) *Pleurotus* b) *Jleurotus*

c) *Rleurotus* d) *Sleurotus*

415. Coir pith manure increases the water holding capacity of soil by ____ times.

a) 5-6 b) 7-8

c) 9-10 d) 11-12

416. The recommended dose of coco peat for organic banana is ________

a) 8 kg/plant **b) 4 kg/plant**

c) 12 kg/plant d) kg/plant

417. Vermicompost content NPK in the proportion_________

a) 1.1:0.86:0.98 b) 2.2:1.6:1.8

c) 3.3:2.4:2.7 d) None of these

418. BD-501 is rich in __________

a) Ca b) S

c) K **d) Si**

419. In general N fixed per ha by red gram is __________

a) 168-200 b) 268-400

c) 368-800 d) 468-900

420. Blue green algae contributes ____kg/ha /season.

a) 25 b) 50

c) 75 d) 100

421. _______is a free living aerobic N-fixing bacterium.

a) *Azolla* **b) *Azotobacter***

c) *Azospirillum* d) *Beijerinckia*

422. *Beijerinckia* production is high in _____ soils.

a Saline b) Alkaline

c) Sodic **d) Acidic**

423. As per standards the expiry period of biofertilizers from the date of manufacturing is

a) Six month b) One year

c) Two month d) Five year

424. It is known that Indian soils are very poor in ______

a) P b) K

c) Ca d) N

425. Frequent pre-monsoon showers facilitate germination of weeds to be destroyed by cultivation is known as____________

a Stale seed bed b) Raised seed bed

c) Flat seed bed d) None of these

426. _______________means the process of collecting and evaluating information on hazards associated with the food under consideration to decide which are significant and must be addressed in the HACCP plan.

a) Biochemical analysis b) Chemical analysis

c) Hazard Analysis d) Nonc of thcsc

427. ____________refers to any of the predominantly anaerobic organisms blended in commercial agricultural amendments.

a) Beneficial organism **b) Effective microorganism**

c) Useful organism d) None of these

428. Flooding is done to control _______ weeds.

a Annual b) Biennial

c) Perennial d) None of these

429. The principle behind _____is to exclude light completely to the growing weeds to preven photosynthesis and further growth.

a) Mulching b) Shading

c) Terracing d) Mowing

430. Harvesting of solar energy through soil_____ will be the key proposition for controlling soil borne pests including weeds.

a Sterilization b) Burning

c) Solarization d) Mowing

431. Problems associated with the use of chemical pesticides are______

a) The development of pest resistance to pesticides

b) Environmental pollutions

c) Disruption in biodiversity

d) All above

432. Yellow sticky traps can be used to monitor____________

a) **Aphids and whiteflies** b) Jassids and mealy bugs

c) Thrips and mites d) Semiloopers and moths

433. Hot water treatment for 10 minutes at 50° C temperature or 30 minutes at 47.8° C to grape rooted for control of ____________

a) *Tylechulus semipenetrans*

b) *Radopholus similis*

c) *Melidogyne* spp.

d) *Praticlenchus penetrans*

434. Growing of susceptible or preferred hosts as trap crops along with the main crop will attract the pests in large numbers and these can be selectively killed is ________

a) Trap cropping b) Drap cropping

c) Srap cropping d) Krap cropping

435. Bio-pesticides are ______

a Predators b) Parasitoids

c) Pathogens **d) All**

436. _______ irrigation should be preferred over flood irrigation to conserve moisture and reduce the weed infestation.

a) Drip b) Sprinkler

c) Bed d) None of these

437. Biological suppression of *Amritodus atkinsoni* was achieved by release of predator__________

a) *Bacillus thuringiensis* **b) *Mallada boninensis***

c) *Chrysoperla carnea* d) *Amblyseius fallecis*

438. For effective control of *Helicoverpa armigera* in tomato the egg parasitoid ___________ is used.

a) *Chrysoperla carnea*

b) *Amblyseius fallecis*

c) *Trichogramma pretiosum*

d) *Bacillus thuringiensis*

439. Long form of VAM is————————

a) Vinyl Acetate Monomer **b) Vesicular Arbuscular Mycorrhizae**

c) Ventilation Air methane d) Virginia Association of Museums

440. Most effective biological control of mealy bug in grape ——————————is used

a) *Verticilium leccani* b) *VAM*

c) *Azotobacter* d) *Tricoderma veridi*

441. Correcting soil pH using agricultural————————————based on soil test values, once in2-3 years is required.

a) Lime b) Calcium carbonate

c) Sodium hypochlorite d) Calcium hypochlorite

442. ———————————— is effective microbial agent for annihilating Eriophyid Mite of Coconut

a) Pyrecon-E

b) Baculovirus

c) *Metarrhizium anisopliae*

d) *Hirsutella thompsonii*

443. ———— number of principles in the Codex Guideline (1997) in HACCP

a) Eight **b) Seven**

c) One d) Three

444. ———————————— is organic certification agency.

a) CIPHET **b) APEDA**

c) MRDBS d) CITA

445. NSKE is useful for control of ________________

a) Mites b) Termites

c) Mealy bug **d) Thrips**

446. VERMI WASH is ____________________

a) Growth regulator **b) Liquid fertilizer**

c) Chemical fertilizer d) Insecticide

447. Head quarter of APEDA located at ____________________

a) Mumbai b) Chennai

c) Delhi d) Kolkata

448. Application of ____________ is effective control of root knot nematodes

a) Caster cake b) Bone meal

c) Neem cake d) Saw dust

449. _____________ is effective in controlling the diamondback moth on cabbage

a) Sulphur **b) Biotrol WP**

c) Oil d) Streptocycline

450. Seed treatment with _______________ at 4 g/kg seed to prevent soil borne infection of fungi and nematodes

a) ***T.viride*** b) VAM

c) *Verticilium leccani* d) PSB

451. The use of __________ is effective against many insect pest such as chilli thrips,whitefly aphids etc.

a) Edible oil b) Coconut oil

c) Neem oil **d) Pongamia oil**

452. Glyricidia content ________ %

a) 0.25 **b) 0.30**

c) 0.40 d) 0.45

453. Fixing of plastic bottle traps with wooden blocks impregnated with _________ to capture fruit flies

a) Methyl parathion b) Methyl bromide

c) Ethanol **d) Methyl eugenol**

454. Intercropping with _________with tomato reduced the damage of root-knot and reniform nematodes.

a) Chrysanthemum b) Aster

c) Gaillardia **d) Marigold**

455. Crop rotation with __________ reduce bacterial wilt

a) Cluster bean **b) French bean**

c) Soybean d) Coco bean

456. Bacterial blight (*Xanthomonas compestris* pv. *puniacae*) of pomegranate can be prevented by_______

a) Use of disease free seedlings for planting

b) Application of FYM/compost/vermicomost

c) Taking *hasta bahar*

d) All above

22

Vegetable Science

1. Onion belongs to the family ....
   a) Alliaceae b) Brussicaceac
   c) Crucifereae d) Chno podoceae
2. Pungency in onion is due to ....
   a) Dially / disulphide b) Carbonates
   c) Sulphonates **d) Allypropyl Disulfide**
3. The origin place of onion is ....
   a) Central Asia b) America
   c) Africa d) Mediterarion region
4. The edible potion of onion is ....
   a) Modified flower b) Modified stem
   c) Modified leaf d) Modified root
5. Yellow colour variety of onion is ....
   a) Early Gruno b) N-53
   c) Phule Samarth d) Punjab Naroya
6. .... is a white onion variety.
   a) Phule Suvarna **b) Phule Safed**
   c) Phule Samarth d) Phule Baswant
7. Onion is highly cross pollinated crop due to ....
   a) Dliestogamy **b) Protandry**
   c) Heterostyly d) Herkogany
8. Quality seed in onion is obtained by .... method of seed production.
   a) Seed to seed method b) Transplanting
   c) Bulb to seed method d) Direct seeding

9. Transplanting of onion in late *kharif* or early *rabi* is known as .... season in Maharashtra.
   a) Pol   **b) Rangada**
   c) Rabi   d) Summer

10. .... is F_1 hybrid in onion.
   a) Arka Kirtiman   b) Arka Pitanber
   c) Arka niketan   d) Arka Kulyan

11. For dehxdration purpose, the TSS of onion should be ....
   a) 5-10   b) 2-3
   c) 15-20   d) 5-7

12. The pungency in garlic is due to ....
   a) Sulphonates   b) Carbonates
   c) Diallyl disulphide   d) Allyl proply disulfide

13. Seed rate for Garlic is .... kg/ha.
   a) 500-600   b) 1500-2000
   c) 100-200   d) 1000-1500

14. Recovery of cloves in the garlic bulbs ranges from ....%.
   a) 86-96   b) 5-10
   c) 10-20   d) 20-30

15. Radish is cross pollinated due to ....
   a) Saprophytic self incompatibility
   b) Male sterility
   c) Genetic sterility
   d) Cytoplasm sterility

16. Kashi Sweta is variety of ....
   a) Turnip   b) Beet root
   c) Carrot   **d) Radish**

17. Pusa Chandrima is variety of ....
   a) Turnip   b) Beet root
   c) Carrot   d) Radish

18. Pusa Kesher is variety of ....
   a) Carrot   b) Beet root
   c) Turnip   d) Radish

19. Crimson Globe is variety of ....

    a) Carrot **b) Beet root**

    c) Radish d) Turnip

20. Potato is a native of tropical ....

    a) North America **b) South America**

    c) Europe d) Africa

21. CPRI is located at ....

    a) Ludiayana **b) Shimla**

    c) Hissar d) Kashmir

22. Kufri Chipsona is a variety of ....

    a) Turnip **b) Potato**

    c) Beet root d) Carrot

23. Potato is prorogated through ....

    a) Tubers b) Roots

    c) Bulbs d) Rhizomes

24. Seed accounts for nearly ....% cost of potato cultivation.

    a) 10 b) 5

    c) 40 d) 15

25. True potato seeds required for one hectare is ....

    a) 100-150 g/ha b) 10-15 g/ha

    c) 1000-1500 kg/ha d) 5-10 kg/ha

26. Origin place of sprouting broccoli is ....

    a) Italy b) Iran

    c) Egypt d) Malaysia

27. Pride of India is variety of ....

    a) Cabbage b) Cauliflower

    c) Knol-khol d) Brussels sprout

28. All the cole crops are originated from a common parent ....

    a) *Brassica Oleracea Var. Capiteta*

    b) *Brassica Oleracea Rubra*

    c) *Brassica Oleracea Gongilodes*

    d) *Brassica Oleracea Var. Sylvestris*

29. Cauliflower is botanically known as ....
    a) *Brassica Oleracea var.. botrytis*
    b) *Brassica Oleracea var. rubru*
    c) *Brassica Oleracea var. gongylodes*
    d) *Brassica Oleracea var. capiteta*

30. Hisar-1 is a self-blanched variety of ....
    a) Cauliflower b) Cabbage
    c) Brussels sprout d) Sprouting broccoli

31. Whiptail in cauliflower is due to deficiency of ....
    a) Boron **b) Molybdenum**
    c) Zinc d) Copper

32. Cauliflower is a .... pollinated crop.
    a) Cross b) Self
    c) Often cross d) Nane of above

33. Phule Priya is variety of ....
    a) Dolichos bean **b) Pea**
    c) Cluster bean d) Cow Pea

34. The basic chromosome numbe of pea 2n = ...
    a) 18 **b) 14**
    c) 20 d) 22

35. Peas with .... tendrometer reading is offered for high price.
    a) Low b) High
    c) Medium d) None of above

36. Botanical name of Broad bean is ....
    a) *Vicia faba L.*
    b) *Phaseolus lanatus L.*
    c) *Vigna uniguiculata L.*
    d) *Cyamopsis tetragonoloba L.*

37. Botanical name of Cabbage is ....
    a) *Brussica Oleracea var. capitata*
    b) *Brussica Oleracea var. gongyloides*
    c) *Brussica Oleracea var. botrytis*
    d) *Brussica Oleracea var. Acephala*

38. Pusa Snowball is variety of

a) Cabbage **b) Cauliflower**

c) Knol-khol d) Sprouting broccoli

39. White Vienna is variety of ....

a) Knol-khol b) Cabbage

c) Sprouting broccoli d) Cauliflower

40. Hilds Ideal is an OP variety of ....

a) Sprouting broccoli b) Cabbage

c) Cauliflower **d) Brussels sprouts**

41. Palam Samridhi is variety of ....

a) Sprouting Broccoli b) Brussels sprouts

c) Cabbage d) Cauliflower

42. Virginia Savoy is variety of ....

a) Spinach b) Turnip

c) Carrot d) Radish

43. The family of coriander is ....

a) Chinopodiaceqe **b) Apiaceae**

c) Brassicaceae d) Leguminaceae

44. The Botanical name of coriander is ....

a) *Coriandrum sativaum* b) *Atriplex hortense*

c) *Chemopodium album* d) *Brassica spp.*

45. Lettuce is .... pollinated crop.

a) Cross **b) Self**

c) Often cross d) None of above

46. The soft tender shoot of asparagus is known as ....

a) Leaf **b) Spears**

c) Shoot d) Stem

47. Asparagus is a ....nature.

a) Monoecieous **b) Dioeceous**

c) Andromonoeceous d) Gynoeceous

48. Mary Washington is variety of ....

a) Asparagus c) Turnip

b) Carrot d) Radish

49. Kanji, an appetizing drink is prepared from .... roots.

a) Carrot b) Turnip

c) Radish d) Asparagus

50. Pungency in radish is due to ....

a) Anthocynins b) Disulfides

c) Isothiocynates d) Sulphonates

51. Pusa Kanchan is variety of ....

a) Turnip b) Radish

c) Carrot d) Asparagus

52. Botanical name of Knol Khol is ....

a) *Brassica Oleracea var. gongylodes*

b) *Brassica Oleracea var. capiteta*

c) *Brussica Oleracea var. rubra*

d) *Brussica Oleracea var. sylvestris*

53. .... is not day neutral vegetable crop.

a) Chilli b) Tomato

c) Brinjal **d) Okra**

54. Chilli has .... chromosome number.

a) 2n = 24 b) 2n = 22

c) 2n = 20 d) 2n = 26

55. Chilli is richest source of vitamin ....

a) vit-B-1 b) vit-B-12

c) vit-C d) vit-D

56. Capsaicin content in Indian chilli varieties ranges from ...... to ......%.

a) 0.02 to 2.0 b) 0.02 to 1.86

c) 0.002 to 1.86 d) 0.002 to 0.86

57. .... is multiple disease resistance variety of chilli.

a) Phule Jyoti b) Pant C-1

c) Punjab Lal d) Andra Jyoti

58. Chilli is a .... pollinated crop.
    a) Self pollinated
    b) Cross pollinated
    c) Often cross pollinated
    d) None
59. .... is leading chilli growing state in India.
    a) Maharashtra
    b) Karnataka
    c) Tamil Nadu
    d) Andra Pradesh
60. .... is principle colouring pigment in chilli.
    a) Capsaicin
    b) Capsanthin
    c) Beta Carotine
    d) None
61. .... form nitrogen is preferred by capsicum crop.
    a) Nitrate
    b) Nitriate
    c) Amonical
    d) Di-amonical
62. Oleoresin is extracted from ....
    a) Chilli
    b) Turmeric
    c) Ginger
    d) All
63. Pant T-3 is variety of .... crop.
    a) Chilli
    b) Tomato
    c) Capsicum
    d) Brinjal
64. .... is variety of Tomato suitable for processing purpose.
    a) Pusa Gaurav
    b) Roma
    c) Punjab Chuhara
    d) All
65. Fruit cracking in tomato is caused by .... factor.
    a) Genetic
    b) Environmental
    c) Genetic & environmental
    d) None
66. For tomato processing pH of fruit should be ....
    a) Low
    b) Medium
    c) High
    d) None
67. .... of following not a physiological disorder of Tomato.
    a) Fruit cracking
    b) Bolssom end rot
    c) Puffiness
    d) Pillow

68. .... and .... styled flower of brinjal act as male flowers and there is no fruit setting.

a) Long styled
b) Medium styled
c) Long and medium styled
d) Short and pseudoshot styled

69. Aruna is variety of .... crop.

a) Chilli
b) Brinjal
c) Tomato
d) Cucumber

70. For increasing fruit set in brinjal crop .... growth regulator is used.

a) Basalin
b) Ethrel
c) 2-4-D
d) Goal

71. Cross pollination in brinjal crop is due to ....

a) House fly
b) Wind
c) Honey and bumble bees
d) All

72. .... is major pest of brinjal crop.

a) Aphid
b) Beetal
c) Mite
d) Shoot and fruit borer

73. .... is a cucurbit crop having less seed.

a) Chow chow
b) Bitter gourd
c) Bottle gourd
d) Cucumber

74. The highest concentration of cucurbitacin is observed in .... and ....

a) Stem and leaves
b) Stem and root
c) Fruit and root
d) Flower and leaves

75. .... cucurbit crops has white flowers.

a) Snake gourd
b) Pinted gourd
c) Bottle gourd
d) All

76. The dioeceous vegetable crops is ....

a) Pointed gourd
b) Sweet gourd
c) Ivy gourd
d) All

77. The botanical name of scarlet bean is ....

a) *P. Vulgasis*
b) *P. Lunatus*
c) *P. Coccineus*
d) *P. Acutifolius*

78. .... is following cross pollinated bean crop.

a) French bean **b) Scarlet bean**

c) Lima bean d) Tapery bean

79. .... is hybrid variety of brinjal developed by MPKV., Rahuri.

a) Phule Raja **b) Phule Arjun**

c) Phule Kirti d) Phule Gauri

80. The botanical name of scarlet gourd is ....

a) *Coccinia indica* b) *Cucurbita pepo*

c) *Benincasa hispida* d) *Cucumis melo*

81. The cromosome number of cucumber is ....

a) 2n = 14 b) 2n = 24

c) 2n = 40 d) 2n = 22

82. Ooty is variety of .... crop.

a) Cow pea b) Dolichos bean

c) French bean d) Cluster bean

83. Sharad bahar is variety of .... crop.

a) French bean b) Lima bean

c) Cluster bean d) None

84. French bean is also called as ....

a) Fresh bean b) String bean

c) Snap bean d) All

85. ...... is vegetable crop is called as vegetable of the twentieth century.

a) Winged bean b) French bean

c) Broccolli d) Lettuce

86. .... Part of Guar is used for preparation of guar gum.

a) Seed flour b) Stem

c) Leaves d) Roots

87. .... crop is used as cover crop.

a) Cow pea b) Sword bean

c) Jack bean **d) All**

88. .... is induced mutant from Pusa Sawani using EMS in Okra.

a) Punjab-8 b) Punjab Padmini

c) Parbhani Kranti d) Punjab-7

89. In .... vegetable crops anthesis takes place during late night hours.

a) Bottle gourd b) Ivy gourd

c) Snake gourd **d) All**

90. Straight Eight is variety of .... crop.

a) Cucumber b) Bottle gourd

c) Water melon d) Snake gourd

91. .... growth regulator is used for induction of staminate flowers in gynoecious lines of cucumber.

a) 2-4-D b) Ethrel

c) Ethephon **d) Silver nitrate**

92. Sweet gourd is propagated by ....

a) Cuttings b) Suckers

c) Tubers or Seeds d) None

93. .... crop is treated as king of vegetable.

a) Pointed gourd b) Sweet gourd

c) Snake gourd d) Bitter gourd

94. Punjab Sadabahar is variety of .... crop.

a) Sponge gourd **b) Ridge gourd**

c) Bottle gourd d) Bitter gourd

95. .... growth regulator dayled flowering in Okra.

a) GA **b) MH-40**

c) 2-4-D d) Ethrel

96. Foliar spray of .... growth regulator inhibit female flower production in muskmelon, however increased female flower produciton in water melon.

a) GA_3 b) $AgNO_3$

c) Ethepon d) Ethrel

97. .... growth regulator is used as gamatocides.

a) MH-40 b) $AgNO_3$

c) 2-4-D d) Ethrel

98. In tissue culture .... growth regulators are used in MS nutrient medium.

a) BA b) IAA

c) IBA **d) All**

99. Bermuda grass and wild sugarcane are .... weeds.

a) Perennial monocot b) Perinnial dicot

c) Annual monocot d) Annual dicot

100. The annual dicot weed is ....

a) Pig weed b) Datura

c) Prickly poppy **d) All**

101. Cuscuta species is .... weed.

a) Aquatic weed **b) Parasitic weed**

c) Aquatic and parasitic weed d) Non

102. .... is a pre-emergance herbicide used in vegetable crop.

a) Oxyflurofen b) Pendimethelin

c) Fluchloralin **d) All**

103. .... is post emergence hervicide.

a) Paraquat b) Glyphosate

c) 2-4-D **d) All**

104. .... post harvest treatment given to vegetable produce to remove field heat.

a) Washing b) Drying

c) Waxing **d) Pre-cooling**

105. .... is the process of decomposing green colour in fruits by applying ethylene to give characteristic colour to fruits.

a) Greening **b) De-greening**

c) Colouring d) None

106. Premature bolting in amaranth is due to deficiency of ....

a) Potassium b) Copper

c) Calcium **d) Nitrogen**

107. .... Oleoresin is used in snackes, curries, pickles.

a) Pepper b) Vanilla

c) Ginger d) None

108. "Arka Saurbh" variety of Tomato is resistant to which stress?

a) Early blight
b) Furasuium wilt
c) Mosaic disease
d) Fruit cracking

109. "Arka Tinda" variety of round gourd is tolerant to which pest (s)?

a) Fruit fly
b) Downy mildew
c) Furasium wilt
d) Aphids

110. A phenomenon in which a gene has more than one phenotypic effect

a) Polymorphism
b) Penetrance
c) Expressivety
d) Pleiotropism

111. Advance form of sex in cucurbits is

a) Monoecious
b) Dioecious
c) Hermaphrodite
d) Andromonoecious

112. Agrifound Parvati (G 313) variety of Garlic is tolerant to which disease?

a) Soft rot
b) Purple blotch
c) Stemphyllum blight
d) Smut

113. Agrifound White (G-41) Yamuna Safed-K (G-1) Yamuna Safed-2 (G-50), G-282 and and Agrifound Parvati (G-313) are newly released varieties of which crop?

a) Onion
b) Garlic
c) Multiple onion
d) Potato

114. All cole crop belongs to which of the family?

a) Cruciferae
b) Umbelliferae
c) Brassicae
d) None of the above

115. All the cole crops are originated from which common parent?

a) ***Brassica oleracea var. sylvestris***
b) *Brassica oleracea var. rapa*
c) *Brassica compestrils*
d) *Raphanus sativus*

116. Alternate form of gene at the same locus are called ?

a) Chromosome
b) Plasid
c) Allele
d) Dominant

117. Amaranth belongs to which family?
a) Chenopodiaceae **b) Amaranthaceae**
c) Portulaceae d) None of the above

118. Amaranth is which type of plant?
a) C3 **b) C4**
c) CAM d) None of the above

119. Amaranth originated from which region of world ?
a) Barzil **b) India**
c) Europe d) Asia

120. An asexual progeny of a single homozygous plant is known as_
a) Variety b) Race
c) Strain **d) Clone**

121. Arka Abhay is a variety of which crop?
a) Brinjal b) Chilli
c) Tomato **d) Bhindi**

122. Arka Ajit is a variety of –
a) Tomato **b) Pea**
c) Botte gourd d) Chilli

123. Samrat is a variety of which crop?
a) Tinda b) Pumpkin
c) Bottle gourd d) Bitter gourd

124. Kokan Harita is a variety of which of the following crops?
a) Amaranth b) Bottle guard
c) Bitter guard d) Brinjal

125. Arka Jyoti is an improved variety of which crop ?
a) Musk melon **b) Watermelon**
c) Bottle gourd c) snap melon

126. Arka Kalyan variety of onion is local collection of what?
a) IIHR-193 b) IIHR56-1
c) Pusa Red **d) IIHR-145**

127. Arka Manik, a variety of watermelon is resistant to which disease (s) ?
a) Downy mildew **b) Powdery mildew**
c) Wilt d) All of the above

128. Arka Nishant' is a resistant for

a) Grape **b) Radish**

c) Carrot d) Beet leaf

129. Arka Nishant variety of radish is resistant which disorder?

a) Pithiness disorder b) Branching disorder

c) Forking disorder d) Zoning disorder

130. Arka Suryamukhe is an improved variety of which crop?

a) Summer spuash **b) Winter squash**

c) Pumkins d) Muskmelon

131. Arkel is an early season variety introduction from which region ?

a) Germany b) UK

c) USA d) Netherlands

132. Ash gourd is originated in which region?

a) Africa b) India

c) America **d) Java and Japan**

133. At present the headquarters of AICVIP is situated in which city?

a) Bangalore b) New Delhi

c) Pune **d) Varanasi**

134. At what time a day anthesis in tomato flowers start?

a) 6:00 AM b) 10:00 AM

c) 11:00 AM d) 12 Noon

135. Beta vulgaris (Beet root) belongs to which family?

a) Convolvulaceae **b) Chenopodiaceae**

c) Cruciferae d) Compositeae

136. Bharat is the first hybrid of capsicum released by which agency?

a) MAHYCO **b) IAHS**

c) Bio-seed d) Sugrow

137. Betterness is brinjal is due to presence of

a) Glycoproteins **b) Glycoalkaloids**

c) Olcoresins d) None of the above

138. Bitterness in cucumber due to effect of external pollens and is called?

a) Glucosides b) Acids

c) Alkaloids **d) Metaxenia**

139. Krishna is Hybrid of which crop ?

a) Tomato b) Okra

c) Brinjal d) Sweet potato

140. Botanical name of which crop is Cucurbita moschata Poir

a) Tomato **b) Pumpkin**

c) Cucumber d) Ridge gourd

141. Bottle gourd originated in which continent?

a) Africa b) America

c) India d) None of the above

142. Brinjal is native of which country?

a) Africa b) South America

c) India and Africa d) Korea

143. C. annuum x C. pubescens are completely –

a) Self-fertile **b) Cross-fertile**

c) Self-incomplete d) Cross-compaitible

144. Cabbage belongs to which of the botanical variety?

a) Botrytis **b) Capitata**

c) Gongylodes d) None of the above

145. Callifornia Wonder, Chinese Giant and World Beater are varieties of which crop?

a) Chilli **b) Capsicum**

c) Okra d) Tomato

146. Capsicum varieties, 'Arka Mohini', Arka Gaurva and 'Arka Basant' are bred by

a) Dr. G. Kalloo b) Dr. K.V. Peter

c) Dr. D.P. Singh d) Dr. K.L. Chanda

147. Capsicum variety "Yolo Wonder" is tolerant to which of following?

a) TMV b) Leaf spot

c) Fruit rot d) None of the above

148. Carrot belongs to which of the family?

a) Malvaceae
b) Solanaceae
c) Umbeliferae
d) None of the above

149. Carrot' is originated from-

a) Europe
b) China
c) Afghanistan
d) Mexico

150. Cauliflower originated in which region?

a) Eastern Mediterranean region
b) South and Central America
c) Iran (Persia)
d) None of the above

151. Challanger is a variety of which crop?

a) Indian bean
b) Lima bean
c) Custer bean
d) Tomato

152. Chenopodiaceae is the family of which crop ?

a) Potato
b) Okra
c) Sweet potato
d) Spinach

153. Chinese cabbage and kale are resistant to which of followings pests ?

a) Powdery mildew
b) Anthracnose
c) Downey mildew
d) Leaf spot

154. *Citrullus lanatus* Mansf is botanical name of which crop ?

a) Muskmelon
b) Watermelon
c) Pumpkin
d) Round melon

155. Co-10 variety of Indian Bean is a

a) Selection from local germplasm
b) Macro-mutant
c) An introduction from U.S.A
d) None of the above

156. Complete genetic heterozygosity and heterogeneity is found in which of following ?

a) F1 hybrids
b) Pureline
c) Multilines
d) Synthetics

157. Coriander is a member of which family?

a) Lauraceae
b) Labiateae
c) Myristicaceae
d) Umbelliferate

158. Coriander is a native of which region?

a) Mediterranean region
b) South Asia
c) Africa
d) South America

159. Coriander is basically which type of crop?

a) Cross-pollinated crop
b) Self-pollinated crop
c) Often Self pollinated crop
d) Often-cross pollinated crop

160. Crossing over during meiosis results in which of following?

a) Promoting linkage
b) Breaking linkage
c) Help in mutation
d) None

161. Cucumis anguira is mutant of which spp.?

a) *C. sativus*
b) *C. longipes*
c) *C. melo*
d) *C. pepo*

162. Cucurbita moschata is cross-fertile with which of following ?

a) Cucurbita pepo
b) Cucurbita maxima
c) Cucurbita ficiloia
d) None of the above

163. Curd' of cauliflower is an example of

a) Hypertrophy
b) Hypotrophy
c) Hyperplasea
d) Hypoplasea

164. *Cyanopsis tetragonolobus* is the botanical name of –

a) Cluster bean
b) Winged bean
c) Kidney bean
d) Hyacinth bean

165. Cytoplasmic male sterility' is found in-

a) Carrot
b) Onion
c) Sugarbeet
d) Tomato

166. Family of sweet potato is

a) Euphorbiacae
b) Aizoiaceae
c) Agavaceae
d) Convolvulaceae

167. First hybrid in vegetable was released in –

a) Bottle gourd (1971) b) Brinjal (1976)

c) Tomato (1965) d) Chilli (1982)

168. First seedless (triploid) variety of watermelon was developed by –

a) Dr. Kihara (1951) b) Baily (1949)

c) Freidlander (1977) d) Heslope (1963)

169. First time cytoplasmic genetic male sterility is used in

a) Onion b) Pea

c) Groundnut d) Carrot

170. Flavour in cabbage leaves is due to the glucoside called?

a) Capsicinoids **b) Sinigrin**

c) Cucurbitacin d) Xanthophyll

171. Florida Market variety of brinjal is resistant to which disease?

a) Damping off b) Bacterial wilt

c) Fusarium wilt d) Anthracnose

172. For hybridization in tomato, mature buds are emasculated how many hours before their opening?

a) 12-16 hr b) 2-6 hr

c) 3-4 hr d) 10-12 hr

173. For what purpose transgenic are produced in tomato ?

a) Modified ripening b) Resistance to herbicides

c) Resistance to virus **d) All the above**

174. French bean is a native of which region?

a) Asia b) India

c) South and Central America d) Mediterranean region

175. French bean is resistant of which stress?

a) Salanity **b) Drought**

c) Frost d) Cold

176. French Bean variety "Contender" is tolerant to which disease?

a) Anthranose **b) Powedery mildew**

c) Stem blight d) None of the above

177. French Breakfast, Pusa Chetki, Arka Nishant and Bombay Red are the varieties of which crop?

a) Carrot **b) Radish**

c) Beet root d) Turnip

178. From where Arka Komal, French bean has been introduced from?

a) USA b) Phillipines

c) Denmark **d) Australia**

179. From where Arkel, pea has been introduced from?

a) France b) Phillipines

c) Denmark d) Israel

180. From where Asahi Yamati, watermelon is introduced from?

a) USA **b) Japan**

c) Denmark d) Israel

181. From where Bonneville'pea has been introduced from?

a) USA b) Phillipines

c) Denmark d) Israel

182. From where Dward Money Maker, tomato is introduced in India?

a) USA b) Phillipines

c) Denmark d) Israel

183. From where Great Lakes, lettuce has been introduced from?

a) USA b) Phillipines

c) Denmark d) Israel

184. From where improved Japanese, cauliflower has been introduced in India?

a) USA b) Phillipines

c) Denmark **d) Israel**

185. From where Indian spicach (palak) is originated?

a) South Africa **b) Northern India**

c) Tropical America d) Indo-Chinese region

186. From where Sugar Baby, watermelon has been introduced in India?

a) USA b) Phillipines

c) Denmark d) Israel

187. From where Golden Acre, cabbage has been introduced from?

a) USA b) Phillipines

c) Denmark d) Israel

188. Fruit setting in brinjal usually occurs in the flower having

a) Long and medium style b) Medium style

c) Short and medium style d) Short style

189. Garden pea belongs to which sub species?

a) Arvense **b) Hortense**

c) Elatius d) None of the above

190. Garden pea variety "Bonnville" is an introduction from which region?

a) Australia b) Canada

c) U.S.A d) None of the above

191. Garlic belongs to which species?

a) Cepa b) Porrum

c) Sativum d) None of the above

192. Give the alternate name of broad bean?

a) French bean **b) Faba bean**

c) Cluster bean d) Hyacinth bean

193. Give the publisher of 'Hort-Science'?

a) ICAR **b) Horticulture Society of India**

c) ASHS d) Govt. of India

194. GMS in chilli is maintained through-

a) Heterozygous Pollinator b) Homozygous pollinator

c) Mutation d) Polyploidy

195. Gynoecious lines are common in

a) Water melon b) Muskmelon

c) Long melon **d) Cucumber**

196. H-64, a cabbage hybrid developed at IARI Regional Station Katrain, Kullu involved use of which type of plants?

a) Self incompatibility **b) Cytoplasmic male sterility**

c) Genic male sterility d) None of the above

197. Herkogamy favours

a) Self pollination **b) Cross pollination**

c) Mutation d) Wide hybridization

198. Heterobeltiosis is estimated over which of the following?

a) Wild parent **b) Better parent**

c) Popular variety d) Popular hybrid

199. Hetermorphic self- incompatibility is found in-

a) Carambola b) Sweet Potato

c) Brinjal **d) All of them**

200. Heterostyle condition is observed in-

a) Tomato **b) Brinjal**

c) Potato d) Chilli

201. Hissar Lalit and SL-12 varieties of tomato are resistant to which pest?

a) Fusarium b) Bacterial wilt

c) Root knot nematode d) Leaf curl virus

202. Hissar Sugandha is the latest released variety of which of following crop?

a) Coriander b) Fennel

c) Fenugreek d) Clove

203. How are synthetic seeds in vegetable produced?

a) Embryo rescue **b) Somatic embryogenesis**

c) Micropropagation d) Anther culture

204. How are the cabbage cultivars can be classified into?

a) White cabbage b) Red cabbage

c) Savoy cabbage **d) All of the above**

205. How Brinjal variety MDU-1 was evolved through?

a) X rays b) EMS

c) Gamma rays d) MMS

206. How distant interspecific hybrids in vegetables are produced?

a) Anther culture b) Somaclonal variations

c) Embryo culture d) Micropropagation

207. How diverse cytoplasm can be fused together?
   a) Embryo rescue
   b) Protoplast fusion
   c) Micropropogation
   d) Anther culture
208. How Genic male sterility in chillies is maintained under heterozygous conditions?
   a) Back crossing with recessive parent
   b) Mass selection
   c) Inbreeding
   d) Pure line selection
209. How haploids are produced and maintained?
   a) Anther culture
   b) Somaclonal variations
   c) Embryo culture
   d) Micropropagation
210. How incompatibility barriers of distant species can be overcome?
   a) Embryo rescue
   b) Somatic hybridization
   c) Micropropagation
   d) Anther culture
211. How is GMS in chilli maintained through?
   a) Heterozygous pollinator
   b) Mution
   c) Homozygous pollinator
   d) Polyploidy
212. How is multiplication of male sterile line in onion done?
   a) Anther culture
   b) Somaclonal variations
   c) Embryo culture
   d) Micropropagation
213. How the tomato variety PKM 1 is evolved through?
   a) X-rays
   b) Gamma rays
   c) EMS
   d) MMS
214. How was tomato variety CO3 evolved?
   a) X-rays
   b) Gamma rays
   c) MMS
   d) EMS
215. How was tomato variety Pusa Lal meeruti evolved?
   a) X-rays
   b) Gamma rays
   c) MMS
   d) EMS
216. In which of following crop Hayes and Jones (1916) firstly reported heterosis ?
   a) Cucumber
   b) Watermelon
   c) Muskmelon
   d) Lone melon

217. In which vegetable " Solasodine" is present ?

a) Tomato
b) Onion
c) Brinjal
d) Garlic

218. International Institute of Horticulture (IIH) is located in-

a) U.S.A
b) China
c) Brazil
d) Rye

219. Jades cross hybrid belong to which crop ?

a) Cabbage
b) Broccoli
c) Cauliflower
d) Brusseles sprout

220. Japanese white variety of radish was developed by which organization?

a) IIHR
b) IARI
c) PAU
d) None of the above

221. "Kufri Badshah" variety of potato is a derivative of cross between whom?

a) Kufri Red x Gineke
b) Kufri Jyoti x Kufri Alankar
c) Kufri Bahar x Kufri Kuber
d) Kufri Sindhuri x Kufri Red

222. K-2 variety of chilli is tolerant to which disease?

a) Baterial leaf spot
b) Powdery mildew
c) Fusarium wilt
d) Fruit rot

223. Kohlrabi (knoll-khol) belongs to which of following botanical variety ?

a) Gemmifera
b) Italica
b) Gongylodes
c) None of the above

224. Kt-1 (Pusa Deepti) developed at IARI, Regional Station Katrain belongs to which crop?

a) Tomato
b) Brinjal
c) Chilli
d) Capsicum

225. Kufri Jyoti Variety of Potato is resistance to which disease?

a) Early Blight
b) Late blight
c) Wart disease
d) Both early blight & wart diseases

226. Maleness in gyno-ecious lines of cucumber is induced by which treatment?

a) Silver nitrate b) NAA

c) IAA d) ABA

227. Mass selection has been employed to develop which of the following radish varieties?

a) White Icicle **b) Arka Nishant**

c) Japanese White d) Chinese Pink

228. MDU-1 is a variety of which of following?

a) Mutant in snakgourd and okra, bitter gourd

b) Cluster bearing mutant chilli

c) Pureline selection of brinjal

d) All of these

229. Mention crop (s) in which self incompatibility is found?

a) Cabbage b) Knol-khol

c) Cauliflower **d) All of above**

230. Mention the botanical name of bitter gourd (Karela) is

a) Citrullus vulgaris b) Luffa cylindrical

c) Momordica charantia d) Lagenaria siceraria

231. Mention the botanical name of swet pepper?

a) Capsicum frutescens L. b) Capsicum nigram L.

c) Capsicum annum L. d) None of the above

232. Mention the cabbage variety developed at IARI which is suitable for high temperature?

a) Pusa Sambandh b) Pusa Mukta

c) Pusa Drum head **d) Pusa Ageti**

233. Mention the country which is the origin of Dolichus bean?

a) China **b) India**

c) Mexico d) Mediterranean region

234. Mention the country which is the origin place of ridge gourd?

a) Ethopia **b) India**

c) China d) Brazil

235. Mention the crop in which the mechanism of protogyne is observed?

a) Onion **b) Cabbage**
c) Carrot d) Radish

236. Mention the crop of which Pant Kakari is a variety?

a) Muskmelon **b) Long melon**
c) Snapmelon d) Watermelon

237. Mention the crop of which nantes is the variety?

a) Radish **b) Carrot**
c) Onion d) Turnip

238. Mention the crop of which Pride of India is a variety?

a) Cabbage b) Cauliflower
c) Radish d) Turnip

239. Mention the crop of which Pusa Jyoti is a variety?

a) Fenugreek **b) Palak**
c) Spinach d) Capsicum

240. Mention the crop of which Pusa Naveen is a variety?

a) Brinjal **b) Bottlegourd**
c) Spongegourd d) Ridgegourd

241. Mention the crop of which Phule Raja is a Hybrid?

a) Bittergourd **b) Tomato**
c) Bottlegourd d) Brinjal

242. Mention the crop of which Swaranrekha is a variety?

a) Snakegourd **b) Pointedgourd**
c) Ridgegourd d) Waxgourd

243. Mention the genus of Gherkins?

a) Cucurbita **b) Cucumis**
d) Citrullus d) None

244. Mention the method used for breeding for disease resistance?

a) Backcross b) Mass selection
c) Pure line selection d) All

245. Mention the name of the common Pumpkin grown throughout India?

a) C. maxima
b) C. moshata
c) C. pepo
d) None of the above

246. Mention the primary center of diversity for drumstick?

a) Chinese-Japanese
b) Hindustan Center
c) Indo-Chinese
d) Mediterranean region

247. Mention the primary center of diversity for radish?

a) Chinese-Japanese
b) Hindustan Center
c) Indo-Chinese
d) Mediterranean region

248. Mention the Primary center of diversity for sweet potato?

a) Central Asia
b) Africa
c) Near East
d) Central America

249. Mention the technique employed for developing Pusa Parvati, a variety of French bean?

a) Conal selection
b) Mass selection
c) Mutation breeding
d) None

250. Mention the techniques used in potato breeding?

a) Intervarietal hybridization
b) Interspecific hybridization
c) Inter conal hybridization
d) Both a and c

251. Mention the tomato varieties that are resistant to bacterial wilt ?

a) Arka Abha
b) Arka Alok
c) Arka Shresha
d) All of the above

252. Mention the tomato varieties which are resistant to "Buckeye rot"?

a) Money Maker
b) Red Cherry
c) Flat Large Red
d) All of these

253. Mention the tomato variety which sets fruit at low temperature?

a) Pusa Ruby
b) Pant Bahar
c) Hissar Arun
d) Pusa Sheetal

254. Mention the types of self incompatibility observed in radish and turnip?

a) Sporophytic
b) Both a & c
c) Gametophytic
d) None of these

255. Mention the variety which is a cross between Chappan Kaddu x Early Yellow Proflific

a) **Pusa Proflific** b) Australian Green

c) Patty Pan d) None of these

256. Mention to which is Pant Bahar "Tomato" resistant to?

a) Verticillium wilt **b) Both a & c**

c) Fusarium wilt d) None of the above

257. Mention to which of following Punjab Lal chilli is resistance to?

a) CMV b) Bacterial wilt

c) CMMV **d) All of these**

258. Mention to which peruvianum hirsutum chesmanii landulosum and pissivi belongs to?

a) Eriopersicon b) Lycopersicon

c) Eulycopericon d) Esculentum

259. Mention which crop shows protandry ?

a) Carrot b) Tomato

c) Chilli d) Brinjal

260. Mention which is a hybrid between sugar beet and local palak ?

a) Jobner Green b) All green

c) Pusa Jyoti **d) Pusa Harit**

261. Mention which is a tropical radish?

a) Arka Nishant b) Scarlet Globe

c) White Icicle d) French Breakfast

262. Mention which of following is drought resistant crop?

a) Sweet potato b) Okra

c) Cauliflower d) Poto

263. Mention which of the following are tolerant to salt stress in tomato?

a) *L. Peruvianum* b) *L. Pennelli*

c) *L. cheesmani* **d) All of above**

264. Mention which of the following belongs to Eulycopersicon?

a) Esculentum **b) Both a and b**

c) Pimpinelifolium d) None of these

265. Mention which of the following Capsicum are resistant to Anthracnose furit rot?

a) Chinese Giant
b) Sparton Emerald
c) Yellow Wax
d) All of these

266. Mention which of the following pea variety is edible podded?

a) Early Badger
b) Khapar Kheda
c) Rachna
d) Sylvia

267. Mention which of the following pea variety is resistant to rust?

a) JP-3
b) Both a and c
c) JP-4
d) None of the above

268. Mention which variety is the result of hybridization between Kufri Red x Kufri Kundan?

a) Kufri Sindhuri
b) Kufri Dewa
c) Kufri Sheetman
d) Kufri Badshah

269. Muskmelon is said to be native of which region?

a) Tropical Asia
b) Mediterranean region
c) South America
d) Tropical Africa

270. Multplier onion is botanically known as?

a) Benincasa hispada
b) Allium cepa var.sativum
c) Allium cepa
d) Allium cepa var. aggregatum

271. Name the crop having Cocumis hardwicki; C. callosus; C. melo;C. Prompnaterum and C. dispaceus as its relatives?

a) Cucumber
b) Muskmelon
c) Watermelon
d) Ridged gourd

272. Name of the crop which Durgapur Meetha, Durgapur Kesar and Pusa Bedana are improved varieties?

a) Muskmelon
b) Watermelon
c) Sweet potato
d) Beet

273. Name of the crop which Palam Samridhi is a known variety?

a) Knol khol
b) Sprouting Broccoli
c) Brussels sprout
d) None

274. Name the crop of which Pusa Phalguni, Pusa Barsati, Pusa-Do-Fsali and Pusa Rituraj are the improved variety?

a) Cowpea b) Pea

c) French bean d) Broad bean

275. Name the crop of which Pusa Rasraj is a variety?

a) Pureline variety of muskmelon

b) Hybrid of muskmelon

c) Hybrid of watermelon

d) Seedless watermelon

276. Name the crop of which Pusa Sadabahar is a variety suitable for both stress condition and low temperature fruit setting?

a) Chilli **b) Tomato**

c) Okra d) Capsicum

277. Name the crop of which Pusa Sawani, Pusa Makhmali, and Punjab Padmini are the varieties?

a) Okra b) Onion

c) Garlic d) Tomato

278. Name the crop of which Pusa Sneha, Phule Prajakta, Pusa Chikani are the variety?

a) Ridgegourd **b) Spongegourd**

c) Bittergourd d) Snakegourd

279. Name the crop of which Phule Green Gold, Hirkani, and Pusa Vishnesh are the variety of?

a) Spongegourd **b) Bittergourd**

c) Snakegourd d) Ridgegourd

280. Name the family to which Okra belongs?

a) Solanaceae **b) Malvaceae**

c) Tiliaceae d) Crucirerae

281. Name the genous to which Radish belongs?

a) Brassica **b) Raphanus**

c) Daccus d) None of the above

282. Name the hybrids of onion developed by using cytoplasmic male sterility?
   a) Pusa Red and Pantana Red
   b) Pusa Nasik
   c) Arka Pitamber and Arka Kirtiman
   d) N-53

283. Name the most closely related species of cultivated okra?
   a) *A. tuberculatus*   b) *A. manihot*
   c) *A. ficalens*   d) None of the above

284. Name the muskmelon variety which is a result of cross between Kutana x Cantaloupe
   a) Pusa Sharbati   b) Pusa Madhuras
   c) Punjab Sunehari   d) Punjab hybrid

285. Name the potato varieties that are resistant to wart disease?
   a) Kufri Shrepa   b) Kufri Muthu
   c) Kufri Jyoti   **d) All of these**

286. Name the stress to which Lycopersicon chessmanil of tomato is resistant?
   a) TLCV   b) Bacterial wilt
   c) **Salt tolerance**   d) nematode

287. Name the varieties to which Pea varieties New Line Perfection, Market Prize and Duke of Albany are tolerant to?
   a) Waterlodging   **b) Salinity**
   c) Acidity   d) Near wilt

288. Name the stress to which Solanum acaule, a potato species is resistant?
   a) Frost   b) Heat
   c) Nematode   d) Water stagnation

289. Name the thermo-insensitive varieties of cauliflower?
   a) Pusa Katki   b) Pusa Synthetic
   c) Pusa Deepali   **d) All of these**

290. Name the variety of muskmelon which is cross of Hara Madhu x Edisto
   a) Sugar Baby   b) Arka Manik
   c) **Punjab Sunehari**   d) Hara Madhu

291. Name the varieties of Cabbage which are salt tolerant?

a) Golden Acre
b) Proidge of Indian
c) Pusa Synthetic
d) All of these

292. Name the vegetable of which Phule Shubangi is an improved variety?

a) Cucumber
b) Broad bean
c) Lima bean
d) French bean

293. Name the vegetable which are protoandrous?

a) Beet
b) Leek
c) Celery
d) All of these

294. Pant Gobi-3, a Cauliflower variety has been developed through?

a) Selection
b) Inbreeding
c) Introduction
d) Synthetic variety

295. The classic example of practical use of colchicine in crop improvement is

a) F1 hybrid seed production
b) Seedless watermelon
c) Parthenocarpic fruit production
d) Resistant variety development

296. What is the alternate name of "Four angled bean?

a) Broad bean
b) French bean
c) Winged bean
d) Hyacinth bean

297. What is the bitter principle in bitter gourd?

a) Cucurbitacin
b) Momordicin
c) Solanin
d) None

298. What is cause of resistant to Fusarium wilt in pea?

a) Single gene inheritance
b) Polygene inheritage
c) Oligo gene inheritance
d) All the above

299. What is the cause of resistance to nematodes in tomatoes?

a) Single gene inheritance
b) Polygene inheritage
c) Oligo gene inheritance
d) All the above

300. Which is seedless watermelon?

a) Diploid **b) Triploid**

c) Tetraploid d) Hexaploid

301. Which is the best method for population improvement in any crop?

a) Pureline selection b) Pedigree selection

c) Mass selection **d) Recurrent selection**

302. Which is the most effective method for the transfer of ollgogenic character?

a) Bulk breeding b) Pedigree breeding

c) Back cross breeding d) None

303. Which mucilaginous substance is found in cluster bean?

a) Allantoin b) Allantonic acid

c) Mannogalacton d) Glycoprotein

304. Which of following causes bitterness in parwal

a) Leutein **b) Trichosanthin**

c) Memordiacin d) None of the above

305. Which of the following is a variety of chilli, resistant to Powdery mildew

a) Pusa Jawala b) NP-46

c) KA-2 **d) Phule mukta**

306. Which of the following is botanically known as B. napus subgroup napobrassica (n = 19)?

a) Cabbage b) Turnip

c) Rutabaga d) Radish

307. Which of following is botanically known as B. oleracea sub group sabauda?

a) Red cabbage **b) Savoy cabbage**

c) Cabbage d) Turnip

308. Growth is a .... increase in size of a cell, organ or whole organism.

a) Irreversible b) Reversible

c) Sustainable d) Constant

309. The whole series of changes which an organism goes through during its life cycle is called as ....

a) Growth **b) Development**

c) Differentiation d) Growth analysis

310. The collection of growth measurement and its subsequent examination and interpretation is called as ....

a) Growth curve
b) Growth response
c) Canopy architecture
d) Growth analysis

311. The basic measurement of growth is the ....

a) Growth curve
b) Dry weight
c) Growth analysis
d) Wet weight

312. Is the terminal point in the life cycle of the mother plant as well as starting point in the life cycle of the plant that follower it.

a) Seed
b) Leaf
c) Growth curve
d) Stem

313. The cotyledons of seed emerged above the ground surface is called as ....

a) Hypogeal germination
b) Epigeal germination
c) Viviparous germination
d) None of above

314. The seed coat of hard seeds was softened by mechanical or chemical means is called as ....

a) Stratification
b) Illumination
c) Scarification
d) Alternation

315. Dormanancy results in unsatisfactory, vigorous but late in maturity is called as ....

a) Senile degeneration
b) Pathological degeneration
c) Physiological degeneration
d) Juvenile degeneration

316. The reduction in yield caused by the unsuitable age of seed tubers is termed as ....

a) Juvenile degeneration
b) Physiological degeneration
c) Pathological degeneration
d) Senile degeneration

317. The sprouting and subsequent growth are comparatively quick but less vigorous and short lived is called as ....

a) Senile degeneration
b) Pathological degeneration
c) Juvenile degeneration
d) Physiological degeneration

318. .... is precursser of IAA.

a) Isopentyl allenine
b) Tryptophan
c) Kaurene
d) Zeatin

319. .... is precursser of gibberellins.

a) Tryptophan b) Isopentyl allenine

c) Zeatin **d) Kaurene**

320. .... is also known as juvenile harmone.

a) Gibbrellins b) Auxins

c) Cytokinin d) Ethylene

321. .... is used as herbicide in higher concentrations.

a) 2-4-D b) 3 CPA

c) 4 CPA d) GA_3

322. .... is used as growth retardant.

a) GA_3 **b) T1BA**

c) IBA d) IAA

323. A green pigment found in plants essential for the process of photosynthesis is called as ....

a) Anthocyin b) Lycopene

c) Chlorophyll d) Limonene

324. The response of the light to the timing of light and darkness is called as ....

a) Senescence **b) Photoperiodism**

c) Dormanancy d) Juvenility

325. The plants in which the flowering is induced readily by exposure to short days is known as ....

a) Day neutrul plants **b) Short day plants**

c) Long day plants d) None of above

326. The plants in which flowering is favored by long days is known as ....

a) Long day plants b) Short day plants

c) Day neutrul plants d) None of above

327. The plants in which the day length doesn't markedly affect flowering known as ....

a) Short day plants **b) Day neutral plants**

c) Long day plants d) None of above

328. .... are the day neutral vegetables.

a) Tomato & Cucumber b) Carrot & Potato

c) Spinach & Radish d) Beet & Lettuce

329. .... is a short day plant.

a) Cucumber **b) Amranths**

c) Tomato d) Spinach

330. .... is the pigment associated with the absorption of light that causes morphogenetic responses.

a) Anthocynin b) Lycopene

c) Phytochrome d) Chlorophyll

331. The developing ovaries belong to the same flower is called as ....

a) Aggregate fruit b) Multiple fruit

c) Climacteric fruit d) Non climacteric fruit

332. The developing ovaries belong to the different flowers is called as ....

a) Climacteric fruit b) Aggregate fruit

c) Non climacteric fruit **d) Multiple fruit**

333. After a fruit reaches maturity, it undergoes some characteristic qualitative changes which are collectively called as ....

a) Fruit ripening b) Fruit growth

c) Fruit set d) Fruit drop

334. Lycopene pigment observed in ....

a) Potato b) Brinjal

c) Chilli **d) Tomato**

335. The fruits which show rise in respiration rate after maturity are called as ....

a) Multiple fruits **b) Climacteric fruits**

c) Non climacteric fruits d) Aggregate fruits

336. The fruits which donot show rise in respiration after maturation are called as ....

a) Non climacteric fruits b) Aggregate fruits

c) Multiple fruits d) Climacteric fruits

337. Tomato is a .... vegetable.

a) Climactric b) Multiple

c) Non climactric d) None of above

338. Brinjal is a .... vegetable.

a) Multiple **b) Non climactirc**

c) Climactric d) Non of above

339. .... is called as ripening harmone.

a) Ethylene c) Lycopene

b) Phytochrome d) Antohocynin

340. Watermelon cells are .... times bigger when expanded.

a) 1,00,000 **b) 3,50,000**

c) 50,000 b) 3,50,000

e) 2,00,000

341. After cell division and before vacuolation starts, the newly formed cell makes some growth is called as ....

a) Plasmic growth b) Development

c) Differentiation d) Growth analysis

342. The deteriorative process which naturally terminate the functional life of an organ; organism or other life unit are collectively celled as ....

a) Fruit ripening b) Fruit growth

c) Juvenility **d) Senescence**

343. Inability of a viable seed to response the favorable environmental condition is known as ....

a) Germination b) Dormanancy

c) Growth d) Development

344. In certain species, seeds have dominancy due to hard seed coat and dormant embryo then it is called as ....

a) Double dormanancy b) Single dormanancy

c) Epicotyl dormanancy d) None of above

345. The different procedures followed to overcome dormanancy in freshly harvested seeds is known as ....

a) Epicotyl dormanancy **b) Seed priming**

c) Seed dormanancy d) seed germination

346. The ability of the plant to develop its fruit without pollination and fertilization is known as ....

a) Parthenocarpy b) Fertilization

c) Sterilization d) Pollination

347. .... are called as power house of the cell.

a) Golgi complex b) Protoplasm

c) Mitochondria d) Chloroplast

348. The initial period in the life cycle of a plant when flowering cannot be induced readily is known as ....

a) Juvenility b) Dormanancy

c) Senescence d) None of above

349. Shoot supplies food and hormones to roots while the roots supply water, nutrients to the shoot that correlation is called as ....

a) Helpful correlation b) Competative correlation

c) Mutual correlation d) None of above

350. One part feeds the other part for its growth i.e. leaf area and fruit size that correlation is called as ....

a) Helpful correlation b) Mutual correlation

c) Competitive correlation d) None of above

351. The correlation observed in between the similar type of parts i.e. fruit thinning – increases size of remaining fruits is called as ....

a) Helpful correlation **b) Competitive correlation**

c) Mutual correlation d) None of above

352. The stage of development when a plant or plant part possess the prerequisites for utilization by consumers for a particular purpose is known as ....

a) Horticultural maturity b) Physical maturity

c) Physiological maturity d) Pre-maturity

353. .... is a special kind of cell division in which the number of chromosomes are reduced to half and four haploid daughter cell are formed.

a) Meiosis b) Mitosis

c) Development d) Differentiation

354. .... is the process in which each of the chromosome separating into two similar groups and two daughter cells are formed.

a) Meisosis b) Differentation

c) Development **d) Mitosis**

355. .... occurs in reproductive cells.

a) Meiosis b) Mitosis

c) Senescense d) Ripening

356. .... occurs in somatic cells.

a) Meiosis b) Ripening

c) Senescense **d) Mitosis**

357. Single fruit which is formed from several flowers is called as ....

a) Collective fruit b) Multiple fruit

c) Climacteric fruit d) Non climacteric fruit

358. Botanically what is seed of potato known as?

a) Berry **b) TPS**

c) Seed potato d) Stolon

359. Breeder seed is the source of

a) Certified seeds **b) Nucleus seed**

c) Foundation seeds d) Registered seeds

360. By seed to seed method, how much is the seed required for planting one hectare crop of onion

a) 8-10 kg b) 5-7 kg

c) 10-12 kg d) 4-5 kg

361. For foundation seed of carrot what should be the isolation distance ?

a) 500 merters **b) 1000 meters**

c) 1500 meters d) None of the above

362. For foundation seed production in radish isolation distance should be

a) 600 m b) 900 m

c) 1200 m **d) 1600 m**

363. For foundation seed what should be the isolation distance between two cultivars of capsicum

a) 100 meters **b) 200 meters**

c) 300 meters d) 400 meters

364. For genetic purity what should be isolation distance for foundation and for certified seed production of Indian spinach ?

a) 400 and 800 m
b) 400 and 200 m
c) 1600 and 1000 m
d) 50 and 25 m

365. For how many years onion seeds are viable ?

a) 1 to 2
b) 2 to 3
c) 3 to 4
d) 4 to 5

366. For hybridization seed production in muskmelon, emasculation is necessary due to

a) Monoecious sex form
b) Andromonoecious sex form
c) Diecious sex form
d) Gynoecious sex form

367. For seed production in chilli, isolation distance should be

a) 50-200 m
b) 200-400 m
c) 800-1000 m
d) 1200-1600 m

368. For seed production of brinjal the isolation distance for foundation and certified seeds should be how many meters, respectively?

a) 50 and 25
b) 100 and 200
c) 200 and 100
d) 200 and 400

369. For seed production of carrot what is the seed rate required for a hectare of land ?

a) 1.5-2 kg
b) 2-2.5 kg
c) 3-4 kg
d) 5-6 kg

370. For seed production purpose, onion is considered as

a) Annual plant
b) Biennial plant
c) Perennial plant
d) Flowering plant

371. For seed production the space recommended for spring summer crop of tomato is?

a) 75x75 cm
b) 75x60 cm
c) 60x75 cm
d) None of above

372. How many days it takes brinjal seeds to germinate?

a) 1 to 2
b) 5 to 6
c) 7 to 8
d) 12 to 18

373. How many quintals of seed yield per hectare are obtained by French bean cultivation?

a) 40-50 **b) 12-18**

c) 100-120 d) 60-70

374. How many seeds are present in one gram seeds of brinjal?

a) 50-60 b) 100-125

c) 150-200 **d) 250-300**

375. How many seeds are there in one gram chilli seeds?

a) 50-60 b) 60-80

c) 120-170 d) 200-300

376. How many seeds can be counted in one gram of onion seed?

a) 180 **b) 240**

c) 300 d) 472360

377. How many seeds could be counted in one hundred gram of okra seed?

a) 600 b) 700

c) 800 d) 900

378. How many years is the viability of vegetable pea?

a) 3 b) 5

c) 4 d) 2

379. How much is the average seed yield per acre of chilli ?

a) 80 to 100 kg b) 30 to 60 kg

c) 120 to 150 kg d) None of above

380. How much is the isolation distance for certified seed of onion ?

a) 200 meters b) 1000 meters

c) 800 meters **d) 400 meters**

381. How much is the isolation distance for foundation seed f French Bean ?

a) 25 meters **b) 50 meters**

c) 100 meters d) None of the above

382. How much isolation distance is recommended for production of foundation seed and Certified seed of pea ?

a) 5 & 10 m **b) 10 & 25 m**

c) 20 & 30 m d) 100 & 150 m

383. How much should be the isolation distance between two cultivars of capsicum for foundation seed and for certified seed production ?

a) 50 and 25 m
b) 800 and 400 m
c) 400 and 200 m
d) 1000 and 1600 m

384. In tomato, for seed production, field inspection and rouging should be done at which stages (s) ?

a) Before flowering
b) Immature stage
c) Mature stage
d) All of these

385. In tomato, seed germination is inhibited due to presence of which compound ?

a) Caffic acid and ferulic acid
b) Mallic
c) Juglone
d) Asperatic

386. In which crop pinching of male flower is effective in hybrid seed production?

a) Bottle gourd
b) Ash gourd
c) Bitter gourd
d) None of above

387. In which crop sporophytic self-incompability is used for commercial hybrid production?

a) Tomato
b) Cabbage
c) Kale
d) Cauliflower

388. What is isolation distance in brinjal for seed production is

a) 100-200 m
b) 10-20 m
c) 200-300 m
d) 500 m

389. Mention the duration for which seed of radish remain viable ?

a) 1-2 years
b) 2-3 years
c) 3-4 years
d) 4-5 years

390. Name the crop in which anthesis takes place in the evening ?

a) Bootle gourd
b) Bitter gourd
c) Musk melon
d) Watermelon

391. National Horticulture Board (NH B) was eastablished during

a) 1976
b) 1980
c) 1984
d) 1986

392. National Seed Project for production of breeder seed of vegetable crops was initiated in which year?

a) 1991 b) 1999

c) 1994 d) None of the above

393. Non-lobing leaf character is used as single recessive marker gene for hybrid seed production in which crop ?

a) Watermelon b) Muskmelon

c) Cucumber d) None of the above

394. Seed production cost in the highest in case of

a) Hybrid seeds b) Foundation seeds

c) Certified seeds d) Registered seeds

395. Seed production of cabbage can be done successfully in

a) Kashmir Valley **b) Kullu Valley**

c) Punjab d) Nilgiri Hills

396. Seed of radish remain viable upto how many years?

a) 1-2 years b) 3-4 years

c) 2-3 years **d) 4-5 years**

397. The isolation distance for certified seed production in radish should be

a) 2000 m b) 1600 m

c) 1000 m d) 400 m

398. The viability of onion seeds is

a) One year b) Two year

c) Three year d) Five years

399. What does cleistogamy favours?

a) Self-pollination b) Cross-pollination

c) Both a and b d) None

400. What does Fenugreek seed contains ?

a) Alicin **b) Diosgenin**

c) Aimacline d) All of the above

401. What is the average seed yield of palak ?

a) 400-500 kg/ha b) 500-600 kg /ha

c) 700-800 kg/ha **d) 1000-1500 kg /ha**

402. What is the colour of the flowers of sponge gourd ?
a) White
b) Purple
c) Orange
d) Deep yellow

403. What is the isolation distance for the foundation seed of fenugreek ?
a) 25 meters
b) 50 merters
c) 200 meters
d) 400 meters

404. What is the isolation distance for certified seed of pumpkin?
a) 200 meters
b) 400 meters
c) 800 meters
d) 1000 meters

405. What is the isolation distance for production of nucleus seed of beetroot crop under open condition?
a) 1 km
b) 2 km
c) 3 km
d) 4 km

406. What is the isolation distance for producing certified seed of cole crops?
a) 0.5 km
b) 1.0 km
c) 1.5 km
d) 2.0 km

407. What is the minimum germination percentage required for high quality of pea seed ?
a) 75
b) 85
c) 95
d) 65

408. What is the number of seeds in one gramme carrot seeds ?
a) 550
b) 650
c) 750
d) 850

409. What is the seed yield of Indian bean per hectare
a) 16-18 q
b) 36-48 q
c) 6-8 q
d) 76-88 q

410. What is the seed yield per hectare for coriander ?
a) 3.5 to 5.5 q (seed)
b) 5.5 to 7.5 q (seed)
c) 7.5 to 9.5 q (seed)
d) None of them

411. What is the weight of 100 seeds of cluster bean?
a) 20 gm
b) 49 gm
c) 45 gm
d) 6 gm

412. What should be isolation distance to maintain genetic purity, for cabbage seed production of foundation and Certified seeds, respectively?

a) 200 m and 400 m
b) 800 m and 1000 m
c) 1000 m and 1600 m
d) 25 m and 50 m

413. What should be minimum isolation distance for potato seed production of foundation and certified seed respectively ?

a) 2 meters
b) 100 and 200 meters
c) 50 and 25 meters
d) 400 and 200 meters

414. What should be the minimum isolation distance between two tomato varieties for producing genetically pure breeder seed?

a) 100 m
b) 200 m
c) 50 m
d) 400 m

415. What type of the inflorescence of tomato is ?

a) Dictomous
b) Monoctomons
c) Polyctomons
d) None of the above

416. What type of inflorescence onion has ?

a) Umbel
b) Spadix
c) Panicle
d) Raceme

417. Which type of seed can be preserved through Cryoperservation (cryobank)?

a) Orthodox
b) Both a and c
c) Recalcitrant
d) None a and c

418. Which type of seed-to seed method is preferred for carrot seed production?

a) Nucleus seed
b) Foundation seed
c) Certified seed
d) All of the above

419. Who developed the seed plot technique in potato ?

a) G. Kalioo
b) Harbhajan Singh
c) Pushkarnath
d) None of above

420. Aim of seed technology is :

a) Rapid multiplication of seeds
b) Assured high quality seeds
c) Timely supply of improve seeds
d) All of the above

421. Breeder seed is produced by :

a) Plant Breeder **b) Government Agencies**

c) Registered Growers d) N.S.C.

422. Certified seed is produced from :

a) Foundation seed b) Registered seed

c) Certified seed d) All of above

423. Foundation seed is obtained from :

a) Certified seed b) Registered seed

c) Farmer's seed **d) Breeder seed**

424. Genetically the purest seed is :

a) Breed's seed b) Foundation seed

c) Certified seed **d) Nucleus seed**

425. Seed testing is done for :

a) Purity b) Germination

c) Moisture content **d) All of the above**

426. Breeder seed is the progeny of

a) Foundation seed b) Registered seed

c) Nucleus seed d) Certified seed

427. Headquarters of the Union for the Protection of New Plant varieties is in

a) Thiland b) USA

c) Denmark **d) Switzerland**

428. Improved seed includes

a) Nucleus seed b) Breeder seed

c) Foundation seed **d) All of above**

429. Plant Breeders Rights are operating in

a) Germany b) Denmark

c) Netherland **d) All of the above**

430. Seed certification requires

a) An improved variety b) Genetic purity

c) Physical purity **d) All of above**

431. Seed is a

a) Immature embryo **b) Mature embryo**

c) Developed embryo d) Undeveloped embryo

432. Presently ICAR has______ breeder seed production agency

a) 45 **b) 54**

c) 92 d) 107

433. The first private seed came into existence in

a) Mumbai **b) Kolkata**

c) Lucknow d) New Delhi

434. Seed Moisture varies from crop to crop in ranges from

a) 15-20 % b) 30-40 %

c) 1-2-% **d) 9-12 %**

435. The hybrid developed by Government agencies or Government Istitutions and Agricultural Univcrsitics are called

a) Private hybrids b) Institutional hybrids

c) Public hybrids d) Government hybrid

436. Pure live seed (PLS) is related to

a) Physical purity b) Genetic purity

c) Germination percentage d) Contamination

437. Standards of germination for seed certification in chillies

a) 70 % b) 90 %

c) 80 % **d) 60 %**

438. First Seed Testing Laboratory was Established at IARI in

a) 1969 **b) 1971**

c) 1981 d) 1991

439. International Seed Testing Association was established on

a) 10 July, 1924 b) 12 July, 1925

c) 12 Febm, 1942 d) 10 Feb, 1924

440. First private seed company was

a) Monsanto b) Namdhari

c) Sutton & Sons d) Takii

441. Seedcoat is derived from

a) Testa b) Embryo

c) Endosperm d) Nucellus

442. Where we have to contact to produce fresh seeds of potao ?

a) New Delhi **b) Shimla**

c) Lucknow d) Darjiling

443. Which of the following method is used for seed production of cabbage ?

a) Head to seed method b) Head intact method

c) Stump method d) All above

444. What is the isolation distance for foundation and certified okra seed production

a) 200-400 m b) 100-200 m

c) 50-100 m d) 250-500 m

445. What is the isolation distance for foundation clusterbean seed production

a) 100 m **b) 50 m**

c) 100 m d) None of these

446. What is the isolation distance for certified Peas seed production

a) 50 m b) 100 m

c) 10 m **d) 5 m**

447. For controlling flowers drop in chilli which PGR is used

a) IBA **b) NAA**

c) GA_3 d) None of these

448. Phule Suvarna, N-2-4-1, Phule Samarth are the cultivar of

a) Onion b) brinjal

c) Cucumber d) tomato

449. Among the following vegetable crops which doesn't require nursery

a) Chilli b) Brinjal

c) Cucumber d) Tomato

450. Himangi is the cultivar of _________ vegegtables crop

a) Cucumber b) Chilli

c) Potato d) None of these

451. Phule Jyoti is the cultivar of _________

a) Chilli b) Brinjal

c) Cucumber d) Tomato

452. Which colour label is used for breeder seed __________

a) Yellow b) Blue

c) White d) Red

453. Which colour label is used for certified seed

a) Yellow **b) Blue**

c) White d) Red

454. In Brinjal seed rate/ha is ________

a) 200 g b) 400g

c) 700-800g **d) 400-500 g**

455. In Methi______kg seed is enough for one ha. Area of seed production

a) 15-20 kg b) 30-32 kg

c) 40-42 kg d) 50-52 kg

456. In methi, seed yield per ha is _________

a) 800-100 kg b) 100-120kg

c) 60-80 kg d) 150-160 kg

457. In cucumber ______ kg seed is requird for one ha area of seed production

a) 5-10 kg b) 10-15 kg

d) 15-20 kg **d) 3-4 kg**

458. In bottle gourd _________ kg seed is required for one ha area

a) 10-12 kg **b) 6-8 kg**

c) 15-18 kg d) 20-22 kg

459. In ridge gourd __________ kg seed is required for one ha area of seed production

a) 5-6 kg b) 7-8 kg

c) 4-5 kg d) 10-11 kg

460. In Sponge gourd _______kg seed is required for one ha area

a) 4-5 kg b) 7-8 kg

c) 10-11 kg d) 11-13 kg

461. In pointed gourd ____ no. of vine cutting are needed for one ha area

a) 2000-2500 b) 3000-3500

c) 3500-4000 d) 4000-4500

462. Degree aliveness is called ___________

a) Vigour b) Vaibality

c) Purity d) Germination

463. Seed act was amended on ________

a) 1966 b) 1969

c) 1972 d) 1975

464. __________ seed handled by breeder to maintain specific genetic purity and identity

a) Breeder **b) Foundation**

c) Certified d) Truthful

465. Trueness type, varietal purity, plants/seed confirming to characteristics of the variety as described by the breeder called_______

a) Genetic purity b) Genetic erosion

c) Genetic isolation d) Genetic advance

466. The prescribed distance for separation of seed plot from the plot of other varieties of the same crop confirming the varietal purity requirement is called _______

a) Isolation b) Isotype

c) Isotherm d) Isogenicative

467. The original seed produced for the first time by the plant breeder is called_______

a) Nucleus seed b) Foundation seed

c) Certified seed d) Truthful seed

468. Foundation seed handled under procedures acceptable to the certifying aganey to maintain satisfactory genetice purity and identity is called

a) Breeder seed **b) Registered seed**

c) Certified seed d) Truthful seed

469. Dormant plant consisting of rudimentary stem and root which are protected with seed coat becames active for germination is called

a) Germination **b) Seed**

c) Seedling d) Dormanly

470. Normally ________ g hybrid seed is required for the planting of one hectare area

a) 125-175 g b) 200-250 g

c) 300-400g d) 400-500g

471. Soaking pea seeds GA3 ________ ppm for 12 hours gives the highest germination

a) 10 ppm b) 50 ppm

c) 100 ppm d) 150 ppm

472. In cucumber ________ PGA may be applied for increasing the femalness

a) Ethrel b) Cycocel

c) NAA d) IAA

473. Maleic hydroxide at ______ ppm promotes the female flower production and fruitset in bottle gourd

a) 200 ppm b) 300 ppm

c) 400 ppm d) 500 ppm

474. Pusa KTS-1 is variety of .... vegetable crop.

a) Broccoli b) Kale

c) Knolkho d) Cauliflower

475. Pointed gourd is propagated by ....

a) Seed **b) Cutting**

c) Runners d) Suckers

476. Four angled bean is also known as ....

a) Broad bean b) Cluster bean

c) Winged bean d) Sword bean

477. Pig weed or Bathua under exploited vegetable crop belong to family ....

a) Rutaceae b) Compositae

c) Chenopodiaceae d) Araceae

478. Elephant Foot Yam an under exploited vegetable crop belong to family ....

a) Araceae b) Rutaceae

c) Chenopodiaceae d) Compositae

479. .... is dioecious vegetable crop.

a) Asparagus b) Pointed gourd

c) Scarlet gourd **d) All above**

480. Asparagus belong to family ....

a) Liliaceae b) Asteraceae

c) Apiaceae d) None

481. Asparagus is propagated by ....

a) Cutting b) Suckers

c) Seeds or Crown d) Roots

482. .... an under exploited vegetable crop belong to family Asteraceae.

a) Globe Artichoke b) Jerusalerm Artichoke

c) Lettuce **d) All above**

483. Lettuce is .... pollinated crop.

a) Self b) Cross

c) Offen cross d) None

484. Chinese Yellow is variety of .... crop.

a) Cabbage b) Chinese Cabbage

c) Lettuce d) Cauliflower

485. Rhubarb is an under exploited vegetable crop belong to family ....

a) Apiaceae **b) Polygonaceae**

c) Asteraceae d) Compositae

486. Basella is propagated by ....

a) Seed b) Stem cutting

c) Seed and Stem cutting d) Root cutting

487. .... is a C_4 under exploited vegetable crop.

a) Basella b) Brussels spront

c) Broccoli d) Kale

488. .... is a edible part of Rhubarb crop used as a vegetable purpose.

a) Petiole b) Leaf

c) Head d) Stem

489. .... is a edible part of Globe Artichoke used as vegetable purpose.

a) Flower bud b) Leaf

c) Fruit d) Root

490. Leaves is edible portion used as vegetable purpose in .... vegetable crop.

a) Celery b) Parsley

c) Spinach **d) All above**

491. In Asparagus .... part is used as vegetable.

a) Root b) Leaves

c) Leaf stalk d) None

492. In celery self pollination within individual flowers is restricted due to ....

a) Protoandry b) Protogyny

c) Cleistogamy d) Hercogamy

493. Amaranth is a .... crop.

a) Monoecious b) Dioecious

c) Trimonoecious d) Andro-monoecious

494. National centre of Organic Farming is located at

a) Faridabad **b) Ghaziabad**

c) New Delhi d) Mumbai

495. Organic farming is a system which avoids the use of

a) Chemical Fertilizer b) Animal manures

c) Crop residues d) Crop rotation

496. The father of bio-dynamics—

a) Pandhariparde b) Purohit

c) Rudolf stenier d) Gehlot

497. The farmer Narayan Devrao Pandharipande has described the method of preparation of compost which is ———

a) Aerobic composting b) Anaerobic composting

c) Both a & b d) None of these

498. Procedure by which an authoritative body gives a formal recognition that a body or person is competent to carry out specific task is

a) Certification body b) Indirect certification

c) Inspection body **d) Accreditation**

499. The Product which has been produced, processed and handled in compliance with organic standard is——

a) **Organic product**
b) Processed product
c) Inorganic product
d) Certified product

500. Vermiwash is a ———— fertilizer

a) Inorganic
b) **organic**
c) Micronutrient
d) Bio-fertilizer

501. Which of the following is a trap crop for the management of Helicoverpa armigera in tomato cultivation

a) Aster
b) **Marigold**
c) Chrysanthemum
d) Agave

502. The crops grown for the purpose of restoring or increasing the organic matter content in the soil are called as ———— crops

a) *In situ*
b) Green manure
b) Both a & b
d) Legume

503. Which is the biofertilizer present in the rhizosphere of plantation crops such as coconut, areacut, etc.

a) Azolla
b) Azospirillum
c) Azotobacter
d) Beigerinkia

504. Biological pest control is an ideal alternative to control pest, using natural enemies such as

a) Predators
b) Parasites
c) Pathogens
d) a,b & c

505. Which is the principle element considered in organic farming

a) Maintaining a living soil
b) Organic mulching for soil conservation
c) Maintaining a living soil
d) a, b & c

506. Chrysoperla carnea is a very potent biocontrol agent of

a) Sucking type of insects
b) Early instars of lepidopterous pest
c) **Both a & b**
d) None of these

507. Which is the base material in BD-500

a) Cowl horn silica **b) Cowl horn manure**

c) Fermental oak bark d) A and B

508. Expliotation of biocontrol agent fauna in pest control is related with ——

a) Quality control b) Certification

c) GATT agreement d) Fertilizer control order

509. The regional centre of organic farming is located at————

a) Jabalpur b) Nagpur

c) Imphal **d) All of these**

510. Phosphate solubilizing micro-organisms include————

a) Bacteria b) Fungi

d) Actinomycetes **d) All of these**

511. In the heavy textured soils with high moisture holding capacity which type of bio-fertilizer will be more effective

a) Azotobacter b) Azospirillum

c) Azotobacter+ PSB **d) Azospirillum + PSB**

512. Sir Albet Howard developed the method of composting

a) Activated composting **b) Banglore method**

c) NADEP method d) A & C

513. Which method of composting is most useful particularly for the offensive material like night soil are to be quickly disposed off is

a) Banglore method b) NADEP method

c) Fowler's method d) Biodung composting

514. The excreta of casting of earthworms are rich in nutrients like

a) Nitrogen b) Phosphate

c) N.P.K. and Mg d) N, P, K

515. The temperature limit of the earthworm feed should be in range of

a) More than 45°C b) Below 0°C

c) 20 to 35°C d) None of these

516. The suitable $_{P}H$ of feeding material for effective multiplication of earthworms should be

a) Extremely acidic

b) Extremely alkaline

b) Neutral

d) Extremely acidic/extremely alkaline

517. The liquid manures prepared with the ———— plants have insecticidal properties

a) Neem b) Pongamia

c) Colotropis **d) All of these**

518. The effective method of weed control in organic farming is————

a) Intercropping b) Use of weedicides

c) A and B d) Zero tillage

519. Intercropping in merigold helps in

a) Reducing harmful microbes

b) Reducing nematode population in soil

c) Enhancing nematode population

d) Enhancement of microbes

520. For reducing damage of root-knot and reniform nematodes in tomato cultivation which intercrops are suitable

a) Mustard b) Merigold

c) Mustard and marigold d) Marigold and cowpea

521. Which type of biofertilizer is mostly used in acidic soils

a) Azotobacter b) Azolla

c) Beijerinckia d) Azospinillum

522. A completely free living organism which takes part in N_2 fixation is

a) Rhizobium b) Azospirillum

c) Azotobacter d) Anabaena

523. Nitrogen fixation is ————

a) N_2 , NH_3 b) N_2 , No_3

c) N_2 ,Amino acid **d) Both a and b**

524. Organism useful in degrading organic pollutants is

a) Actinomycetes **b) Pseudomonas**

c) Nitrosomonas d) VAM

525. VAM is an example of

a) Symbiotic N_2 fixing fungi b) Non-symbiotic N_2 fixing fungi

c) Disease causing fungi d) Amonifying bacteria

526. A free living nitrogen fixing cyanobacterium which can also form symbiotic association with the water fern Azolla is

a) Anabaena b) Chlorella

c) Tolypothrix d) Nostra

527. Which of the following is pair of bio-fertilizers

a) Azolla & BGA b) Rhizobium & VAM

c) Nostac & legume **d) Both a & b**

528. The fungal hyphae develop inside root tissues in VAM is ——— association

a) **Symbiotic** b) Non-symbiotic

c) Free living d) None of these

529. The organic agriculture is based on the principle of___

a) Health and care b) Ecology

c) Fairness **d) All of these**

530. In the live organic soil total microbial load (bacteria, fungi, actonomycetes) should be above________per gm of soil

a) 1×10^{8} b) 1×10^{7}

c) 1×10^{5} d) 1×10^{4}

531. The soil enrichment formulation includes————

a) Jivamrut b) Amritpani

c) Panchgavya **d) All of these**

532. Organic vegetables can be distinguished from conventional vegetables by following characters

a) Shape b) Colour

c) Volume and fairnessd **d) None of the above**

533. For Organic product Irradiation is ————

a) Restricted **b) Prohibited**

c) Allowed d) Strictly followed

534. The material used for packaging of organically produced vegetable must be ————

a) Synthetic b) Ecofriendly

c) Biodegradable **d) Eco-friendly & biodegradable**

535. The material from plant and animal origin used for soil conditioning in organic farming includes ———

a) Vermicompost   b) FYM

c) Green manure   **d) All of these**

23

Ornamental Horticulture

1. Formal garden has a ———— layout.
   a) Odd b) Natural
   c) Symmetric d) Irregular
2. Foutain is located in —— of building.
   a) Backside **b) Front**
   c) Lateral side d) None of these
3. Rockery should be is constructed ——
   a) Below tree b) In vicinity of building
   c) Close to pond **d) Natural elevated place**
4. Perennials are useful as.
   a) Bedding plants
   b) Border plants
   c) Long lasting colour schemes
   d) Temporary fillers
5. Golden Duranta is popular as
   a) Climber b) Avenue
   c) Annual **d) Hedge**
6. Dieffenbahia is —— plant.
   a) Indoor b) Outdoor
   c) Hardy d) Creeping
7. Art of making miniature plants is called as....
   a) Dwarfism **b) Bonsai**
   c) Minitree d) Gems
8. Grand gates are featured in —— gardens
   a) Mughal b) Italian
   c) Public parks d) Bunglow

9. Annuals have life of———

a) **One season** b) Two season

c) Multiseason d) None of these

10. Succulents are propagated by.—

a) **Soft cuttings** b) Hard cuttings

c) By seed d) None of these

11. ——are branchless plants

a) Conifers b) Mangroves

c) Palms d) Shrubs

12. Cacti are characterized by——

a) **Spines** b) Suckers

c) Fruits d) Nitrogen fixation

13. _________ is example of avenue tree.

a) Royal palm b) Bamboo

c) Bougainvillea d) Hibiscus

14. ....are the group of plants which complete their life cycle in one season/ year.

a) Perennials b) Biennials

c) Annuals d) None of these

15. When shrubs are planted on boundary for fencing of garden it is called as......

a) Hedge b) Avenue

c) Shrubery d) Markers

16. The most suitable time for planting hedge in India is....

a) Rainy season b) Winter

c) Summer d) Spring

17. When low growing perennial plants are grown on the borders of the plot or bed is called as.......

a) Borders b) Compound

c) Fence **d) Edge**

18. ....is art of training plants into different shapes

a) Idol b) Model

c) Cartoon **d) Topiory**

19. *Jasminum sambac* is mainly propagated by .....

a) Layering **b) Cutting**

c) Grafting d) Divisions

20. Climbers are equipped with modified organs which help to hold support are........

a) Spines **b) Tendrils**

c) Prop roots d) Stakes

21. *Caryota urens* is a botanical name of.........

a) Royal palm b) Fanpalm

c) Areca palm **d) Fishtail palm**

22. .... contributes major part of landscape in frontage.

a) Lawn b) Borders

c) Steps d) Patio

23. Botanical name of Korean grass is ....

a) Joisa japonica b) *Joisa koreana*

c) *Joisa indica* d) *Joisa barbariana*

24. ....is the science which deals with planting of ornamentals in such a way that it creates a picturesque effect on selected area.

a) Eesthetic horticulture b) Ornamental horticulture

c) Pictureqe horticulture **d) Landscaping**

25. ....is the style of gardening which reflects non symmetric layout and view.

a) Formal b) Normal

c) Informal d) None of these

26. ....is a underground stem with short, fleshy ,vertical axis, covered with dried leaf bases

a) Bulb b) Tuber

c) Corm d) Sucker

27. ....is a place where young plants are raised and nourished.

a) Nursery b) Conservatory

c) Humid chamber d) None of these

28. ……………garden style is raised in symmetrical pattern.

a) Japanese **b) Formal**

c) Wild d) Natural

29. Mughal garden is a example of ……………style of garden.

a) Italian b) Modern

c) Ancient **d) Formal**

30. ………..garden is a example of informal garden.

a) Persian **b) Japanese**

c) Mughal d) None of these.

31. Baradari is one of the features of …………..type of garden.

a) English b) Chinese

c) Greek **d) Mughal**

32. ………..is the important feature of Italian garden.

a) Fountain b) Wall

c) Masonry work d) Pergola

33. ……is a large area in city with created landscape for recreation of people.

a) Museum b) Conservatory

c) Island **d) Public park**

34. …………..is collection and plantation of live plants grown for scientific study.

a) Arboretum b) Garden

c) Nursery d) None of these

35. ………..is an base line in any garden around which garden is created

a) Axis b) Benchmark

c) Marker d) Road

36. The garden at Taj mahal is a good example of………..type of garden.

a) Russian b) Korean

c) Mughal d) Dutch

37. ………..is one of the most attractive element of the garden.

a) Patio b) Steps

c) Retaining wall **d) Focal point**

38. ….. are the plants which posses special structures to hold over support

a) Shrubs b) Herbs

c) Climbers d) None of these

39. …………….are the plants which are unable to climb vertically on support due to weak stem and spread over.

a) Climbers b) Twiners

c) Creepers d) None of these

40. *Jasminum auriculatum* is propagated by …………………..

a) Hard wood cuttings b) Softwood cuttings

c) Seed d) Air layering.

41. …………… are the plants smaller than trees in height and produce many shoots from their base.

a) Shrubs b) Herbs

c) Bush d) None of these

42. Botanical name of bottle brush is …………..

a) *Grivelia robusta* b) *Plumeria alba*

c) *Callistemon lanceolatus* d) *Alistonia* sp.

43. Acalypha hispida is propagated by ……………..

a) Semihardwood cuttings b) Softwood cuttings

c) Leaf cuttings d) Root cuttings

44. …………..is also called as flame of forest

a) *Butea monosperma* b) *Bahunia purpurea*

c) *Ficus bengalenensis* d) *Bombax ceba*

45. Botanical name of gulmohor is ……………

a) *Asansonia digitata* **b) *Erythrina indica***

c) *Delonix regia* d) *Sesbania grandiflora*

46. Commercial method of propagation of miniature rose is………..

a) Grafting **b) Budding**

c) Layering d) Cutting

47. …………… are generally constructed near the gate /paths in the garden.

a) Pagoda b) Cottages

c) Conservatories **d) Arches**

48. ....is the green carpet of the garden.

a) Creeper b) Shrubbery

c) Lawn d) Vines

49. ....is a series of arches joined together.

a) Pergola b) Fence

c) Archery d) None of these

50. ....plants grow well in shade or partial shade

a) Evergreen b) Herbs

c) Indoors d) Outdoors

51. ....are the plants which complete their lifecycle in one season or a year

a) Biennials b) Perennials

c) Annuals d) None of these

52. ....are the plants which have non branched cylindrical stem.

a) Palms b) Conifers

c) Xerophytes d) Succulents

53. The ideal soil pH range for lawn is ....

a) 4.5-5.0 **b) 5.5-6.0**

c) 6.5-7.0 d) 7.5-8.0

24

Floriculture & Landscape Gardening

1. This is fragrant rose variety

   a) Blue Moon b) First Red

   c) Gladiator d) None

2. Rose belong to family

   a) Amaryllidaceae b) Compositae

   c) Rosaceae d) None

3. Calyx splitting is disorder in

   a) Lilium b) Alstroemaria

   c) Carnation d) Gerbera

4. Flower crop commercially suitable for drying

   a) Alpinia **b) Statice**

   c) Bromelia d) Song of India

5. Water requirement of rose under polyhouse condition

   a) 25 l/day/m2 b) 50 l/day/m2

   c) 5 l/day/m2 d) 5 ml/day/m2

6. Cymbidium orchid is

   a) Epiphyte b) Halophyte

   c) Biophyte **d) Lithophyte**

7. This is the Queen of the roses

   a) Polyanthus rose b) Miniature rose

   c) Hybrid Perpetual rose **d) Hybrid Tea rose**

8. This is necessary for keeping enough leaves on the rose for the production of carbohydrates

   a) Disbudding b) Staking

   c) Bending d) Desuckering

9. Plant population of carnation per gross m^2 greenhouse
   a) 6 b) 36
   c) 26 **d) 20**
10. For avoiding flower opening in roses this is used
   a) Shed net **b) Bud net**
   c) Poly bag d) Plug net
11. Pinching operation is followed for production of quality carnations flowers
   a) Six week after planting b) Six month after planting
   c) Six days after planting **d) After six node**
12. Basamid is used for soil sterilization in polyhouses
   a) 30-40 gm/sq m^2 b) 30-40 kg/sq m^2
   c) 5-10 gm/sq m^2 d) 70-80 gm/sq m^2
13. Aerial root system is found on
   a) Alstroemeria b) Cordyline
   c) Anthurium d) Sago palm
14. Suitable plant for cut foliage
   a) Cycades b) Aster
   c) Tuberose d) Orchid
15. Anthurium belongs to sub family
   a) Rosaceae b) Amaryllidaceae
   c) Compositae **d) Pothoideae**
16. National Research for Orchid
   a) Orissa **b) Sikkim**
   c) Kerala d) Himachal Pradesh
17. Avon is red colour rose variety
   a) Hybrid Tea b) Polyantha
   c) Floribunda d) Miniature
18. Bud drop occurs when lilium plants receive insufficient
   a) Water b) Nutrition
   c) Growth regulator **d) Light**

19. Gypsophila (*Gypsophila paniculata*) belongs to family
    a) Caryophyllaceae b) Pothoideae
    c) Amaryllidaceae d) Compositae
20. Which form is exhibiting by Phalaenopsis orchid
    a) Lithopodal b) Halopodal
    c) Monopodal d) None
21. The optimum stage of harvesting of Alstroemaria is
    a) 4-5 florets open b) Fully open
    c) Bud stage d) All
22. In post harvest management of flowers Silver nitrate is most effective
    a) Fungicide **b) Biocide**
    c) Acaricide d) Nimbicide
23. Pinching is done by breaking out the head of the cutting of gypsophila at
    a) 8 to 10 internodes on the plant
    b) 4 to 6 internodes on the plant
    c) 2 to 4 internodes on the plant
    d) 12 to 14 internodes on the plant
24. Pulsing flowers refers to
    a) Post storage b) Nutrition
    c) Pre storage d) All
25. Major disease of gladiolus
    a) Fusarium rot b) Bacterial wilt
    c) Sclerotium rot d) Mosaic
26. Per square meter cost of errection of natural ventilated polyhouse is
    a) Rs. 1000-1200 **b) Rs. 500-600**
    c) Rs. 5000-6000 d) Rs. 200-300
27. Harvesting indices for Aster flower is
    a) Full bloom b) Tight bud
    c) Half bloom d) All
28. Tissue culture is common method of multiplication
    a) Alpine **b) Orchid**
    c) Limonium d) Statice

29. Requirement of light intensity for flowering of Phalenopsis is

a) 15000 to 20000 lux b) 800 to 1500 lux

c) 80000 to 150000 lux **d) 8000 to 15000 lux**

30. Gross plant population of Gypsophila in polyhouse is

a) 9 plants/m^2 **b) 5 plants/m^2**

c) 15 plants/m^2 d) 12 plants/m^2

31. Origin of gladiolus

a) South Africa b) France

c) America d) Germany

32. Which of the following operation is followed in carnation

a) Pruning **b) Disbudding**

c) De suckering d) Cutting

33. Swarna Rekha is mutant of

a) Gladiolus b) Chrysanthemum

c) Carnation **d) Tubrose**

34. Chromosome number of double type of tuberose is

a) 50 b) 40

c) 70 d) 60

35. Dendrobium orchid is propagated by

a) Seed **b) Division**

c) Cutting d) Sucker

36. Flower colour of Bromelia

a) Red b) Green

c) Blue d) None

37. Most commonly used cut foliage

a) Lilium b) Alstroemaria

c) Bromelia **d) Springeri**

38. Water requirement of lilium is

a) 4 to 5 lit/m^2/day b) 8 to 9 lit/m^2/day

c) 2 to 3 lit/m^2/day d) None

39. International registration authority for rose is situated in
    a) USA b) Delhi
    c) Belgium d) Denmark
40. Concrete in single petal tubrose
    a) 1.12-1.80 % b) 1.5-2.0 %
    c) 2.2-3.0 % **d) 0.08-0.13 %**
41. Flower colour of Tropic Sea variety of gladiolus
    a) White b) Yellow
    c) Blue d) Pink
42. This disease is found on lilium bulb during storage of bulbs.
    a) Fusarium **b) Penicillium**
    c) Damping off d) All
43. Native of Gypsophila is
    a) Eastern Europe b) South Africa
    c) Indo Burma d) Peru
44. Gypsophila is an extremely hardy perennial plant with
    a) Shallow root system **b) Deep tap root system**
    c) Fibrous root system d) None
45. Rose is national flower of
    a) India b) Japan
    c) Spain **d) England**
46. Among the following spp. Of orchid which is temperate one
    a) Dendrobium b) Venda
    c) Cymbidium d) None
47. Chromosome number of carnation
    a) 18 b) 20
    c) 14 **d) 30**
48. Thrips management is effective with
    a) Triazophos
    b) Penconazole
    c) Metalaxyl 8% + Mancozeb 64%
    d) Acetamiprid

49. Parentage of Phule Ganesh variety of gladiolus

a) Sancerre X Oscar b) Tropic Sea X Oscar

c) Suchitra X Sancerre d) Friendship X Yellow Stone

50. Family of carnation

a) Caryophyllaceae b) Compositae

c) Rosaceae d) Amaryllidaceae

51. Rose is national flower of

a) America **b) England**

c) France d) India

52. Rose damascena commonly grown rose species for

a) Cut flower b) Protected cultivation

c) Rose oil d) Hanging baskets

53. Rose water is obtained from

a) Petals b) Sepals

c) Leaves d) Seed

54. The produce prepared by pouring equal proportions of petals and white sugar is called

a) Rose water b) Rose oil

c) Gulkand d) Cold drink

55. Dried rose petals are known as

a) Pankhuri b) Gulkand

c) Rose water d) Gul Roghan

56. Who introduced the Damask rose in India

a) British **b) Babar**

c) Shahjahan d) Shivaji

57. Who introduced Edouard rose in India

a) Janhangir b) Shivaji

c) British d) Babar

58. Rose developed from cross between Hybrid Tea and Polyantha

a) H.T. b) Teas

c) Floribanda d) Grandiflora

59. Fruit of rose is called as

a) **Hip**
b) Berry
c) Thalamus
d) Spadix

60. Bull head is a disorder in the flower of

a) Marigold
b) Tuberose
c) Rose
d) Carnation

61. How many times rambler type of roses produces flowers in a year

a) Four
b) Three
c) Two
d) One

62. Standard type of roses are differentiated in to full standard, half standard and weeping standard on the basis of

a) Budding method on root stock
b) budding height on root stock from ground level
c) Type of root stock
d) Type of variety

63. Full standards are prepared by budding on root stock at a height of __________ from the ground level.

a) Below 1 mt.
b) 1.0 to 1.15 mt.
c) 1.5 to 2.0 mt.
d) Above 2.0 mt.

64. Half standards are prepared by budding on root stock at a height of __________ from the ground level.

a) Below 40 cm
b) Above 70 cm
c) 45 to 60 cm
d) 70 cm to 1 mt

65. Weeping standards are prepared by budding on root stock at a height of __________ from the ground level.

a) 80 cm to 1.0 mt
b) 1.0 to 1.15 mt.
c) Below 80.0 cm
d) 1.5 mt & above to 1 mt

66. Native of tuberose is

a) India
b) South Africa
c) Mexico
d) Taiwan

67. Tuberose varieties are classified on the basis of

a) Plant height
b) Flower colour
c) Number of flowers/stalk
d) Number of rows of petals

68. Arka Nirantra variety of tuberose is classified under

a) Variegated
b) Semi-double
c) Single
d) Double

69. Rajat Rekha and Swarna Rekha varieties of tuberose are differentiated on the basis of

a) Variegated leaves
b) Number of flowers
c) Plant height
d) Flower colour

70. Tuberose flowers with 2-3 rows of corolla segments are classified under

a) Double
b) Semi-double
c) Variegated
d) Single

71. Vaibhav verity of tuberose have flowers with

a) 2-3 rows of corolla
b) **More than 3 rows of corolla segments**
c) Single rows of corolla segments
d) Seven rows of corollasegments

72. Most suitable temperature at the time of tuberose planting is

a) 10-15^{0}C
b) 16-18^{0}C
c) 24-27^{0}C
d) 38-40^{0}C

73. Variety having pinkish tinch on flower bud is

a) Shringar
b) Phule Rajani
c) Calcutta Local Single
d) Vaibhav

74. Tuberose Variety suitable for loose flower production is

a) Suvasini
b) Vaibhav
c) Phule Rajani
d) Hydrabad Double

75. Proper depth of planting for tuberose bulb is

a) 4-8 cm
b) 2-3 cm
c) 10-15 cm
d) More than 15 cm

76. Optimum time of tuberose bulb planting is

a) Oct - Nov
b) Aug - Sept
c) April - May
d) Dec - Jan

77. Chromosome number in single type of tuberose is

a) 60
b) 50
c) 38
d) 40

78. Chrysanthemum are mainly classified under two categories on the basis of

a) Size of flower **b) Colour of flower**

c) Duration of flowering d) Size of plant

79. Large flowered Chrysanthemum are classified into

a) 10 classes b) 13 classes

c) 08 classes d) 10 classes

80. Small flowered Chrysanthemum are classified into

a) 5 classes b) 8 classes

c) 10 classes d) 15 classes

81. Ball, Quilled, Spider and Regular Incurve are different classes of Chrysanthemum belong into

a) Yellow flowered **b) Large flowered**

c) Small flowered d) White flowered

82. Birbal Sahani variety of Chrysanthemum belonging into class

a) Pompon b) Quilled

c) Decorative d) Stellate

83. Sonali Tara variety of Chrysanthemum belonging into class

a) Cineraria b) Semi quilled

c) Decorative d) Pompon

84. Flower colour of Kikubiori and Mountaineer cultivars of Chrysanthemum is

a) White **b) Yellow**

c) Pink d) Bronze

85. For good vegetative growth Chrysanthemum requires

a) Low temperature **b) Long days condition**

c) Short days condition d) Low intensity of light

86. For flowering Chrysanthemum requires

a) Long day condition b) High light intensity

c) Short days condition d) Proper nutrition

87. How many types of pinchings are performed in Chrysanthemum

a) Four b) Three

c) One **d) Two**

88. Many of the standard type of Chrysanthemum varieties are disbudded in which

a) Large terminal bulb is reserved and all auxiliary buds are removed

b) 2-3 auxiliary buds are reserved and large terminal buds are removed

c) Large 2-3 buds are reserved and all auxiliary buds are removed

d) All auxiliary buds are reserved and large terminal bud is removed

89. Arka Aradhana is a colonel selection of

a) *Jasminum grandiflorum* b) *Jasminum auriculaturm*

c) *Jasminum sambae* d) *Jasminum multiflorum*

90. Arka Surabhi is a colonel selection of locally grown

a) Jasminum grandiflorum b) Jasminum auriculaturm

c) Jasminum sambae d) Jasminum multiflorum

91. Variety Parimullai released by TNAU, Coimbatore is belonging into

a) *Jasminum grandiflorum* **b) *Jasminum auriculatum***

c) *Jasminum sambae* d) *Jasminum multiflorum*

92. Arka Arpan is a variety of

a) *Jasminum grandiflorum* b) *Jasminum auriculaturm*

c) *Jasminum sambae* **d) *Jasminum multiflorum***

93. Diploid number (2n) of *Jasminum sambae cv. Gundumalli* is

a) 39 b) 52

c) 62 d) 54

94. Jasmine is commercially propagated by

a) Hard wood cutting **b) Soft wood cutting**

b) Semi hard wood cutting d) Budding

95. The ideal conditions for successful cultivation of Jasminum are

a) Warm summer and cool winter

b) Dry summer and cool winter

c) Warm summer and mild winter with ample of water and sunny days

d) Cool and dry winter

96. In Jasmin the operation manipillate growth and flowering

a) Harvesting b) Topping

b) Disbudding **d) Pruning**

97. Jasminum flowers are harvested for concrete extraction at

a) Daily after 9:30 p.m.

b) Fully open in early hours of days

c) Unopened high bud stage

d) Fully opened at night hours

98. Shelf life of Jasminum multiflorum flowers, from harvested at tight bud stage to withering is

a) 24 hours b) 28-35 hours

c) 48-60 hours d) 15-18 hours

99. Useful methods of Jasmin oil extraction is

a) Solvent b) Stem

c) Alcohol d) Vapour

100. Botanical name of China Aster is

a) ***Calllistephus chinesis*** b) *Calllistephus grandi florum*

c) *Calllistephus erecta* d) *Calllistephus morifollium*

101. The flower colour of aster is well developed in the temperature range of

a) 40-42°C during day and 20-22°C during night with 50-60% relative humidity

b) 20-30°C during day and 15-17°C during night with 50-60% relative humidity

c) 38-40°C during day and 20-25°C during night with 65-70% relative humidity

d) 34-36°C during day and 10-15°C during night with 70-80% relative humidity

102. Aster seeds have ________ dormancy

a) One month b) Six months

c) Three months **d) No dormancy**

103. Flower colour of Kamini variety of Aster is

a) White b) Deep blue

c) Deep pink d) Deep violet

104. Poornima variety of Aster have flower colour as

a) Pink b) Violet

c) White d) Purple

105. Growth habit of Phule Ganesh white is

a) Spreading b) Dwarf

c) Semi spreading **d) Erect**

106. Botanical name of Gaillardia is

a) *Gaillardia tatarium* b) *Gaillardia acutifolia*

c) *Gaillardia pulchella* d) *Gaillardia chinancis*

107. Gaillardia is propagated by

a) Seed b) Cutting

c) Grafting d) Air layering

108. Diploid number (2n) of Gaillardia pulchella is

a) 62 b) 18

c) 46 **d) 36**

109. Marigold is indigenous to

a) Mexico b) China

c) South Africa d) France

110. African Marigold are grouped on the basis of plant height, growth habit, flower shape, size and colour into

a) 3 groups b) 5 groups

c) 7 groups d) 8 groups

111. French Marigold are grouped into

a) 4 groups **b) 6 groups**

c) 8 groups d) 10 groups

112. The critical photo period for *Tagetes erecta* is between

a) 8-9 hours b) 6-7 hours

c) 12.5-13 hours d) 10-11 hours

113. Removal of apical portion of growing shoot is called

a) Pinching b) Pruning

c) Cutting d) de-shooting

114. Damping off disease in Marigold is caused by

a) *Rhizotonia solani* b) *Alternaria tagetica*

c) *Botrytis cinerea* d) *Fusarium oxysporum*

115. Which of the following loose flowers can not be stored in cold storage below 15^0C

a) Carnation b) Rose

c) Crossandra d) All of these

116. Which of the following loose flower is not fragrant

a) Jasmine b) Tuberose

c) Crossandra d) Chrysanthemum

117. Harvesting indices of Hibiscus flowers

a) Tight bud stage b) Half blooming stage

c) Fully bloom stage d) Paint brush stage

118. ______ is defined as the use of plants in the outdoor to fulfill the aesthetic and functional purpose.

a) Arboriculture b) Aforestation

c) Cafeteria **d) Landscaping**

119. _____ is an activity in which beautification and functional use of plant is achieved.

a) Outdoor Scaping **b) Landscaping**

c) Designing d) None of these

120. The person who designs a landscape is called as_____.

a) Civil designer **b) Landscape designer**

c) Architect d) Civilian

121. ______ garden is an example of specialty landscaping

a) Botanical b) Wild

c) Persian d) English

122. ______ refers to the object's feel with respect to sense of touch

a) Rhythm b) Axis

c) Texture d) Balance

123. ______ represents three dimensional shape of the plant canopy

a) Form b) Canopy

c) Line d) None of these

124. _____ is the boundary elements in landscape design

a) Topiary b) Carpet

c) Step **d) Wall**

125. _____ is the basic principle of landscape design

a) Line b) Focalization

c) Scale d) None of these

126. ____ aims to guiding the viewer to the must see exhibits in the landscape

a) Texture b) Rockery

c) Cacti **d) Focalization**

127. The ability of plant to survive in the low temperature in the given area is called as___

a) Rivers tolerance **b) Cold hardiness**

c) Temperate hardiness d) None of these

128. Using various ornamental plants in outdoors to fulfill garden establishment is called as____

a) Landscaping b) Hedge

c) Avenue d) Bedding

129. ____ is measure of a plant ability to survive in winter

a) Winter resistance b) Winter adaptability

c) Cold hardiness d) None of these

130. _____ is technique used in landscape design to select plants which are water efficient in its maintenance.

a) Plantscaping **b) Xeriscaping**

c) Arboring d) Indexing

131. _____ is defined as the decoration of the tract of land with plants and other garden materials to create a picturesque and natural effect in a limited space.

a) Arboreum b) Beautification

c) Focalization **d) Landscape gardening**

132. _____ relates to coarseness or fineness of leaf roughness and smoothness of bark

a) Texture b) Canopy

c) Form d) Shape

133. Repetition of same object at equidistance is called as _____

a) Sequence **b) Rhythm**

c) Simplicity d) Complexity

134. _____ is the traits pattern and structure of a metropolitan cities specific geographic area including its biological composition, physical environment and social patterns

a) City survey b) City look

c) Urban landscape d) Topography

135. _____reffers to the facilities of rides and other entertainment attractions assemble for the purpose of entertaining large number of people.

a) Amusement park b) Public park

c) Private park d) Informal park

136. The oldest amusement park in the world is situated in ____

a) India b) China

c) Greece **d) Denmark**

137. ____ is responsible travel to natural areas that conserve the environment and improves the well being of local people.

a) Safari b) Ecotoeorism

c) Welfare park d) Social park

138. _____ consist of the inanimate elements of the landscaping especially civil construction work.

a) Hardscape **b) Landscape**

c) Design d) None of these

139. ____ are the affordable elements of hardscaping

a) Concrete walls b) Fountains

c) Decks **d) Paving**

140. The art of growing houseplants inside a house is called as ____

a) Housekeeping **b) Indoor gardening**

c) Amateur gardening d) Novelty

141. _____ are the plants which are attractive and having good aesthetic value and can tolerate in house conditions

a) Indoor plants b) Garden plants

c) Annuals d) Biennials

142. ____ is the unique method of adding fog effects to water feature and garden areas

a) Fogging b) Sprinkling

c) Mist scaping d) Showering

143. _____ is an outdoor garden space that has been specifically design to meet the physical, psychological, social and spiritual needs of the people using the garden.

a) Medicinal b) Allopathic

c) Therapeutic d) None of these

144. ____ are the large water feature typically set on underground reservoirs that keeps recirculating the water.

a) Bubbling urns b) Sunken garden

c) Marsh garden d) None of these

145. _____ type of garden has been developed in Switzerland.

a) Water garden b) Public park

c) Wild garden **d) Vertical garden**

146. Bough garden is also called as _____

a) Italian garden b) Mughal garden

c) Marsh garden d) Water park

147. The garden which is laid below the ground level is called as ____

a) Underground garden b) Subsurface garden

c) Secret garden **d) Sunken garden**

148. _____garden can not be created at elevation less than 2000-2500 meters.

a) Temperate garden **b) Alpine garden**

c) Hanging garden d) Rock garden

149. ____ is the museum of living plants in the garden where propagation of various plants is undertaken and plants are grown for scientific study.

a) Arboretum b) Herbarium

c) Conservatory d) Plant bank

150. Formal garden is laid out in a ______ pattern.
   a) Natural
   b) Asymmetrical
   c) Symmetrical
   d) Free style

151. Japanese gardens are laid out _____ style.
   a) Informal
   b) Formal
   c) Universal
   d) Conventional

152. The combination of formal and informal garden style is called as____
   a) Natural style
   b) Free style
   c) Standard style
   d) Japanese style

153. ____ is placed in frontage of the building of institutional gardens.
   a) Pergola
   b) Lantern
   c) Steps
   d) Lawn

154. ____ is the main feature Italian garden.
   a) Flower beds
   b) Pagoda
   c) Fountain
   d) Baradari

155. The presence of running water is important feature of_____ type of garden.
   a) English
   b) Informal
   c) French
   d) Mughal

156. ___ is main feature of Japanese styles of garden.
   a) Stone lantern
   b) Rockery
   c) Pergola
   d) Arches

157. Lining of a flower bed, paths, lawns and shrubbery with bricks and low growing plants is called as ____
   a) Hedge
   b) Edge
   c) Border
   d) Fence

158. A series of arch join together is called as _____
   a) Archery
   b) Semicircular house
   c) Pergola
   d) Conservatory

159. ____ means covering an area perfectly in a bed with dense low growing herbaceous plants to set a design.
   a) Bedding
   b) Carpeting
   c) Screening
   d) Sweeping

160. _____ is the most important operation which should be done regularly to maintain the lawn in good form.

a) Wrecking
b) Sweeping
c) Mowing
d) Patching

161. Training and pruning of plants to give particular ornamental shape is called as _____

a) Art
b) Architect
c) Designing
d) Topiary

162. Anthuriums can be grown successfully in the temperature range of ———————

a) 30 to 40^{0}C
b) 15-30
c) 5-10
d) None of these

163. After how many days roses can be harvested post bending ?

a) 60
b) 20
c) 30
d) 45

164. Lime spraying on the cladding material is done during ———

a) Winter season
b) Summer
c) Rainy
d) All seasons

165. What is the optimum pH range for fertigation of flower crops under polyhouses?

a) 5.5 to 6.5
b) 7-8
c) 5-6
d) Any pH

166. Foliar application of sulphur on flower crops in the polyhouses can control ———

a) Both powdery mildew and mites
b) Mites
c) Powdery mildew
d) None of these

167. What is the the economic life of gerbera under polyhouses conditions ?

a) 10 years
b) 4-5 years
c) 10-15 years
d) Perenial

168. What is the rooting media for commercial cultivation of Orchids?

a) Red soil
b) Black cotton soil
c) Rise husk
d) Coco shell

169. Name the crop in which Crown Gall disease appears .

a) Gerbera
b) Rose
c) Carnation
d) Anthuriums

170. Where does the Foundation pipes are placed in the structure of the polyhouses ?

a) On the top
b) On the sides
c) Below the curtains
d) None of these

171. The light intensity in the polyhouse is measured with the help of————

a) Thermometer
b) Salinometer
c) Lux meter
d) pH meter

172. Whether Gerbera can be grown under shade net conditions ?

a) Not at all
b) Only under 50 %
c) Yes
d) Only under polyhouse

173. Which plants are preferred for planting of Rose in the polyhouses ?

a) Top grafted plants
b) Budded plants
c) Cuttings
d) Seeds of Roses

174. After how many days fertigation is done after planting of Carnation and Gerbera in the polyhouse?

a) 45
b) 60
c) 21
d) None of these

175. Lillium can be grown successfully in the temperature range of———— degree centigrade.

a) 30 to 40
b) 5-10
c) 20-30
d) 1-10

176. Bull headed flowers are seen in roses due to

a) Deficiency of boron
b) Mites
c) Physiological disorder
d) Excess water

177. Spraying of water along the path in the polyhouse can control ————

a) Mildew and mites
b) Mites
c) White flies
d) All diseases

178. The economic life of carnation under polyhouses is ________

a) 10 years
b) 15 years
c) 3 yrs
d) One year

179. Amongst the following is not the type of greenhouse based on the shape.

a) Lean to type greenhouse
b) Uneven span,
c) Quonset type
d) Glass greenhouses

180. Plastic film is most popular as a cladding material because

a) It transmits light
b) It is cheap
c) It is light in weight
d) None of these

181. Amongst the following ________ is the greenhouse type based on utility.

a) Greenhouse for active heating
b) Quonset type
c) Wooden framed
d) Ridge and furrow type

182. The night temperature of greenhouse crops is generally in the range of ______________ degree centigrade.

a) 7 to 21
b) 10 to 20
c) 15 to 25
d) None of these

183. Which of the following is the automatic device used to regulate temperature in greenhouse.

a) Thermometer
b) Thermostats
c) Sensor
d) All of these

184. Which of the following is the effective cooling system in the greenhouse.

a) Fan and pad cooling
b) Fog cooling
c) Misting
d) None of these

185. In fan and pad system, fan and cooling pads are placed on

a) One side of polyhouses
b) Top of the polyhouses
c) At the bottom
d) None of these

186. The naturally ventilated polyhouses are mostly suited for ____.

a) Temperate region
b) Tropics
c) Sub-tropics
d) All of these

187. To prevent shadows on the crop in the polyhouses trees should be located ———————— times their height.

a) 3 times **b) 2.5**

c) 2 d) 4

188. The floriculture has average growth potential of ________ percent.

a) 10-20 **b) 25-30**

c) 30-14 d) 2-5

189. Amongst which of the following is practically used acid for pH maintenance.

a) Phosphoric acid b) Sulphuric acid

c) Nitric acid d) All of these

190. No ventilation is required for one of the following greenhouse.

a) Naturally ventilated

b) Quonset

c) Fan & Pad system polyhouse

d) None of these

191. Amongst the following is not a media for hydroponics.

a) Perlite b) Cocopeat

c) Red soil d) None of these

192. In nutrient film technique plants are fertilized with ______.

a) Organic manures b) **Liquid fertilizers**

c) Water d) Enriched coco peat

193. Which of the following crop need pinching.

a) Gerbera b) **Carnation**

c) Anthurium d) Standard rose

194. Which of the following crop require heading back.

a) Gypsaphilia **b) Roses**

c) Gerbera d) Orchids

195. The Roses grow well in the temperature range of ______ °C.

a) 15-30 b) 30-40

c) 10-15 d) 5-10

196. Soil sterilization in the greenhouse is done using ________.

a) **Formalin**
b) Chlorpyriphos
c) Methyl bromide
d) None of these

197. In which of the following crop green bending is followed.

a) Gerbera
b) **Rose**
c) Carnation
d) Orchid

198. Carnation belongs to the family _________.

a) Asteraceae
b) **Caryophylaceae**
c) Aracea
d) Plumbaginaceae

199. Which of the following are types of the carnation.

a) Standard and mini
b) **Sim and spray**
c) Spray and standard
d) None of these

200. For better yield with quality flowers at 14-15°C, carnation should be supplied with __________ppm CO_2.

a) 1000
b) **500**
c) 1500
d) 2000

201. Carnation is commercially propagated by__________

a) Seed
b) Grafting
c) **Stem cutting**
d) Budding

202. The ideal night temperature for gerbera in polyhouses should be________°C.

a) 5 to 10
b) **10-15**
c) 15-20
d) 20-25

203. Gerbera can be propagated by________________

a) Sexual
b) Asexual
c) **Both sexual & asexual**
d) None of these

204. Gerbera start flowering after ______________days of planting.

a) 30
b) 60
c) **80**
d) 120

205. Which of the following orchids flower mostly in high temperatures?

a) Cymbidiums
b) **Cattleya**
c) Dendrobiums
d) None of these

206. Commercially Orchids are grown in ____________

a) Read soil
b) Coco shell
c) Coco-peat
d) Sand

207. Amongst which of the following crops disbudding is not followed.

a) Gerbera
b) Roses
c) Orchids
d) Carnation

208. In which of the following crops snail cause sever damage.

a) Roses
b) Anthurium
c) Crysanthemum
d) Gerbera

209. The cheapest and easiest way to control mites in the greenhouse is________

a) Regular chemical sprays
b) Watering paths, keeping moisture
c) Opening of curtains
d) All of above

210. Which of the following crop needs maintenance of photoperiod in protected cultivation

a) Roses
b) Chrysanthemum
c) Gerbera
d) Orchids

211. Amongst which of the following crop require support?

a) Anthurium
b) Chrysanthemum
c) Carnation
d) All abode

212. _____are nothing but pieces of earth with compact grasses on them.

a) Plug
b) Runners
c) Sod
d) Turf

213. _____is the most important operation which should be done regularly to maintain lawn in good form.

a) Weeding
b) Mowing
c) Scraping
d) Rolling

214. _____ is quickest method of developing lawn.

a) Turf plastering
b) Turfing
c) Dibbling
d) Seedling

215. _____ is green carpet for a landscape.

a) Turf
b) Garden
c) Lawn
d) Grass

216. ____ is the common method practiced for cool season turf grasses lawn.

a) Dibbling
b) Hydro seeding
c) Seeding
d) Plugging

217. Hydro seeding is also known as ____

a) Sprigging
b) Hydraulic mulch seeding
c) Plugging
d) Astroturfing

218. ____ refers to a brand of synthetic carpeting designed to look like natural grasses

a) Lawn
b) Turf
c) Plug
d) Austroturf

219. ____ is the method where water is supplied from beneath the soil surface directly to root.

a) Surface irrigation
b) Overhead irrigation
c) Subsurface irrigation
d) Basin irrigation

220. ____ is chemical employed to killing the weeds.

a) Antitransperent
b) Herbicide
c) Insecticide
d) Acaricide

221. ____ is the plant growing where it is not desirable.

a) Runner
b) Weed
c) Lawn
d) Climber

222. Stress caused by one of the factors below is abiotic stress. .

a) Stress due to insect attack
b) Stress due to disease attack
c) Stress due to animal attack
d) Stress due to excess temperature

223. _____ stress caused by fungus or disease pathogen.

a) Biotic
b) Abiotic
c) Residual chemical
d) None of these

224. ____ is the removal cut grasses on the surface of lawn.

a) Mowing | b) Racking
c) Weeding | **d) Sweeping**

225. ____is the special practices where garden soil, land, leaf mould spread over the lawn.

a) Mowing | b) Scrapping
c) Soil top dressing | d) Sweeping

226. ___ is the practices of turf management where to break or loose old runners and create the surface of soil in the lawn.

a) Scraping | b) Irrigation
c) Soil top dressing | **d) Racking**

227. ____ is grass suitable for shade area.

a) Bermuda grass | **b) Korean grass**
c) Poa grass | d) Zoysia grass

228. ____is the ideal pH of soil for lawn.

a) 6-7 | b) 7-8
c) 5.5-6 | d) 6.6-7.5

229. ___ is important grass for lawn and grazing for livestock

a) Bent grass | **b) Rye grass**
c) Poa grass | d) Zoysia grass

230. ___ involves use of pieces of runners cut of from mature turf.

a) Hydro seeding | b) Austroturfing
c) Dibbling | **d) Sprigging**

231. ____ is the drought tolerant species of turf grass.

a) Bermuda grass | b) Zoysia grass
c) Fescue grass | d) Bent grass

232. Botanical name of ketuchy blue grass is _____

a) *Cynadon dactilon* | b) *Dichandhia micranilla*
c) *Poa pratensis* | d) *Zoysia japonica*

233. Warm season grass starts growth when initial temperature is _____

a) 8^0C | b) 10^0C
c) 9^0C | d) None of these

234. Cold season grass starts when initial temperature is ________.

a) 5^0C **b) 0^0C**

c) 2^0C d) 3^0C

235. ____ is the grass is mostly control the soil erosion.

a) Bent grass b) Bermuda grass

b) St. Augstine grass **d) Rye grass**

236. ___ is the common method practiced for development of cool season turf grass lawn.

a) Turfing b) Sodding

c) Seeding d) Dibbling

237. ____ Kg seeds are required to development of lawn for 1 ha.

a) 20 kg **b) 30 kg**

c) 15 kg d) 25 kg

238. Botanical name of doob grass is _____

a) *Zoysia japonica* **b) *Cynadon dactylon***

c) *Festuca alpine* d) *Lolium edwardii*

239. ____ is the grasses becomes dormant and losses in colour in cold weather.

a) Zoysia grasses b) Ketuchy grasses

c) Bermuda grasses d) Poa grasses

240. ____ is cheapest but time consuming method to establishment of turf.

a) Sodding b) Seeding

c) Dibbling d) Plugging

241. ____ is the method where slurry of seeds and mulch slurry is used to establishment of turf.

a) Sprigging b) Austroturfing

c) Hydro seeding d) Sodding

242. ____ is the irrigation method where irrigation channels flows across the turf grass

a) Overhead **b) Surface**

c) Subsurface d) Basin

243. The requirement of micronutrients for grass is in __________

a) Small quantity b) Large quantity

b) In traces d) None of these

244. The requirement of macronutrients for grass is in___________

a) Flowering stage only b) Initial stage

c) Through out growth d) Senescence

245. Plant produce natural compounds that inhibit or control growth are__________

a) Hormones b) Synthetic compounds

c) Chemicals d) None of these

246. ___________promotes stem growth through cell elongation and cell division.

a) A BA b) Ethylene

c) Gibberellins d) Inhibitors

247. ________growth inhibitor closes the stomata of plants under water stress.

a) Auxins b) Cytokinins

c) Gibbrelins **d) ABA**

248. Plant responds towards light is called as___________

a) Geotropism b) Apical dominance

c) Phototropism d) None of these

249. Lawn is not mowed when it is ________________

a) Over grown **b) Wet**

c) Winter d) Summer

250. Temperate grass like perennial rye and blue grass are mowed at height of__________

a) 1-2 inch **b) 2.5-3.0 inch**

c) 3.5-4.0 inch d) Above 5 inch

251. ____________type of weedicide kills all types of lawns.

a) Selective **b) Non selective**

c) Natural d) None of these

252. Iron is important in formation of _________________

a) Chlorophyll b) Hormone

c) Growth regulator d) Xanthophil

253. Plant growth inhibitors are widely used on _____________

a) Turf grass b) Blue grass

c) Golf courses d) Carpets

254. Pop-up sprinklers should be placed at ___________height.

a) Mowing **b) Below mowing**

c) Above mowing d) Deep 10-20 cm.

255. _______is followed for good anchorage of grass.

a) Sweeping b) Mowing

c) Racking **d) Rolling**

256. ___________is a method of establishing a new turf by transplanting small pieces of sod plugs into holes in the seed bed.

a) Sodding b) Dibbling

c) Turfing **d) Plugging**

25

Plantation Crops, Spices, Aromatic and Medicinal Plants

1. Botanical name of All spice is__________ _________.

    a) *Piper nigrum* b) *Zinziber officinale*

    c) *Curcuma longa* d) ***Pimenta dioica***

2. Saffron belongs to family _________

    a) Piperaceae b) Myrtaceae

    c) Iridaceae d) Orchidaceae

3. The ginger oleoresin is commercially called as _________.

    a) 6-gingerol b) **Gingerin**

    c) Gingeron d) Gingeril

4. Directorate of Arecanut and Spices is located at ______________.

    a) Kozikode **b) Calicut**

    c) Kasargod d) Kochi

5. For *Kumkum* preparation ________ _________ species of turmeric is commercially used)

    a) ***Curcuma aromatica*** b) *Zinziber officinale*

    c) *Curcuma longa* d) *Cucuma domestica*

8. The flavouring compounds ____________ and _________ are present in Nutmeg.

    a) Piperine and S-3-Carone b) **Sabinine and Myristicin**

    c) Turmerone and Zingiberene d) Myristicin and Piperine

9. The saffron of commerce is _________.

    a) Pistil b) Androcium

    c) Petals d) Sepals

10. In mace, commercially used plant part as a spice is _________.

    a) Aril b) Pistil

    c) Bud d) Berry

11. The fiber content in ginger variety, Rio-de-Janeiro is _____________ percent.

    a) 3.43 **b) 5.19**

    c) 3.8 d) 4.4

12. The clove of commerce is _________.

    a) Unopened Flower Bud d) Fruit

    c) Opened flower bud d) Bark

13. The chief chemical constituent present in ginger is

    a) Gingerin **b) Gingerol**

    c) Zinziberin d) Curcumin

14. The cylindrical fingers are peculiar characteristics of__________ginger variety.

    a) Suruchi d) China

    c) Suprabha **d) Surari**

15. The origin of nutmeg is _____________

    a) Moluccas b) Jawa

    c) India d) Madagaskar

16. Pick out the odd from the given nutmeg varieties

    a) Konkan Sugandha b) Konkan Swad

    c) Konkan Tej d) Konkan Shrimanti

17. The botanical name of Golden spice is _________ __________.

    a) ***Curcuma longa* L.** b) *Zinziber officinale* Roscoe

    c) *Piper nigrum* L. d) *Syzygium aromaticum* L.

18. For *Kumkum* preparation, __________ variety of turmeric is commercially used)

    a) Suguna b) Krishna

    c) Kasturi d) Amruthpani

19. India is known as '**Land of Spices**' because
    a) Most of the spice are native of India
    b) India grows variety of spices
    c) India has monopoly in majority of International Spice Trade
    d) All the above
20. Indian Institute of Spice Research is located at
    a) Cochin b) **Calicut**
    c) Thiruvanthapuram d) Kozikode
21. The fruit of ginger is of ___________ type.
    a) Capsule b) Berry
    c) Drupe d) None of the above
22. The yellow orange colour of turmeric is due to __________.
    a) Curcumin b) Turmerone
    c) Zingiberene d) Gingerin
23. The typical spicy flavour of turmeric is due to _______
    a) Curcumin b) **Turmerone**
    c) Zingiberene d) Gingerin
24. The botanical name of East Indian Arrow root is
    a) *Curcuma longa* b) *Curcuma aromatica*
    c) *Curcuma angustifolia* d) *Curcuma amada*
25. In the following given species of *Curcuma*, the maximum starch content in rhizome is present in
    a) *Curcuma longa* b) *Curcuma aromatica*
    c) *Curcuma angustifolia* d) *Curcuma amada*
26. The botanical, name of mango ginger is
    a) *Curcuma longa* b) *Curcuma aromatica*
    c) *Curcuma angustifolia* **d) *Curcuma amada***
27. The Mahatma Phule Krishi Vidyapeeth, Rahuri has released turmeric variety
    a) Suguna b) **Phule Swaroopa**
    c) Roma d) Rajendra Sonia

28. Katte disease in Cardamom is transmitted by

    a) Banana thrips   b) **Banana aphids**

    c) White fly   d) None of the above

29. Katte disease in cardamom is __________ disease

    a) Viral   b) Fungal

    c) Bacterial   d) Any other

30. The Cinnamon variety released by Dr. BSKKV, Dapoli is

    a) Konkan Tej   b) Konkan Sugandha

    c) Navsree   d) Konkan Shrimanti

31. Coriander of commerce is

    a) Fruits only   b) Tender green leaves only

    c) Both a and b   d) None of the above

32. Coriander belongs to family_________

    a) Liliaceae   b) **Apiaceae**

    c) Crucifereae   d) Umbellifereae

33. Swathi is variety of _________

    a) Coriander   b) Fenugreek

    c) Mint   d) Nutmeg

34. The fruits of coriander are _____________.

    a) Schizocarp   b) Legume

    c) Berry   d) Capsule

35. The fruits of fenugreek are _____________.

    a) Schizocarp   b) **Legume**

    c) Berry   d) Capsule

36. The cardamom is a ___________ plant

    a) Pseophyte   b) Xerophyte

    c) Helophyte   d) None of the above

37. The coffee beverage flavoured with cardamom is called as ___________.

    a) Lemonade   b) Pinacolada

    c) **Gawa**   d) Cappuccino

38. Among the spice given below, ___________ is known as National spice of India)

a) Black Pepper b) Nutmeg

c) Cardamom **d) Turmeric**

39. The cardamom of commerce is _________.

a) Dried rhizome b) Dried berries

c) **Dried capsule** d) Dried bud

40. The common name of 'Queen of spices' is

a) Ginger b) Nutmeg

c) **Cardamom** d) Cinnamon

41. The botanical name of 'Grains of Paradise' is

a) *Aframomum melegueta* b) *Aframomum korarima*

c) *Aframomum hanburyi* d) *Aframomum augustifolium*

42. The 'Grains of Paradise' belongs to ___________

a) Lesser cardamom group b) Greater cardamom group

c) Large cardamom group d) None of the above

43. The chromosome number of cultivated cardamom is _________.

a) 2n=48 b) 2n=32

c) 2n=14 d) n=14

44. The inflorescence of cardamom is of __________ type.

a) Cymose b) Catkin

c) **Racemose** d) Umbel

45. The fruits of cardamom are_______.

a) Berry b) Drupe

c) Etario of Berries d) **Capsule**

46. Botanically cardamom is ___________ crop

a) Bulb b) **Rhizome**

c) Corm d) None of above

47. In cardamom, _________ type is known as a natural hybrid)

a) Mysore b) Malabar

c) **Vazhukka** d) None of above

48. National Cardamom Research Station is located at _________.

a) Calicut b) Panniyur

c) **Appangala** d) Myladumpara

49. Indian Cardamom Research Institute is located at _________.

a) Calicut b) Pampadumpara

c) Appangala d) **Myladumpara**

50. Out of the following given cardamom varieties, __________ is Mysore type cardamom

a) ICRI-1 b) CCS-1

c) **ICRI-2** d) SKP-14

51. The most unsuitable shade tree in cardamom estate is

a) *Erythrina indica* b) *Diospyrous elengi*

c) *Cedrella toona* d) *Artocarpus fraxinifolius*

52. The predator *Mallada sp.* is commonly used against _________ pest in cardamom.

a) Cardamom thrips b) Aphids

c) **White fly** d) Mites

53. The cardamom chirke disease is caused due to ____________.

a) Bacteria b) Fungi

c) Mycoplasma **d) Virus**

54. The full form of ECCARD is

a) Economical Cardamom Drier

b) Economical Cinnamon Drier

c) Economical Clove Drier

d) European Centre for Cardamom Research and Development

55. The fruit type of *Myristica fragrans* Houtt is ________.

a) Drupe b) Berry

c) Balausta d) Capsule

56. The products prepared from nutmeg includes

a) Essential oil b) Oleoresin

c) Nutmeg Butter d) **All the above**

57. The nutmeg butter is commercially used
    a) To impart spicy flavour to perfumes
    b) In confectionary
    c) In flavouring foods
    d) None of the above
58. Botanically nutmeg is classified as________
    a) Herbal spice b) Root spice
    c) Tree spice d) Rhizome spice
59. The bright red coloured aril exposed after opening fully ripe nutmeg fruit is commercially called as _________.
    a) Capsule **b) Mace**
    c) Rind d) Pod
60. In epicotyl grafting of nutmeg, for getting normal shaped Nutmeg tree, straight growing scions called _________ are used)
    a) Plagiotropic shoots b) Geotropic shoots
    c) Lateral shoots **d) Chupon**
61. For making jam, jellies and pickles from nutmeg, _______ of the fruit is used)
    a) Rind b) Mace
    c) Pericarp d) Seed
62. The botanical name of 'Sweet wood' is ____________.
    a) *Cinnamomum verum* b) *Myristica fragrans*
    c) *Pimeta dioica* d) *Tamarindus indica*
63. The 'Sweet wood' belongs to family __________.
    a) Myrtaceae b) Myristicaceae
    c) Lauraceae d) Leguminaceae
64. The botanical name of Tejpatta is
    a) *Cinnamomum verum* **b) *Cinnamomum tamala***
    c) *Cinnamomum cassia* d) *Cinnamomum burmannii*
65. The bark obtained from *Cinnamomum cassia* is popularly known as __.
    a) False cinnamon b) Chinese cinnamon
    c) Bastard cinnamon **d) All the above**

66. The chief chemical constituent of true cinnamon leaf oil is _________.

a) **Eugenol** b) d-Linalool

c) Cinnmaldehyde d) Sabinine

67. The chief chemical constituent of false cinnamon leaf oil is _________.

a) Eugenol b) d-Linalool

c) **Cinnmaldehyde** d) Sabinine

68. The largest producer of cinnamon bark with best quality is ________.

a) **Sri Lanka** b) Seychelles

c) India d) China

69. The small pieces of cinnamon bark, left after preparing quills are grades as ______.

a) Featherings b) Unscraped chips

c) **Quillings** d) Scraped chips

70. The very thin dried inner pieces of cinnamon bark are known as ________

a) **Featherings** b) Unscraped chips

c) Quillings d) Scraped chips

71. The cinnamon quills of finest quality are graded as ________.

a) **00000** b) 0

c) 00 d) 1

72. The allspice of commerce is _________.

a) Dried bark b) Dried leaves

c) **Dried immature fruits** d) Dried mature fruits

73. The allspice has its centre of origin in __________.

a) India d) China

c) Java d) **West Indies**

74. The fruits of *Pimenta dioica* are

a) Drupe b) **Berry**

c) Capsule d) Legume

75. The flavour of Pimenta resembles to the blend of

a) **Nutmeg, Clove and Cinnamon**

b) Clove, Cinnamon and Cardamom

c) Ginger, Pepper and Clove

d) Ginger, Clove and Cinnamon

76. The Pimenta is commercially propagated by

a) Seed b) Rhizome

c) Cuttings d) Epicotyl grafting

77. The all spice or pimento berry oil contains

a) Eugenol b) d-Linalool

c) Gingerol d) Myristicin

78. The inflorescence of pepper is __________

a) Racemose **b) Catkin**

c) Umbel d) Cymose

79. The biting taste of black pepper is due to __________

a) Eugenol **b) Piperine**

c) Sabinin d) d-Linalool

80. The fruits of pepper are

a) Trilocular capsule b) Legume

c) Single seeded berry d) Single seeded drupe

81. The main adulterant used in black pepper is

a) Papaya seed b) Coffee particles

c) French bean seed d) Cardamom capsules

82. The black pepper adulteration with papaya seeds can be identified by using morphological as well as microscopic inspection. The major points of differentiations includes

a) Papaya is dicot while pepper is monocot

b) Papaya seed shows a line or suture but pepper does not

c) Pepper shows a hollow cavity

d) All the above

83. The most biting ingredient of pepper is ________.

a) **Chavisine** b) Piperine

c) Piperidine d) Piperic acid

84. The pungency of pepper is due to ___________.

a) Piperine b) Chavicine

c) Piperattine **d) All the above**

85. The Directorate of Arecanut and Spices is located at __________.

a) Cochin
b) **Calicut**
c) Kasargod
d) Kozikode

86. Match the pairs

A)	B)
i) Black pepper	a) Green Gold
ii) Cardamom	b) Golden spice
iii) Turmeric	c) Sweet Wood
iv) Cinnamon	d) King of spice

a) i-d, ii-a, iii-b) iv-c
b) i-c, ii-a, iii-b) iv-d
c) i-a, ii-d, iii-b) iv-c
d) i-d, ii-b, iii-a) iv-c

87. Arrange proper chronology of turmeric processing technology

i) Polishing
ii) Colouring
iii) Boiling
iv) Drying
v) Grading
vi) Packaging

a) iii, iv, i, ii, v, vi
b) ii, iv, i, iii, vi, v
c) iv, iii, i, ii, v, vi
d) iii, i, iv, ii, v, vi

88. Match the pairs

A)	B)
i) Black pepper	a) Curcumin
ii) Nutmeg	b) Eugenol
iii) Turmeric	c) Chavisine
iv) Cinnamon	d) Myriticin

a) i-d, ii-a, iii-b) iv-c
b) i-c, ii-d, iii-a) iv-b
c) i-a, ii-d, iii-b) iv-c
d) i-d, ii-b, iii-a) iv-c

89. Pick out the odd group from the following

a) Turmeric, herb, rhizome crop, capsule fruit, boiled, cured fingers

b) Ginger, herb, rhizome crop, capsule fruit, bleached or unbleached dried rhizomes

c) Clove, herb, tree spice, unopened flower bud

d) Nutmeg, tree spice, shallow rotted crop, fruit fleshy drupe, dried seed and mace

90. Match the pairs

A)	B)
i) IISR	a) Puttur
ii) CPCRI	b) Anand
iii) DCR	c) Kasargod
iv) DMAPR	d) Calicut

a) i-d, ii-a, iii-b) iv-c

b) i-c, ii-d, iii-a) iv-b

c) i-a, ii-d, iii-b) iv-c

d) i-d, ii-c, iii-a) iv-b

91. Match the pairs

A)	B)
i) DOPR	a) Ajmer
ii) CPCRI	b) Bangalore
iii) IIHR	c) Kasargod
iv) NRCSS	d) Pedavegi

a) i-d, ii-c, iii-b) iv-a

b) i-c, ii-d, iii-a) iv-b

c) i-a, ii-d, iii-b) iv-c

d) i-d, ii-c, iii-a) iv-b

92. Directorate of Medicinal and Aromatic Plant Research is located at __________.

a) Ajmer

b) Lucknow

c) Purara

d) **Anand**

93. National Research Centre on Seed Spices is situated at __________.

a) Bikaner b) Jodhpur

c) **Ajmer** d) Anand

94. Central Institute of Medicinal and Aromatic Plants has its headquarters at _____.

a) Anand b) Pusa

c) **Lucknow** d) Ajmer

95. Directorate of Cashew Research is located at _________.

a) Banglore b) Pullal

c) **Puttur** d) Vengurla

96. Directorate of Oil Palm Research is situated at ________.

a) Pedavegi b) Hyderabad

c) Puttur d) Trivandrum

97. Central Plantation Crops Research Institute is located at__________.

a) Munnar b) Calicut

c) **Kasargod** d) Panniyur

98. The fruit type of *Piper nigrum* is _________.

a) **Single seeded berry** b) Two seeded berry

c) Fleshy drupe d) Trilocular capsule

99. The most suitable pepper variety for intercropping as well as for high density planting is __________.

a) **Karimunda** b) Panniyur-I

c) Kalluvally d) Krishna

100. The pepper hybrids Panniyur-1 and Shima are F_1 between ______ X _______.

a) Uthirankottah X Cheriyakaniakadan

b) Balankaotta X Uthirankotah

c) Karimunda X Kuthravally II

d) Karimunda X Chriyakody

101. Indian Institute of Spices Research is located at——

a) Ootacamund, Tamil Nadu **b) Kozhikode, Kerala**

c) Dapoli, Maharashtra d) Darjeeling, Kolkata

102. Central Plantation Crops Research Institute is located at—

a) Tamil nadu **b) Kerala**

b) New Delhi d) Maharashtra

103. Alkaloid 'Piperine' in Black pepper forms ——— by weight of the seed)

a) 1-2 % **b) 5-8 %**

b) 50-60 % d) 15-20 %

104. Inflorescence of black pepper is ———

a) Catkin b) Spike

b) Panicle d) Spadix

105. Sreekara variety of Black pepper is developed through———

a) F1 hybrid **b) Selection**

b) Introduction d) Mutation

106. Black pepper is commercially propagated through———

a) Runner b) Tissue culture

b) Multiple stem d) Grafting

107. Rostellum is found in ———— crop.

a) Black pepper b) Cardamom

b) Vanilla d) Nutmeg

108. Pollu flea beetle is a serious pest of ———— crop.

a) Black pepper b) Cardamom

b) Clove d) Nutmeg

109. Black pepper is a————

a) Vine b) Tree

b) Herb d) Shrub

110. Black pepper attains full bearing after ——— years.

a) 7-8 b) 1-2

b) 10-15 d) 15-20

111. Fruit of cardamom is known as————

a) Syconus **b) Capsule**

b) Berry d) Achene

112. Large cardamom is cultivated in ———

a) Kerala **b) Sikkim**

b) Maharashtra d) Rajasthan

113. 'Katte' disease of cardamom is transmitted by ————

a) Bub borer **b) Aphid**

b) Leaf eating caterpiller d) Stem borer

114. Mango ginger is ——

a) *Curcuma longa* b) *C. aromatica*

b) *C. amada* d) *Alipinia galanga*

115. Phule Swaroopa is a variety of ————

a) Nutmeg **b) Turmeric**

b) Clove d) Garlic

116. Suruchi is a variety of ————

a) Turmeric **b) Ginger**

b) Clove d) Black pepper

117. Clove is ——— tree spice.

a) Evergreen b) Deciduous

b) Semi-deciduous d) Caudocus

118. Optimum stage for picking clove is ————

a) Colour change from green to dark green

b) Colour change from green to pink

b) Colour change from green to black

d) Colour change from pink to brown

119. Spice determining factor in clove is ———

a) Fruit **b) Eugenol**

b) Odour d) Heat units

120. Nutmeg is ————

a) Monoecious **b) Dioecious**

b) Both d) None of this

121. Konkan Swad is variety of ———

a) Black pepper b) Clove

b) Nutmeg d) Cardamom

122. Cinnamon belongs to family————

a) Compositae **b) Lauraceae**

b) Solanaceae d) Poacae

123. Essential oil content of coriander is ——— per cent.

a) 1-10 **b) 0.1-1.0**

b) 2-4 d) 5-6

124. Contribution of India to world spice production by volume is

a) <15% b) 15-30%

b) 30-50% d) 70-80%

125. Most exported item from Indian market is

a) Black pepper **b) Chilli**

b) Turmeric d) Cardamom

126. Major challenge/s in Indian spice industry is/are

a) Low yielding varieties b) Competitive market

b) Diseases **d) All of the above**

127. First pepper research scheme was started at

a) Ajmer b) Ratnagiri

b) Penniyur d) Baptla

128. CPCRI stands for

a) Central Plantation Cash Research Institute

b) Central Plantation Crops Research Institute

b) Central Consortium Crops Research Institute

d) Central Controlled Crops Research Institute

129. Pungency in blak pepper is due to

a) Piperine b) Capsaicin

b) Withanin d) Ajamalicine

130. Black pepper species resistant to phytophthora and root knot nematode is

a) *Piper nigrum* b) *P. longum*

b) *P. betle* **d) *P. ornatum***

131. Botanically fruit of black pepper is known as

a) **Drupe** b) Berry

b) Syconus d) Balusta

132. IISR- Malabar variety of black pepper is obtained by ———— breeding method)

a) OP selection **b) F_1 hybrid**

b) Clonal selection d) Mutation

133. Black pepper is commercially propagated by

a) Runner b) Seed

b) 5 node cutting d) Tissue culture

134. Percent Moisture content for safe storage of black pepper is

a) 1-2 b) 5-7

b) 10-12 d) 15-20

135. Malabar Garbled is important grade of

a) Black pepper b) Turmeric

b) Cardamom d) Clove

136. Queen of spices is

a) Clove **b) Cardamom**

b) Turmeric d) Saffron

137. Second costliest spice is

a) All spice b) Saffron

b) Vanilla d) Turmeric

138. IISR Vijetha is a variety of

a) Vanilla **b) Cardamom**

b) Saffron d) Turmeric

139. Tree suited for temporary shading in spice crops is

a) *Quiscalis indica* **b) *Erythrina indica***

b) *Lagerstromea indica* d) *Saraca indica*

140. Turmeric is

a) Haploid b) Diploid

b) Triploid d) Tetraploid

141. Per ha seed rate of turmeric is

a) 1500 kg **b) 2500 kg**

b) 3000 kg d) 3500 kg

142. Turmeric comes to harvest after ———months after sowing.

a) 4 months b) 6 months

b) 9 months d) 12 months

143. No seed set in ginger is due to ————

a) Self incompatibility **b) Spiny stigmatic surface**

b) Male sterility d) Polyploidy nature

144. Surari is———— cultivar of ginger.

a) Introduced b) Selection

b) Hybrid **d) Mutant**

145. Pungency of ginger is due to

a) Gingerol b) Shagol

b) Zingerone **d) All of these**

146. Yield of dry ginger is ———— per cent of fresh ginger.

a) 5-10 b) 11-15

b) 16-20 **d) 21-25**

147. Clove is obtained from

a) Unopened flower bud b) Bark

b) Root extract d) Seed

148. The name 'Saffron' is derived from ——— word)

a) English **b) Arabic**

b) Latin d) Greek

149. Konkan Tej is a variety of ————

a) Clove **b) Cinnamon**

b) Black pepper d) All spice

150. All spice tree combines flavour of———— spices.

a) Two **b) Four**

b) Six d) Eight

151. Medicinal plants are rich in ———— metabolites.

a) **Primary** b) Secondary

b) Tertiary d) Binary

152. ———— obtained from Dioscorea tubers is the major base chemical of several steriod harmones.

a) Diosgenin **b) Tropane**

b) Robasin d) Serpentine

153. The husk :seed ratio in Isabgol is———— by weight.

a) 75: 25 b) 30: 75

b) 25:75 d) 75:30

154 Belladona is an important source of———— alkaloid

a) Barbaloin b) Tropane

b) Serpentine **d) Diosgenin**

155. Isabgol belongs to family————

a) Rubiaceae b) Solanaceae

b) Dioscoreaceae **d) Plantaginaceae**

156. *Dioscorea alata* is known as ———— yam

a) Greater b) Lesser

b) Smaller d) Minute

157. Dioscorea is commercially propagated by————

a) Seed b) Corms

b) Bulbs **d) Tubers**

158. Rauvolfia can be intercropped with ———— in monsoon season

a) Soybean b) Wheat

b) Cabbage d) Cauliflower

159. Chief constituent of lemon grass oil is————

a) Diosgenin **b) Citral**

b) Robasin d) Tropane

160. Mentha belongs to family————

a) Solanaceae b) Rubiaceae

b) Labiatae d) Dioscoreaceae

161. ———— found in the leaves of periwinkle has antifibrillic and hypertensive properties

a) **Serpentine** b) Sennosides

b) Solasodine d) Quinidine

162. ———— is used in preparation of antimalarial drug

a) Geraniol **b) Quinine**

b) Citronellol d) Limonene

163. ———— is an annual twining plant.

a) Rauvolfia b) Senna

b) Ipomea d) Cinchona

164. Lemon grass is ———— pollinated in nature.

a) Cross b) Self

b) Often cross d) Often self

165. Asparagus belongs to family————

a) Lilliaceae b) Apocynaceae

b) Labiatae d) Solanaceae

166. Oil recovery in case of Patchouli is————

a) 1.8 to 3% b) 2-2.5%

b) 3-4% d) 10-15 %

167. Dried roots of Rauvolfia serpentina are commonly known as ———— roots.

a) Robasin roots b) Dehydrated roots

b) Serpentine roots d) Cured roots

168. Harvested roots of Rauvolfia should be artifically dried to reduce the moisture content to ———— %

a) 5% b) 7%

b) 3% d) 8%

169. Mentha is harvested at———— stage.

a) Bloom b) Tender

b) Mature d) Pre bloom

170. *Dioscorea esculentus* is known as ———— yam

a) Greater **b) Lesser**

b) Thicker d) Tender

171. Asparagus is also known as a ———— agent
a) Dehydrating b) Hydrating
b) Healing **d) Cooling**

172. Periwinkle is planted at a spacing of ———— cm.
a) 30x30 **b) 45x30**
b) 45x45 d) 60x60

173. Bitter component of Aloe juice is known as————
a) Alonin b) Verinin
b) Alovernin **d) Barbaloin**

174. Chinchona belongs to family————
a) Rubiaceae b) Solanaceae
b) Apocyanaceae d) Dioscoreaceae

175. Pin, thrumb and Pitchi are different types of————
a) Patchouli b) Rose
b) Palmarosa **d) Jasmine**

176. Oil from sandalwood is obtained from————
a) Heartwood b) Bark
b) Seed d) Flowers

177. Geranium is propagated by————
a) Seed **b) Tip cutting**
b) Root d) Buds

178. Material which slows down the rate of evaporation is————
a) Fixative b) Oleoresin
b) Absolute d) Extract

179. ———— is a prefered slovent for extraction of flower oil
a) Heaxane **b) Benzene**
b) Propane d) Tropane

180. Botanical name of Ashwagandha is————
a) *Valeriana officinalis* **b) *Withania somnifera***
b) *Urginea indica* d) *Tylophora indica*

181. ———— is one of the three constituents of the famous Indian preparation Triphala
a) Tamarind b) Jamun
b) Sandal wood **d) Bahera**

182. Rauvolfia belongs to family————

a) Apocynaceae	b) Fabaceae
b) Berberidaceae	d) Plantaginaceae

183. The root drug of Rauvolfia is used as————

a) Rejuvenating agent	b) Cooling agent
b) Tranqualising agent	d) Accelerating agent

184. ———— is very useful in several kinds of chronic dysentery.

a) Isabgol	b) Periwinkle
b) Adulsa	d) Long Pepper

185. Botanical name of Isabgol is————

a) *Piper longum*	b) *Ocimum sanctum*
b) *Madhuca indica*	***d) Plantago ovata***

186. Plants belonging to genus Mentha are aromatic————

a) Shrubs	**b) Herbs**
b) Trees	d) Climbers

187. Peppermint oil is obtained from————

a) Tulsi	b) Geranium
b) Mentha	d) Palmarosa

188. ———— is a Japanese variety of Mentha

a) Mentha arvensis	b) *Mentha longifolia*
b) *Mentha piperita*	d) *Mentha spicata*

189. Mint is commonly propagated by————

a) Cuttings	b) Layering
b) Tissue culture	**d) Suckers**

190. Leaves of ———— are astringrnt in nature.

a) Isabgol	b) Citronella
b) Periwinkle	**d) Henna**

191. ———— is a large genus of twining herbs.

a) Datura	b) Digitalis
b) Dioscorea	d) Cymbopogon

192. Tubers of *Dioscorea deltoidea* are rich in————

a) Diosgenin b) Robasin

b) Serpentine d) Vincristine

193. Oil extracted from grasses of genus Cymbopogon is used as———— agent

a) Cooling **b) Flavouring**

b) Rejuvenating d) Tranqualising

194. ———— grass is grown on hill slopes as it has good soil binding properties

a) Palmarosa **b) Lemon**

b) Citronella d) Vetiver

195. Qunine is the most important constituent of———— bark

a) Asparagus b) Belladona

b) Cinchona d) Adulsa

196. ———— is used as an antidote in certain types of poisoining cases

a) Belladona b) Neem

b) Bael d) Sweet flag

197. ———— brings about quick relief in bronchitis

a) Ashwagandha b) Shatawari

b) Adulsa d) Isabgol

198. ———— is used to prevent abortion and excessive blood loss in women.

a) Belladona b) Periwinkle

b) Rauvolfia **d) Asparagus**

199. ———— is used for curing gout

a) Dioscoria **b) Belladona**

b) Cinchona d) Vetiver

200. ———— has boat shaped seeds.

a) Periwinkle b) Senna

b) Henna **d) Isabgol**

26

Post Harvest Management of Horticultural Crops

1. The goal of ———— is to gather commodity from the field at proper stage of maturity With minimum damage.
   a) **Harvesting** b) Grading
   c) Sorting d) Handling
2. Harvesting in rose is done at ———— stage
   a) Loose bud b) **Tight bud**
   c) Fully open d) Partially open
3. Gerbera is harvested by ———— the stalk
   a) Cutting b) Uprooting
   c) Twisting d) Pinching
4. Solidago is harvested with secateur when ———— percent of flowers are open
   a) 5% b) 15%
   c) 20% d) **25%**
5. Major disease of cut flowers after harvest is————
   a) Powdery mildew b) **Botrytis**
   c) Downy mildew d) Anthracnose
6. In non climatric fruits there is no upsurge of————
   a) **Respiration** b) Photosynthesis
   c) Transpiration d) Senescence
7. Enzymes are made up of————
   a) Fats b) Carbohydrates
   c) **Proteins** d) Vitamins
8. The material released during chlorophyll degradation is used for caratenoid synthesis increasing vitamin———— content in fruits
   a) **"A"** b) " B"
   c) "C" d) " D"

9. Relative rate of respiration in pea is
   a) **High** b) Moderate
   c) Low d) Very low
10. Vegetables taste sour, bitter and saltish if stored at
   a) **Low temperature**
   b) High temperature
   c) Temperature has no effect
   d) Alternate low and high temperature
11. Storage life of knoll khol is——— days
   a) 52 b) 60-80
   c) 84 d) **98**
12. Carrots are best stored with the help of
   a) House celler b) **Mounds**
   c) Trenches d) Cold storages
13. Gas used for refrigeration is——
   a) **Ammonia** b) CO2
   c) SO2 d) NO2
14. Pinching chemical used for chrysanthemum is known as
   a) **Emgard 2007** b) Ancymidol
   c) Chloremquat d) GA3
15. Flower rot disease of chrysanthemum is caused by
   a) Fungus b) **Grey mould**
   c) Virus d) Bacteria
16. Gladiolus is propagated through——
   a) Cuttings b) Layering
   c) **Corms** d) Grafting
17. Polyembryonic variety of mango is
   a) Bangalore b) Goa
   c) Alphanso d) **Himsagar**
18. Which variety of banana is essentially used for cooking
   a) **Monthan** b) Lal Kela
   c) Kunnan d) Amritsagar
19. Low content of——— in fruits and vegetables play an important role in maintaining texture, flavour and pigments
   a) Carbohydrates b) **Lipids**
   c) Proteins d) Vitamins

20. Vitamin——— content increases during ripening and thereafter decreases
    a) A b) B
    c) **C** d) D
21. Physiological loss in weight (PLW)——— after harvest of most of the fruits
    a) **Increases** b) Decreases
    c) Remains constant d) None of the above
22. ——— is a predominant acid present in grape
    a) Malic acid b) Citric acid
    c) Oxalic acid d) **Tartaric acid**
23. ——— is the sequential change in the sensory factors of colour, texture and taste of fruits
    a) **Ripening** b) Senescence
    c) Growth d) Maturity
24. The concentration of ethylene required for ripening of various fruits is in the range of———
    a) 0.5-1ppm b) 0.4-1 ppm
    c) 0.2-1 ppm d) **0.1-1 ppm**
25. ——— is most useful to rehydrate flowers after harvest
    a) **Acid** b) Alkali
    c) Sugar d) Salt
26. Pulsing treatment with——— percent sucrose solution for 24 hours has been found effective for extending vase life of gladiolus.
    a) 15% b) **20%**
    c) 10% d) 25%
27. ——— is a simple process where flowers are kept loosely in a big container
    a) **Conditioning** b) Holding
    c) Pulsing d) Impregnation
28. Spray type chrysanthemum is not graded as———
    a) Gold b) Silver
    c) Make up d) **Utility**
29. ——— is a cut flower
    a) **Rose** b) Jasmine
    c) Gallardia d) Marigold

30. The flat sour spoilage of canned vegetables is due to.............
    a) Development of sour odour without gas production by microorganism
    b) Corrosion of the tin plate
    c) Gas formation by the miocroorganism
    d) A decrease in pH
31. Which of the following are responsible for the postharvest deterioration of fruits and vegetables.
    a) Respiration b) Temperature
    c) Ethylene d) Their high temperature content
32. Zero energy cool chamber operates on the principle of ....
    a) Second law of thermodynamics
    b) Evaporative cooling
    c) Stannous chloride
    d) Ascorbic acid
33. The heat treatment given before canning of vegetables without boiling water or steam followed by cooling is termed as...............
    a) Blanching b) Brining
    c) Clinching d) Exhausting
34. Which one of the following is the permanent method of preservation of fruits and vegetables
    a) Canning and bottling b) Pasteurization
    c) Exclusion and moisture **d) Blanching**
35. Pectin is measured by ....
    a) Thermometer b) Refractometer
    c) Jelli meter d) All of these
36. Vegetables are canned in ....
    a) Syrup **b) Brine**
    c) Distilled water d) None of these
37. Exhausting temperature of canned fruit is ....
    a) 70-72°C, **b) 80-82°C,**
    c) 90-92°C d) 100-102°C
38. Food Product Order was passed by Government of India in the year..........
    a) 1920 **b) 1955**
    c) 1945 c) 1975

39. Which one of the chemical is used to keep the fruit and vegetable firm
    a) Sodium chloride
    b) Sodium benzoate
    c) Ascorbic acid
    d) Calcium chloride
40. Which one of the following does occur in fruits and vegetables by blanching process
    a) Driving out the air from tissue
    b) Hardening the tissue
    c) Getting rid of the material of micro- organism
    d) Inactivating the enzyme system
41. Refractometer is used to determine ....
    a) Minerals
    b) TSS
    c) Vitamins
    d) None of these
42. Permissible limit of synthetic color in food preservation is ....
    a) 300 ppm
    b) 200ppm
    c) 250 ppm
    d) 350 ppm
43. Radiation which is mostly used for disinfection of food
    a) Alpha rays
    b) UV rays
    c) Gamma rays
    d) X rays
44. Which of the following chemical is used as surface fertilizers?
    a) Hgcl2
    b) KN03
    c) Kcl3
    d) None of these
45. Sulphur containing foods are stored in ....
    a) AR cans
    b) SR cans
    c) Both
    d) None of these
46. Which of the following principle is used in freezing?
    a) Condensation
    b) Crystallization
    c) Sublimation
    d) None of these
47. For vegetable canning, time and temperature for processing is depend upon ....
    a) Microbial load on vegetables
    b) Texture of the product
    b) Nutrient present in vegetables
    d) All of these
48. Which one of the following method is the permanent method of preservation?
    a) Canning
    b) Deareation
    c) Pasteurization
    d) Dehydration

49. Modified atmosphere packaging of fruit and vegetables prevent the built up of following

a) CO_2 and O_2
b) CO_2 and C_4H_4
c) Sugars
d) Proteins

50. Which one of the following is not a food preservative?

a) Glacial acetic acid
b) Benlate
c) KMS
d) Sodium Benzoate

51. Which one is a ripening hormone

a) GA_4
b) B_4
c) GA_3
d) Ethylene

52. The best storage temperature for onion is

a) 2 °C
b) -5 °C
c) 5 °C
d) 10 °C

53. Waxing of fruit is mainly to reduce ....

a) Respiration
b) Transpiration
c) Ripening
d) Transpiration and respiration

54. .... is recommended for maintaining freshness in cut leafy vegetables

a) Auxin
b) Cytokinin
c) Gibberalin
d) Ethylene

55. CIPHET is situated at ....

a) Punjab
b) Ludhiana
c) Bangalore
d) Hyderabad

56. Which one of these kill microorganism in food

a) Cold processing
b) Heat processing
c) Thermal processing
d) None of these

57. Lactic acid bacteria are used in ....

a) Jam
b) Jelly
c) Pickle
d) Wine

58. Precooling is meant to ....

a) Absorb field heat
b) Remove field heat
c) Decrease the temperature
d) Increase the temperature

59. .... is the minimum content of juice in RTS beverage
   a) 10% b) 15%
   c) 12% d) 8%

60. Potato contains .... of protein (mg/100g of edible portion)
   a) 2 b) 3
   c) 1.6 d) 1.5

61. Relative rate of respiration in pea is ....
   a) Low **b) High**
   c) Moderate d) Very low

62. Relative humidity of beet root is ....
   a) 60-80% b) 70-80%
   c) 85-87% d) 80-90 %

63. Cool season crop with the exception of white potatoes should be stored at..............
   a) 32°F b) 40°F
   c) 10-15°F d) 60-70°F

64. Vegetables taste sour, bitter and saltish is stored at ....
   a) Low temperature
   b) High temperature
   c) Temperature has no effect
   d) Alternate low and high temperature

65. Storage life of Knol Khol is.............
   a) 50 days b) 60-80 days
   c) 84 days **d) 98 days**

66. Carrot is best stored with the help of ....
   a) House Celler, **b) Mounds**
   c) Trenches d) Cold storages

67. Garlic can be stored best at the temperature range of ....
   a) 55-55° F, b) 45-55°F,
   c) 36-40°F **d) 32° F**

68. Gas used for refrigeration is.............
   a) Ammonia b) CO_2
   c) SO_2 d) No_2

69. .... sprayed 4-5 days before harvest prevents the loss of chlorophyll
a) 2,4-D
b) **2,4,5-Trichlorophenoxiacetic acid**
c) Ethylene
d) Acetylene

70. Loss in weight of onion bulbs during storage at room temperature is caused by............
a) Sprouting
b) Long term storage
c) CO_2
d) SO_2

71. Garlic freezes at average temperature of ....^{0}C.
a) -5
b) -4
c) -3
d) -2

72. Tomato sauce must have not less than ....
a) 16% TSS
b) 10% TSS
c) 5% TSS
d) 12 % TSS

73. What is TSS of Jam
a) 68.5
b) 60
c) 65
d) 75

74. Which one of the following vegetable is the richest source of protein
a) Pea
b) Fenugreek
c) Palak
d) Cucumber

75. Which one of the following vegetables gives maximum calories per 100 gram of edible matter
a) Spinach
b) Watermelon
c) Sweet potato
d) Tomato

76. Yellow coloured vegetables are rich source of ....
a) Vitamin E
b) Vitamin C
c) Vitamin A
d) Vitamin B

77. The best quality 'Oleoresin' is extracted from-
a) Onion
b) Castor
c) Chilli
d) Coconut

78. The Indian Institute of Vegetable Research is located at
a) Ranchi
b) Delhi
c) Varanasi
d) Bangalore

79. The pungency of chillies is due to which compound?
a) Coumarin
b) Resin
c) Capsaicin
d) Cucurbitacin

80. The red colour in chilli fruits at the ripening stage is due to which pigment?
    a) Capsaicin **b) Capsanthin**
    c) Alkaglucoside d) Mimosine
81. According to All India Medical Science report, how much is the per capita vegetable requirement in India
    a) 500g b) 400g
    c) 200g **d) 300g**
82. According to ISI tomato has been graded into how many grades?
    a) 4 grades b) 3 grades
    c) 2 grades d) 1 grade
83. Acid content in tomato is lower in which fruit?
    a) Mature fruits **b) Immature fruits**
    c) When colour appeared d) None of the above°
84. After how many days of sowing watermelon crop is ready for harvesting
    a) 45-60 b) 70-75
    c) 75-100 d) 100-120
85. Ascorbic acid is another name for which of following
    a) Vitamin A b) Vitamin D
    c) Vitamin C d) Vitamin B6
86. At what temperature and RH cabbage heads store well
    a) 15°C at 60-70% RH b) 5°C at 70-80% RH
    c) 0°C at 90-95% RH d) None of these
87. At what temperature and RH cauliflower curds can be stored for 30 days?
    a) 10°C at 70-80% RH b) 5°C at 70-80% RH
    c) 0°C at 85-90% RH d) None of these
88. At what stage tomato fruits are picked for processing tomato ?
    a) Immature stage b) Pink stage
    c) Hard ripe stage d) Over-ripe stage
89. At what temperature onion is stored
    a) 4-5°C **b) 0°C**
    c) 6-8°C d) 10°C
90. Bitterness in chilli is due to..........
    a) Capsanthin b) Capsinoid
    c) Capsaicin d) Carotenoid

91. Browning disdorders occurs in ....

a) **Cauliflower** b) Cabbage

c) Okra d) Brinjal

92. Chemical formulae of Potassium meta- bisulphate is ....

a) KMS b) K_2SO_4

c) KSO_2 **d) $K_2S_2O_5$**

93. Cracking of tomato fruit is brought about by ....

a) Restricted watering

b) A period of drought followed by sudden watering

c) Over watering

d) Insufficient watering

94. Curing of onion bulbs after harvesting is essential for which purpose?

a) For drying b) For dehydration

c) For better storage d) a and b both

95. Daily requirement of vitamin –D for a healthy adult is ....

a) 200 I.U. b) 400 I.U.

c) 600 I.U. d) 800 I.U.

96. Daily requirement of vegetable per capita /day is ....

a) 150 gram b) 200 gram

c) 285 gram d) 400 gram

97. Delayed harvesting in radish may lead to ....

a) Forking **b) Pithiness**

c) Deformed roots d) All of the above

98. For controlling sprouting of onions in storage it is advantageous to apply preharvest foliar spray of maleic hydrazide (MH-40) at which concentration.

a) 500 ppm b) 1500 ppm

c) 2500 ppm d) 2000 ppm

99. For how long Brussels sprout can be stored at 0 to 1°C temperature and 90-95 % RH?

a) 15 days after transplanting

b) 30 days after transplanting

c) Two months

d) 3-5 weeks

100. For how many days brinjal can store in fairly good condition at 7.2°C to 10°C with 85-95 % RH?

a) 1to 3 b) 3 to 4

c) 4 to 5 **d) 7 to 10**

101. For how many days cabbage can be stored at 0°C and 90-95 per cent RH?

a) 15 days after transplanting

b) One month

c) 2 to 8 months

d) 45 days

102. For how many days can okra green pods be stored for in 400 gauge polythene bags under room temperature (32 ± 20°C) and 70-75 per cent RH as against 2-3 days without package

a) 4 b) 5

c) 7 **d) 9**

103. For how many days mature green tomato fruits can be stored at 10-15°C

a) 10 b) 15

c) 30 d) 20

104. For how many days parwal fruits after harvesting can be stored under ordinary conditions

a) 7-10 b) 10-15

c) 3-4 d) 15-20

105. For how many days under ordinary conditions, harvested fruits of snake gourd can be easily kept?

a) 10 b) 15

c) 3 d) 15-20

106. For how many days under ordinary conditions, harvested fruits of round gourd can be easily kept?

a) 10 b) 15

c) 3 to 4 d) 15-20

107. For how many years under good management, once planted crop of pointed gourd give economic return?

a) 2 b) 3

c) 4 d) 1

108. For long storage potato tubers should be kept at which temperature?

a) 5-10°C b) 10-15°C

c) 15-20°C d) None of these

109. For longer storage of cucumber fruits the temperature should be kept at which level?
a) 5°C b) 15°C
c) 10°C d) 7°C

110. Freeze drying is also called as...............
a) Lyophilization b) Iceing
c) Precooling d) Pesteurization

111. Good storage require..............
a) High temperature and high humidity
b) Low temperature and high humidity
c) High temperature and low humidity
d) None of these

112. How much is the recommended daily consumption of leafy vegetables?
a) 50g **b) 116g**
c) 250g d) 285g

113. How much is the vitamin A content in pumpkin fruits?
a) 25mg/100g b) 30mg/100g
c) 84mg/100g d) 60mg/100g

114. Immediately after harvest, the tubers of potato have how long a rest or a dormant period?
a) 3 to 4 months **b) 2 to 3 months**
c) 1 to 2 months d) None of these

115. Mention the onion variety suitable for dehydration?
a) Udaipur-101 **b) Udaipur-102**
c) Udaipur -103 d) Phule Safed

116. Mention the purpose for which blanching in vegetable processing is done?
a) Micro-organism removal
b) Inactive enzyme
c) For softening the vegetables
d) All of these

117. Mention what will br the colour when snake gourd fruit becomes ripe?
a) Dark green b) Pale green
c) Light yellow **d) Orange yellow**

118. Mention which crop contributes maximum in export of fresh vegetables?
a) Potato **b) Onion**
c) Tomato d) Garlic

119. Mention which is non- climacteric vegetable?

a) Muskmelon b) Watermelon

c) Tomato **d) Cucumber**

120. Mention which is not a recognized stage of harvesting of tomato?

a) Mature green stage

b) Fully ripe stage

c) Pink stage or turning stage

d) Fully mature stage

121. Mention which is the richest source of Vit A?

a) Turnip leaves b) Carrot

c) Pumpkin yellow d) Drumstick leaves

122. Mention which is the source of vit C?

a) Tomato **b) Cabbage**

c) Turnip d) Radish

123. Mention which of the following is rich in iron?

a) Muskmelon b) Watermelon

c) Bottlegourd **d) Bittergourd**

124. Name the acid of which green leafy vegetables are rich source ?

a) Citric acid b) Malic acid

c) Folic acid d) All of above

125. Name the elements which acts as anti-oxidants ?

a) Selenium b) Iodine

c) Boron d) Calcium

126. Name the enzymes which converts starch to sugar in potato ?

a) Starch phosphorylase **b) Glucose-1- Phosphate**

c) Both a and c d) None of a and c

127. Which is the pigment present in watermelon ?

a) Carotenoid b) Anthocyanin

c) Lycopene **d) Both B and C**

128. Onion is the richest source of which vitamin ?

a) Vanidium b) Calcium

c) Magnesium d) Sodium

129. Pungency in onion is due to ……………….

a) Allyl propyle disulphide

b) Di allyl disulphide

c) Capasaicin

d) None of these

130. Which colour brinjal is good for diabetic patient ?

a) Purple b) Green

c) White d) Black

131. Which of the potato variety is more suitable for chips making ?

a) Kufri Naveen b) Kufri jyoti

c) Kufri Badshah **d) Kufri Chipsona**

132. Select the correct answer using the code given below

a) 1 and 2 b) 1,2 and 3

c) 2,3 and 4 **d) 1,2,3 and 4**

133. According to Spencer's theory of jelly formation, pectin is having-

a) +ve charge **b) -ve charge**

c) Neutral d) None of these

134. ________is the instrument used for measuring strength of syrup in terms of ^{0}Brix.

a) Jelmeter b) Hand Refractometer

c) Salinometer **d) Brix Hydrometer**

135. If extract is rich in pectin, __________ of sugar is to be added for Jelly preparation.

a) Equal quantity b) ½ quantity

c) ¾ quantity d) None of the above

136. If pressure gauge shows no vacuum inside a can it is called as ____________.

a) **Breather** b) Leaker

c) Springer d) Flipper

137. The sparkling clear liquid free from suspended solids is known as ___________.

a) Squash b) Jam

c) Nector **d) Cordial**

138. ________is the heat treatment generally above 100^0c aimed at the destruction of all viable microorganisms.
   a) Pasteurization   b) Blanching
   c) Sterilization   d) None of the above
139. Browning in apple is due to the presence of ______.
   a) PPO   b) Tyrosine
   c) Hydrogenise   d) None of these
140. Cryo-preservation is related to _________.
   a) Liquid Oxygen   **b) Liquid Nitrogen**
   c) Liquid CO_2 d) Liquid Potassium
141. Aonla fruits are not suitable for fresh consumption as they are ________.
   a) Sour and bitter
   b) Pungent
   c) Highly acidic & astringent
   d) None of these
142. Whisky is a fermented product, which is prepared from_________.
   a) Apple   **b) Malt**
   c) Coconut   d) Cashewnut
143. Loquat fruit is botanically known as ________.
   a) Drupe   b) Berry
   c) Nut   **d) Pome**
144. Pricking process is related to ________.
   a) Papaya   b) Mango
   c) Aonla   d) Guava
145. The term three quarterful or full three quarter is used to denote fruit maturity in which crop in the following.
   a) Banana   b) Mango
   c) Pineapple   D) Tomato
146. Most suitable packaging material for cut flowers is ________.
   a) Wooden boxes   **b) CFB**
   c) Plastic boxes   d) Carets
147. The point at which the the dried products just become lumpy is known as _________.
   a) Danger point   b) Saturated point
   c) Critical point   d) Safety point

148. Chemical used for removing the spray residues of Arsenic and lead from the fruit is ________.

a) NaOH **b) HCl**

c) NaCl d) H_2SO_4

149. Ready-to-serve (RTS) contains ________.

a) 10% Juice and 15% TSS

b) 15% Juice and 15% TSS

c) 10% Juice and 10% TSS

d) 15% Juice and 10% TSS

150. Best degreening temperature and RH for citrus fruit is ________.

a) 27 °C and 85-95 % b) 15 °C and 80-85 %

c) 38 °C and 90-95 % d) 10 °C and 80-85 %

151. In which of the following process, enzyme is inactivated?

a) Canning b) Asepsis

c) Sulphitation **d) Blanching**

152. Sublimation is associated with _______.

a) Vacuum drying b) Spray drying

c) Freeze drying d) Foam mat drying

153. Albinism is an important physiological disorder of________.

a) Plum b) Peach

c) Strawberry d) Cherry

154. Citric acid is commercially produced by _________.

a) *Aspergillus niger* b) *Penicillium*

c) *Bacillus* d) *Clostrium*

155. The chemical commonly used for prolonging vase life of cut flower is ________.

a) Potassium nitrate **b) Sucrose**

c) MH d) Benzyl adenine

156. Which bean is used for extraction of gum?

a) Broad bean b) French bean

c) Hyacinth bean **d) Cluster bean**

157. Which of the following fruit is canned after halving?

a) Mango b) Litchi

c) Peach d) Strawberry

158. Which of the organization is engaged in exporting of processed products?

a) NAFED **b) APEDA**

c) NABARD d) CFTRI

159. Fruit which is used for preparation of good quality jelly is _______.

a) Mango b) Jamun

c) Aonla **d) Guava**

160. What is the maximum level of SO_2 permitted in squash?

a) 250 ppm **b) 350 ppm**

c) 450 ppm d) 400 ppm

161. A device for measuring spread or flow of semi solids foods in specified length of time is called as _______.

a) Consistometer b) Salinometer

c) Refractometer d) Tenderometer

162. How much pectin should be present in finished jelly?

a) 2% **b) 1%**

c) 3% d) 6%

163. Under normal conditions, Orchid can be stored up to two weeks at _________.

a) 2-4 °C **b) 5-7 °C**

c) 10-12 °C d) None of these

164. In Lye peeling, how much caustic soda (NaOH) is used?

a) 1-2 % b) 3-4 %

c) 4-5 % d) 7-8 %

165. Which of the following is strongest senescence stimulator?

a) GA b) PBA

c) IAA **d) ABA**

166. Botanically mulberry fruit is known as ________.

a) Berry **b) Sorosis**

c) Ballusta d) Syconium

167. The term 'pulsing' is related to ________.

a) Preservation b) Storage

c) Cut flowers d) Freezing

168. Traditional drying of onion in the field is called as _______.

a) Windrowing b) Curing

c) Vacuum drying d) Freeze drying

169. According to FPO, permissible limit of Tin content in processed foods is ________.

a) 2 ppm **b) 5 ppm**
c) 10 ppm d) 20 ppm

170. Find out Minimum Fruit Content and TSS for a fruit jelly according to FPO?

a) 45 % and 65 °B b) 50 % and 70 °B
c) 55 % and 65 °B d) 60 % and 75 °B

171. ________ is obtained by blending thin pulp of the fruit with sugar and citric acid resulting in 15-20° Brix sugar and mild acid taste.

a) Syrup b) Squash
c) Juice **d) Nectar**

172. ________ is used to preserve naturally coloured juices.

a) Potassium metabisulphite
b) Antibiotic preservative
c) Antiseptic preservative
d) Sodium Benzoate

173. ________ia an antibiotic used in the food industry especially for preservation of acid foods in which it is more stable.

a) Potassium metabisulphite **b) Nisin**
c) Subtilin d) Pimaricin

174. Storage of fruits below recommended temperature results in ________.

a) Browning injury **b) Chilling injury**
c) Decaying d) None of these

175. During controlled atmospheric storage composition of which of the following set of gases is controlled.

a) $O_2 + N_2$ b) $CO_2 + N_2$
c) $C_2H_4 + N_2$ **d) $CO_2 + O_2$**

176. Which of the following is biodegradable plastic?

a) Polypropylene b) LDPE
c) Polyethylene **d) Polyhydroxy butyrate**

177. What should be the head space in can for canning of fruits and vegetables?

a) 0.32-0.47 cm b) 0.5-1.5 cm
c) 1.0-2.0 cm d) 3.0-5.0 cm

178. Zero Energy Cool Chamber is developed by-
   a) M. K. Rai and R. N. Singh
   b) S. K. Roy and D. S. Khurdiya
   c) R. P. Roy and D. K. Khurana
   d) None of these

179. "Jelly Seed" is a physiological disorder of _______.
   a) Apple b) Guava
   c) Mango d) Papaya

180. Commercially, the chemical used to scrub ethylene from fruit storages is _______.
   a) Potassium oxalate b) Potassium sodium titrate
   c) Potassium dichromate **d) Potassium permanganate**

181. Softening of fruits during ripening is due to the breakdown of __________.
   a) Starch **b) Pectic substances**
   c) Organic acids d) Sugar

182. Which of the following test is used to test the non-mechanical damage in package?
   a) Vibration test b) Field test
   c) Accelerated test **d) Both A & C**

183. ———— can decorate the office or home from months to years.
   i) Cut flowers **ii) Dry flowers**
   iii) Cut foliage iv) All of these

184. ———— is characteristic of dry flowers.
   i) Aesthetics ii) Longevity
   iii) Nobility **iv) All of these**

185. ———— is the largest importer of dry flowers.
   i) UK ii) Spain
   iii) UAE iv) Russia

186. ———— is/are the exporters of dry flowers.
   i) India ii) Australia
   iii) South Africa **iv) All of these**

187. ———— flowers is not grown for dry flowers.

i) Straw flower ii) Paper flowers

iii) Tulip iv) Statice

188. Indian export of dry flowers constitute about ——— %.

i) 10-15 **ii) 50-60**

iii) 20-30 iv) 80-90

189. The main dry flower product being exported from India is————

i) Lotus pods ii) Hybrid lilies

iii) Rose iv) None of these

190. Most of the companies exporting dry flowers are situated at————

i) Cosco flora ii) Ramesh Flower Ltd.

iii) Deccan Flora iv) Kasturi Flowers Ltd.

191. ———— a famous product of dry flowers is very common in Europe.

i) Wall sceneries ii) Potpourries

iii) Pot plants iv) Flower arrangement

192. The plant material suitable for drying should be resistant to————

i) Moulds **ii) Toxins**

iii) Noxious odours iv) All of these

193. ———— means to dry something under artificially produced heat through controlled temperature, humidity and air flow.

i) Cooling **ii) Dehydration**

iii) Desiccation iv) None of these

194. ———— of the following has beautiful dried seeds.

i) Amaltas ii) Bael

iii) Pines **iv) All of these**

195. ———— of the following is most suitable for air drying.

i) Paper flower ii) Anaphalis

iii) Straw flower **iv) All of these**

196. Any material which removes moisture without reacting with it is known as ————

i) Desiccant ii) Dehydrator

iii) Absorbent iv) Drier

197. The desiccant should have an ideal size of ————mm.

i) 1-2 **ii) 0.02-0.2**

iii) 2-5 iv) All of these

198. ————— is suitable desiccant for flower drying.
   i) Silica gel
   ii) Sand
   iii) Boric acid
   iv) All of these
199. Optimum temperature for flower drying in hot air oven is————^{0}C
   i) 30-40
   ii) 80-90
   iii) 40-60
   iv) Any of these
200. ————— is the quickest method of flower drying.
   i) Microwave
   ii) Hot air oven
   iii) Solar drier
   iv) Room drying
201. ————— drying is done at very low temperature up to -35^{0}C.
   i) Vacuum
   ii) Freeze
   iii) Cool
   iv) Air
202. ————— dried by water drying method.
   i) Hydrangea
   ii) Corn flower
   iii) Baby's breath
   iv) All of these
203. ————— dried flowers are used for making greeting cards.
   i) Air
   ii) Embedded
   iii) Press
   iv) Freeze
204. ————— is not used for preserving flowers.
   i) Sugar
   ii) Polyols
   iii) KCl
   iv) H_2SO_4
205. ————— is not a serious pest of dry flowers.
   i) Mice
   ii) Silver fish
   iii) Book lice
   iv) Caterpillars
206. ————— discovered rose oil in 9th century.
   i) Ibraham
   ii) Babur
   iii) Akbar
   iv) Avi Cena
207. ————— Rosa species is not grown for oil extraction.
   i) *Indica*
   ii) *Damascena*
   iii) *Bourboniana*
   iv) *Centifolia*
208. ————— is not a cultivar of *Rosa damascena.*
   i) Noor jahan
   ii) Sherbat
   iii) Himroz
   iv) Jawala

209. One kg rose oil is extracted from ——————— flowers.

i) 10 q **ii) 3-5 T**

iii) 1.5 T iv) 50 Kg

210. Himroz cultivar of *Rosa damascena* is developed at————

i) IHBT, Palampur ii) IARI, New Delhi

iii) NBRI, Lucknow iv) IIHR, Bangalore

211. ———— species of *Jasminum* is not grown for oil extraction.

i) S*ambac* **ii) H*umile***

iii) G*randiflorum* iv) A*uriculatum*

212. ————is not method of extraction method in perfumery.

i) Enfleurage ii) Maceration

iii) Propelier iv) Solvent extraction

213. Most commonly used solvent in oil extraction is ————

i) Petroleum ether ii) Tarpene

iii) Acetone iv) Distilled water

214. ————seeds are used in extraction of jasmine oil.

i) Mustard ii) Wheat

iii) Sesame iv) Castor

215. One ton flowers of jasmine yield————kg absolute oil.

i) 0.5 **ii) 1.3-1.5**

iii) 4-5 kg iv) 10-12 kg

216. Damask flowers should be harvested between———— for more oil extraction.

i) 8-10 am ii) 10-12 am

iii) 4-6 am iv) Any time

217. ———— species of *Tagetes* is commonly grown for oil extraction.

i) T*enuifolia* ii) *Erecta*

iii) P*atula* **iv) M*inuta***

218. ———— flower is not grown for perfumery.

i) Rose **ii) Lilium**

iii) Geranium iv) Carnation

219. Roots of ———— are used for oil extraction.

i) Sweet pea **ii) Iris**

iii) Gardenia iv) Rose

220. ———— annual is grown for oil extraction.

i) Pansy ii) Paper flowers

iii) Sweet pea iv) Salvia

221. ———— is essential for storing perfume.

i) Cool temperature ii) Dark

iii) Air tight container **iv) All of these**

222. ———— shrub is grown for oil extraction.

i) Gardenia ii) Cestrum

iii) Hibiscus iv) Sambuscus

223. End point of ketch up is judged by————

i) Flakes test ii) Sheets test

iii) Lump test **iv) Absence of free flowing water.**

224. ———— is the most important constituent in jelly making.

i) Carbohydrates ii) Proteins

iii) Amino acids **iv) Pectin**

225. Pasteurization temperature for ketch up is———— for 30 mins.

i) 80-90 °C ii) 30-40 °C

iii) 20-30 °C iv) 50-60 °C

226. ———— consists of strained juice with moderate amount of fruit pulp.

i) Syrup **ii) Squash**

iii) Jelly iv) Cordial

227. ———— is the process of dipping fruits or vegetables in boiling water to loosen the skin.

i) Straining ii) Dipping

iii) Blanching iv) Boiling.

228. Salt solution is also known as.

i) Brine solution ii) Brix solution

iii) Salt solvent iv) Salt solute

229. Products prepared from acidic fruits are stored in ———— cans

i) S.R.cans ii) R enamel cans

iii) P enamel cans iv) Q.R. cans.

230. ———— means complete elimination of microrganisms.

i) Pasteurization **ii) Sterilization**

iii) Asepsis iv) Fermentation

231. ———— is considered as the most important microorganism responsible for Spoilage of processed products

i) Bacteria ii) Fungi

iii) Yeast iv) Mould

232. End point of jam is judged by———— test.

i) Flakes ii) Lump

iii) Pectin iv) None

233. ———— is low in pectin and acids.

i) Guava ii) Woodapple

iii) Pomegranate iv) None

234. ———— is a method of temporary preservation.

i) Sterilization ii) Pasteurization

iii) Drying iv) None

235. ———— is a concentrated beverage.

i) Juice **ii) Syrup**

iii) Jam iv) Jelly

236. Strength of salt solution is measured with help of————

i) Refractometer ii) Gelmeter

iii) Salinometer iv) Thermometer

237. Quantity of citric acid to be added to 1 kg fruit pulp for making jam is ———g

i) 8 ii) 10

iii) 12 iv) 14

238. ——— per cent citric acid helps in strengthening the pectin fibres.

i) 0.5 % **ii) 1.0 %**

iii) 1.5% iv) 2.0 %

239. ———— is slightly bitter in taste.

i) Jam ii) Jelly

iii) Marmalade iv) Syrup

240. ———— pickles are most preferred in Indian markets.

i) Mango ii) Lime

iii) Chilli iv) Cauliflower

241. Rapidly lowering the temperature of harvested produce to near storage temperature is known as ————

i) Room cooling **ii) Precooling**

iii) Evaporative cooling iv) Vaccum cooling

242. Tomato ketch up has a tendency to separate into pulp and clear juice which largely Depends on the amount of———— present in it.
   i) Pectin ii) Sugar
   iii) Acids iv) Seeds
243. ———— peeling is used for onion and garlic.
   i) Hand ii) Machine
   iii) Lye **iv) Flame**
244. Hand peeling is done in case of————
   i) Sweet orange ii) Sweet potato
   iii) Apple **iv) Papaya**
245. During canning the syrup or brine should be added to the can at a temperature of———
   i) 60-62 °C **ii) 79-82 °C**
   iii) 85-87 °C iv) 70-72 °C
246. Lidding has now been modernized by the———— process.
   i) Exhausting ii) Sealing
   iii) Cooling **iv) Clinching**
247. A——— sound on striking the top of the can with a short iron rod indicates a leakage.
   i) Dull ii) Ringing
   iii) Metallic iv) Clear
248. A can with a mild positive pressure is called as———
   i) Swell **ii) Flipper**
   iii) Springer iv) Hydrogen swell
249. Bacteria are active in ———— media
   i) Alkaline ii) Acidic
   iii) Non acidic iv) Sugary
250. Bacteria are killed below a pH of——
   i) 4.5 ii) 5.5
   iii) 6.0 iv) 7.0
251. Low temperature used for preservation varies between————
   i) 5-5.4 °C **ii) 0-4.4 °C**
   iii) 3.5-5.5 °C iv) 5.5-7.5 °C
252. ——— is a precursor of Vitamin A
   i) β Ccarotene ii) α Carotene
   iii) Tartazine iv) Edicol orange

253. Ketch up contains not less than—— per cent total solids

i) 25% ii) 23%

iii) 22% **iv) 28%**

254. Observing strict cleanliness during handling, processing, sealing and storage of cans is known as———

i) Pasteurization ii) Sterilization

iii) Asepsis iv) Acidification

255. Process of killing of all forms of microbial life is called as————

i) Pasteurization **ii) Sterilization**

iii) Asepsis iv) Acidification

256. ———— is a type of forced air cooling.

i) Hydro cooling **ii) Serpentine cooling**

iii) Vacuum cooling iv) Evaporative cooling

258. Grapes are cooled by——— method.

i) Room cooling ii) Vaccum cooling

iii) Evaporative cooling **iv) Forced air cooling**

259. ——— is the first step in good temperature management

i) Pre cooling ii) Washing

iii) Sorting iv) Packaging

260. A prelimanary———— of produce helps to remove unmarketable produce and foreign Matter

i) Cleaning ii) Handling

iii) Sorting iv) Packaging

261. ————— is an effective method to reduce water from the horticultural produce

i) Restricting air movement **ii) Increasing humidity**

iii) Packaging iv) Sorting

262. ———— refers to a small container of 5 kg capacity

i) Bag ii) Box

iii) Case iv) Tray

263. The fully mature fruits when harvested show———— catalase activity during storage

i) Lower **ii) Higher**

iii) Constant iv) No

264. Knol khol is harvested when the knob attains a size of——— cm
i) 5-7 **ii) 8-10**
iii) 10-12 iv) 12-14

265. "C" enamel cans are used for packing——— foods.
i) Bitter ii) Acidic
iii) Salty **iv) Non acidic**

266. ——— caps are used for sealing long necked bottles.
i) Screw ii) Plastic
iii) Crown iv) Lid

267. 100 per cent acetic acid is known as———
i) Vinegar **ii) Glacial acetic acid**
iii) Pure acetic acid iv) A grade acetic acid

268. The process of sealing food stuffs hermeatically in containers and sterilizing them by Heat for long storage is known as———
i) Canning ii) Pasteurization
iii) Sterilization iv) Asepsis

269. ——— multiply by fission or division of cells
i) Yeast **ii) Bacteria**
iii) Mould iv) Virus

270. ——— is caused due to under sterilization of canned products
i) Swell ii) Springer
iii) Flipper **iv) Flat sour**

271. Central Food Technological Research Institute is located at———
i) Bangalore **ii) Mysore**
iii) Delhi iv) Mumbai

272. ——— has a very low rate of respiration
i) Pea ii) Beans
iii) Cabbage **iv) Onion**

273. ——— is a active ingredient of vinegar
i) Acetic acid ii) Citric acid
iii) Malic acid iv) Tartaric acid

274. A fruit is said to be physiologically mature when it is _________.
a) Attains maximum size
b) **Continues ontogeny even after detachment.**
c) Possess prerequisites for utilization for a particular purpose.
d) Begins to ripen.

275. Softening of fruits during ripening is due the breakdown of.................

a) Starch **c) Peptic substances**

b) Sugars d) Organic acids.

276. The predominant organic acid present in grapes is.

a) Maleic b) Citric

b) Tartaric acid d) Quinic acid

277. The lowest safe temperature for the storage of banana is..........

a) 8 °C b) 10 °C

c) 14 °C d) **12°C**

278. Pre-cooling refers to the cooling of fruits and vegetables................

a) **Immediately after harvest**

b) Immediately before harvest

c) During storage

d) During marketing

279. Blanching of fruits and vegetables prior to canning is necessary as it helps in .....

a) Inactivating enzymes b) Eliminating microorganisms

c) Close filling of cans **d) All of these**

280. Treatment of fruits and vegetables with boiling water/ steam for short periods followed by cooling is

a) Blanching b) Pulping

c) Exhausting d) Sterilization

281. Exhausting of cans prior to their sealing is done at a temperature of

a) **79 to 82 °C** b) 39 to 42 °C

c) 59 to 62 °C d) 99 to 102 °C

282. Processing plant should be established at a place which meets the requirements——

a) Availability of fruits &vegetables

b) Proper transport facilities.

c) Environment is clean

d) All of these

283. Water for processing plant should not ......

a) Alkaline b) Contain organic matter

c) Contain iron and sulphur d) **All of these**

284. Process of removal of air from the cans is known as

a) Brining b) Lye peeling

c) Blanching **d) Exhausting**

285. As compared to fruits and acid vegetables, the processing temperature for non-acid vegetables is usually..........

a) Higher b) Lower

c) The same d) It makes no difference

286. Sugar syrup flavoured with artificial essences of fruits /herbs is known as __________.

a) Squash **b) Sharbet**

c) Cordial d) None of these.

287. Which of the following is a chemical preservative used in processed products?

a) **Sodium benzoate** b) Sodium chloride

c) Sodium nitrate d) Sodium bicarbonate.

288. ________ is the chemical used to release of SO_2 as a preservative.

a) Potassium sulphide b) **Potassium metabisuphate**

c) Potassium sulphate d) Sodium sulphate

289. TSS content of jam should not be less than ....

a) 70.5% b) 66.5%

c) **68.5%** d) 72.5%

290. According to FPO the residual SO_2 in the jam should not exceed........

a) 40 ppm b) 30 ppmt

c) 50 ppm d) 60 ppm

291. A jelly may fail to set due to and

a) Lack of acid or pectin

b) Addition of too much sugar

c) Cooking below the end point

d) All of theses

292. The oldest method of preservation of food is

a) Canning b) **Drying**

c) Fermentation d) Processing

293. The best jelly can be made from__________.

a) Papaya b) Mango

c) **Guava** d) Pecan -nut

294. A fruit impregnated with cane sugar and then drained is....

a) Candy b) Jam

c) Marmalade d) Syrup

295. The term which gives idea about the nature of the medium is written as ....

a) PH **b) pH**

c) ph d) Ph

296. The storage life of fruits is reduced by highe.........

a) Respiration b) Transpiration

c) Ethylene **d) All of these**

297. A brix hydrometer measures the concentration...........

a) Sugar b) Acid

c) Salt d) None of these

298. A mild heat treatment used to reduce the total micro flora, especially pathogenic bacteria is called ___________.

a) Refrigeration b) Sterilization

c) **Pasteurization** c) None of these

299. Foods are refrigerated to reduce both as well as activities.

a) Microbial b) Enzymatic

c) Both (a) and (b) d) None of these

300. Which of the following substance is useful in increasing firmness of fruits?

a) **$CaCl_2$** b) KCL

c) NaCl d) All of these

301. Firmness of fruits can be measured by a

a) Altimeter b) Refractometer

c) **Penetrometer** d) Technometer

302. Which of the following is the most effective in initiating ripening of fruits.

a) **Ethylene** b) Calcium carbide

c) Propylene d) Acetylene

303. Liquid which absorbs heat on expanding to a gaseous state is called_____________.

a) Refrigerants b) Coolant

c) Absorbent d) None of these

304. To preserve foods by dehydration, water activity must be below___________ per cent.

a) 0.9 b) 0.8

c) 0.7 d) 0.6

305. In freeze- drying, water is removed from the product by

a) Sublimation b) Evaporation

c) Transpiration d) None of these

306. The storage system in which the exact concentration of different gases in the storage environments are maintained is called as

a) Hypobaric storage **b) Controlled atmosphere storage**

c) Cold storage d) Modified atmosphere storage

307. Which of the following storage method results in retention of best quality of fruits?

a) Refrigerated storage **b) Controlled atmosphere storage**

c) Ambient storage d) Modified atmosphere storage

308. Which of the following methods is more suitable for pre-cooling of leafy vegetables?

a) Vacuum pre-cooling b) Hydro-cooling

c) Forced air cooling d) Ice- cooling

309. The minimum TSS content in RTS beverage is

a) 8 % **b) 10%**

c) 12.5 % d) 15.0 %

310. The minimum juice content in squashes should be

a) 10% b) 15%

c) 20% **d) 25%**

311. The amount of SO_2 in squashes should not exceed

a) 150 ppm b) 250 ppm

c) 350 ppm d) 450 ppm

312. Food with a pH of more than 4.5 must be processed at or above

a) 101°C b) 106 °C

c) 111 °C **d) 116 °C**

313. Which of the following is categorized as Class- I preservatives?

a) Citric acid b) Sulphur dioxide

c) Benzoic acid **d) Sugar**

314. Which is the latest technique in food preservation?

a) Canning **b) Freezing**

c) Hurdle technology d) Drying

315. Minimum juice content in squash according to FPO

a) 10 % b) 20 %

c) 15 % d) 25 %

316. A hard stone like sensation, usually caused by the presence of sand particles on stone cells is known as

a) Mealy b) Chewiness

c) Firmness **d) Gritty**

317. Those properties of foods stuffs apprehended by the eyes and by the skin muscle senses of the mouth, including the roughness, smoothness, graininess is known as____________.

a) Flavour b) Colour

c) Taste **d) Texture**

318. Benzoic acid is most effective against

a) Yeasts and moulds b) Moulds

c) Yeast d) None of these

319. The Fruit Products Order (FPO) license is given by———

a) NHB b) ICAR

c) Government of India d) State Government

320. The chemical preservative is most suitable for coloured juices.

a) **Sodium Benzoate** b) Potassium meta- bisulphite.

c) Acetic acid d) Sorbic acid

321. Impact of bruising to fruits may be caused by ....

a) Filling under sized fruits in a container

b) Filling over sized fruits in a container

c) Sudden jerks to the fruits in a container

d) None of the above

322. Which of the following is not a physical method of food preservation?

a) Removal of heat b) Addition of heat

c) Removal of water **d) Addition of salt**

323. The energy required by fruits and vegetables is supplied ____________.

a) Water **b) Aerobic respiration**

c) Nutrients d) Anaerobic respiration

324. The quickest method of pre-cooling the produce__________.

a) Hydro-cooling b) Vacuum cooling

c) Cooling in shade d) Forced air cooling

325. Canning is a method of ____________.

a) Sterilization b) Non heat processing

c) Heat processing d) Cold processing/ cooling

326. Failure of jelly setting occurs due to ________.

a) Lack of acid b) Lack of pectin

c) Too much sugar **d) All of these**

327. For tomato ketch-up tomato should have ________.

a) Green colour b) Yellow colour

c) High TSS d) Fully ripe

328. The chemical formula of potassium meta-bisulphite is ____________

a) KMS b) K_2SO_4

c) $K_2S_2O_5$ d) KSO_2

329. Potassium meta-bisulphite (KMS) contains________% SO_2.

a) 25.5 % b) 75.5 %

c) 57.7 % d) 78.2%

330. In jelly making, pectin acts as a ____________.

a) Stabilizer b) Buffers

c) Preservative d) Flavouring agent

331. Marmalades can be prepared from__________.

a) Citrus fruits only b) Any fruit having pulp

c) Temperate fruits only d) Fruits which contain pectin

332. Paper shreds are one the types of ____________material.

a) Packaging b) Lining

c) Cushioning d) None of these

333. Which of the following fruit is not suitable for jam making?

a) Banana b) Mango

c) Aonla **d) Lemon**

334. Jelly can be prepared from_________.

a) Citrus fruits only
b) Pome fruits only
c) Sub-tropical fruits
d) Fruits which contain pectin

335. PFA is name given to

a) Prevention of Fruit Produce Adulteration Act
b) Prevention of Food Products Act
c) Prevention of Fruit Adulteration Act
d) **Prevention of Food Adulteration Act**

336. FPO refers to?

a) Fruit Products Order
b) Fruit Processing Organization
c) Fruit Processing Order
d) None of these

337. ''MAP'' stands for _________________.

a) Modified Atmosphere Permeability
b) Modified Atmosphere Packaging
c) Modified Atmospheric Packaging
d) Medium Atmosphere Packaging

338. Which of the following treatments helps to improve appearance and prolonged shelf life of fruits?

a) Washing with salt solution
b) Pre-cooling
c) Waxing
d) IBA Treatment

339. Jam comes under _____________.

a) Concentrate
b) Sugar concentrate
c) Any other
d) Non heat processing

340. Commercial source of tartaric acid is ______________.

a) Grape
b) Grape fruit
c) Karonda
d) Sour orange

341. Which of the following is diluted before serving?

a) RTS
b) Juice
c) Squash
d) Cordial

342. Lemon squash is preserved for a longer period without any discoloration by using________.

a) Benzoic acid
b) Citric acid
c) Potassium metabisulphite
d) Both a and b.

343. High concentration of sugar in jam facilitates________________.
a) Good setting
b) Preservation
c) Improve flavour
d) None of these

344. Specific gravity used as maturity indices for mango is _________.
a) 2.01-2.02
b) 1.5-2.0
c) 2.0-2.5
d) 1.01-1.02

345. Sweetest sugar in fruits is ____________.
a) Glucose
b) Fructose
c) Sucrose
d) None of these

346. Fruits those can ripen on tree are known as _________.
a) False fruits
b) Non-climacteric
c) Climacteric
d) True fruits

347. Which of the following is climacteric fruit?
a) Litchi
b) Orange
c) Papaya
d) Grape

348. Hypobaric storage is also known as ________________.
a) Low temperature storage
b Modified atmospheric storage
c) Controlled atmospheric storage
d) All of these

349. Sheet test is performed in ____________.
a) Jam
b) Cordial
c) Squash
d) Murabba

350. Can with a mild positive pressure is called ________
a) Bursting of can
b) Swell
c) Springer
d) Flipper

351. Exhausting is done _____________.
a) To improve the taste of products
b) To reduce the risk of corrosion tin plates
c) To inactivate the enzymes
d) To eliminate micro-organisms

352. Bulging of cans takes place due to _________.
a) Excess exhausting
b) No vacuum in cans
c) Excess head space
d) High temperature

353. Which of the following preservative is added in tomato products?
a) Potassium meta-bisulphite b) Sodium benzoate
c) Acetic acid d) Sodium chloride

354. Preservative used in jelly making__________.
a) Sugar b) Salt
c) Unripe d) Over ripe

355. Most suitable fruit making squash __________.
a) Tomato b) Jack fruit
c) Guava **d) Lemon**

356. How much sugar is recommended for making of Jam by FPO?
a) Above 30 % b) Above 40 %
c) Above 60 % d) Above 70 %

357. How much sugar is recommended for making of Jam by FPO?
a) Above 30 % b) Above 40 %
c) Above 60 % d) Above 70 %

358. Preservative used in jelly making__________.
a) Sugar b) Salt
c) Unripe d) Over ripe

359. For processing tomato fruits are picked at__________.
a) Immature Stage b) Pink stage
c) **Hard ripe stage** d) Over ripe stage

360. For pickle making one can use maximum ____________.
a) 40 % salt b) 30 % salt
c) 25 % salt d) 35 % salt

361. Asepsis means________.
a) Exclusion of air
b) Exclusion of moisture
c) Exclusion of micro-organisms
d) Exclusion of dust

362. 'Clinching' a term related to __________.
a) Freezing **b) Canning**
c) Fermentation d) Drying

363. Solution of salt in water is called as________.
a) Vinegar b) Cider
c) Juice **d) Brine**

364. The chemical ___________ is used to prevent sprouting during storage of onion.
   a) NAA b) GA_3
   c) MH d) Thiourea
365. Tenderometer is used to measure maturity of ________ vegetable.
   a) French bean b) Cowpea
   c) Dolichos bean **d) Garden pea**
366. Almost all fruits can be processed satisfactorily at a temperature of ___________.
   a) 80 °C b) 110 °C
   c) 100 °C d) 98 °C
367. Sun drying is slow as evaporation takes place____________.
   a) Uniformly **b) Non-uniformly**
   c) Continuous d) Intercepted
368. Vacuum cooling is most suitable for________.
   a) Fruits b) Tubers
   c) Leafy vegetables d) Flowers
369. The term "cold sterilization" is also known as _________.
   a) Freezing b) Cold storage
   c) Pasteurization **d) Irradiation**
370. Which are major respiratory substrates found in fruit__________.
   a) Starch and acid b) Minerals and fat
   c) Protein and CHO d) None of these
371. Sugar acts as a preservative in fruit preservation by ______________.
   a) Hydrolysis b) Imbibition
   c) Osmosis d) Fermentation
372. After processing, cans are cooled rapidly up to a temperature of __________.
   a) 10 °C b) 25 °C
   c) 39 °C d) 49 °C
373. Vegetables are subjected to drying after_________.
   a) Blanching b) Sulphuring
   c) No blanching d) Any other means

27

Animal Science and Dairy Science

1. The normal gestation period of buffalo is

   a) 280 days   b) 290 days

   c) 300 days   **d) 310 days**

2. The best crop of silage making is

   a) Maize   b) Jowar

   c) Bajra   d) Lucerne

3. The chief Energy source of cattle ration is:

   a) Protein   **b) Carbohydrate**

   c) Mineral   d) Fat

4. Spermatogenesis takes place in:

   a) Ovary   b) Placenta

   c) Kidney   **d) Testes**

5. Sudden heritable change is

   a) Epitasis   **b) Mutation**

   c) Chromosomal aberration   d) None of the above

6. Milk fever is due to deficiency of:

   a) Ca   b) co

   c) Na   d) Mg

7. Most wool producing state of India is:

   a) Gujarat   b) Punjab

   c) Rajasthan   d) Bihar

8. The highest protein is found in:

   a) Maize   b) Guar

   c) Jawar   **d) Gram**

9. The heaviest cattle breed of India is:
   a) Ongole b) Sahiwal
   c) Kankraj d) Gir
10. I V.R.I is located at:
   a) Mumbai b) Pantnagar
   c) Karnal **d) Izatnagar**
11. The offspring of cross between jack and a mare is called:
   a) Hinny **b) Mule**
   c) Yak d) All of the above
12. Which type of mating should be preferred for the improvement of non-descript animals?
   a) Inbreeding b) Line breeding
   c) Upgrading d) All of the above
13. The semen volume of bull per ejaculate ranges from:
   a) 10 to 15 ml b) 20 to 40 ml
   c) 5 to 12 ml d) 75 to 100 ml
14. AGMARK is:
   a) A cooperative society for egg production
   b) Regulatory body for agricultural market
   c) An association of poultry farming
   d) A quality guarantee stamp for commodities like egg, ghee etc.
15. Major constituents of egg are:
   a) Carbohydrate **b) Protein**
   c) Fat d) Vitamins
16. Standard fat percentage of double toned milk is:
   a) 3 b) 2
   c) 1.5 d) 2.5
17. Bacteriological test of milk is judged by:
   a) Reductase test **b) M.B.R.Test**
   c) Sediment test d) Alizarin test
18. Which method of milking avoided:
   a) Full hand method b) Machine milking
   c) Knuckling d) Stripping

19. Grass tetany in cattle is due to deficiency of:
    a) Mn **b) Mg**
    c) Cu d) Ca
20. Chromosome number of Swamp buffalo:
    a) 52 b) 50
    c) 54 **d) 48**
21. Normal range of temperature of cattle is:
    a) 97-99^{0}f **b) 99-101 ^{0}f**
    c) 103-105^{0}f d) 107 ^{0}f
22. In dry fodder, crude fibre range is:
    a) 8-10% b) 15%
    c) 5-15% **d) 18 and above**
23. Rank of India in world egg production:
    a) 10 b) 12
    c) 3 d) 5
24. Cross breeding increases:
    a) Vigour b) Breeding merit
    c) Both A and B d) None
25. Which breed cattle is known as milch breed:
    a) Gir b) Hariyana
    c) Kankraj d) Amrit Mahal
26. Young one of poultry is:
    a) Chick b) Poult
    c) Hen d) Cock
27. Excellent Silage PH is:
    a) 3.7-4.2 b) 4.7-5.2
    c) 4.5-5.0 d) 5.0-5.5
28. Calf ration Contains:
    a) 18-25% DCP; 70-75% TDN b) 10-15% DCP; 80% TDN
    c) 30% DCP; 70-75% TDN **d) 18% DCP; 60-70% TDN**
29. In Cotton seed cake Anti nutritional factor is present:
    a) Gossypol b) Tannin
    c) Saponin d) Cyanogon

30. The biggest and most majestic breed of goats in India is:
    a) Surti b) Mehsana
    c) Jamunapari d) Sirohi

31. FMD is type of disease:
    a) Viral b) Protozoa
    c) Bacterial d) None

32. Act of Mating in Sheep:
    a) Crossing **b) Tupping**
    c) Kidding d) Copulation

33. Half of Herd is refers to:
    a) Bull b) Management practices
    c) Calf d) None

34. Which is known as Merino of India?
    a) Magra b) Gaddi
    c) Chokla d) Bhakarwal

35. Most prolific animal is:
    a) Sheep **b) Pig**
    c) Dog d) Goat

36. Camel is considered an animal, which is:
    a) Non-ruminant b) Ruminant
    c) Pseudo-ruminant d) Omnivorous

37. The central institute of Research of Goats is located at:
    a) Makhdoom b) Dantivara
    c) Izzatnagar d) Rishikesh

38. Livestock feeds generally divided in to two classes-Roughages and:
    a) Concentrate b) Supplement
    c) Additives d) Silage

39. The colour of egg of Minorca poultry breed is
    a) White b) Brown
    c) Black d) Red

40. 1st milk is:
    a) Skimmed b) Toned
    c) Homogenised **d) Colostrum**

41. Oxalate in high amount is present in:
    a) Paddy straw **b) Gram**
    c) Cow pea hay d) Oat fodder
42. pH of rumen content n normal diet may be:
    a) 2-2.5 **b) 3.5-5**
    c) 6.7-7.2 d) 8-8.5
43. Protein content in fish meal:
    a) 15 b) 25
    c) 35 **d) 60**
44. No enzyme found in saliva of:
    a) Dog b) Cow
    c) Pig d) Camel
45. Keratin is protein of:
    a) Connective tissue **b) Wool**
    c) Blood d) None of these
46. Find out legume fodder:
    a) Green panic fodder b) Pear millet fodder
    c) Cowpea fodder d) Maize fodder
47. Dry matter intake for normal healthy animal is:
    a) 2.5% of body wt. b) 50% of body wt.
    c) 10% of body wt. d) 0.5% f body wt.
48. Which of the following animals has maximum fat contents in their milk?
    a) Whale b) Cat
    c) Buffalo d) Goat
49. In ruminant stomach 'Honey comb 'is which of the following:
    a) Rumen **b) Reticulum**
    c) Omasum d) Abomasum
50. Which of the following is the rate of respiration per minute in heifer?
    a) 26 **b) 20**
    c) 30 d) 34
51. Mammary glands are modification of which of the following:
    a) Sebaceous gland b) Sudoriferous gland
    c) Oil gland **d) None above**

52. Buffalo milk is not yellow in colour:

a) It contain more fat
b) It contains no lactose
c) It contains no carotene
d) It contains more calcium

53. Require time for removal of milk:

a) 3-5 min
b) 5-7 min
c) 7-8 min
d) 2-3 min

54. Lactation period of cow is which of the following:

a) 40 weeks
b) 43 weeks
c) 46 weeks
d) 37 weeks

55. Rate of the milk feeding to calf should be about:

a) 5-6 lit/day
b) 7-8 lit/day
c) 2-3 lit/day
d) 8-9 lit/day

56. Surface tension of milk (Dyne/cm) is which of the following:

a) 46
b) 50
c) 55
d) 65

57. Refractive index of milk at 20 °C is which of the following:

a) 1.31
b) 1.32
c) 1.33
d) 1.34

58 Which of the following has maximum milk production?

a) Sahiwal
b) Red Sindhi
c) Rathi
d) Gir

59. Pulsation rate of machine milking (cycle/min):

a) 10-40
b) 40-120
c) 120-150
d) Above 150

60. Flavouring agent of butter is which of the following:

a) Diacetyl
b) Volatile fatty acid
c) Butter protein
d) All above

61. For Passurization of milk require Degree centigrade and Second:

a) 74 and 7
b) 72 and 15
c) 150 and 3/4
d) 63/15

62. Segregation of genes takes place during which phase:
    a) Metaphase b) Anaphase
    c) Prophase d) Embryo formation

63. Who described the details of mitosis in 1892?
    a) Altmann **b) Walter Flemming**
    c) Hugo de vries d) Darwin

64. Hardy Weinberg law was formulated in the year:
    a) 1809 **b) 1908**
    c) 1918 d) 1928

65. Moisture content in hay should not be more than:
    a) 15% b) 28%
    c) 38% d) 40%

66. Legal Standard for solid not fat in cow milk is:
    a) 8% **b) 8.5%**
    c) 9% d) 9.5%

67. To which animal hay should not fed:
    a) Cattle **b) Pig**
    c) Goat d) Sheep

68. Length of estrus cycle of Goat is:
    a) 20 b) 17
    c) 21 d) 28

69. Time of ovulation of cow is:
    a) 10-15 hrs after end of estrus
    b) 10-15 hrs before end of estrus
    c) 12-24 hrs after end of estrus
    d) 12-24 hrs before end of estrus

70. Age of dehorning in cattle is:
    a) 7 b) 16
    c) 13 d) 20

71. How does the meat of cow is known:
    a) Chevon b) Mutton
    c) Beef d) Pork

72. In poultry eggs too large air cell may be possibly due to:

a) Variable room temperature b) High humidity

c) Low humidity d) All of the above

73. In which portion of milk from udder bacterial content is highest:

a) Secretary phase **b) Fore milk**

c) Mid milk d) Stripping

74. Jersy is native of which country:

a) Denmark **b) England**

c) Holland d) USA

75. Jamunapari goat breed is usually found in the Etwah district of which region?

a) M.P. b) A.P.

c) Punjab **d) U.P.**

76. Let down of milk in cow is due to:

a) Ingestion **b) Secretion of Oxytocin**

c) Secretion of thyroxin d) Over eating

77. Leghorn is:

a) Mediterranean class b) Asiatic class

c) English class d) None

78. Late lactation milk contains:

a) More Chloride b) More fat content

c) More lactose d) More water

79. Law of inheritance were postulated by whom:

a) Robert Koch **b) Mendel**

c) Priestley d) Lush

80. Livestock census is done after how many years:

a) 5 b) 10

c) 12 d) 7

81. Length of dry period of well-fed cows should be how many days:

a) 20-40 b) 90-120

c) 60-100 **d) 40-80**

82. Khoa contains milk fat not less than:

a) 20% **b) 25%**

c) 30% d) 35%

83. Nurse cells for sperm are called:

a) RBC **b) Sertoli cell**

c) WBC d) All

84. NFE refers to:

a) Non fat extract b) No fibre extract

c) Nitrogen free extract d) None above

85. Queen of Milk producing goat breed is

a) Jamunapari b) Rambullete

c) Sannen d) Beetal

86. Mention the stage when animal comes in heat

a) Proestrus **b) Estrus**

c) Metaestrus d) Diestrus

87. Mention the sugar present in milk

a) Fructose b) Maltose

c) Sucrose **d) Lactose**

88. The rate of application of urea to treated with dry fodder

a) 1% b) 2-3%

c) 4-5% d) 5-8%

89. The protein present in Cow milk

a) 5.2% b) 4.8%

c) 4.2% **d) 3.6%**

90. The respiration rate of the cow per min

a) 12-20 b) 8-12

c) 12-16 d) 10-30

91. The zoological name of buffalo is

a) *Bos indicus* b) *Bos tourus*

c) *Bubalus bubalus* d) *Capra hircus*

92. Yorkshire is breed of

a) Pig b) Poultry

c) Goat d) Cattle

93. What is the average size of bull shed?

a) 12 in to 15 **b) 10 into 15**

c) 8 into 10 d) 10 into 11

94. What is the approximate water percent in cow milk?

a) 80% **b) 87%**

c) 90% d) 75%

95. What is the acidity content of fresh dahi?

a) 0.25% b) 0.40%

c) 0.50% **d) 0.75%**

96. What is Ranikhet?

a) Nematode disease **b) Viral Disease**

c) Fungal Disease d) Bacterial Disease

97. Vasectomised male of cattle is called

a) Stag b) Steer

c) Teaser d) Bullock

98. What is paneer?

a) Concentrated milk product b) Fermented milk product

c) Coagulated milk product d) Dried milk product

99. What is Culling of Poultry?

a) De–Beaking b) Branding

c) Tagging **d) Disposal of undesired birds**

100. What is the no. of pair of chromosome in goat

a) 25 b) 23

c) 30 d) 26

28

List of ICAR Institutes & Universities

1. Institutes under ICAR
   i) Deemed Universities - 4
   ii) Institutions - 64
   iii) National Research Centres - 15
   iv) National Bureaus - 6
   v) Directorates/Project Directorates - 13
      State Agricultural Universities

Institutes under ICAR

Deemed Universities - 4

1. Indian Agricultural Research Institute, New Delhi
2. National Dairy Research Institute, Karnal
3. Indian Veterinary Research Institute, Izatnagar
4. Central Institute on Fisheries Education, Mumbai

Institutions - 64

1. Central Agricultural Research Institute, Port Blair
2. Central Arid Zone Research Institute, Jodhpur
3. Central Avian Research Institute, Izatnagar
4. Central Inland Fisheries Research Institute, Barrackpore
5. Central Institute Brackish water Aquaculture, Chennai
6. Central Institute for Research on Buffaloes, Hissar
7. Central Institute for Research on Goats, Makhdoom
8. Central Institute of Agricultural Engineering, Bhopal
9. Central Institute of Arid Horticulture, Bikaner
10. Central Institute of Cotton Research, Nagpur
11. Central Institute of Fisheries Technology, Cochin

12. Central Institute of Freshwater Aquaculture, Bhubneshwar
13. Central Institute of Research on Cotton Technology, Mumbai
14. Central Institute of Sub Tropical Horticulture, Lucknow
15. Central Institute of Temperate Horticulture, Srinagar
16. Central Institute on Post harvest Engineering and Technology, Ludhiana
17. Central Marine Fisheries Research Institute, Kochi
18. Central Plantation Crops Research Institute, Kasargod
19. Central Potato Research Institute, Shimla
20. Central Research Institute for Jute and Allied Fibres, Barrackpore
21. Central Research Institute of Dryland Agriculture, Hyderabad
22. Central Rice Research Institute, Cuttack
23. Central Sheep and Wool Research Institute, Avikanagar, Rajasthan
24. Central Soil and Water Conservation Research & Training Institute, Dehradun
25. Central Soil Salinity Research Institute, Karnal
26. Central Tobacco Research Institute, Rajahmundry
27. Central Tuber Crops Research Institute, Trivandrum
28. ICAR Research Complex for Eastern Region including Centre of Makhana, Patna
29. ICAR Research Complex for NEH Region, Barapani
30. ICAR Research Complex Goa
31. Indian Agricultural Statistical Research Institute, New Delhi
32. Indian Grassland and Fodder Research Institute, Jhansi
33. Indian Institute of Agricultural Biotechnology, Ranchi
34. Indian Institute of Horticultural Research, Bangalore
35. Indian Institute of Natural Resins and Gums, Ranchi
36. Indian Institute of Pulses Research, Kanpur
37. Indian Institute of Soil Sciences, Bhopal
38. Indian Institute of Spices Research, Calicut
39. Indian Institute of Sugarcane Research, Lucknow
40. Indian Institute of Vegetable Research, Varanasi

41. National Academy of Agricultural Research & Management, Hyderabad
42. National Biotic Stress Management Institute, Raipur
43. National Institute of Abiotic Stress Management, Malegaon, Maharashtra
44. National Institute of Animal Nutrition and Physiology, Bengaluru
45. National Institute of Research on Jute & Allied Fibre Technology, Kolkata
46. Sugarcane Breeding Institute, Coimbatore
47. ICAR-Vivekananda Parvatiya Krishi Anusandhan Sansthan, Almora
48. ICAR-Central Institute for Research on Cattle, Meerut, Uttar Pradesh
49. ICAR-National Institute of High Security Animal Diseases, Bhopal
50. ICAR-Indian Institute of Maize Research,New Delhi
51. ICAR- Central Agroforestry Research Institute , Jhansi
52. ICAR-National Institute of Agricultural Economics and Policy Research, New Delhi
53. ICAR- Indian Institute of Wheat and Barley Research, Karnal
54. ICAR- Indian Institute of Farming Systems Research, Modipuram
55. ICAR- Indian Institute of Millets Research, Hyderabad
56. ICAR- Indian Institute of Oilseeds Research, Hyderabad
57. ICAR- Indian Institute of Oil Palm Research, Pedavegi, West Godawari
58. ICAR- Indian Institute of Water Management, Bhubaneshwar
59. ICAR-Indian Institute of Rice Research, Hyderabad
60. ICAR- Central Institute for Women in Agriculture, Bhubaneshwar
61. ICAR-Central Citrus Research Institute, Nagpur
62. ICAR-Indian Institute of Seed Research, Mau
63. ICAR-Indian Agricultural Research Institute, Post Box No. 48, Hazaribag 825 301, Jharkhand

National Research Centres - 15

1. National Centre for Integrated Pest Management, New Delhi
2. National Research Centre for Banana, Trichi
3. National Research Centre for Citrus, Nagpur
4. National Research Centre for Grapes, Pune

5. National Research Centre for Litchi, Muzaffarpur
6. National Research Centre for Pomegranate, Solapur
7. National Research Centre on Camel, Bikaner
8. National Research Centre on Equines, Hisar
9. National Research Centre on Meat, Hyderabad
10. National Research Centre on Mithun, Medziphema, Nagaland
11. National Research Centre on Orchids, Pakyong, Sikkim
12. National Research Centre on Pig, Guwahati
13. National Research Centre on Plant Biotechnology, New Delhi
14. National Research Centre Seed Spices, Ajmer
15. National Research Centre on Yak, West Kemang

National Bureaus - 6

1. National Bureau of Plant Genetics Resources, New Delhi
2. National Bureau of Agriculturally Important Micro-organisms, Mau, Pradesh
3. National Bureau of Agriculturally Important Insects, Bangalore
4. National Bureau of Soil Survey and Land Use Planning, Nagpur
5. National Bureau of Animal Genetic Resources, Karnal
6. National Bureau of Fish Genetic Resources, Lucknow

Directorates/Project Directorates - 13

1. Directorate of Groundnut Research, Junagarh
2. Directorate of Soybean Research, Indore
3. Directorate of Rapeseed & Mustard Research, Bharatpur
4. Directorate of Mushroom Research, Solan
5. Directorate of Onion and Garlic Research, Pune
6. Directorate of Cashew Research, Puttur
7. Directorate of Medicinal and Aromatic Plants Research, Anand
8. Directorate of Floriculture Research, Pusa, New Delhi
9. Directorate of Weed Science Research, Jabalpur
10. Project Directorate on Foot & Mouth Disease, Mukteshwar
11. Directorate of Poultry Research, Hyderabad

12. Directorate of Knowledge Management in Agriculture (DKMA) New Delhi
13. Directorate of Cold Water Fisheries Research, Bhimtal, Nainital